PSYCHOLOGY LIBRARY EDITIONS:
COMPARATIVE PSYCHOLOGY

I0130418

Volume 16

ANIMAL NATURE AND HUMAN NATURE

ANIMAL NATURE AND HUMAN NATURE

W.H. THORPE

Routledge
Taylor & Francis Group

LONDON AND NEW YORK

First published in 1974 by Methuen & Co. Ltd

This edition first published in 2018
by Routledge
2 Park Square, Milton Park, Abingdon, Oxon OX14 4RN

and by Routledge
711 Third Avenue, New York, NY 10017

Routledge is an imprint of the Taylor & Francis Group, an informa business

British Library Cataloguing in Publication Data
A catalogue record for this book is available from the British Library

ISBN: 978-1-138-50329-8 (Set)
ISBN: 978-1-351-12878-0 (Set) (ebk)
ISBN: 978-1-138-55977-6 (Volume 16) (hbk)
ISBN: 978-1-138-55983-7 (Volume 16) (pbk)
ISBN: 978-0-203-71226-9 (Volume 16) (ebk)

Publisher's Note
The publisher has gone to great lengths to ensure the quality of this reprint but
points out that some imperfections in the original copies may be apparent.

Disclaimer
The publisher has made every effort to trace copyright holders and would welcome
correspondence from those they have been unable to trace.

ANIMAL NATURE

AND

HUMAN NATURE

W. H. THORPE, Sc.D., F.R.S.

EMERITUS PROFESSOR OF ANIMAL ETHOLOGY

UNIVERSITY OF CAMBRIDGE

METHUEN & CO LTD

Based on the Gifford Lectures
St. Andrews University 1969–71

First published in Great Britain in 1974
by METHUEN & CO LTD
11 NEW FETTER LANE, LONDON EC4
© 1974 W. H. THORPE
Printed in the United States of America
ISBN 41676310 3

ACKNOWLEDGMENTS

In preparing a work such as this, one received so much help from so many that to express one's gratitude to everybody becomes impossible. Nevertheless, at the risk of appearing invidious, I must mention a few.

I am particularly grateful to Mr. Leslie Barden for his photography of many of the illustrations; his work has ensured that the best possible results have been achieved. To Mr. David Bygott I owe the exquisite painting of the inverted display of Prince Rudolph's Bird of Paradise (*Paradisornis rudolphi*), which adorns the cover.

Dr. Erskine Hill has been most helpful in tracing the exact source and context of some of the quotations. Among the many who have kindly allowed me to quote from their works, I must particularly mention Professor R. E. Ulrich, Professor P. W. Anderson, Pofessor John Hick, Sir John Eccles, and Sir Karl Popper. To the latter I owe especial gratitude for readily agreeing to my using some paragraphs from his pen which are still in the press.

Finally my wife attended, and survived, all the lectures and provided valuable direct internal information as to the reactions of my audience—quite apart from help in many other ways.

I am also grateful to the following publishers for their permission to use illustrations of which they own the copyright:

Figure 1. After Guy Murchie, 1955, *The Song of the Sky*, p. 202. London: Secker & Warburg; Boston: Houghton Mifflin Company.
Figure 2. After H. R. Byers, 1949. *Science* 110, pp. 291–4, American Association for the Advancement of Science.
Figure 3. After Jean Brachet, in *Scientific American*, September 1961, p. 55. Copyright © 1961 by Scientific American, Inc. All rights reserved. San Francisco: W. H. Freeman & Company.
Figure 4. From L. H. Hyman, *The Invertebrates*, Vol. 2, p. 69. Copyright © 1951 by McGraw-Hill Book Company. Used with permission of McGraw-Hill Book Company.

Figure 5. Cartoon by Roy Mumme from *The Worm Runner's Digest*, 7 (1965), p. 85.

Figure 6. After P. Ullyott in *Journal of Experimental Biology*, 13 (1936), pp. 265–78. The Company of Biologists Ltd.

Figure 7. After V. B. Wigglesworth, 1941, *Parasitology*, 33, p. 105. New York: Cambridge University Press.

Figure 8. After S. O. Mast, 1911, *Light and the Behavior of Organisms*. London: John Wiley & Sons.

Figure 9. After Muller, 1925, in *Zeitschrift für vergleichende Physiologie*, 3, pp. 113–44. Berlin: Springer-Verlag.

Figures 10, 11, 12. From J. C. Eccles, 1970, *Facing Reality*. New York: Springer-Verlag.

Figure 14. After E. O. Wilson and W. H. Bossert in *Recent Progress in Hormone Research*, 19 (1963), pp. 673–716. New York: Academic Press.

Figures 15, 17. From R. D. Alexander in W. E. Lanyon and W. N. Tavolga, 1960, *Animal Sounds and Communication*. Washington, D.C.: American Institute of Biological Sciences.

Figure 16, Plate 3. From R. D. Alexander in T. A. Sebeok, 1968, *Animal Communication*. Bloomington: Indiana University Press.

Figures 18, 19. From P. Marler in P. R. Bell, 1959. *Darwin's Biological Work*. New York: Cambridge University Press.

Figure 22. From R. W. Doty and J. F. Bosma in *Journal of Neurophysiology*, 19 (1956), pp. 44–60. American Physiological Society.

Figure 23. After E. J. Batham and C. F. A. Pantin in *Quarterly Journal of Microscopic Science*, 92 (1951), pp. 27–54. The Company of Biologists Ltd.

Figures 24, 25. From P. Marler and W. J. Hamilton, 1966, *Mechanisms of Animal Behavior*. New York: John Wiley & Sons.

Figure 26. After H. and H. Schone in *Zeitschrift für Tierpsychologie*, 20 (1963), pp. 641–56. Copyright © 1963 by Verlag Paul Parey, Berlin and Hamburg.

Figure 27. After J. Crane in *Zoologica*, 42 (1957), pp. 69–82. New York Zoological Society.

Figure 28. From N. E. and E. C. Collias in *University of California Publications in Zoology*, 73 (1964), p. 136. Originally published by the University of California Press; reprinted by permission of the Regents of the University of California.

Figures 29, 30. From N. E. and E. C. Collias in *Auk*, 79 (1962), pp. 568–95.

Figure 31. After D. Morris in *Behaviour*, 6 (1954), pp. 274, 276, 277; and suppl. VI (1958), pp. 20, 21. Leiden: E. J. Brill.

Figure 34. Modified after R. A. Hinde, 1970, *Animal Behavior*, p. 636. Copyright © 1970 by McGraw-Hill Book Company. Used with permission of McGraw-Hill Book Company.

Figure 35. After E. C. Tolman and C. H. Honzik in *University of California Publications in Psychology*, 4 (1930), pp. 215–32. Originally published by the University of California Press; reprinted by permission of the Regents of the University of Calilfornia.

Figure 36, Plate 9. After A. D. Blest in *Behaviour*, 11 (1957), pp. 257–309. Leiden: E. J. Brill.

Figure 38. After L. R. Aronson in *American Museum Novitates*, 1486 (1951), pp. 1–22. Courtesy of the American Museum of Natural History.

Figure 39. From B. T. Scheer in *Quarterly Review of Biology*, 14 (1939), p. 422.

Figure 40. From R. A. Hinde, *Animal Behaviour*, p. 474. Copyright © 1970 by McGraw-Hill Book Company. Used with permission of McGraw-Hill Book Company.

Figure 41. From P. Marler and W. J. Hamilton, *Mechanisms of Animal Behaviour*, 1966, p. 349. New York: John Wiley & Sons.

Figures 43, 44. After R. L. Fantz in A. M. Schrier et al., 1965, *Behavior of Nonhuman Primates*, Vol. 2. New York: Academic Press.

Figure 45. After R. Held and A. Hein in *Journal of Comparative and Physiological Psychology*, 56 (1963), pp. 872–6. Copyright © 1963 by the American Psychological Association. Reprinted by permission.

Figure 46. From G. V. T. Matthews, 1953, *Bird Navigation*, p. 67. New York: Cambridge University Press.

Figure 47. After G. V. T. Matthews in *Journal of Experimental Biology*, 30 (1953), p. 251. The Company of Biologists Ltd.

Figure 48. After B. G. Tunmore in *Proceedings of the XIIth International Ornithological Congress* (Tilgmannin Kirjapaino), 1960. Through the courtesy of Lars von Heartman, Secretary General of the XIIth International Ornithological Congress.

Figure 49. From C. Walcott and M. Michener in *Proceedings of the XIVth International Ornithological Congress* (Blackwell, 1967), p. 315.

Figure 50. After W. W. Cochran et al. in *Living Bird*, 6 (1967), pp. 213–25. Cornell Laboratory of Ornithology.

Figures 51, 52. From A. Koestler and J. R. Smythies, 1969, *Beyond Reductionism*. London: Hutchinson Publishing Group Ltd.

Plate 1. From L. A. Borradaile, 1923, *The Animal in Its Environment*. New York: Oxford University Press.

Plate 2. From I. Eibl-Eibesfeldt, 1967, *Grundriss der vergleichenden Verhaltensforschung*, R. Piper & Co. Verlag.

Plate 4. From R. E. Hutchison, J. Stevenson and W. H. Thorpe in *Behaviour*, 32 (1968), pp. 150–7, Leiden: E. J. Brill.

Plate 5. After Konrad Z. Lorenz in *Scientific American*, 199 (1958), pp. 71, 72–3. Copyright © 1958 by Scientific American, Inc. All rights reserved. W. H. Freeman & Company.

Plate 6. From J. H. Crook in *Ibis*, 105 (1963), p. 239. British Ornithologists Union.

Plates 7, 8. From H. B. Cott, 1940, *Adaptive Coloration in Animals*. London: Methuen.

Il est dangereux de trop faire voir à l'homme combien il est égal aux bêtes, sans lui montrer sa grandeur. Il est encore dangereux de lui trop faire voir sa grandeur sans sa bassesse. Il est encore plus dangereux de lui laisser ignorer l'un et l'autre. Mais il est très avantageux de lui représenter l'un et l'autre.

PASCAL

It is dangerous to show man too clearly how much he resembles the beast without at the same time showing him his greatness. It is also dangerous to allow him too clear a vision of his greatness without his baseness. It is even more dangerous to leave him in ignorance of both. But it is very profitable to show him both.

(No. 186 in H. F. Stewart's edition and translation, 1950)

CONTENTS

and Meaning / Call notes of birds / Call notes
adapted to signalling different types of danger / Bird
song—signals indicative of both species and individual
/ Neural templates for song—innate and acquired /
Song learning by imitation in birds / Sea birds—The
fullest development of individual recognition by voice /
The perfection and complexity of the aural sense in
birds as compared with that of man / Imitative ability in the Indian Hill Mynah / Summary of vocal auditory communication in birds / Bird language and
human speech / The song of the Humpbacked Whale
/ Audio-perception in bats.

The problem of instinct / The history of the instinct
concept / The influence of Darwin / The rise of
ethology / The characteristics of instinct / The relation between environmentally stable and environmentally labile behaviour / The two natural divisions
of a life history / Fixed action pattern, consummatory
acts, and consummatory stimuli / Nesting behaviour /
The analysis of bird songs / Drives / Neurophysiological aspects / Hormones and motivation / The effects of specific and non-specific stimuli / The relation
to genetic factors / Instinct and information / The
estimation of complexity / Preliminary statement on
learning.

The types of learning relevant to perception and perceptual organisation / Insight, or exploratory learning
/ Latent learning, or exploratory learning / Field
observations on insects and birds / Laboratory observations / Recognition of pattern / Rate of perceptual
development—laboratory animals versus those in their

/ Man as a religious animal / The concept of the
soul / The knowledge of death / The concept of creation / Fitness of the environment / Idea of the
supernatural / Natural religion / The supreme duty
of man.

PREFACE

I should probably never have undertaken to write a work of this kind had it not been for the honour conferred upon me by the University of St. Andrews in appointing me Gifford Lecturer for the years 1969–71. The will of Lord Gifford instructed the Lecturers to deal with natural religion and "to treat their subject as a strictly natural science, the greatest of all possible sciences. . . ." It is also specifically stated that the Lecturers shall be under no restraint whatever in the treatment of their themes. Faced with an opportunity of this kind one naturally gives careful thought to the topic and scope of one's lectures, and I chose my title, bearing in mind several related reasons.

Firstly our views on human nature are fundamental to the whole development, indeed the whole future, of society in this epoch of an overpopulation catastrophe. It is only too clear, and not in the least surprising, that human life appears to be less generally valued than at any time in the past hundred years or more. There are a number of possible reasons for this, but two of them are I think particularly clear. Firstly there are already too many people in the world so that, however humane and benevolent we may be, one cannot help feeling a twinge of satisfaction (if the disaster is not too near us, personally) at anything which reduces the population a little, however trivially. Secondly the widespread, often subconscious, acceptance of the outdated view of science, that man is simply the product of vast machine-like evolutionary forces, can easily lead to a hopeless loss of faith in the value of human beings and a consequent sense of the futility and purposelessness of our existence. It accordingly seemed to me that the position of Man in the animal kingdom, his evolutionary relationships to the rest of the living world, as far as these can be reasonably presumed, is one of the most important and significant topics to which a biologist can address himself. And granting this, it is essential that people should be shown both the characteristics in which the animal world approaches, and in some cases greatly exceeds, mankind in achievement and those characteristics of man that cause us sometimes to feel that we are brutes and at other times that we are gods.

I felt convinced that it would be futile to talk in general terms about the similarities and differences between animal and human nature because, in spite of many popular works on both, the field is vast and complex; moreover knowledge is accumulating at a formidable rate. This means that the particular facts that are relative to such a discussion must be selected and marshalled with the immediate ends of the discussion constantly in mind.

A matter of prime importance emerged as soon as I began to think seriously about lecturing and writing on such a topic—namely this: it would be useless to launch into a consideration of man, how far he is unique and how far he is just an exceptional animal, without first examining the question of the origin of the lower animals and indeed of life itself; for if the lowest forms of life are fully explicable in terms of non-living existence—that is to say if all the features of any living organism can be fully described in terms of chemistry and physics—then it would be that much more probable that Man himself could be "explained" in purely animal terms, and thus, as a further remove, in terms of the world of physics and chemistry. So the problem of the nature and origin of life at once became basic to the whole enquiry.

As will be seen, the answer becomes surprisingly definite. The general trend of the work of philosophers of science in the last half century has been increasingly to make clear that in spite of the enormous progress of science in explaining the complex in terms of the simple, and special cases as instances of general laws, there are big and seemingly unbridgeable discontinuities in the account of the world as we range from the supposed "primordial gases" and particles to this stupendously complex and awesomely great universe which we now realise we inhabit.

Thus it now seems clear that however perfect our knowledge of the details of any supposed "primordial nebula" might have been, and however thorough our understanding of the particles of which such a nebula could have been constituted, it would still have been logically impossible to have foretold the development of the world of heavy atoms such as carbon and iron on which life as we know it must depend. That is to say the world which the chemist studies can, it seems, never be *fully* explained and interpreted in terms of physics. Rather there seems to be a real discontinuity—a real unforeseeable emergence of something new. Similarly the marvellous epoch of discoveries of the genetic code through which we have recently lived seems, quite contrary to the popular belief, to make it far less comprehensible how life might have arisen from non-living than it was before. The possibilities of this having happened "by chance" are, so far as we can see, so infinitely improbable that science as such can hardly have an opinion to express. Life may have arisen many times in the history of the cosmos; it may on the other hand be absolutely unique and have arisen only once. Science has, as yet, *no grounds* for considering one alternative more probable than another. Similarly when we come to the other great frontier of knowledge, the relation between the private world of personal consciousness and the world picture resulting from the application of the scientific methods of, for instance, physics, biochemistry, genetics and physiology, we are again confronted with a seemingly unbridgeable gap where something truly and completely new appears to have emerged over the horizon.

Now it is clear that the scientist must always try to interpret and explain the complex in terms of the simple, the "higher" in terms of the "lower"; for that—reductionism as it is called—is of the very nature, the basic technique, of the scientific enterprise.

Indeed all of us working scientists regard this as our universally applicable conceptual tool. Yet we have compelling logical reasons for believing that science, from its very nature, can never yield a complete self-coherent picture of the world. There will always be a residue, something behind and beyond, which science is unable to grasp.

The Lectures from which the book arose were given to a stimulating and rewarding audience which included undergraduate and graduate students and staff from several different faculties —scientific, philosophical, and theological. With such an audience comprising such a range of age, interests, and approaches I naturally strove for eclecticism, and this has inevitably influenced the form and content of the book. It also meant that the treatment had often to be cursory, and many topics might certainly have profited by much fuller discussion than I have given them. However the book is already larger than I intended it to be and to have extended it still further would have involved a two-volume work at least and a much longer delay in publication. Where I have gone into fuller detail, e.g., Chapter 3, it is because I feel that while the non-specialist reader may be fairly well acquainted with, say, the recent developments in the study of monkeys and apes, he is likely to know far less about the astounding behavioural and sensory abilities of some of the "lower animals." Yet the study of birds and fish and also of some of the invertebrates such as insects and sea anemones, and even humbler creatures, reveals facts which, in their way, are just as important as evidence for "animal nature."

I have tried to give references to the more important general works for more detailed study, without overburdening the bibliography unduly. However, Chapter 3 is something of an exception in that it contains so much new factual material, as yet little available in works of general reference. So here I felt more detailed citations and explanations to be desirable.

W. H. THORPE
Cambridge, November 1972

PART ONE

ANIMAL NATURE

Chapter 1

LIVING AND NON-LIVING

INTRODUCTION

My objective in this book is to show the living world, and especially the animal world, as part of, yet distinct from, the inanimate world and to consider particularly the animal world especially as it appears to approach the human world in behaviour and capabilities. Then I propose to consider man firstly as part of the animal world and secondly as in some respects uniquely different from the animals and to discuss the nature and extent of this uniqueness. I am only too aware of the immensity of this undertaking, involving as it does incursions into many branches of science both physical and biological. And as if that were not enough, I must attempt substantial raids into the territories of various branches of psychology, philosophy, linguistic, and other arts, and, not least, theology! Though parts of this book must inevitably be complex I have chosen a simple title, *Animal Nature and Human Nature*. In this title I use the word "nature" in its ordinary everyday meaning, as denoting the qualities of anything which make it what it is, and this implies that we are trying to discover the essential quality, character, or disposition of the beings we talk about.

There are two key questions to be asked at the outset, questions which are continually debated by scientists and to which the answers are very far from clear: Is there a real unbridgeable gap between (1) the living and the non-living and (2) between man and the rest of the living world?

Just because the relationship, or lack of relationship, between animals and men is central to my whole theme I have, in choosing the examples of animal behaviour that I discuss, often selected the more complex, the "higher" or what appear to be the more "intelligent" instances. But I am anxious not to give the impression that all the animal world is like this; and so it is essential to start with an aspect of the whole subject which is more technical and difficult than most—that is, the relations between the animate and the inanimate, between the approaches of the physicist chemist and engineer on the one hand and the biologist, naturalist, and psychologist on the other.

Whenever we discuss the sciences and particularly how to teach them, even when we just think about them, most of us tend to place them in our minds in a linear series. Mathematics and physics are at the top and the others arranged down the rungs of a ladder up which they are proceeding as they become more exact. The so-called descriptive sciences are at the bottom of the ladder, perhaps not even standing on it at all, but still waiting for the first lucky throw as in a dice game (Pantin, 1968). In fact, a little thought shows that this linear arrangement is certainly wrong. We have only to consider astronomy, geology, and biophysics to see that much. The divisions we make are in fact arbitrary, and the divisions between physical science and biological science at first appear as merely those of practical convenience. Obviously the sciences form a multidimensional network—some of them complex, some of them apparently much simpler, some of them highly precise and exact, some with a lot of fluff round the edges.

The Relations Between the Sciences

A hundred years ago it was customary to divide sciences into the observational and the experimental (Pantin, op. cit.). When we merely note and record phenomena which occur around us, in the ordinary course of nature, we are said "to observe." When we change the course of nature, by the intervention of our will and manipulative powers producing new or unusual combinations of phenomena, we are said "to experiment." Sir John Herschel suggested that these two modes would be better called passive and active observation. Obviously observations are made in both cases; experiment is therefore just observation plus the controlled alteration of conditions. There are, of course, "natural experiments" such as the occurrence of eclipses or the appearance of super nova stars; and the astronomer, even today, has to wait for the appropriate time, or journey to the appropriate place, in order to find the conditions most fitted to allow firmer conclusions to be drawn. In the mid-nineteenth century it was frequently said that geologists ought only to observe and not to theorise—in response to which argument Charles Darwin remarked that at this rate a man might as well go into a gravel pit and count the pebbles and describe their colours. He even went so far as to say, and we should all agree with him today, that even to be a good observer one must be an active theoriser.

But the physical scientists are unwilling to deal with any project where they cannot in at least some, and often a very high, degree manipulate the conditions. In doing this they are in fact abstracting from the richness and complexity of the natural world and focussing their attention on small parts of it—with the spectacular results that we all know today. Carl Pantin (1968) said that physics and chemistry had been enabled to become exact and mature just because so much of the wealth of natural phenomena is excluded from their study. So there is no need for the classical physicist or chemist as such to go to biology for data; he in fact restricts himself to certain types of material and situations which his techniques and theories can deal with, and for this reason Pantin, in fact following Clerk Maxwell (in 1877), calls such sciences "restricted." In contrast, biology and geology are "unrestricted." Scientists devoted to these latter fields may have to follow the analysis of their problems into every other kind of science; whereas the physicist can stick to his last. This selection

5

or restriction enables the physical scientist to make rapid progress, with the help of mathematical models of high intellectual quality. To quote Carl Pantin again, "Very clever men are answering the relatively easy questions of the Natural Examination Paper. Intellectually magnificent though the attack upon these problems has been, the problems they present are easier than those of the unrestricted sciences, of which biology is the obvious example."

At first sight it might seem that the fact that sciences like geology deal with gross phenomena is an indication of immaturity. Similarly with psychology. Indeed, during the last twenty-five years, experimental psychologists have again and again pleaded that the reason why their results are not more satisfactory and firmly established is because their science as yet lacks an Isaac Newton. It should therefore, so they argue, be their aim to make psychology as precise and exact as physics. But it is an error to suppose that it is only micro-events, such as the behaviour of electrons and of molecules, which are worthy of the consideration of the true scientist. Indeed the astronomer and geologist would heartily agree with the biologist that there is much to be learned from the study of slow-acting systems of relatively large size; these systems simply cannot be examined with the precision and exactitude characteristic of the work of the chemist and physicist. Nonetheless it is, and of course must be, the aim of all branches of science to render themselves as exact as possible; and so, as the various disciplines mature, mathematics is brought more and more into the picture—even nowadays in such apparently unmathematical subjects as taxonomic botany. New mathematical techniques are continually being produced to answer questions which have become too intractable for the old-fashioned methods of observation and description. This is of course just as it should be and reveals another important point: namely that, since mathematics is really the study of relations, so also is science to a very large extent the study of relationships; and we may find important relations displayed in the interaction of species of animals at one level of size, in the movements of strata and the drift of the continents at another level of size, as well as in the unimaginable distances of the stellar universes. This does not mean that these sciences are simply becoming new branches of physics and chemistry! On the contrary they are revealing new features and new laws as they become more exact—features and laws which the chemist and physicist by themselves are powerless to investigate.

Knowledge of the "Objective" World

To say that science investigates relationships is of course only one aspect of the truth. The word science formerly meant the whole of knowledge; but by popular usage it has become more or less restricted to knowledge about objects in the natural world—that is the task of the natural sciences. This brings us to the next important question, namely—what are the "objects" which the scientist investigates? Nature presents itself to us in one aspect as a continuum. In studying this continuum we recognise complexes of phenomena which retain identity and show a high degree of stability and persistence of pattern, in contrast to examples with less cohesive features (Weiss, 1969). In practice the scientist, like everyone else, accepts the reality of descriptions of the external world as in some sense made up of "real" objects. We may all be confused at the first sight of an entirely new object or of an old object in an unfamiliar situation. A curved stick in the forest may look like a snake, a toadstool may look like a delightfully sticky bun, and we have to look quite carefully before we can decide what it is we are really seeing. At first glance we may be quite certain of our identification, only to find, perhaps to our embarrassment, how wrong we have been. A favourite dog of mine, who was fond of chasing cats, was not prepared for the fact that a neighbour had acquired a highly miniaturised Yorkshire Terrier which at a distance looked to her like a cat. She chased it, and her confusion when it turned and barked at her was comical to behold.

As scientists we must beware of following the psychologists of a previous generation and looking upon sense data as a substance "out of which we build perceptions." Rather sense data are highly intellectual abstractions from it, robbed of those relationships which are the basis of our conviction of reality. But above all, the scientist, whatever he may say, always believes that he is investigating a real world consisting of "objects" whose relationships he can study. Now the most striking feature of the everyday world of objects is the enduring character of the things in it. Apart from cyclical changes, daily and seasonal, the world is full of things which we see as objects; some of them like the hills and the oceans are constant over immense periods of time; others like snowflakes and lightning flashes and many radio-active atoms and elementary particles may have very brief, even infinitesimal, existences. So the "real world" is built up of objects that endure, though (with the exception of certain primary physical particles) decaying slowly or rapidly, and other objects displaying dynamic equilibria (as does our atmosphere), which may endure for an immense period of time. And indeed most of the objects which, as biologists, we study *are* in a state of dynamic equilibrium. For though both a man and a mollusc may be presented to our senses as a continuing individual for a long time, the tissues of which they are composed are for the most part in a continual state of flux; like a river, whose form may remain substantially constant even though the water is continually changing, they can be composed of an entirely different set of molecules after the lapse of a few years. So our choice as to what we call "objects" obviously depends on our senses and on the fact that these senses only cover a certain range; our perceptions are in fact limited by what may be called our "sensory spectrum." We only see with light over a certain range of wavelengths. Bees have a good colour sense, but it corresponds to quite different divisions of the visible spectrum from our own and includes a region of sensitivity in ultraviolet. It is difficult for us to imagine what the bee is "seeing" when it can be trained to respond differentially to two white papers that are to our vision identical, but one of which reflects ultraviolet and the other does not. Again

8

with our unaided senses we do not perceive things which are too small, or too vast, or which endure for too short a time. The endurance of an enduring object is to be measured against the time scale of our own lives and senses. Events which are too small, too large, too quick, or too slow are not perceived, and unless our attention is drawn to them by indirect means we know nothing about them.

The Approach of the Physicist

But while we must have objects to study and "facts" about them—nevertheless, in all branches of science, we find that as we analyse, so the facts and objects tend to disappear and become systems of relations. It has always been so and very disturbing it is too. Scientists have at times been moved by a robust sense of a reality waiting to be studied, of nature as bringing to them an intelligible message which they only have to decipher (Toulmin, 1966). Yet at other times the programme of science has been modified so fast as to leave many almost in a state of shock. The popular and semi-popular writings of Eddington in the 1930s played a great part in helping the ordinary man to understand what was going on as the safe material world of Victorian physicists seemed to be dissolving under his very eyes. This is no new problem. Some deplore change, some welcome it; and the changes that have taken place in theoretical science may indeed be welcomed, even though they may seem to conflict with common sense, since by and large they undoubtedly constitute immense advances in our understanding of the very nature of the natural world. But we always feel some pangs for the disappearance of the worlds we knew, just as did Newton and Galileo in their last years, a feeling which was well expressed by John Donne in 1611 who wrote,

> And new Philosophy calls all in doubt,
> The Element of fire is quite put out;
> The Sun is lost, and th'earth, and no man's wit

Can well direct him where to looke for it.
And freely men confesse that this world's spent,
When in the Planets, and in the Firmament
They seeke so many new; then see that this
Is crumbled out againe to his Atomies.
'Tis all in peeces, all cohaerence gone;
All just supply, and all Relation.[1]

Ever since Victorian times it has been the changes in physics and in astronomy which have in fact seemed so appalling and disconcerting to many thoughtful men. Many of our most cherished beliefs have gone by the board. Atoms were thought to be permanent unchanging elements of nature. Now, far from remaining unaltered, they appear to be created, destroyed, and transmuted. What do remain enduring are certain abstract attributes of particles, of which the electric charge and the wave aspects of elementary physical particles are the most familiar. Edmund Whittaker (1949) has described what he calls *postulates of impotence*, but which Bronowski (1969) has cleverly entitled *the laws of the impossible*, a break-up of which is particularly disturbing. Thus a great part of mechanics can be derived from the single assertion that perpetual motion is impossible. A great part of electro-magnetism follows from the assertion that it is impossible to induce an electric field inside a hollow conductor. Again, in special relativity it is impossible to detect one's motion if it is steady, even by measuring the speed of light. In general relativity it is impossible to tell a gravitational field from a field set up by one's own motion. In quantum physics there are several laws of the impossible which are not quite equivalent: *the principle of uncertainty* is one, another is that it is *impossible to identify the same electron in successive observations*. At bottom all the quantum principles assert that there are no devices by which we can wholly control what state of a system we will observe next: Bronowski translates that into the statement, "It is impossible to ensure that we shall copy a specified object perfectly." And this disturbing process of change seems to be accelerating, till one wonders how it will end, if end it will! As J. B. S. Haldane once said (not long before his death), "My own suspicion is that the universe is not only queerer than we suppose, but queerer than we *can* suppose."

Indeed the inevitable conclusion from quantum theory seems to be that nature is fundamentally non-mechanical. Some experts go so far as to suggest, on the basis of their knowledge of quantum theory and its effectiveness, that it is better (that is to say more rational) to start by being indeterministic in general (Linney and Von Weizsäcker, 1971). Von Weizsäcker suggests that belief in quantum theory is similar to the belief that nature is indeterministic. But of course one must not suggest that quantum theory in its present form is final. Indeed at the present time there are strong criticisms of it coming from philosophers and philosophically minded physicists. This tendency is based upon the conviction that ideas like complementarity, correspondence, uncertainty, and indeterminacy have always been indefensible on philosophical grounds. Therefore such physicists all propose the idea that there must be hidden variables in quantum theories and so they proceed to indulge in perfectly respectable and allowable speculation as to what is needed, beyond quantum theory, to provide a satisfactory philosophical picture. Of course speculation is essential in research as it is in any field of thought which is not fixed by rigid dogma. Theoretical physicists are an exceptionally able and intelligent group. Indeed they exemplify the dictum that an intelligent man is one who can hold two contradictory concepts in his mind simultaneously. The trouble however is that speculation, no matter how rational and revealing it may seem, is not an alternative to a working theory, however imperfect that theory may be. It must be said that the physicists who stick to quantum theory find that it is still an indispensable tool in research. That is to say it turns out results expressible in numerical terms. So far the speculations aimed at refining or replacing quantum theory have not produced results in this way, and until they do they are hardly likely to emerge victorious.

One of the most striking differences between physics and biology arises in just this context. I think one can say that in biology there are no *genuinely biological* postulates of impotence *except* that spontaneous generation is impossible. Any other postulates of impotence which may appear to be part of biology are in the end I think reducible to physics, and it is from that discipline they really come.

But there is another side to all this. There are assumptions which we cannot do without, even though all seems to be dissolving. One of these is that there is a *real world which we in some measure apprehend by our senses: that is to say that knowledge is possible*. And (as Bronowski, 1969, points out) in the field of science this means that it is *rational*. But this is not to imply that nature is necessarily therefore all machine-like. And this idea of a great machine is one of the great misconceptions of our age, haunting the biologist now as it haunted the thinkers of the nineteenth century when Tennyson wrote, "The stars, she whispers, blindly run." But let us come back to biology, and particularly to the ideas of modern biology as affecting man's views of nature and his own place in it.

Thunderstorms and Organisms Compared

In 1944 Professor Schrödinger wrote a little book entitled *What Is Life?* This treatise of less than a hundred small pages has perhaps had more influence on recent thinking on this topic, among both physicists and biologists, than almost any other recent study. Schrödinger points out that when a piece of matter is said to be alive, it is because it goes on "doing something"—moving, exchanging material with its environment, and so on. Moreover, it goes on doing this for a much longer period than we would expect an inanimate piece of matter to "keep going" under similar circumstances. A system that is not alive, if isolated or placed in a uniform environment, usually ceases all motion very quickly as a result of various kinds of friction. Temperature becomes uniform by heat conduction and after that the whole system fades away into a dead, inert "lump of matter." A permanent state has been reached in which no *macroscopically* observable events occur, a state which the physicists speak of as thermodynamical equilibrium or "maximum entropy." During a continued stretch of existence, it is by avoiding rapid decay into the inert state of equilibrium that an organism appears so enigmatic; so much so that from the earliest stages of human thought some special non-physical or supernatural force was claimed to be operative in the organism.

Pantin, in discussing such statements, points out that almost everything that Schrödinger has said about life could at least in some measure be said about a thunderstorm. A thunderstorm goes on doing something, moving, exchanging material with the environment, and so forth; and that for a much longer period than we would expect of an inanimate system of comparable size and complexity. It is by avoiding the rapid decay into an inert system of equilibrium that a thunderstorm appears so extraordinary. But the parallels between living organisms and thunderstorms, and indeed some other meteorological phenomena, are remarkable. It is true that thunderstorms arise by spontaneous generation, and since they are incapable of sexual reproduction natural selection can only act upon them by selecting individuals and not by acting upon the whole species. Like living organisms, they require matter and energy for their maintenance. This is supplied by the situation of a cold airstream overlying warm, moist air. This situation is unstable and at a number of places vertical up-currents occur. Once these have developed they are maintained, at least for a while, through the liberation of heat consequent upon the formation of rain as the warm damp air rises. Each up-current "feeds" upon the warm and damp air in its neighbourhood and is thus in competition with and can suppress its neighbours. A storm is in fact parasitic on the increase of entropy which would result from the mixing of warm moist and cold air to form a uniform mass. Moreover the storm itself has a well-defined anatomy of what can almost be called functional parts. The two accompanying (Figures 1 and 2) illustrations show this better than would a long, detailed description. But although certain non-living systems, of which the thunderstorm is such a striking example, do show what we can call "organismal characters." This property is nowhere found in so high a degree as it is in living organisms.

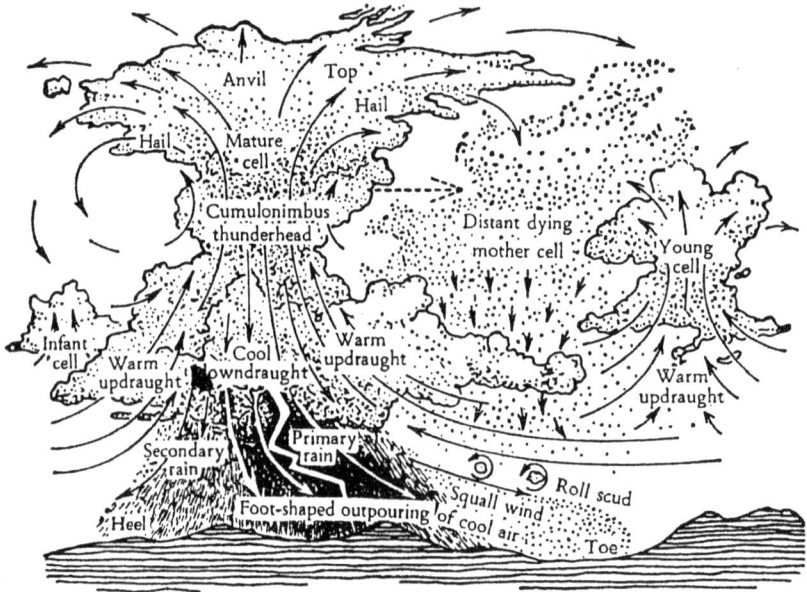

Figure 1 Diagram of the organisation of a thunderstorm as a system of individual cells. As the drawing shows, the storm has "a well-defined morphology of what can almost be called functional parts." As the descending central downpour of rain increases, the mature stage of the original cell passes into the dissipating stage. This presently culminates in the total cessation of updraughts. The process is meanwhile being repeated in the offspring thunderstorm cells and cloud towers, each of which in turn passes through the same process of "development, maturity and decay." (From Pantin, 1968, after Murchie, 1955.)

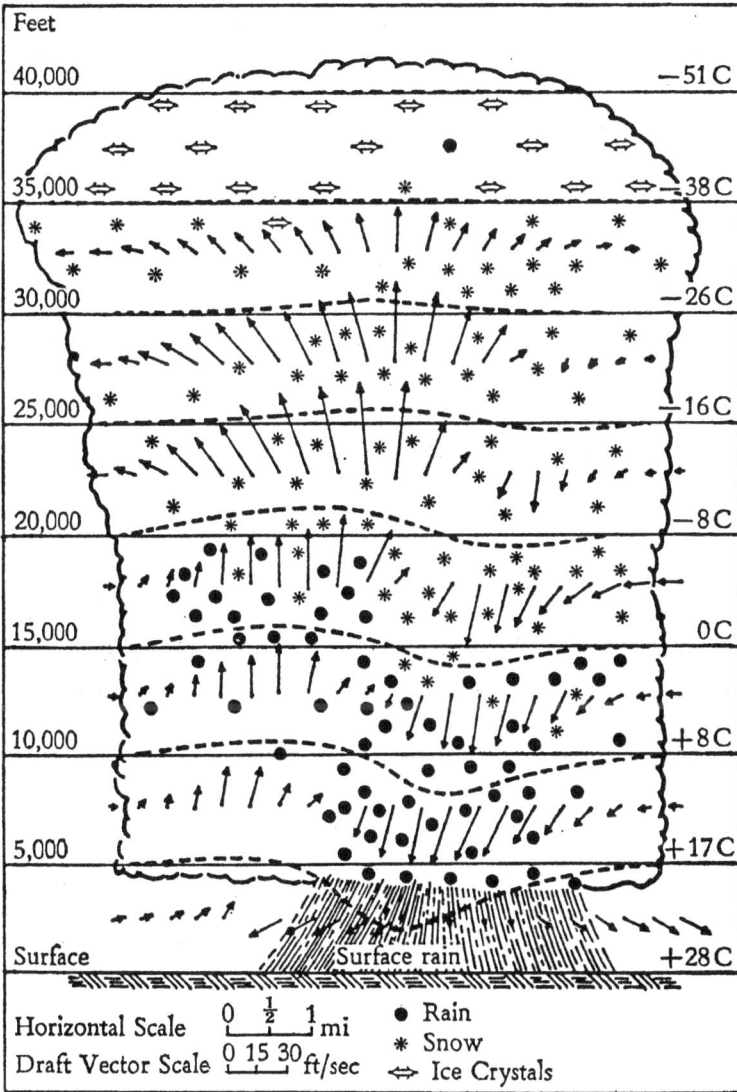

Figure 2 Sketch of a vertical cross section through a thunderstorm cell in a mature stage, showing vectorially the air circulation. The temperature distribution shown is typical of summer thunderstorms in the eastern United States. (From Pantin, 1968, after Byers, 1949.)

Woodger (1960) pointed to the importance of the fact that living things have parts which stand in a relation of existential dependence to one another—e.g., limbs, digestive organs, circulatory systems and brains. And even in a single cell (Figure 3)

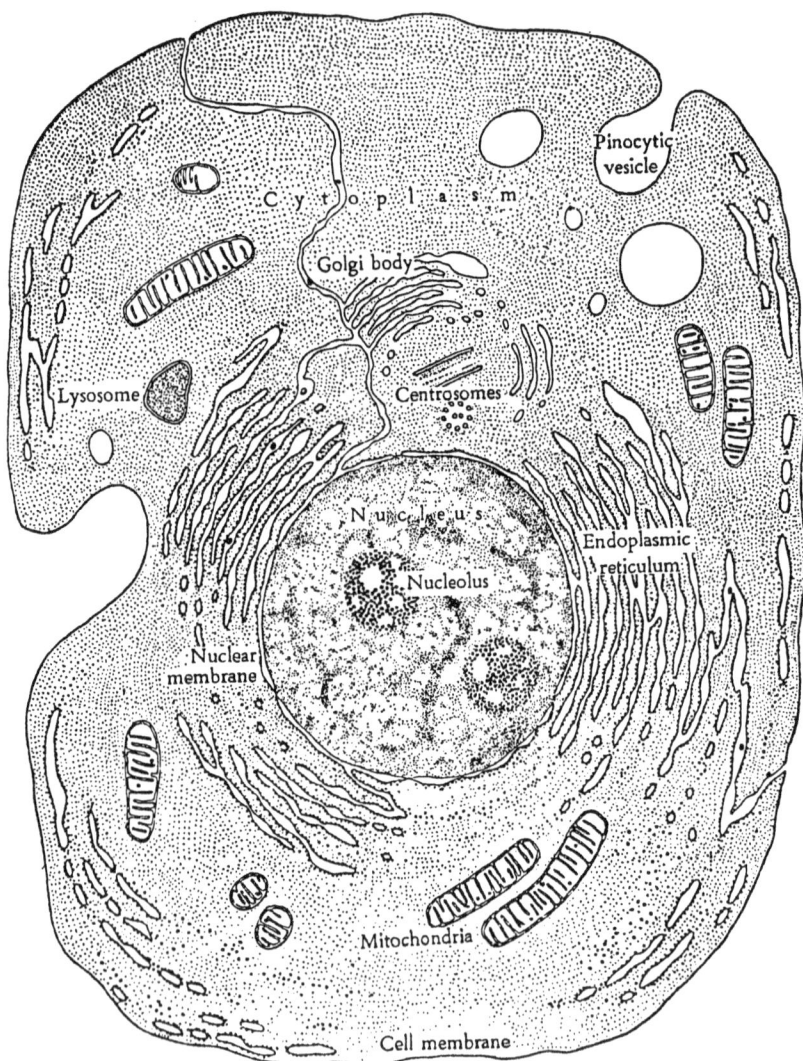

Figure 3 Diagram of a cell showing the organelles which form essential parts of its machinery. (From Pantin, 1968, after J. Brachet, 1961.)

we find organelles, so to speak micro-organs, all of which seem to constitute some essential part of the cell's machinery. So we can ask of the structures in a living organism, just as we can ask of the structures in a man-made machine, what is this for? We can often give fairly exact and plausible answers. It has been argued, I think convincingly, that we cannot sensibly ask that kind of question of natural non-living systems. It is surely nonsense to ask of a solar system or its parts, or of a nebula or an atomic structure, or of the parts of a mineral, "What is this for?" Any answer which we think we can give is an answer of an entirely different kind from that which we can give in the case of a man-made machine or the parts of a living organism. Another distinction, of course, concerns reproduction. If we compare this in living and non-living systems we find that in non-living systems (e.g., thunderstorms or vortex rings) new examples are generated, but the new ones do not exactly reduplicate the old. In the reproduction of living organisms, however, reproduction is essentially reduplication of all the essential features of the design (Pantin, 1968). It is the fact that the organisation of living creatures, whether great or small, is determined by a molecular and therefore precisely repeatable template that makes biological reproduction possible. So we can say (a) what organisms *do* is different from what *happens to* stones. (b) The parts of organisms are functional and are interrelated one with another to form a system which is working in a particular way or appears to be designed for a particular direction of activity. In other words the system is directive, or if we like to use the word in a very wide and loose sense, "purposive." (c) The material substances of organisms on the one hand and inorganic materials on the other are in general very different. And there is still another difference (d) which seems to me of great importance, and that is that organisms absorb and store information, change their behaviour as a result of that information, and all but the very lowest forms of animals (and perhaps these too) have special organs for detecting, sorting, and organising this information—namely the sense organs and specialised parts of the central nervous system. I shall return to this very important aspect later.

First we must make it clear, as of course Michael Polanyi (1967) has done, that we adhere to the basic assumption that all local structural or physiological organisations and events inside the living being occur according to a local biochemical determinism. That is to say that there is no firm evidence whatever against, and an immense amount of evidence for, the view that the "ordinary" laws of physics and chemistry are holding within the organism just as they do within a man-made machine. The problem is how to explain the stability and reproduction of even the simplest organism in space and time in terms of the organisation of the structure itself.

The Approach of the Biologist

It is a claim of molecular biologists, a claim with which we can in general agree, that they have made very large steps towards reducing the problem of the organisation of the living being (including even the problem of its hereditary processes) to physical laws. Some indeed would claim to have accomplished the whole task already. We shall come back to the question of the hereditary organisation later. Here we can say that what has been done by the molecular biologists is to develop a model of the cell which behaves very much like a classical man-made machine, or an automaton, but one in which the "secret of heredity" is found in the normal chemistry of nucleic acids and enzymes. The implication of this is that parts functioning like a machine can be described as a machine even though these parts may be single molecules; and machines are understood in terms of elementary physical laws. This is an attractive analogy and is indeed one which we have all been using for a long time. As has been explained above, we repeatedly and successfully ask the question, "What is this for?" when considering the different structures in living organisms—quite as successfully and legitimately as we can ask this of a piston, a lever, or an electric circuit in any machine designed by man.

The Nature of the Organisation Shown by Living Beings

But we can easily be trapped by this useful analogy into losing sight of two basic aspects of living beings which are clearly evident to the physicist but, curiously enough, overlooked by the biologist. It is, of course, no satisfactory answer to respond to the question, "How does a man-made machine or living machine work?" by saying that it obeys the laws of physics and chemistry. As Pattee (1971) points out, if we ask, "What is the secret of a computing machine?" no physicist would consider it in any sense an answer to say, what he already knows perfectly well, that the computer obeys all the laws of mechanics and electricity. If there is any problem in the organisation of a computer, it is the unlikely constraints which, so to speak, harness these laws to perform highly specific and directive functions which have of course been built into the machine by the expertise of the designer. So of course the real problem of life is not that all the structures and molecules in the cell appear to comply with the known laws of physics and chemistry. The real mystery is the origin of the highly improbable constraints which harness these laws to fulfil particular functions. This is in fact the problem of hierarchical control. And any claim that life has been reduced to physics and chemistry must in these days, if it is to carry conviction, be accompanied by an account of the dynamics and statistics and the operating reliability of enzymes ultimately in terms of present-day groundwork of physics, namely quantum mechanical concepts. So we have two questions, "How does it work?" and "How does it arise?" The second question has in fact, two facets: (a) how does it arise in the development of the individual organism during the process of growth from the moment of fertilisation of the egg and (b) how does the egg itself come to get that way; that is to say, how can we conceive of evolution as having "designed" the cell?

19

The Idea of Hierarchy

It is the necessary concept of hierarchy in biology which pin-points the problem. And the problem is one of hierarchical inter-faces. In common language a hierarchy is an organisation of individuals with levels of authority—usually with one level sub-ordinate to the next one above and ruling over the next one below. For an admirable account of this, see Koestler and Smyth-ies (1969). So any general theory of biology (which must in-clude the concept of hierarchy) must thereby explain the origin and operation, the reliability and persistence of these constraints which harness matter to perform coherent functions according to a hierarchical plan. Pattee (1970, 1971) says

> it is the central problem of the origin of life, when aggregations of matter obeying only elementary physical laws first began to con-strain individual molecules to a functional, collective behaviour. It is the central problem of development where collections of cells control the growth or genetic expression of individual cells. It is the central problem of biological evolution in which groups of cells form larger and larger organizations by generating hierarchical constraints on subgroups. It is the central problem of the brain where there appears to be an unlimited possibility for new hier-archical levels of description. These are all problems of hierarchical organization. Theoretical biology must face this problem as funda-mental, since hierarchical control is the essential and distinguishing characteristic of life (1970, p. 120).

He goes on to point out that a simpler set of descriptions at each level will not suffice. Biology must include a theory of the levels themselves.

I have said above that even the simplest biological mechanism is to a superlative degree more complex than the most complex of humanly constructed machines. It is perhaps instructive to consider this complexity as it appears when we look at the human body and brain. Professor Paul Weiss (1969) has put this very dramatically by pointing out that the average cell in our bodies contains about 10^5 macromolecules. The brain alone contains 10^{10} cells, hence about 10^{15} macromolecules. To get these figures themselves into perspective, it is worth remembering that the age of the galaxy in which our solar system resides is estimated at 10^{15} sec! This is to say each of us has in our brains about as many cells as there have been seconds since our part of the cosmos began to assume its present form. Paul Weiss says:

> Could you actually believe that such an astronomical number of elements shuffled around, as we have demonstrated them to be in our study of cells, could ever guarantee to you your sense of identity and constancy in life without this constancy being insured by a superordinated principle of integration? Well, if you could for instance by invoking a "micro-precisely" predetermined universe, the following consideration should dispel that notion. Each nerve cell in the brain receives an average of 10^4 connections from other brain cells, and, in addition, recent studies on the turnover of the molecular population within a given nerve cell have indicated that, although the cells themselves retain their individuality, their macromolecular contingent is renewed about 10^4 times in a lifetime. In short, every cell of our brain actually harbours and has to deal with approximately 10^9 macromolecules during its life. But even that is not all. It is reported that the brain loses on the average 10^3 cells per day irretrievably rather at random, so that the brain-cell population is decimated during the life span by about 10^7 cells, expunging 10^{11} conducting cross-linkages. And yet, despite that ceaseless change of detail in that vast population of elements, our basic patterns of behaviour, our memories, our sense of integral existence as an individual have retained throughout their unitary continuity of pattern (p. 13).

This is just another way of putting the problem that Schrödinger poses in his book *What Is Life?* The problem is mainly that of the contrast between the degree of potential freedom on the one hand and on the other hand the perseverance and the essentially invariant pattern of the functions of such systems. (By "degrees of freedom" we mean simply the number of variables necessary to describe or predict what is going on. Thus there is a potential freedom amongst trillions of molecules making up the brain, or for that matter the whole body.)

Consider this for our nervous system, and following this our thoughts, our ideas, our memories. Schrödinger was forced to the conclusion that, as he put it, "I . . . that is to say, every conscious mind that has ever said or felt I . . . am the person, if any, who controls 'the motion of the atoms' according to the laws of nature." This puts the problem of the boundary conditions, which have to be maintained all the time in both simple and complex examples of biological mechanisms, as it appeared to one of the most able physicists of his time who had given particular thought to these problems. Polanyi as we have seen assumes that all molecules work according to natural laws, but concludes that since no one has accounted for hierarchical organisation by these laws there must be principles of organisation which will in due course be found not to be reducible to the laws of physics and chemistry. Many others would be rather more cautious. Thus the physicist Pattee (1970) expresses himself as neither satisfied with the claim that physics explains how life *works* nor the claim that physics cannot explain how life *arose*. In his view (I) the concept of autonomous hierarchy involves collections of elements which are responsible for producing their own rules as contrasted with collections which are designed by an external authority to have hierarchical behaviour. He then (II) assumes, of course, that they are part of the physical world and that all the elements obey the laws of physics. He limits his definition of hierarchical control (III) *to those rules or constraints which arise within such a collection of elements but which affect individual elements of the collection.* Finally, and perhaps most important, he points out (IV) that collective restraints which affect individual elements always appear to produce some integrated function of the collection. In common language this is to say that such hierarchical constraints produce specific actions or are "designed for" some purpose.

It is in considering the third of the above four statements, in relation to classical mechanics, that the difficulties are seen to be at their greatest. Classical physics appears to provide no way in which an explanation can be reached because it requires a "collection" of particles which constrains individual particles in a manner not deducible from their individual behaviour. However, it has been pointed out that in quantum mechanics the concept of the particle is changed and the fundamental idea of a continuous wave description of motion produces the stationary state or local time-independent collection of atoms and molecules. So it seems to be not impossible that hierarchical structures could be reducible to quantum mechanics, although as we shall see later the whole scheme of quantum mechanics is now in such confusion that, to the outsider, it seems far from clear to what extent they will be able to help. But even if structural hierarchies can be explained ultimately in this way, there is still something missing when we come to biological systems. Complexities of physical structure seldom if ever, by themselves, provide any feature which seriously suggests to biologists that such structures are in any sense alive. As has been said above, what organisms do is different to what happens to stones. The piece missing in the hierarchies of the non-biological world is, once again, function. What is so exceptional about enzymes and what creates their hierarchical significance is the simplicity of their collective function which results from their very detailed complexity. This is the core of what is meant by integrated behaviour.

Self-programming

We are generally content with the view that a physical system, at least a macrophysical system, may appear completely deterministic; but the attempt to reduce living systems to such, that is to say *formal reductionism,* fails in part because the number of possible combinations or classifications is generally immensely larger than the number of degrees of freedom. And then, as we have seen, and as we shall see more clearly later, living systems are *self-programming;* this means that the particles of which they are composed form an internal simplification, or *self-representa-*

tion; and these systems of self-representation which assume control of the whole seem utterly baffling in many cases because they appear to originate spontaneously. Again this means that the organism is self-programming. This concept of *living organisms being uniquely different from non-living systems in having internal self-representation* raises a point of most profound importance. As will be argued later in this book, it is difficult to know if and where in the animal kingdom one has the need to postulate "self-consciousness," "self-awareness" or, to use Eccles' phrase, "the experiencing self." We come to the conclusion that as we proceed from man downwards through the animal series, the lower we go the less useful (as predictive of animal behaviour and as leading to an understanding of animal nature) the concept becomes. Until with the lowest animals and with the plants the usefulness of the idea becomes vanishingly small. But if it be true that all living organisms have internal self-representation, does this not amount to saying that the seeds of self-consciousness are present in all living creatures—from the virus and the bacterium upwards?!

Another theoretical physicist, Walter M. Elsasser (1966), has approached some of these problems in an original manner by considering the number of internal configurations in which a complex system may exist in theory. Astronomers assume the existing finite total of atomic nuclei is of the order 10^{80} but, as we have seen, the lifetime of our galaxy is assumed to be no more than 10^{18} sec. Elsasser (1966) argues that the number of distinguishable events which can occur in a finite universe is correspondingly limited. In considering these systems of increasing complexity we must soon reach a point where a number of internal configurations in which the system may exist will vastly exceed the number of actual examples of any one given class that can possibly be collected in our universe. It follows that if the discrepancy between the number of possible states and the number of possible samples is large enough, we can assert without fear of contradiction that no two members of a class, e.g., no two members of an animal or plant species, not even two bacteria, can *ever* be in the same internal state. This leads Elsasser to suggest another characteristic of living organisms as distinct from non-living. He says that in physics the classes of things, e.g., atoms, protons, electrons, etc., are very homogeneous. It is a fundamental assumption that all the helium atoms in the universe are identical; though when we come to larger aggregations, however fully homogeneous the class, the objects would have to be not only chemically equivalent but also in the same quantum state. That is to say, for complete homogeneity all the members of a class have to be at the absolute zero point of the temperature scale so that their molecules are in the ground state. But the point is that in principle we do have, and can work with, the idea of homogeneous classes in physics. And all fundamental questions of theory may be evaluated in terms of these. This can never be the case in biology, even in principle, as the number of individuals in any class in existence at one time is far too small to allow statistical prediction to have any physical significance. The resulting conclusion is that while *physics is a science dealing with essentially homogeneous systems and classes, biology is a science of inhomogeneous systems and classes.* In physical terms one may say that an organism must be a system that is endlessly engaged in producing, regenerating, or increasing inhomogeneity, and thereby the phenomenon of individuality, at all levels of its functioning.

Polanyi seems so convinced of the impossibility of the physical explanation of these biological constraints that he often appears to be speaking as a vitalist. That is to say he is coming near to returning to the original idea of indwelling vital principle guiding the organism in some manner completely independent of its physical nature. Elsasser does not go as far as this, and he suggests that there is room for (and we must assume the existence of) separate laws—biotonic laws, as he calls them—which are compatible with the quantum laws but not deducible in principle from them. Two other physicists have considered this matter carefully (E. H. Kerner, in Waddington, 1970, and D. Bohm, in Bastin, 1971). Bohm indeed appears to find not only room for,

25

but, even within physics itself, a necessity for "hidden variables," which the usual scheme of quantum theory has ruled out as a matter of principle. Kerner, considering this, hesitates as yet to espouse either biotonic law or the incompleteness of quantal law, for he feels that no clear set of observations seem thus far to compel either. And we must not forget that a quantum-mechanical calculation even on one particular bacterial cell would be incorrect for every other cell, even of the same species—a point clearly made by Elsasser in his conclusions about the heterogeneity of the material with which the biologist has to deal. Finally one must here bring in again the most important biological discovery of recent years, and this is the discovery that the processes of life are directed by programmes. And not only directed by programmes and not only manifesting activity, but in some extraordinary way producing their own programmes. Professor Longuet-Higgins (in Waddington, 1970) sums this up from the biological point of view by showing that it results in the biological concept of the programme being something different from the purely physical idea of the programme; and we can now point to an actual programme tape in the heart of the cell, namely the DNA molecule. Even more remarkable is that programmed activity which we find in living nature will not merely determine the way in which the organism reacts to its environment; it actually controls the structure of the organism and its replication including the replication of the programmes themselves. This is what we mean by saying once again (a statement that can hardly be reiterated too often) that *life is not merely programmed activity but self-programmed activity.*

Monod (1971) has suggested that the combination of processes which must have occurred to produce life from inanimate matter is so extremely improbable that its occurrence may indeed have been a unique event (an event of zero probability). Monod also rightly points out that the uniqueness of the genetic code could be the result of natural selection. But even if we assume this, the extraordinary problem remains that the genetic code is without any biological function unless and until it is translated, that is unless it leads to the synthesis of the proteins whose structure is laid down by the code. Now Monod shows that the machinery by which the cell (or at least the non-primitive cell, which is the only one we know) translates the codes "consists of at least fifty macromolecular components which are themselves coded in DNA." Thus the code cannot be translated except by using certain products of its translation. As Sir Karl Popper (1972) comments, "this constitutes a really baffling circle: a vicious circle, it seems, for any attempt to form a model or a theory, of the genesis of the genetic code." In fact this undreamed of breakthrough of molecular biology, far from solving the problem of the origin of life, has made it, in Sir Karl Popper's opinion, a greater riddle than it was before. Thus we may be faced with a possibility that the origin of life, like the origin of the universe, becomes an impenetrable barrier to science and a block which resists all attempts to reduce biology to chemistry and physics. So difficult does it now seem to suppose that this earth can have supplied the necessary conditions for long enough to allow even a reasonable probability of the origin of life here that Crick and Orgel (1973) have been carefully and seriously considering the possibility that some simple form or forms of life may have been deliberately transmitted to this planet by intelligent beings on another!

The Concepts of Information

I have already used the terms "communication" and "information" and shall do so more as we proceed. And already we see that a recording and a read-out of information are both ideas fundamental to the concept of "life." So, from the behavioural point of view, it is very important to get our minds clear as to what we mean by communication. Here and in what follows I shall try to use the term "communication" only in the sense of interactions between organisms. This is different from the use of communication by many communication engineers, who use it loosely to mean the transmision of information regardless of its origin or destination. They will happily speak of a rock or a hill-side as communicating with an observer if some light reflected from the rock reaches his eyes. Worse still, as Donald MacKay has pointed out, the engineer's definition of a communication channel does not even require a causal connexion between the two points in question! Provided that the sequence of events at A shows some degree of correlation with the sequence at B, authors are ready to define a channel capacity "between A and B," regardless of the possibility that the correlation is due to a third common cause and not, after all, to any interaction. So in their sense, communications between A and B may imply (a) correlation between events at A and B; (b) causal interaction between A and B; (c) transmission of information between A and B, regardless of the presence of a sender or recipient, and/or finally (d) a transaction between organisms A and B.

MacKay (1972) gives a delightful example. If we see a man walking in the street carrying sandwich boards, can we legitimately say that he is communicating a message to all who see the sandwich boards? Surely not! The man may have his eyes on the ground and not see most of the people who look at the boards. Some people may be foreigners who cannot read the boards, and the man himself may be unable to read! On the other hand most people when they speak (or if they signal by Morse code) are directing their signals to some individual, known or unknown, with the expectation that communication will be established. It seems then that it is best to restrict the term "communication" to the sense in which a person, or animal A, communicates with a person, or animal B, only when A's action is goal-directed towards B. When I say "goal-directed," I mean either programmed by heredity or experience to be appropriate to perception by B or to be deliberately emitted in order to affect B or individuals of a similar class or type. If this relationship between A and B does not exist, then it is better simply to say that B perceives this or that about A or that "information flows" from A to B.

There is another criterion relevant to the attempt to define a living organism—namely that the organism is primarily something which perceives. And in saying this we mean that an organism (however simple and primitive it may be) in some sense searches for information and has some means of organising and storing its perceptions. This conclusion has been reached independently by a number of different workers, as for instance by Agar (1943), an investigator with a wide zoological and philosophical knowledge and having especial experience of the zoologically lower animals, namely the invertebrates. It was espoused also by Woodworth (1938), a comparative psychologist of broad outlook and wide experience, who was too well informed to consider, as did many of his psychological colleagues, rats as "lower animals." (See Thorpe, 1963.) I do not propose in this context to discuss the very simplest organisms of all, such as viruses and bacteria. But when we come to the protozoa and then to the somewhat high invertebrate animals, it is very instructive to consider perceptual abilities and in what sense, if any, communication is taking place.

Perception and Learning in Organisms

Information storage must be occurring in some form or another in all organisms which show a predictable change of behaviour as a result of the impact of environmental conditions encountered by the individual—provided of course that this change in behaviour is not a mere loss of information resulting from traumatic injury. A change of behaviour as a result of individual experience comes very near to the most general definition of learning which has been put forward. I myself, in order to rule out the effect of injury, included in my first definition of learning the word "adaptive"; and by this I meant adaptive to the conditions of life of the organism over a considerable period of time. However, an objection can be raised to this in that it includes as learning a great deal of homeostatic or self-regulative response of the non-sensory systems, the result of say the direct effect of temperature, light, chemical stimuli, especially

29

hormones, etc., on the animal body. This is not what is usually meant by learning, and to avoid this diffculty, I now define learning as *"adaptive change in behaviour as a result of individ-ual sensory experience."* This does leave a difficulty in that, as in the lower organisms, where there are no certainly identified special sense organs, it is difficult and sometimes impossible to tell what is sensory and what is not. However, by sensory, I in-tend to imply a process of co-ordinating and structuring sense experience in some sort of systematic way, in short what in a higher organism we should call *perceptual learning*—an organisa-tion of what the psychologists used to call "raw sense data" into a systematic organised unit of information upon which behaviour can subsequently be based. This of course is a kind of process which is continuing unceasingly in all of us as we build up a perceptual world by the use of our eyes, ears, and other sensory systems. I shall have a good deal more to say about this later in respect of higher animals and in man. But I think for the im-mediate problem of our understanding of the storage and use of information, it is best to consider how far animals can learn. So in the next chapter we shall commence with the most primitive animals such as the protozoa, sea anemones, and their relatives; then proceeding to the slightly higher type of organism, namely the harmless necessary flatworm, about which so much ink has been spilled, both in professional journals and in the newspapers in recent times.

Chapter 2

STORAGE, CODING, AND ACCUMULATION OF INFORMATION IN SIMPLE ORGANISMS AND THEIR RELATION TO THE PROCESSES OF EVOLUTION

In the last chapter we made clear some of the basic differences between living and non-living matter. Now we come to two related questions: (1) Given the existence of living matter in its simplest forms we ask the question, "How have these relatively simple systems given rise to the astounding pageant of nature as we know it, culminating in Man?" And then we must ask the cognate question (2), "Can the methods we postulate as sufficient to explain evolution amongst living organisms also be plausibly involved as sufficient to have produced living from non-living?"

BIOLOGICAL REPRODUCTION AND NATURAL SELECTION

Natural selection can be regarded as a device for giving reality and persistence to new and possibly adaptive structures and other features of organisms. As everyone knows, this action depends upon heredity on the one hand and variation on the other. If the offspring had no similarity to the previous generation, then obviously nothing could be conserved and chaos would result. Indeed there could have been no continuing life under these circumstances. Again, if all offspring were the *exact* copy of the parent, there could be no adaptive change, or indeed change of any kind, except that which takes place in the individual during its life; and again, it is virtually certain that life could never even have reached its lowliest present manifestations, let alone anything more complex. So, for evolution by natural selection one must have offspring that are extremely similar to but not absolutely identical with the parent. That is to say that *"reproduction"* must basically imply *"reduplication."* But no chick, puppy, or child grows up to be exactly like its parent; there are always differences between offspring and parent, which if they are to be conserved by natural selection must of course be in some degree hereditary or at least have a hereditary basis. This means that for natural selection to act there must be successive generations; and the quality of the species and of its individual varieties must be coded so that by a sequence of events the coding of the initial configuration can lead to the adult individual. As Pantin (1968) has pointed out, codes of this sort are possible in gross matter, as in the templates and moulds from which machine parts are reproduced according to human design. However, as all engineers and manufacturers realise only too vividly, even the hardest and most robust template or mould wears out.

For living beings the construction of a code capable of adaptation is impossible within the atomic level for two reasons—first, atoms cannot reproduce their like, and second, one cannot impress new features upon the individuality of atoms. There is one level of material organisation alone at which these two difficulties can be overcome, and that is the molecular. Just by virtue of its atomic structure a particular molecule can be repeated precisely (as it is in crystal growth) and of course it can be destroyed; but it cannot in any ordinary sense of the term be worn out. Moreover, complex molecules, particularly if they are arranged in chains, can be constructed from sequences of more or less similar parts. So we get the situation that families of very closely related molecules with closely related properties can arise. The realisation that the nucleic acids with their chain structure provided particularly good, indeed one could almost say uniquely good, possibilities for the development of very closely related molecules was the first major step in the great advance which resulted in the establishment of the genetic code. Further it was found that in the nucleic acid family every molecule in a cell was capable, under certain conditions, of reproduction by the construction of another code as a mould in a negative image of the first. From this "template" the original can be re-formed without any wear and tear. It follows from this that the code can be dynamically maintained, for if a link be destroyed during the changes and chances of the violent metabolic activity that is continuing throughout every instant, without cessation, in living organisms, it may be replaced by a new and identical link.

Storage and Coding of Information

It will be quite unnecessary for me here to attempt to describe and explain the immense development of "macromolecular biology" in recent years. Nor need I say anything about the importance of this in relation to the storage and coding of information in simple organisms. Practically the whole of the work in this field has been done, and is being done, with simple organisms such as viruses and bacteria. Both the scientific press and the popular press of the world have been filled with it for years, and there is no doubt that the molecular biologists have proved their main argument, that macromolecules are indeed the means of storing and coding information, and proved it up to the hilt. Still it must be said that certain points are not yet clear—for example how far other methods are also employed; whether the DNA store is adequate for all purposes; how far is there a quantitative relation between the amount of DNA in the germ cell and the amount the organism must be presumed to need in order to transmit the necessary details of structure and biology to its offspring?

In this last case there appears not to be such a close relation. In fact the number of chromosomes and the quantity of chromatinic material often seem to show no particular relationship with the degree of complexity of the organism.[2] Indeed in plants the relationship often appears to be an inverse one; highly elaborate plants having the small chromosome numbers. Thus in ferns chromosome numbers tend to be in the hundreds, whereas in the Labiatae (Mint, Thyme, Lavender, etc.) and the Compositae (Daisies, Thistles, etc.) they number five, six, or seven. Even in animals we find a similar situation. The chromosome number of the fruit fly (*Drosophila*) is four, and there is no genetic evidence whatever for genes being present which encode the main structural differences which distinguish, say, a fruit fly from a blowfly (*Calliphora*). One is at present forced to the conclusion that the characteristics of the true flies (Diptera) and of the family groups such as Muscidae and Drosophilidae must be coded in some mechanism which is outside the nucleus—although this does not of course mean that it need be coded by something other than nucleic acid (Thorpe, 1965 and Wolpert, 1970).[3]

As a non-specialist in this field of molecular genetics and the coding of information, I like to employ a down-to-earth example which perhaps may be helpful to others.[4] The layman in these matters can gain much from a vivid simile which likens the information store in the DNA chains to instruction books which can be closed and put away or opened and read out. Thus it has been suggested that a bacteriophage, or virus, with a DNA chain, say 200,000 bases long, has in its molecular instruction book 60,000 words, which would be roughly thirty pages of an instruction book written in English. The instruction book for a bacterium would be 10 to 100 times larger than this. Pratt (1962) continues, "And for man, the genetic information in the forty-six chromosomes of each somatic cell is not so much a book as a very large encyclopedia with forty-six volumes, and about six times 10^9 base pairs, two times 10^9 words and a million pages—an average of about 20,000 pages for each of the forty-six volumes!" And it must be remembered that such an instruction book does not of course specify the detailed positions, actions, and functions of the great hordes of molecules in each cell, still less any questions of atomic species and activity. It presumably supplies instructions for the structural and biochemical organisation and functioning of the main type of cell (Pantin, 1968). Yet we are still largely ignorant of the mechanisms which enable it to do even this. How far, and by what means, it specifies the position and organisation of tissues and organs, their development and ultimate fate, is a far larger and extremely difficult question which, I believe, we are not yet within sight of being able to answer (Thorpe, 1965).[5]

The Accumulation of Information in Lower Organisms

I need therefore say no more about the basic evidence for the functioning of DNA as an information store in simple organisms (Wolpert, 1970). But it seems appropriate to consider here a controversy which seems now to have been brought to some degree of conclusion, and that concerns the much-questioned power of a very simple invertebrate animal, the planarian or flatworm, *Dugesia doroteocephala,* to display learning abilities. (See Figure 4.) These delightful little worms which glide about on

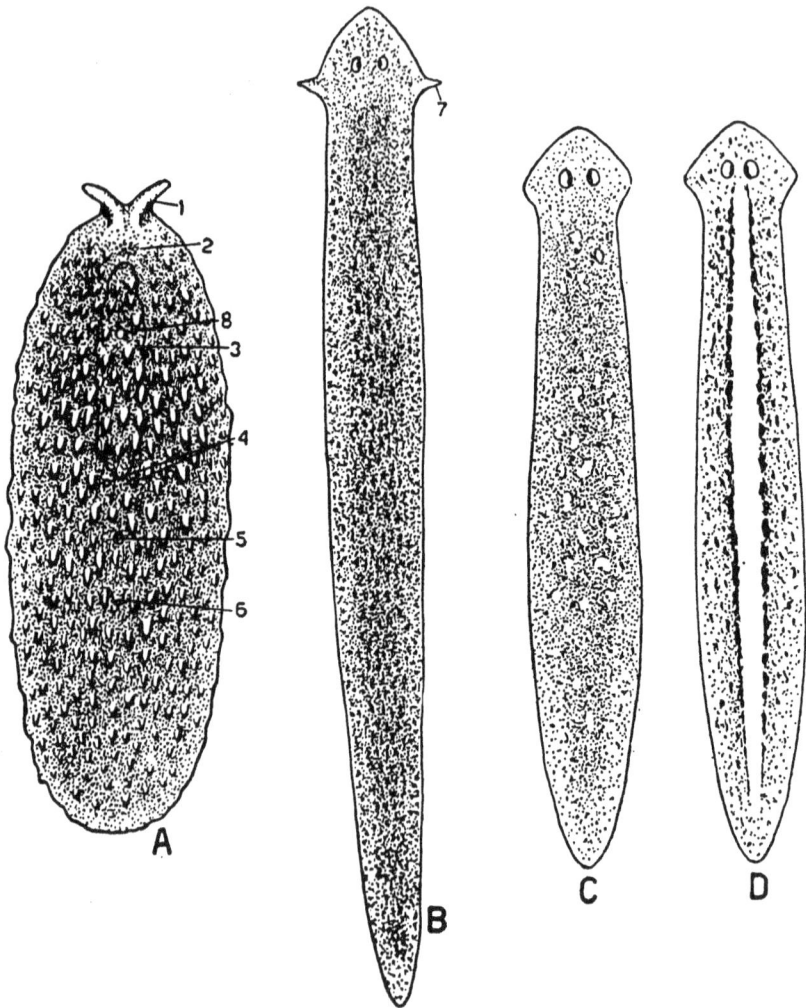

Figure 4 Types of Turbellaria. A. Cotylean polyclad. *Thysanozoon nigrum* from life. Bermuda, black, with marginal tentacles, dorsal papillae, and double male apparatus. B–D fresh-water planarians of the genus *Dugesia* with triangular head and definite auricles, from life. B. *Dugesia doroteo-cephala,* common United States planarian, dark brown to black to 30 mm. long may have light middorsal stripe, found in springs. C-D colour variants of *Dugesia tigrina* (=*Planaria maculata*), most common United States planarian, brown, 10 to 20 mm. long, found in ponds, lakes and streams. 1, marginal tentacles; 2, cerebral eyes; 3, outline of ruffled pharynx; 4, double male pores; 5, female pore; 6, adhesive disk ("sucker"); 7, auricles; 8, mouth. (From Hyman, 1951.)

stones, etc., at the bottom of brooks and other clear, relatively un-polluted water sources such as streams and springs, have turned out to be valuable experimental animals for the study of learning and the transfer of information. They are useful for many reasons, but mainly because their laboratory requirements are, at least at first sight, very simple. If cut into halves, or even into small pieces, each piece will regenerate itself into a whole worm, though if given insufficient food the worms tend to be cannibalistic. There are well over a hundred important recent papers concerned with their study, and indeed a lighthearted journal, *The Worm Runners' Digest*, together with both the runners and their worms (Figure 5), has now been running for over ten years.

Figure 5 The lighter side of studies on the learning of flat-worms. (From *Worm Runners' Digest*.)

The initial experiments involve the teaching of the animals to run very simple mazes or to make a choice in a choice-chamber and then see whether the rewarded choice would, with experience, be learned. The early papers led to a welter of conflicting results—very largely due to misunderstanding of the needs of the animals when in the laboratory, the stimuli to which they normally respond in the wild, and their normal behaviour in the wild. However, some sort of concensus of opinion of the results has now been achieved (Corning and Riccio, 1970).

The most important questions posed by this planarian work have been *first* the general question of whether learning is possible with animals of this grade of organisation, and *second* whether adequate experimental techniques have been used to study it. Following on this there is the question: If learning is established, can we be sure that regeneration studies—that is, experiments in which a trained worm has been bisected or fragmented and allowed to regenerate new individuals—have shown that the learning of the old worm has in fact been transferred to the new ones? Can we be sure that transfer of "memory" has really taken place? Because, if so, it appears probable that this has been done by transfer of a specially modified RNA molecule.

As a result of all these studies we can now say, I think, without fear of any further contradiction, that planarians do possess the capacity to learn. One precise series of experiments has now been replicated in two independent laboratories, with congruent and parallel results, and there seems no reason to doubt these conclusions. As to the question of transfer of memory, the injection of RNA has shown quite convincingly that the performance of animals receiving the RNA from trained animals was different from that of animals which received it from untrained groups or from those which had been pseudo-conditioned. If, however, the RNA was chemically degraded and then injected, the differences did not appear. These experiments seem then to show that RNA from experienced animals bears some quality which enables the animals receiving it to do better in the experiments. However, this does not, in my view, at present amount to an indication of the real transfer of a precise memory by RNA, and it does not seem (to me) to provide any evidence at all for the theory that memories in the brains of higher animals are coded by nucleic-acid derivatives. However, there has been some recent work on rats which *seems* to point that way, and I shall return to the discussion of this later.

Essential Differences Between Plants and Animals in Relation to Their Evolution

We now come to a basic matter which is fundamental to the topic of this book, and that is the differences between plants and animals. There are many possible ways of making a distinction, each of them indicating points of real importance yet none of them being altogether satisfactory. And indeed there are groups of organisms which, on almost any definition, can at one stage of their life cycle be regarded as plants and at another as animals. The outstanding example is the group of organisms which the botanist calls Myxomycetes and the zoologist Mycetozoa. In the days when I, as a boy, was first interested in these topics, the British Museum guidebook to the group considered them as animals and called them Mycetozoa, whereas the specimens themselves were housed in the Department of Botany!—an unusual example of our supposed national tendency to compromise. However, from our point of view, the most striking difference between animals and plants is that plants are, on the whole, sedentary and animals, on the whole, mobile. Animals are in fact essentially predatory-behaviour machines which have to go out and find and catch their food; or at least they must be equipped with special devices, as in so many marine organisms, for filtering food out of water, sweeping it towards themselves, and ingesting it in some form or another. This emphasis on the importance of movement in animals is absolutely fundamental.

Once an animal starts to move as distinct from being passively carried along by currents in the lake or sea or by wind, it has two choices. It can either move in an entirely random manner, in which case we must assume that the movement itself will bring it in contact with all that it needs (including of course food, oxygen and water) and will ensure the normal development and survival of a sufficient proportion of the species. Or if this kind of random movement is not enough, there must be directed movement. As we shall see, this can be of many different kinds. But the first essential of directed movement is that there must be some special devices for detecting objects in the environment which can give guidance, either direct or indirect. And the more precise and elaborate these movements have become the greater will be the pressure behind the tendency to develop more and more precise sense organs. If an animal is going to move in a particular direction, it will be able to perform much better if it is elongate, perhaps to some extent "streamlined." And this will of course imply that the most acute sense organs as well as the point at which food is absorbed will be at the front end, i.e., the animal should have some kind of a "head." Even before this stage has been reached it is obviously important for the animal that information collected about past events can be used as a guide to the course of events in the future. This amounts to saying that the rules, which seem so far to have governed the universe experienced by the animal, will not abruptly change and make nonsense of past experiences as a guide. There is another important point which may be mentioned here (Pantin, 1968). However different another organism is from ourselves and however different the sources of information which it appears to utilise, on analysis its behaviour is completely consistent with the occurrence of the external objects and events presented to us by the same naïve realism implicit in our own everyday behaviour. To quote Pantin: "However private is the world of an ant, of *Paramoecium* and of another man; individual stones, puddles, plants and men exist for them all, experienced in varying degrees of precision and complexity depending on the sensory equipment of each creature."

There is a second point which here arises as of fundamental importance. It is abundantly clear that the geological record of the succession of animal forms throughout the 800 million years— from the pre-Cambrian to the present day—in spite of great and distressing gaps and great difficulties of interpretation, does show an overall progress towards greater complexity of organisation.

There are of course examples to the contrary where promising lines have dwindled and slowly or suddenly become extinct, and we have clear evidence for the degeneration in structure and organisation of many groups of animals which have become parasites. Nevertheless these exceptions merely serve to emphasise the truth of the main premise that there has been striking overall advance in complexity both of organisation and (so we may fairly assume) of behaviour. One almost feels like saying at times that there is a "tendency towards complexity." Now if we look at plants, we see little or no such tendency. Can we really say that a pine tree is less complex and efficient than a willow tree? Can we aver that a fern is less complex, less well adapted to its environmental needs than is a thistle or a poppy? There seems to me to be no real sense in which these questions could be answered in the affirmative. After all, the bracken, which is a fern, is one of the most wide-ranging plants on earth, and many species of fungi are so widespread as to be practically ubiquitous, at least in the climatic zone—whether it be temperate or tropical— to which they are adapted.

One of the great problems is posed by the fact that the biochemical characteristics of higher plants are in addition to their morphological and floristic characters—for example the presence of alkaloids in the Solenaceae (Thorpe, 1965). These are certainly not biochemical accidents in the sense that the occasional occurrence of haemoglobin (one of the oxygen-carrying proteins) in many insects, where it often appears to have no respiratory functions, is a biochemical accident. Alkaloids are highly complex biochemical substances and are extremely difficult to synthesise in the laboratory. Far from being a simple biochemical accident, these occurrences must be the result of a very elaborate series of highly controlled processes. The argument that many of these substances may have, or have had, a protective effect is based on very little evidence; in many cases it seems impossible to have any confidence in it at all. Thus plants are on the whole characterised by being able to produce whole series of peculiar chemical compounds. It is probably this biochemical originality which

41

has been the driving force in the evolution of the plants, a process which those insects specialised for life on, or in, particular plants have been forced to follow. Although a great many species and genera of plants are biochemically peculiar, it does not seem possible to say that the higher plants are biochemically more complex than the lower. Heterospory* in the Pteridophyta (ferns, club-mosses, etc.) is a supreme example of the "originality" of plants. There is no conceivable function for this phenomenon, yet one of its types has led to the evolution of seed plants. And in connexion with heterospory, structures of fantastic similarity have developed independently, e.g., the carboniferous club-mosses (the Lycopodiales) and the ferns proper (the Filicales). Another extraordinary problem is posed by the main algal groups, for there is no known adaptive significance in the presence of the brown pigment which characterises the brown algae and distinguishes them from the green algae. Yet a whole host of morphological and other characters is related to these colour differences; and the original early classification based on colour has stood the test of time and shown itself to be a "natural classification." Here there would seem to be no selective mechanism whatever ensuring that the colour characteristics of these main groups of plants are maintained. Whatever mechanism it is must be completely and absolutely resistant to all destructive circumstances, e.g., thermal noise,† which of course threatens the integrity of the DNA code, independently of the protecting effect of natural selection.

The Development of Ideas Concerning the Movements of Animals

But to return finally to the animals. We seem almost forced to the conclusion that the greater complexity of animals as compared with plants is related to their greater mobility. Another point is (Waddington, in Koestler and Smythies, 1969) animals more often utilise other animals as part of their living space,

---

* The product of two types of spores which respectively give rise to male and female prothalli in ferns.
† The random heat motions of molecules and small particles which have a disruptive effect on the larger and more highly organized systems.

that is to say foxes eat rabbits. But one "higher" plant does not usually live off another "higher" plant except for the relatively few parasitic species. Of course many plants such as epiphytes do live *on* other plants, utilising them as platforms on which to grow; but a really active interaction between two species is far more usual in the animal world. The question then arises as to what possible genetic mechanism could account for this generally increasing complexity amongst animals. Waddington suggests that if we have an ecosystem involving several different species, it is always possible to imagine a new species of animal evolving which utilises several of them. Once you have snails in the streams, and men walking into the streams to bathe, you can get trematode parasites that live half their lifetimes in the snail and the other half in man. Thus an animal which exploits other species can always go one degree better than the existing system. Waddington even goes so far as to suggest that this may be the general explanation for the increase in complexity in the animal world. It does not mean, of course, that (and this tendency is quite general) everything *has* to get more complex. It only means that, as evolution goes on, the most complex animals existing are likely to be more complex at later stages than they were at earlier stages; but, even if this is so, it is certainly not a universal tendency.

This discussion has been designed to lead on to the question of animal movement, for it is not only that movement, as we have seen, is fundamental to the structure and evolutionary history of the animals, it is fundamental to their whole appearance, their whole biology, life history, their brain and "mental development," in short to their very nature. So it is that the nature of animal movement is bound to be a basic topic in the consideration of animal nature and human nature.

Around the turn of the century, and indeed for some time afterwards, there were many highly learned students of animals, and not merely students but acute observers of and experimenters with animals, who did not hesitate to regard the apparently purposive movements of even the lowest animals as evidence for some kind of mental life. Thus Binet (1891), Bouvier (1918), and many others wrote quite freely about the "mental life" of Protozoa, echinoderms, sea anemones, etc. Perhaps the most distinguished of these as a biologist, and indeed a very great one, was H. S. Jennings, one of the pioneers in the modern study of animal behaviour. In 1899 he produced a paper which was concerned in the main with *Paramoecium*. This paper, of Jennings, was something of a landmark in that the behaviour of *Paramoecium* was studied more intensively and more scientifically by Jennings than any before him. He ended his paper by showing that the reactions of *Paramoecium* are comparable in all essentials to those of an isolated muscle, and in neither case has the direction of motion any relation to the position of the source of stimulus. He concludes, "While we cannot deny that *Paramoecium* is an organism, the fact shows the machine-like nature of its activities! An animal that learns nothing, that exercises no choice in any respect, that is attracted by nothing and repelled by nothing, that reacts entirely without reference to the position of external objects, that has but one reaction for the most varied stimuli, can hardly be said to have made the first step in the evolution of mind, and we are not compelled to assume consciousness or intelligence in any form to explain its activities." Yet in a book which is one of the real classics of biology, Jennings (1906) produced some evidence, which he regarded as convincing, that *Paramoecium* and some other Protozoa can in fact learn, and this conclusion has been on the whole substantiated by many subsequent workers, although the picture is not altogether clear (Thorpe, 1963).

In those days none of the workers concerned had any doubt that the existence of some ability to learn, even of the most elementary kind, was evidence of "mental faculties," however dim. And Jennings (1906) boldly said, "The writer is thoroughly convinced, after a long study of the behaviour of *Amoeba*, that if *Amoeba* were a large animal, so as to come within the everyday experience of human beings, its behaviour would at once call forth the attribution to it of states of pleasure and pain, of hunger, desire, and the like, on precisely the same basis as we attribute these things to the dog." This natural recognition is exactly what Münsterberg (1900) has emphasised as the test of a "subject." "In conducting objective investigations we train ourselves to suppress this impression; but thorough investigation tends to restore it stronger than at first." This viewpoint was held in some quarters until about the 1920s, and it is indeed interesting to note that J. Arthur Thomson (1920) in his Gifford Lectures delivered in St. Andrews, in the years 1915 and 1916, gives an admirable account of it. But at the same time that Arthur Thomson was delivering his lectures, that great and too-long-neglected philosopher, L. T. Hobhouse (1913, 1915), began to adopt a much more critical attitude to the evidences for mind and arrived at a much more critical and precise evaluation of the concept, and of the meaning of the word, when he used it in relation to the animal kingdom. The writings then of the turn of the century on this topic appear now to us, and rightly so, very dated and often naïve. But it is salutary to consider, even today, how readily we assume (and indeed with much justification) that the movements and movement systems of an animal are a key to its basic nature.

The quotation I have given from Jennings about the *Amoeba* is worthy of consideration, even now. As Pantin (1968) says, "The characteristic look of an animal is largely due to its motor machinery. The eyes and brains make for similarity; the octopus is obviously staring at you—it is its arms that make it so inhuman and uncouth." The researches of Pantin showed that the behaviour of even a sea anemone is vastly more complicated than anyone had previously supposed. Not only is there a great deal of spontaneous movement but there are elaborate patterns of apparently purposive activity which, though they *may* consist of uncoordinated contraction of different parts, more usually take the form of periodical contractions commencing with the longitudinal musculature and followed by peristaltic waves running down the column and resulting in elongation. Batham and Pantin (1950) became aware of these astonishingly complex pieces of behaviour by employing lapse-rate photography, so that the behaviour of the anemone could be studied speeded up sixtyfold. When this is done, one can really "see what is happening." The ordinary behaviour of the sea anemone is much too slow for the unaided human eye to take in, however great the patience of the observer. Just as an *Amoeba* the size of a dog might well strike us as providing a new revelation of its nature, so for strictly scientific reasons the speeded-up motions of the sea anemone *Metridium* do the same. Recently this has become obvious in all dimensions. The behaviour of many animals, such as the flight of insects or of the hummingbirds, can only be studied by stroboscopic or ultrarapid cinematographic techniques which slow it down to a point at which it can be measured and interpreted. Moreover it is commonplace today to slow down the tape recordings of the vocalisations of birds in order to measure and fully evaluate them. In the case of the birds this is entirely reasonable because the present evidence suggests very strongly, if it does not prove, that the temporal resolution of the bird ear is about ten times as good as that of the human ear.

Complexity of Movements and "Perceptions" in a Simple Animal

As another outstanding example of complexity of behaviour in a very small animal, *Microstomum,* an aquatic, free-living flatworm of the order Rhabdocoela, is worth careful consideration. This minute creature represents an evolutionary stage in which the nervous system is hardly more complex than that of the sea anemone. Its "brain" is little more than a thickening of each ventral cord or a bilobed mass springing from the dorsal surface of these cords. Yet, as Lashley (1938) says, "Here in the length of half a millimetre are encompassed all the major problems of dynamic psychology." This worm is equipped with nematocysts, or stinging cells, like those of the hydroids, which it discharges in defence and in capture of prey. It does not grow its own weapons but captures them from another microscopic animal, a freshwater *Hydra,* which is eaten and digested until the undischarged stinging cells lie free in the *Microstomum's* stomach. These cells are then picked up by the amoeboid processes in the stomach and passed through the walls into the mesoderm where they are again picked up by wandering tissue cells and carried to the skin. When the cell carrying the nematocyst gets to the surface, it turns around so as to aim the poison tube outwards; it then grows a trigger and sets the apparatus to fire on appropriate stimulation. When *Microstomum* has no stinging cells, it captures and eats *Hydra* voraciously. When it gets a small supply of cells, these are distributed uniformly over the surface of the body. As more cells are obtained they are interpolated at uniform intervals between those already present. When a sufficient concentration of the cells is reached, the worm loses its appetite for *Hydra*, and in fact will starve to death rather than eat any more of the polyps, which are apparently not a food but only a source of weapons.

Here, then, is a specific drive or appetite satisfied only by a very indirect series of activities, a recognition and selection of a specific object, recognition of the undischarged stinging cells by the wandering tissue-cells, and some sort of "perception" of its form so that it may be aimed. The uniform distribution of the nematocysts over the surface suggests a *Gestalt.* So striking are these facts that Kepner[6] was driven to postulate a group mind amongst the cells of the body to account for the internal behaviour of the *Microstomum.* Such a conclusion seems to us absurd; but it is to be remembered that behaviour such as this, while striking the ethologist with amazement, is a commonplace of embryology—though the embryologist has often no better theory for explaining it than has the ethologist.

THE ORIENTING MOVEMENTS OF ANIMALS

It is important to be clear in our minds as to how and why different animals move in the different ways that we see since, as has been said, animal movement is in a very large degree the key to their nature. We are not here going to consider the details of the mechanism of movement, but rather the functions of the movements and the circumstances in which they occur. That is to say we are going to consider animal movement as part of the process of finding particular goals or achieving particular objects —in other words, as *orienting movements*. So we ask how it is that the animal controls its movements in such a way as to become appropriately oriented to various environmental stimuli that it must cope with—visual, olfactory, tactile, and so on. To do this we need some sort of classification, for the phenomena are so diverse as to be otherwise impossible to cope with. However, a word of warning is necessary; namely to say that it is not possible to classify all the phenomena in a wholly satisfactory way, and the system which is given here is simply the one that has been found most useful over the years for the orientation responses of a large series of animals, particularly the lower animals, although all these responses can be found in the higher animals when we look for them, even in man himself. Indeed we can say at once that in evolutionary development new means of managing and controlling movement have been added step by step on top of the earlier ones as the sense organs have been developed and refined. So we find that man, when deprived of particular sensory means of reference, either in the circumstances of physiological or psychological experiment or through disease, will drop back immediately to the evolutionarily earlier types of behaviour. In other words, if you restrict his sense organs sufficiently, man will behave exactly like *Amoeba* or a flatworm in finding what he requires.

Animals as Machines

The first and simplest kind of movement is what is called kinesis. In this there is no orientation of the body relative to the source of stimulation. That is to say the animal has not the sensory powers to guide it directly towards a sound stimulus or a light stimulus. There are many different subdivisions of this category. We need only mention two. Woodlice are very sensitive to drying out since their skin is not well waterproofed, so they have to remain in air of high humidity if they are to keep alive. If you place a woodlouse in a chamber in which the humidity is controlled, you find that, other things being equal, it walks slower when in the higher humidity and faster if the air is dry. In nature this means they will tend to aggregate in the damper places since they will tend to slow up there.

This kind of kinesis is called *orthokinesis* in that the animal does not necessarily need to turn at will to the right or left, nor is it necessarily capable of doing so. All it need do is change its rate of walking.

The next and more important kind of kinesis is *klinokinesis*. This phenomenon is shown very beautifully by the flatworms (*Dendrocoelum*) when crawling about on the bottom of a glass dish of water, the one end of which is more highly illuminated than the other but with diffuse *indirect* lighting. In this situation we find that, although the animals do not seem to be walking consistently in any one direction, nevertheless, in due course, they all end up in the darker end of the dish. Investigations show that with a given temperature they all have a given *rate of change of direction*. This is to say that in a given time they will make a predictable average number of turns, totalling a given angular amount of turning, but indiscriminately to the right and left. At the start of the experiment it is found that those worms which are in the more intense light show a higher probability of turning. In this situation, sensory adaptation to the intensity of the light occurs fairly rapidly. The given light intensity therefore induces a higher probability of turning in an animal not yet adapted to that intensity, and moving up the gradient, than it does in one moving down the gradient which has already started to become adapted to even higher intensities. The result of this is that the paths of the worms tend towards the darker regions. That is to say such paths tend to be longer than paths away from it. Paths which expose the animals to gradually increasing light intensity result in the animals again turning more and so aggregating in the dark. This is because the rate of turning decreases with decreasing stimulation. Figure 6 will make this clear. Partly because the light-sensitive organs of the flatworms cannot perceive direction but only intensity, and partly because of the conditions of this experiment, it is quite impossible for the worm to orient

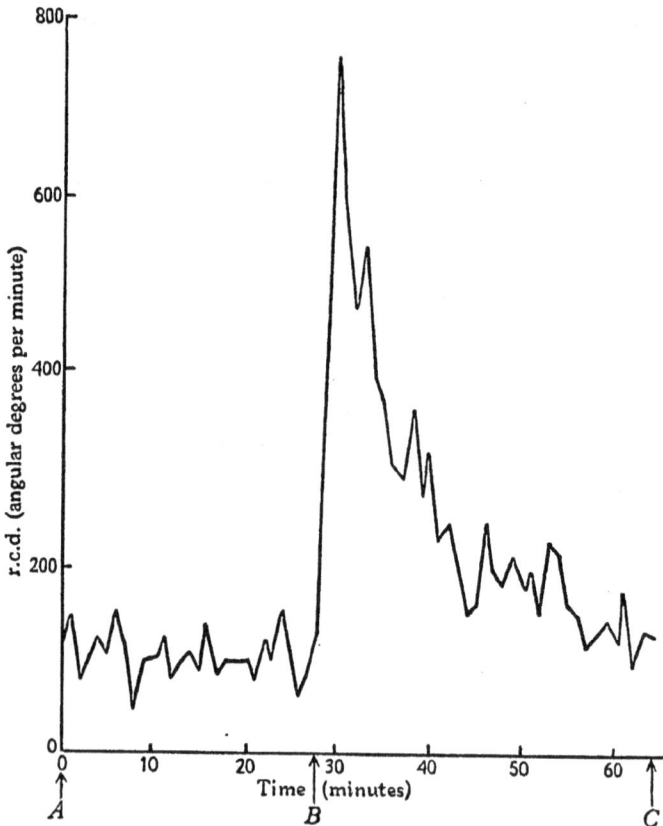

Figure 6 Relation between light intensity and rate of change of direction (r.c.d.) of *Dendrocoelum.* A–B in darkness. At B, the light was switched on, the r.c.d. increased, but slowly returned to the basal value. (After Ullyott, 1936.)

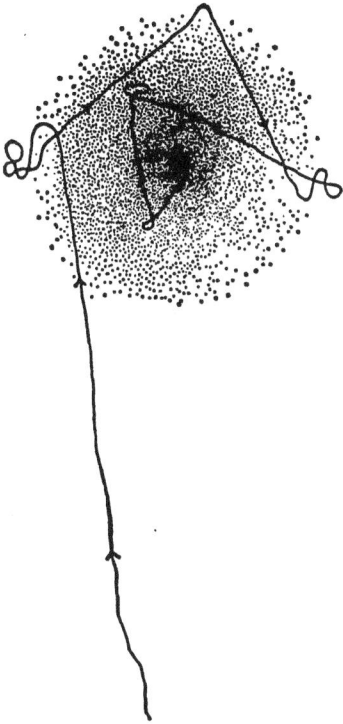

Figure 7 Hypothetical track of a louse approaching the centre of some favourable diffuse stimulus. (After Wigglesworth, 1941.)

itself towards the light. Figure 7 shows the same sort of behaviour in response to a chemical stimulus diffusing or spreading out uniformly in all directions from a given centre. It is very well seen in animals such as lice, e.g., the human louse (*Pediculus humanus*). For with a given "attractive" physical substance the rate of turning decreases with an increase in intensity of stimulation. The result is that the animal tends to walk straighter when increasing its sensory stimulation and more crookedly when moving away from it—with the inevitable result that it ends up at the source of the odour.

It will readily be seen that we should ourselves behave in just the same way under conditions where we had no means of deciding what direction to take. Imagine oneself in a large, cold, dark, empty hall, preferably a circular hall with absolutely smooth walls and no furniture. Imagine that one small area of the floor is warm. Our only hope of finding the warm place would be to go on walking at random. When we found ourselves getting warmer we would go straight on and if we found ourselves getting cooler we would turn more, so sooner or later we would find the warmest spot in the hall. In that case the rate of turning would decrease with increase in intensity of stimulation.

Then we come to directed movements which are known as *taxes,* where orientation of the body with respect to the source of stimulation is attained. Thus there is klinotaxis where the animal still need not have sense organs discriminating direction, but only discriminating intensity. Figure 8 shows that a fly maggot swings its body from side to side, comparing intensities of light on different sides at successive instances. This enables it to approach a source of light, even though (unless perhaps very close) it has no means of detecting the direction from which the light is coming. Klinotaxis is in fact rare to light because if animals get as far as developing eyes they usually soon reach the stage of having eyes that respond to direction *as well as* intensity. Klinotaxis is in fact more usual to chemical stimuli. Thus planarian worms seeking food may start with the convoluted path of klinokinesis; then as they get nearer the stimulus, one may see that the worms swing the front of their bodies from side to side just as does the blowfly maggot comparing intensity successively with time.

Tropotaxis is shown in animals with paired sense organs which are far enough apart and sufficiently sensitive to allow *simultaneous comparison* of intensity. This is to say they do not have to swing from side to side but can go straight. Thus a beetle or a wasp walking towards a light is able with its two eyes to compare intensity registered by the two sense organs continuously and simultaneously (Figure 9). Coming to more complicated means of orientation we have *telotaxis.* This does not depend upon a simple balance. In this case the animal can "choose" one, *or* the other, of two sources. That is to say it can inhibit the response of the sense organ on one side and direct itself towards the stimu-

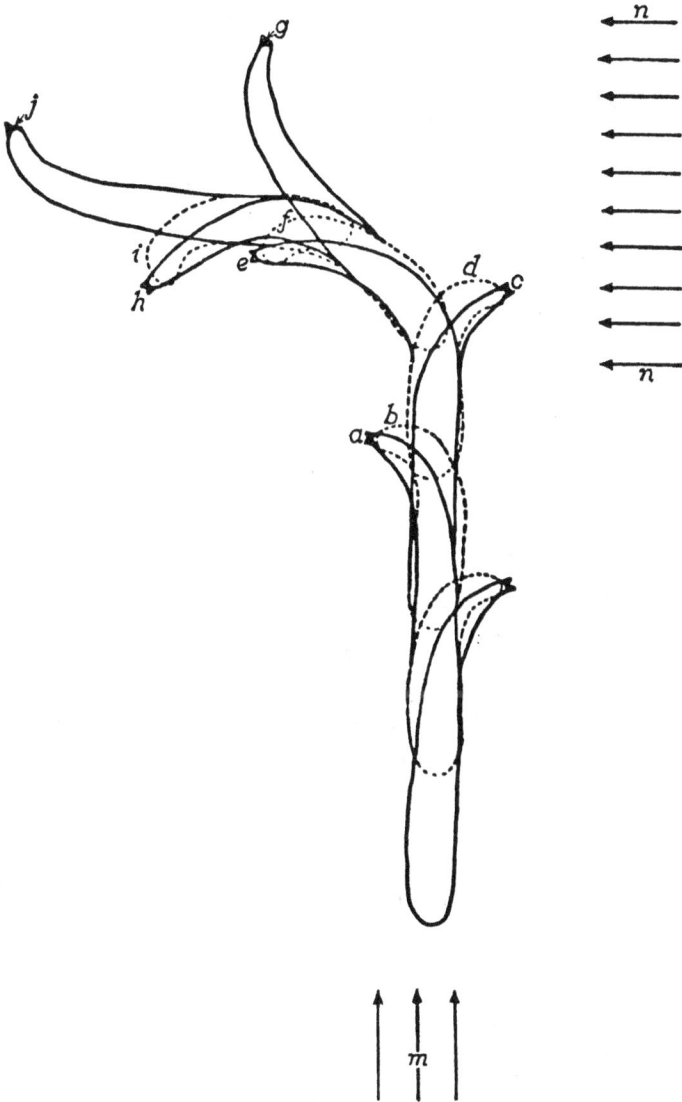

Figure 8 Klinotaxis in the maggot. (After Mast, 1911.) At *d* the light *m* was switched off and *n* switched on.

Figure 9 Tracks of photopositive *Armadillium* with two equal lights. (After Müller, 1925.)

lation of the other. Quite simply one can say it no longer behaves like the proverbial donkey between two bales of hay, but "makes up its mind" that it will go to one or the other. Then comes *menotaxis*, sometimes called the light compass reaction. Here the animal can not only move to or away from the stimulus but can instead maintain a constant angle towards it. This is very well shown by ants which are able to maintain a particular track from, say, nest to foraging ground, by keeping the sun at a definite angle to the axis of the body. From the recent work on ants it looks as if this menotaxis is an acquired method superimposed upon a pre-existing tropotaxic response.

Finally we have *mnemotaxis*. This kind of orienting response can be shown only by animals which have eyes sufficiently well developed to detect a pattern or configuration. We see this very well in insects such as hunting wasps and honeybees where there is extremely precise and accurate recognition of visual pattern as a result of experience. In this case, the animal, like ourselves, is able to choose one pattern rather than another and make straight towards it.

Natural Selection as an Explanation of the Origin of Animal Mechanisms

In the previous chapter we considered the possibility and the difficulty of explaining the structure and activities of living organisms in terms of simple physical mechanisms. But now that we have examined to some degree the idea of information being stored, coded, and transmitted by the organism, it is worth coming back to this problem to consider how far it is reasonable to suppose that the animal organism could have *arisen*, and achieved the forms and behaviour we now find all around us, by the Natural Selection of purely random variations alone. So we ask, "How have the mechanisms we observe everywhere in the study of life been produced?" It is indeed absurd to suppose that an *Amoeba* has thought them out for itself—even if we go so far as to suppose *Amoeba* or *Paramoecium* contain an element of mind. And it is quite evident that many mechanisms—consider the bird's wing, for example—can be plausibly explained as the result of natural selection. And this natural selection will give a direction to the course of evolution. Indeed we can say with Bronowski (1969) that time in the large, open time, takes its direction from the evolutionary processes which mark and scale it. This is essentially the concept which I have been accustomed to label "directiveness." He goes on to say that it is pointless to ask why evolution has a fixed direction in time and to draw conclusions from the speculation. For it is physical change in biological evolution that gives time its direction.[7] So Bronowski would argue that progression from simple to complex, the building up of stratified stability, is a necessary character of evolution. (And in the sense, and only in the sense, that we are talking about the evolution of animals, I agree with him.) It is thus not a forward direction in the sense of a thrust towards the future; it is a headed arrow and nothing more. "What evolution does is to give the arrow of time a barb which stops it from running

55

backwards; and once it has this barb, the chance play of errors will take it forward of itself."

It is always possible to defend micromechanism in principle by making your mechanism complicated enough and by postulating enough submechanisms to meet all contingencies. You can do this in the cell until there comes a point to which the argument can neither be verified nor refuted. But if you go on making your postulated mechanisms smaller and smaller, there comes a further point at which the very concept, in the original sense, vanishes. This is because at the level of electron orbits the idea of shape begins to disappear until finally the very idea of "occupation of space" loses meaning. I do not wish to dive any further into these tenuous regions at this point except to add that there is a point at the other end of the evolutionary scale—namely in man himself (and probably earlier)—where it is no longer possible to defend "mechanism" in any useful sense as a basis for the full understanding of life and its activities.

To think up plausible models, and then to produce some degree of evidence for them, is not one of the most difficult aspects of biology at the present time. (For support for this assertion, one can suggest a perusal of recent volumes of *The Journal of Theoretical Biology* as instructive and rewarding.) For the more promising of these models, the next step is for them to become provisionally regarded as "established." In this phase they are liable to be expounded in the textbooks; but a generation later the workers in the field discover that these models were grossly oversimplified and that biological reality is vastly more complex. This seems so frequent an experience in biology that one is led, purely empirically, to suspect a basic problem—one which is perhaps characteristic of the physical sciences as well. Commoner (1968) has given a number of examples to show how complicated the process of DNA reproduction really is, indicating that there is far more to it than replication by template. In addition there seem to be complicated enzymatic feedback cycles which, to say the least, are a great complication for a purely mechanistic scheme of heredity. Commoner's conclusions have been vigorously attacked (Fleischman, 1970, and Hershey, 1970), many of them certainly with some justice. But there seems no doubt at all (and I think Commoner is right in saying so) that this is a universal experience in biology, that the picture is more complex than before, and this may now well be an expression of Elsasser's view (which indeed is self-evident) of the inhomogeneity of all organismic systems.

Next I propose to consider more deeply than we have yet done the basic problems posed by the concept of Natural Selection of random variation as an all-sufficient explanation not of the mere *maintenance* of living mechanisms but for their origin. How in fact, granting the *existence* of living self-programming organisms, can we envisage their origin and evolution? How can we suppose that evolution has been achieved by the natural selection of adaptive genes that are originally produced by random mutations? This is coupled with the concept of the gene as part of a molecule of DNA, each gene being unique in the order of arrangement of its nucleotides. If life really depends on each gene being as unique as it appears to be, then it is too unique to come into being by chance mutations. There would be nothing for natural selection to act upon.

Salisbury (1969) has shown with overwhelmingly conclusive mathematics that in the evolution of life on earth we are dealing with millions of different life-forms, each based on many genes. Yet the mutational mechanism as at present imagined could fall short by hundreds of orders of magnitude of producing, in a mere four million years, even a single required gene. Salisbury, considering the fantastic information content of a nucleus, arrives at a comparable total to that estimated by Pratt. (See p. 35 above.) He concludes that the DNA in man contains about 10^9 nucleotide pairs per nucleus and in other organisms from 10^7 to 10^{11}. Written in standard type this would occupy about a thousand volumes (10^9 bits at 2,000 bits per page and 500 pages per volume). It has been shown that certain DNA sequences recur anywhere from a thousand to a million times per cell. Hence much is redundant. Work on amino-acid sequences within a given protein also implies a high redundancy. Yet if only one tenth of the gene supply in man is relevant, this is still 10^8 bits of information (still 100 volumes of our encyclopaedia). Could the mutation process account for it?

The problem has further been considered by Spetner (1970). His conclusion, after examining the various arguments which have been brought forward, including Salisbury's, is that the latter's contention still seems to stand. The concept of evolution by random mutation and natural selection and the concept of the uniqueness of the gene are apparently contradictory. Either mutations are not random or genes are not unique. If genes are not random, then there might be some inherent interaction between atoms and molecules which might raise the percentage of useful mutations by many orders of magnitude. As Salisbury says, "Special creation or a *directed* evolution would solve the problem of the complexity of the gene; but such an idea has little scientific value in the sense of suggesting experiments." Salisbury suggests that perhaps there is some fallacy in the concept of natural selection which will give a way out. But this seems to me personally the most unlikely of the possible loopholes. There the matter must rest for the moment, and time will no doubt help in due course to clarify the picture. But this suggestion certainly provides one of the most surprising and disturbing jolts to evolutionary theory in recent times.

The Dualism of Matter and Mind as Seen by Neurophysiologists

The universal, or almost universal, reaction to the dualism of Descartes has, in the past century or so, led to an overwhelming preference of most scientific people for mechanistic explanations; for the very good reason that the adoption of mechanistic theories has made possible and is making possible vast progress in the field of science. But recently there has been an increasing tendency for those scientists who have any philosophical understanding at all, and in particular those who have any understanding of the problems of epistemology (i.e., of the nature of knowledge and of knowing), to change their views on this. As an example of this, and one which will be amplified later in this work, it is now time to discuss the recent papers of a very distinguished scientific philosopher, Sir Karl Popper (1968a, b).

Sir Karl Popper comes down with all the weight of his great learning and experience heavily on the side of dualism; for he sees that no explanation of the physical world can be valid which regards the self-consciousness of man as being merely an epiphenomenon—an accidental outcome of the mechanical workings of a machine which we call the brain. That is, there must be in fact *two worlds—the world of consciousness*, of self-knowing, and the physical world which is known by the operations of the scientific method. And of course the scientific method can only be carried out by a "knowing" being. Popper's recent papers amount in fact to something more—to a *three-world plan*, and this three-world plan has fairly recently been developed or elaborated, from the neurophysiological point of view, by Eccles (1970) (Figures 10–12). Popper's three worlds are first the world

World 1 ⇄	World 2 ⇄	World 3
Physical objects and states	States of consciousness	Knowledge in objective sense
1. Inorganic Matter and energy of cosmos	Subjective knowledge Experience of: perception,	1. Records of intellectual efforts: philosophical, theological,
2. Biology Structure and actions of all living beings— human brains	thinking, emotions, dispositional intensions, memories,	scientific, historical, literary, artistic, technological
3. Artifacts Material substrates of human creativity: tools, machines, books, works of art, music	dreams, creative imagination	2. Theoretical systems: scientific problems, critical arguments

Figure 10 Tabular representation of the three Worlds. (From Eccles, 1970.)

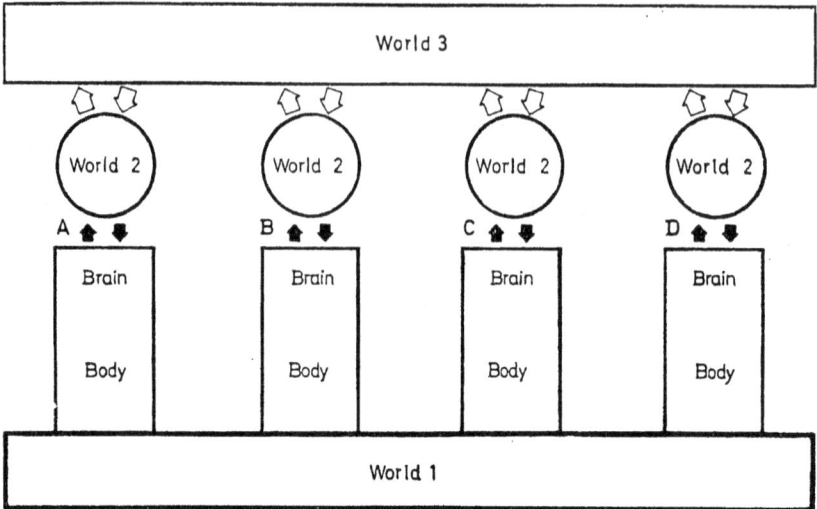

Figure 11 Information-flow diagram showing interaction between Worlds 1, 2 and 3 for four individuals. World 3 is represented as being "impressed" on a special part of World 1 (books, pictures, films, tapes, etc.) that forms an indefinitely extending layer. It is to be understood that any individual is able to move into relationship with any particular part of World 3 that is of interest to him. Further description in text. (From Eccles, 1970.)

of physical objects and states. As such, this "world 1" comprises not only inorganic matter and the energy of the cosmos but also all biology—the structures and actions of the bodies of all living beings—plants and animals and even human brains. It also comprises the material substratum of all man-made objects or artifacts—machines, books, works of art, films, and computers. *The second world* is the world of states of consciousness or of mental states. (Here we are for the time being dealing solely with human consciousness, but I shall have a good deal to say in later chapters about the evidence for animal consciousness.) "World 2" is thus the world that each of us knows at firsthand only for himself and in others by inference. It is the world of knowledge in the subjective sense and comprises the ongoing experiences of perception, of thinking, of emotions, of imaginings, of dispositional intentions, and of memories. But by contrast there is another world,

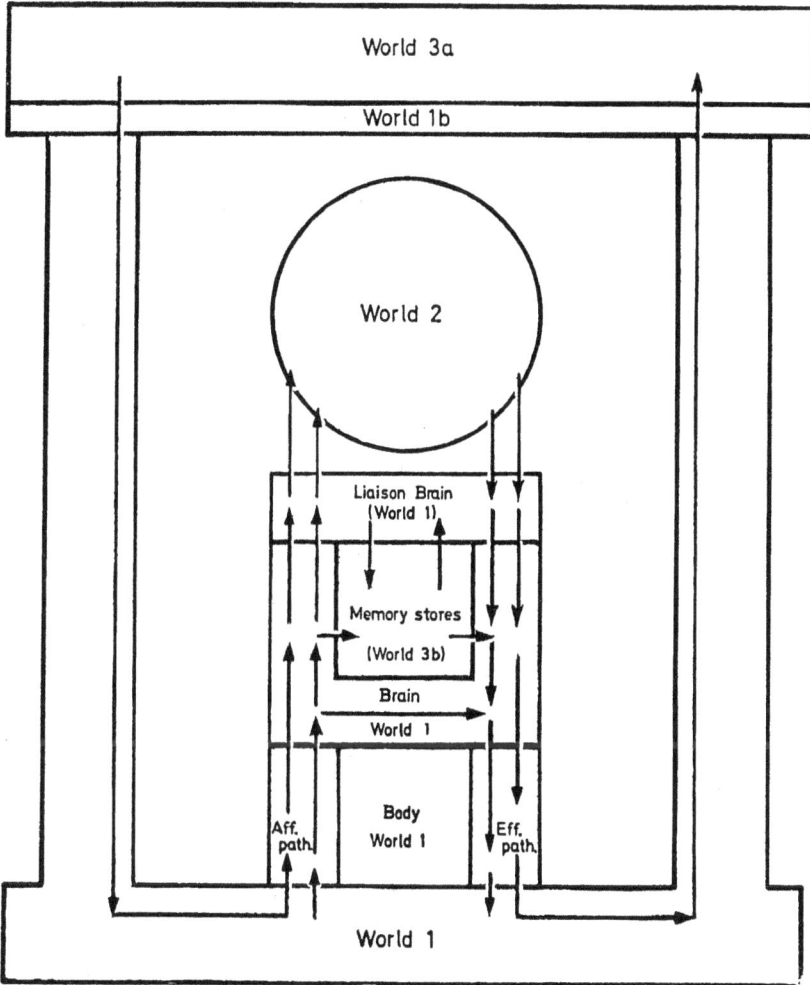

Figure 12 Information-flow diagram representing modes of interaction between the three Worlds as shown by the pathways represented by arrows. It is to be noted that, except for the liaison between the brain and World 2, all of the information occurs in the matter-energy system of World 1. For example, in the reading of a book, communication between the book and the receptor mechanisms of the eye is subserved by radiation in the band of visual wavelengths. As in Figure 11, it is to be understood that any individual can at will range widely in his relationship to World 3. (From Eccles, 1970.)

61

and it is here I think philosophers may look askance at Popper's conclusions. "World 3," the world of knowledge in the objective sense, has an extremely wide range of contents. For example, it comprises the expressions of scientific, literary, and artistic thoughts codified in libraries and museums and all the records of human culture. Material compositions, paper and ink, are of course in "world 1," but the knowledge conveyed by these artifacts is in "world 3." According to Popper the most important components of "world 3" are the theoretical systems comprising scientific problems and the critical arguments generated by the discussion of these problems. So "world 3" comprises the records of the intellectual efforts of mankind through all ages up to the present, that is to say the cultural heritage of mankind. This view will perhaps be made clearer by the diagram on page 61. In order to illustrate the independent existence of this third world, I ask the reader to carry out (as suggested by Popper) two "thought experiments."

EXPERIMENT ONE. Imagine that all our machines and tools are destroyed, and also all our subjective learning, including our subjective knowledge of machines and tools and how to use them. *But libraries and our capacity to learn from them survive.* In theory, after much suffering, our world may get going again.

EXPERIMENT TWO. As before, machines and tools and our subjective learning are destroyed, including our subjective knowledge of machines and tools and how to use them. But this time, *all libraries are destroyed also,* so that our capacity to learn from books becomes useless.

As Popper says, if we think about these two experiments, the reality, the significance, and the degree of autonomy of the "third world" (as well as its effects on the second and first worlds) may perhaps become a little clearer. For in the second case there will be no re-emergence of our civilisation for many millennia. As Eccles says, if we think of the history of the human race, we note that in *experiment two* man would be transported far back into prehistory and would have to begin again the long upward

climb that characterised the tens of thousands of years from
Neanderthal man, through Cro-Magnon man, and so eventually
to the epochs of history. He points out that even the great destruction of the Roman Empire was incomplete, for there were
islands of culture with written records that survived, and
eventually the recovery of classical literature came partly
through the isolated monastic centres and the scholars of Arabia.
Here again we must realise that knowledge in the objective sense
is a product of human intellectual activity and, although it has
an existence independent of a knowing subject, it must be potentially capable of being known. That is to say, though it is
largely autonomous, it is not absolutely and finally autonomous.
Eccles gives as an example the Linear B scripts of the Minoan
civilisation so brilliantly deciphered by Michael Ventris. The information symbolically carried by the scripts was nevertheless in
"world 3" because they were potentially capable of being deciphered.

Popper's Worlds 2 and 3

Popper's claims on this suggest "that a subjective mental
world of personal experiences exists (a thesis denied by the be-
haviourist)[8] . . . that it is one of the main functions of the
'second world' to grasp the objects of the 'third world.' This is
something we all do: it is part of being human to learn a language;
and this means, essentially, to learn to grasp *objective thought
contents* . . . so that one day we will have to revolutionise psychology by looking at the human mind as primarily an organ
for interacting with the objects of the 'third world'; for understanding them, contributing to them, participating in them; and
for bringing them to bear on the 'first world.'"

This is only of course the baldest résumé of an important theory
which I have outlined here so that it may be familiar before it is
further discussed in later chapters. But one additional comment
may be helpful here. It is that since the objects in "world 1," the
natural world, the world of physical objects and states, can, as is

63

obvious, be interpreted, understood and, if you like, "translated" by the activities of organised science, then does it not follow that the physical world which can be so understood and translated is in a sense on a par with Popper's "world 3"? It is a world which has been understood, to a very, very small extent, by the proved experience of scientific man during the last ten thousand years and therefore this understanding is of course in "world 3." Can it not be plausibly argued that what man is understanding is in fact a "pre-existing" knowledge of nature, a plan which in fact ties the whole universe together in a creative unity; and further, that it is this, which by such laborious and painful processes, we may partly come to understand? If then this is so, all the evidences for the understanding of this plan would lie also in the "third world." As Eccles points out, this suggests Plato's world of forms and ideas; but is not Popper's thought quite different? For Plato the third world comprised eternal verities that provided ultimate explanations and meanings for all our experiences, and our efforts were concerned only in trying to grasp and understand these eternal verities. This was a transcendental world, a world of possible objects of thought. Popper's point is that his third world is man-made and arises from our efforts to understand and make intelligible "world 1" and even "world 2." His is the world of civilisation and cultures from all ages to the present. But if we admit, as I shall hope to show we have to admit, that there is some real evidence for consciousness in subhuman types and that there is real evidence for at least the beginnings of culture (in the sense of a transmitted body of knowledge) amongst animals, then perhaps Popper's world will begin to look slightly different.

Popper (1972) believes philosophical reductionism is a mistake due to the wish to reduce everything to an ultimate explanation in terms of essences and substances—an explanation which is incapable of any further explanation. We can of course go on asking the question "Why?" but "Why" questions never lead to an ultimate answer. Popper comes to the conclusion that it is the very nature of science itself to be essentially incomplete, a point of view stressed many years ago by Professor Herbert Dingle and others.

But there is, as Popper says, a further reason why all explanatory sciences are impossible of completion, for to be complete it would have to give an explanatory account of itself. A further result is implicit in Gödel's famous theorem of the "incomplete-ability" of formalised arithmetics. Since all physical science uses arithmetic (and since for a reductionist only science formulated in physical symbols has any reality), Gödel's incompleteness theory renders all physical science incomplete, which to the reductionist should show that all science is incomplete.

"For the non-reductionist, who does not believe in the reducibility of all science to physically formulated science, science is incomplete anyway." Not only is philosophical reductionism a mistake, but the belief that the method of reduction can achieve complete reductions is, so Popper believes, mistaken too. In fact we live, so it appears, in a world of emergent evolution, and of problems whose solutions, if they are solved, beget new and deeper problems. Thus we live in a universe of emergent novelty —a novelty which as a rule is not completely reducible to any of the preceding stages. As Marjorie Grene (1966) says, we can never prove the consistency of the whole, for it is always open-ended. "This is a formal admission which is philosophically of the highest importance."

Chapter 3

ANIMAL LANGUAGES

I. COMMUNICATIONS IN INVERTEBRATES
AND LOWER VERTEBRATES.

ANIMAL COMMUNICATION AS LANGUAGE

We have already briefly considered in Chapter 2 the basic significance of the concept of information in relation to the very nature of life itself—as shown in the organisation of living matter. Now we come to consider in more detail how animals of vastly differing structure and habits, from the relatively simple anemones and worms up to and including (in the latter part of this book) the primates and man himself, communicate with one another concerning matters which are vital to their life and survival in a complex and hostile world. This in fact amounts to a study of various stages in the evolution of language. In one sense all the examples we shall consider may be described as "language," and, in due course, we shall find it quite a problem to decide where and in what sense we are justified in using the word "speech." But this will not bother us at the start.

In this survey we shall consider communication by contact, by gestures, by sounds, and by odours and taste. That is to say information perceived by the senses of touch, vision, hearing, and olfaction and/or chemical senses. The last of these constitutes the field in which knowledge is being most rapidly accumulated at the present time. Yet since, compared to many animals, our own olfactory sense is so poorly developed, this is the type of communication which we find it hardest imaginatively to appreciate. In fact since birds are primarily "visual animals," whilst dogs are primarily "olfactory animals," it is often easier for us to "understand" the behaviour of birds than that of "man's best friend." Dogs endear themselves to us, firstly, owing to their gregarious nature, which is derived from their ancestry as pack animals and explains their readiness, when domesticated, to adopt man as a fellow pack member and leader; and, secondly, as contact animals who respond delightedly to caresses and petting. But even to most dog lovers, the dog's world of smell remains unimagined and misunderstood. G. K. Chesterton realised this when he put into verse his dog's candid and exasperated opinion of man:

> They haven't got no noses
> The fallen sons of Eve,
> Things aren't what they supposes
> For goodness only knowses
> The noselessness of man.

But if we are to make any progress in comparing and evaluating the communicative abilities of animals and men, we must have some basic scheme, or system, by which to order and arrange our evidence.

HOCKETT'S SYSTEM ADAPTED

The most complete system so far developed for attempting such comparisons is that of Hockett (1960a, b). This scheme has been elaborated and developed over a number of years, not only by Hockett himself, but also in collaboration with several of his colleagues (Hockett and Altmann, 1968). I have adapted this system to compare, on the basis of modern knowledge, animal "languages" with those of men. This adaptation is summarised

67

in the accompanying table (Table I). The first column on the left indicates the "design features," all of which are to be found in human verbal language. As will be clear, the other columns deal with the communicative abilities, as compared with the peak example of man, in a number of different groups of animals.

In addition to this, it is to be noted that columns numbered 1 and 10 refer to other aspects of human communication. The first is designated "Human paralinguistics." A word is necessary at the outset as to the meaning of "paralinguistics." Not all the sounds and features of sound produced by articulatory motions in the human being are part of language. As Hockett himself has pointed out (1960a, p. 393), the activity of speaking produces also, besides visible gestures, a variety of sound effects which may perhaps be conveniently termed vocal gestures. Neither the visible signals, perceptible at a distance in the form of gestures or attitudes, nor the sounds which sometimes may accompany these are part of language itself in the true human sense. They are, rather, "paralinguistic phenomena" and are of great importance when we consider the relationship between animal and human communication. For this reason I have included human paralinguistics in the first column. I have also used the term paralinguistics in columns 9 and 10 which refer to the social Canidae and to the Primates. But in these two contexts I have, for convenience sake, omitted all consideration of vocal elements and so am merely speaking about the gestural or postural language of which these animals are capable. Column 10 thus includes the gestural ("deaf and dumb") language which the current work of Gardner and Gardner (1971) has shown to be within the powers of chimpanzees when they are daily exposed to the use of these gestures by human associates, and which they can learn to use in the same way as deficient human beings rely on "deaf and dumb language"—even, it now appears, to the extent of mastering the use of as many as ninety distinct words. This topic, of especial interest in relation to the distinction between animals and man, will be discussed fully in a later chapter.

Now let us consider, one by one, the design features themselves.

It must be emphasised again that all these are shared by all human languages, but that each is lacking in one or another of the animal communication systems which have so far been studied.

1. VOCAL-AUDITORY CHANNEL. This design feature is perhaps the most obvious and hardly needs comment. It has two supremely important features: (a) the production of sound requires very little physical energy, and (b) it leaves much of the body free for other activities that can then be carried on at the same time.

2. BROADCAST TRANSMISSION AND DIRECTIONAL RECEPTION. This feature and, similarly, design feature (3) which follow are the almost inevitable result of the physics of sound. Nevertheless, they are so obvious that they can easily be overlooked and the significance of them, and the benefits derived from them, ignored or underestimated. Broadcast transmission is, of course, inevitable with sound, but directional reception depends upon the structure and design of the auditory organ, which, in animals generally, and obviously in mammals and birds, is clearly an adaptive result of evolutionary development.

3. RAPID FADING. This indicates, of course, that the message does not linger for reception at the hearer's convenience, but quickly vanishes, leaving the communication system free for further messages. This is obviously in strong contrast to such things as animal tracks, spoors, and also the production of messages by means of those scent glands which secrete persistent chemical substances; likewise urine and excreta, which may persist, sometimes, for a very long while.

4. INTERCHANGEABILITY. This is meant to imply that the adult members of any speech community are interchangeably transmitters and receivers of linguistic signals.

69

Table I. A comparison of the communication systems of animals and men, based on the design features of Hockett (From W. H. Thorpe, 1972.)

Design Features (All of which are found in verbal human language)	1 Human paralin-guistics	2 Crickets, grass-hoppers	3 Honey-bee dancing	4 Doves
1. Vocal-auditory channel	Yes (in part)	Auditory but non-vocal	No	Yes
2. Broadcast transmission and directional reception	Yes	Yes	Yes	Yes
3. Rapid fading	Yes	Yes	?	Yes
4. Interchangeability (adults can be both transmitters and receivers)	Largely yes	Partial	Partial	Yes
5. Complete feedback ("speaker" able to perceive everything relevant to his signal production)	Partial	Yes	No?	Yes
6. Specialization (energy unimportant, trigger effect important)	Yes?	Yes?	?	Yes
7. Semanticity (association ties between signals and features in the world)	Yes?	No?	Yes	Yes (in part)
8. Arbitrariness (symbols abstract)	In part	?	No	Yes
9. Discreteness (repertoire discrete not continuous)	Largely no	Yes	No	Yes
10. Displacement (can refer to things remote in time and space)	In part	—	Yes	No
11. Openness (new messages easily coined)	Yes	No	Yes	No
12. Tradition (conventions passed on by teaching and learning)	Yes	Yes?	No?	No
13. Duality of patterning (signal elements meaningless, pattern combinations meaningful)	No	?	No	No
14. Prevarication (ability to lie or talk nonsense)	Yes	No	No	No
15. Reflectiveness (ability to communicate about the system itself)	No	No	No	No
16. Learnability (speaker of one language learns another)	Yes	No(?)	No(?)	No

5 Buntings, finches, thrushes, crows, etc.	6 Mynah	7 Colony nesting sea birds	8 Primates (vocal)	9 Canidae non-vocal communication	10 Primates— chimps, e.g., Washoe
Yes	Yes	Yes	Yes	No	No
Yes	Yes	Yes	Yes	Partly Yes	Partly Yes
Yes	Yes	Yes	Yes	No	No
Partial Yes, if same sex	Yes	Partial	Yes	Yes	Yes
Yes	Yes	Yes	Yes	No	Yes
Yes	Yes	Yes	Yes	Yes	Yes
Yes	Yes	Yes	Yes	Yes	Yes
Yes	Yes	Yes	Yes	No	Yes
Yes	Yes	Yes	Partial	Partial	Partial
Time No Space Yes	Time No Space Yes	No	Yes	No	Yes
Yes	Yes	No?	Partial	No?	Yes?
Yes	Yes	In part?	No?	?	Yes
Yes	Yes	No?	Yes	Yes	Yes
No	No (?)	No	No	Yes	Yes
No	No	No	No	No	No
Yes (in part)	Yes	No	No?	No	Yes

5. COMPLETE FEEDBACK. This simply means that the speaker hears everything relevant in what he himself says. The significance of features 4 and 5 for language becomes clear when we compare them with other systems. In general, a speaker of a language can reproduce any linguistic message he can understand; whereas the mating displays of, for instance, the spiders are usually confined to the male sex only and cannot be executed by the female who receives them. The same lack of interchangeability is often characteristic of those vocal displays which are known generally as "song," female song being the exception rather than the rule in the birds. In contrast, however, directly we come to the "call notes" of birds (which are used for maintaining contact and co-ordinating movements amongst flocks and families not in breeding condition), we see that these signals may be interchangeable in Hockett's sense.

The term "complete feedback" emphasises the important fact that we ourselves, and, presumably, most animals, can hear ourselves as others hear us but cannot see ourselves as others see us. This is a feature of communication systems of great importance in the study of behaviour.

6. SPECIALISATION. Specialisation implies that the direct energy consequences of linguistic signals are biologically unimportant; only the triggering consequences are significant.

7. SEMANTICITY. This refers to the fact that the role of linguistic signals in man is to correlate and organise the life of a community. They can do this because there are associative ties between signal elements and features in the outside world. That is to say, some linguistic forms have denotations. A good many anthropological theorists (e.g., L. A. White, 1959, quoted in Lanyon and Tavolga, 1961) speak as if they believe that only human communicative systems are semantic. A glance at the columns in Table I will show how unjustified such an assumption is.

8. ARBITRARINESS. This simply refers to the fact that the symbols are abstract in the sense that the relation between a meaningful element in a language and its denotation is independent of any physical or geometrical resemblance between the two. For instance, the word "three" is in no sense triple nor is the word "four" quadruple.

9. DISCRETENESS. This implies that the repertoire is discrete, not continuous, and that the possible messages in any language constitute a discrete repertoire rather than a continuous one. This distinction between discrete units and graded units can also be regarded as the difference between digital and analog communication. True language is characterised by its digital information coding system. Thus we may have two words which are acoustically very similar but with entirely different meanings and with no possibility of bridging the gap, e.g., the difference between the English words "smock" and "smog" is discontinuous. If, by contrast, we look at the facial displays or the gestures of human beings and a great many animals, there is a continuum of gradations possible between the two. And although the two ends of the continuum may involve a change of message in between, the cues by which we decide what is meant are not discrete but are graded—the information coding is analog.

10. DISPLACEMENT. Displacement merely implies that signals can refer to things remote in time and space. Human language can refer to things millions of light years distant and aeons removed in time. They can also refer to events here and now taking place in our heads. Here, the difference between human and animal languages is far from concrete and very often may be merely a matter of the length of the time or space gap to be bridged.

11. OPENNESS. Openness implies that new linguistic messages are coined freely and easily and, in context, can be immediately understood. This is sometimes referred to as "productivity" in the

sense that a communicative system in which new messages can be coined and understood is productive. Obviously human communication is open in this sense; we can talk about things never talked about before. But so can a bee by means of its dances, since a worker may report a location which has never been reported before. It will become clear that some bird-song systems are open in the same sense.

12. TRADITION. This indicates that conventions can be passed on, by teaching and learning, from one group or generation to another.

13. DUALITY OF PATTERNING. This essentially implies that though the signal elements themselves may be meaningless, patterned combinations of them are meaningful. This is a feature of the sounds of some birds and also of the paralinguistic communications of animals such as the Canidae and the Primates.

Number 13 completes the design features originally elaborated by Hockett in his papers in the early nineteen sixties. However, Hockett and Altmann (1968, pp. 61–72) have recently given three more which are numbers 14–16 in our table.

14. PREVARICATION. This connotes the ability to lie or talk nonsense with deliberate intent. It is highly characteristic of the human species and hardly found at all in animals. Possible exceptions occur in the play of some mammals and a few birds where we see what appear to be gestures, feints, and ruses designed to mislead.

15. REFLECTIVENESS. Reflectiveness, or reflexiveness, simply indicates the ability to communicate about the communication system itself. This is undoubtedly peculiar to human speech and not found anywhere else, as far as we know, in the animal kingdom.

16. LEARNABILITY. This implies that the speaker of one language can learn another language. This is most obviously true for human beings, for there is no known human language which cannot be learnt by all normal members of the human race. It is much more difficult to decide how to evaluate this in animals. Certainly animals can learn new signals and the meaning of new signals; and learning plays a vital part in many communicative systems of birds and mammals. In birds, of course, "imitativeness," i.e., the ability and tendency to imitate the sounds produced by congeneric associates (or foster parents, as in Mynahs) without specific reward, is an outstandingly important feature. Thus it will be seen that we can give a fairly confident "yes" to this question in columns 1, 2, 5, 6, and 10, and a rather less confident "no" in some of the other columns.

From what has been said, it will be evident that admirable as this outline scheme may be, it raises a number of problems and it is difficult—as the table shows—to decide what answer to give in some of the columns. Hockett and Altmann (1968) are themselves very conscious of this, emphasising two points of difficulty. The first is the one to which I have just referred—that each feature seems to be set forth in an all-or-none manner, whereas, in fact, they are surely matters of degree (e.g., the difficulty of displacement referred to above). The second point is that the sixteen features tie into communicative behaviour in different ways. Some have to do with the channel, others with the repertoire of messages, some with the mechanisms, by means of which the system is passed from generation to generation and group to group, and so on. Accordingly Hockett and his co-workers commenced to look for some superordinate grouping which might suggest further things to be looked for in the communicative behaviour of any one species or society. In order to make headway with this difficulty, they give groupings or, as they call them, "frameworks," which help to indicate what points it makes sense to enquire about in any given situation.

Framework A concerns features relating to the channel or

channels and the points which are suitably enquired into in these circumstances.

Framework B concerns features of the social setting.

Framework C relates to the behavioural antecedents and to the consequences of communicative acts.

Framework D covers continuity and change in communication systems, raising points such as the variations from group to group and community to community in regard to age and sex, and differences between successive generations.

Framework E comprises features of repertoire and of messages for a single system, asking, for example, is the repertoire open or closed, continuous or discrete? Are new messages sometimes transmitted and received and interpreted appropriately? And do the messages of the repertoire differ from one another as total *Gestalts* or are they built out of recurrent partials in some patterned way?

It would be quite out of the question and, indeed, undesirable to go into these five frameworks in any formal detail. They comprise, in fact, circumstances which should at once spring to the mind of any good ethologist or ecologist in considering the significance of, and the differences between, different methods of communication. It is hoped that these points have been sufficiently borne in mind here, to render the discussion meaningful without the necessity of repeated reference throughout.

CHEMICAL RECOGNITION AND COMMUNICATION: PHEROMONES

We now come to consider in very brief summary the communication systems in the vast assemblage of animals included amongst the invertebrates and the lower vertebrates. As there are in all probability more than a million species of insects in the world, it will be realised how tentative and cursory this survey must be. Obviously, to cover it fully, a large volume would be required. So instead of attempting to be exhaustive I propose to take examples from the main groups concerned, to show the range and type of communication employed and to emphasise some of the most interesting features. In doing this I shall try to indicate those points which are particularly instructive when we are trying to compare the behaviour and sensory capacities of man with those of the animals.

It will be obvious that there is a great deal to be said about visual signals, e.g., the communication of information by specialised movements such as the dances and displays of birds and of many insects, where particular structures are patterned and coloured in distinctive ways and moved in particular rhythms to convey information from one member of a pair to another, or from one bird in a flock to another. This is so well known and has been dealt with in so many excellent books that it would seem a waste of space to attempt to cover it fully here. Instead we shall pass from group to group, drawing attention particularly to communication by secretion and dissemination of chemical substances, now called *pheromones*—the subject of a field which is now being explored with greater energy and expertise than ever before and which includes topics of far-ranging and basic significance.

EVOLUTION OF CHEMICAL COMMUNICATION IN PRIMITIVE ANIMALS

Slime Moulds

At first it seems appropriate to mention that in the protozoa, and creatures such as the slime moulds, communication, though simply chemical, may be used in an extraordinarily sophisticated way. In the slime moulds known as *Acrasiales,* cellular aggregation has to take place before the reproductive phase, which leads to the production of spores, can occur. Here communication takes place by means of the discharge of a chemical called acrasin (Bonner, 1959). Acrasin, which may be more than one com-

77

pound, initiates release of further acrasin by other amoebae nearby, which sets up centrifugal wave-like pulses of the material. Acrasin not only induces acrasin discharge but also induces amoebae to stream towards the central producer. Shaffer (1953–57) has studied the properties of extracted acrasin in a cell-free medium. The substance seems to be rapidly destroyed by enzymes produced by the amoebae. In this way a gradient is produced. He has shown, however, that it is not the gradient itself that orients the cells; rather it is the time sequence in which the relaying amoebae produce acrasin which may be responsible. This being so, it is possible that a specific pulse structure is the signal to which the amoebae are responding.

Sea Anemones

The complexity of behaviour of simple animals such as some sea anemones and jellyfish is especially remarkable. For example, certain kinds of anemones (e.g., *Calliactis*) live habitually on the shells of molluscs which are inhabited by hermit crabs (Plate 1). They are never molested by the owner of the shell and benefit by the constant change of feeding ground and by the fragments of food which are let fall by the crab. Several of these anemones take up a particular attitude, standing with the mouth on the lower side of the shell so as to seize food morsels more easily. In return the crab obtains protection from fish which are kept from eating it by the stinging powers of the anemone. Other species of anemone, such as the giant anemone (*Stoichactis* sp.), are almost invariably found to have two or more specimens of the Percoid fish (*Amphiprion* spp.) swimming about unharmed among their tentacles, and when disturbed, taking refuge in the anemone's mouth. Much material of interest is given by Davenport (1966). From this work it seems that precise recognition of specific chemical agents may be part of the normal behavioural biology of these animals. It seems not impossible that in the partnerships between giant anemones and their inquiline fishes, the activity of the fish may in some way be directed to effecting recognition of the fish by the anemone. It even seems likely that an anemone may recognise its own individual fish, for it does not sting when reintroduced to it, whereas another fish of the same species is stung on first contact.

The extracts below from Davenport's work give a varied and intriguing picture of the complexities of behaviour and communication which may be taking place in these "lowly" animals.

The crucial experiment conducted by Ross at Plymouth has direct bearing on coelenterate physiology and behaviour. Here the Hermit crab *Eupagurus* takes little or no part in the activity which results in the change of position of a *Calliactis* from a glass plate or stone to the shell of its host which, from then on, will carry it about. The behaviour of the anemone is so precise and so interesting that it would be best to quote Ross's words directly, in a description of the process:

> The attachment of *Calliactis*, which have been removed from shells, to stones, glass plates, and other objects, is in no way remarkable. An animal lying on its side, or supported in some way, merely secures a foothold by the edge of the pedal disc, and from this foothold the attachment spreads until the whole surface is adherent. The entire process may take many hours and is accomplished by the combined effects of muscular suction and cementing secretions. Essentially this process is the same as the method employed by *Actinia equina* and *Anemonia sulcata*, which are free living and not associated with crabs. Compared to these, however, the pedal disc of *Calliactis* attaches much more slowly, but once the attachment is made it is firmer, and because the attached foot is virtually immobile, it is more permanent.

The attachment of an unattached *Calliactis* to a shell occupied by *E. bernhardus* is very different indeed. Faurot described this briefly, and the following expanded account, based on Davenport's observations, agrees with his in the essential points. First, the tentacles explore the surface of the shell very actively and many of them adhere to the shell, perhaps by glutinant stinging cells or nematocysts, forming an attachment firm enough to hold the anemone on the shell even when the crab moves about. This

79

tentacular attachment develops within a few minutes into a firmer attachment in which the whole oral disc is involved as well. Apparently, the radial musculature contracts and pulls against the expanded margin and its adhering tentacles and so produces an immense suctorial disc. (At no other time does the animal seem so much to deserve its specific name *"parasitica."*) Once this is achieved, the anemone is virtually safe from being dislodged, even by the most active movements of the crab.

All this may take five to ten minutes and is followed by a slow bending of the column which, in another few minutes, brings the pedal disc up to the shell so that the animal is bent double. The pedal disc, meanwhile, becomes greatly distended and begins to adhere to the shell immediately contact is established. Within another few minutes the whole pedal disc has spread out, its swollen surface and edge becoming bedded down firmly to fit the grooved, often encrusted, surface of the shell. Finally, when the pedal disc is firmly attached, the tentacles and oral disc let go, and in the space of another two to three minutes, the column straightens out and the animal assumes its normal extended posture.

A very special type of behaviour on the part of the first *Amphiprion percula* has been described during what is called the "process of acclimation." Very little indeed is known about how frequently this process occurs in nature, how much of the adult life of these fishes is spent in a free state, or how much they move from one host anemone to another. But when the individual "unacclimated" *Amphiprion percula* was introduced into the observation tank with the anemone, a fairly stereotyped series of events occurred which terminated in acclimation. To quote from Davenport and Norris (1958):

> An unacclimated fish introduced into the tank a foot or so away from the anemone usually approached the anemone within a few minutes and began to swim under the disk around the column, and occasionally over the top of the disk a centimeter or more away from the tentacles. Such fish spent most of their time under the disk at this stage and sometimes were seen nibbling at the column

of the anemone. Most fish seemed to "recognise" the anemone within a few minutes and swam towards it. . . . As the process proceeded, passage over the disk became more and more frequent and the "acclimating" fish moved closer and closer to the stinging tentacles. Swimming was accomplished by a distinctive series of slow vertical undulations, in which the tail was usually held a little lower than the rest of the body. Eventually, on one of these trips over the disk, the fish would touch a tentacle or two, usually with the ventral edge of its anal fin or the lower margin of its caudal fin. Commonly this resulted in a moderate adherence of the tentacle to the fin and contraction of the tentacle. The fish then jerked itself free with a violent flexure of its body and usually raced off the disk. Not all newly introduced *Amphiprion* caused clinging upon their first contact with tentacles, but it was the general rule. However, this adherence failed to deter the fish, which nearly always returned immediately to the anemone, either under the disk or over the tentacles. . . .

After this initial contact the fish typically came closer and closer to the tentacles, touching them with increasing regularity. The reaction to the clinging of tentacles became less and less violent until a sudden flexure of the animal's body was the only reaction given by the fish. Mouthing or nipping of tentacles was often observed in this and later stages.

The clinging and contraction of tentacles upon contact with the fish gradually became less until it ceased altogether. At the same time the fish began to swim deeper among the tentacles, using the same slow undulating movements as when it had cruised above the disk.

Once the fish was swimming in fairly constant contact with the tentacles of the anemone, a very striking change in its behaviour occurred. The general speed of swimming suddenly increased until the *Amphiprion* was dashing back and forth over the disk of the anemone, flailing unreactive tentacles aside with violent movements of its body. Often the fish raced beneath the anemone and appeared in one of the folds of the disk margin, its head completely ringed in tentacles. The fish frequently maintained this vantage point for a few seconds, holding position with rapid alternate fanning movements of its pectoral fins, after which it might dash onto the disk again for another foray among the tentacles. The powerful swimming typical of this stage of the acclimation process was accomplished by rapid and strong lateral body flexures. The impression given by the swimming behaviour of the fish after final acclimation was that the fish was "bathing" its entire surface among the tentacles.

This final activity was so marked, so sudden, and so dramatic that upon observing it one was obliged to recall the rejoinder of Chuang-tzu to Hui-tzu,[9] for once an *Amphiprion* reached this level in its behaviour, it exhibited every indication of "joyful" activity in its mad dash in and out of the tentacles of its host (Plate 2).

Marine Worms

When we come to the group Annelida, which includes a vast number of marine worms and also the earthworms and leeches, there is little doubt that in many marine forms the precise synchronization of spawning must be controlled by chemical stimulation. In the land leeches there are some casual observations which suggest mechanical signalling, and it has been noticed that a male may approach a "tapping" female and set up a duet with her. "The two alternatively tap and curl the front ends of their bodies together, this ultimately leading to copulation" (Leslie, 1951, quoted by Frings and Frings, 1968). There are similar suggestive observations with regard to earthworms, but, as far as I am aware, no experimental confirmation. In marine annelids there is one case on record of a signalling system using luminescence. In a Bermudan polychaet, *Odontosyllis enopla*, females rise to the surface of the sea at the swarming season where they form a glowing mass, and the males are attracted to this. If the females stop glowing, the males signal by flashing and the females resume their light (Galloway and Welsh, 1911). Thus even animals as structurally simple as the coelenterates and the echinoderms may show associative learning and patterns of complex behaviour for which precise signals may be necessary. (For a general discussion see Thorpe and Davenport, 1965.)

Molluscs

There is little doubt that many Mollusca, such as land snails and slugs, communicate both by chemical secretions and mechanical stimulation, though the details of the former process have not yet been worked out experimentally. In the oyster *Crasostrea virginica,* Galtsoff (1938) has shown that females release eggs when stimulated by a chemical in the sperms, whereas the male is unspecific and will release sperms as a result of temperature changes and the chemical substances provided by a number of species of invertebrates not even closely related. With the Cephalopoda (octopuses and squids)—a group that is outstanding for mobility, highly developed eyes similar in structure and in action to those of the vertebrates, and high brain development (all, of course, features which are linked with one another)—no definite evidence of chemical communication seems to have been produced, whereas there is every reason to suppose that recognition of sex and readiness to mate is signalled by visual displays. Many octopods are remarkable for their ability to effect rapid changes of colour and pattern, but whether these are of significance in communication is not certainly known.

Crustacea

The Crustacea constitute a group containing a very large number of species, the vast majority of which are marine: a much smaller number live in fresh water and a relatively few are terrestrial. Only a very small proportion of this great total of species has been studied sufficiently thoroughly to allow much to be said about the methods of communication. However, enough is known to indicate that the general situation is broadly similar to that in insects. (A valuable general survey is given by Frings and Frings, 1968.) Visual signalling by means of special gestures

83

has been particularly thoroughly worked out in the Fiddler crabs of the genus *Uca* by Altevogt (1957, 1959) and Crane (1957, 1958). In this genus the males have elaborate and highly specific gestures involving rhythmic waving and other movements of the specially developed large claw on one side of the body. In recent years it has been discovered that a great many crustacea make noises of one kind or another. These involve tapping, bubbling, stridulation, etc., with specially developed structures for the purpose often being involved. Thus the Snapping shrimps, *Alpheidae*, produce loud cracks by the sudden closure of a highly specialised large claw. In some cases this snapping seems to serve to stun potential prey, and it seems likely to be involved in territorial or sexual signalling as well. While there is no clear-cut evidence, Frings and Frings suggest—probably correctly—that it is highly likely that further work will show that these special sounds are used for communication.

There are also many luminescent crustacea, particularly in deep waters, and it looks as if the lights of many of these give warning of the approach of predators; but the possibility remains open that aggregational attraction and sexual attraction and recognition also result from the light signals. Finally, there is little doubt that chemical signalling is also important in this group. Crisp (1961) and Crisp and Mellers (1962) have found that extracts of the bodies or shells of barnacles, when applied to otherwise clean slates and then submerged in waters where the barnacle larvae (*Cypris*) are present, cause a significant degree of settlement. It is thought that the factor here may be a substance known as arthropodin which is a regular constituent of the exoskeleton of these animals and not a specifically produced signalling material. Carlisle and Knowles (1959) find that in many marine crustacea the moult, in which the female is transformed from an immature creature into an adult ready for reproduction, is of a special type which they call the copulatory moult. Females just before or at the time of this moult seem to be recognised by males which often seize them and hold them for mating. In some cases the male is attracted from a distance to the premoult female, while in others it is necessary for him to make antennal contact before recognition can occur.

Spiders: Chemical and Mechanical Signalling

Spiders are remarkable for their dependence upon vibrations conveyed through the threads of the web, combined with visual displays at close quarters and no doubt a good deal of chemical communication. Table II shows the generalised course of display in spiders and summarises the results of a number of papers by Crane (especially 1949). Other important studies include those of Bristowe (1939–41) and Cloudesley-Thompson (1958). In the case of the web spiders the male moves about until he accidentally touches a web of the female; from then on he is capable of detecting the species and sex but generally not the sexual readiness of the female. In other cases the male finds the female by the scent of her dragline which she lays down as she walks. Full precopulatory behaviour depends upon whether the female is in a web or not. If she is, the male generally uses vibrations of the web as signals. These may be taps on the door in Trapdoor spiders or plucks of the thread of the web in Orb-spinning spiders. If the female responds, she may give aggressive signals, in which case the male departs, or if she is mature and sexually ready, she may give signals of a different type or remain passive, whereupon the male enters the web and is able to copulate. In view of the predatory habits of the female when in the web, it is obviously important that means of identification of species and reproductive state should be rapid and unequivocal. (See also Parry, 1965.)

In some of the parasitic water mites (e.g., *Unionicola ypsilophorus*), a chemical is given off by the host—a fresh-water clam—which when responded to brings the parasite into the shell of the host. In other species of water mite, males can apparently recognise females and vice versa by signals which are both chemical and tactile. In one case, *Eylais infundibulifera*, recognition is said to be entirely tactile, no evidence for chemical signals hav-

85

Table II. Generalized course of display in salticid spiders.
(From Crane, 1949; in Sebeok, ed., 1968.)

Male	Female
Becomes aware of female; starts display. Stage 1. *(Minimal releaser:* several sight factors; airborne chemical stimuli also involved.)*	
	Retreats, or watches male, usually in braced, high position, often vibrating palps. Rarely attacks. *(Minimal releaser and director:* several sight factors.)*
Approaches, in zigzags, or follows (if female retreats), continuing or resuming display. *(Minimal releaser and director:* above sight factors, plus type of female motion or lack of it.)* Special female signs, such as vibrating palps and light abdominal spots probably have directive value.	
	Becomes completely attentive; sometimes gives weak reciprocal display. *(Minimal releaser:* summative effect of display motions.)*
Speeds up display tempo. *(Releasers and directors:* reduced motion of female, plus chemical stimuli. Self-stimulation is doubtless also a factor.)*	
	Ceases motion and, usually, crouches low, legs drawn in.
Enters stage 2. *(Releasers:* primarily, proximity of female; also involved, usually, her lack of motion, low position, and doubtless, reinforced chemical stimuli.) Copulation follows unless female withdraws. *Director:* sometimes a pale abdominal crossbar.)*	

ing been detected (Böttger, 1962, quoted by Frings and Frings, 1968). To complete this brief survey of the Arthropoda (excluding the Insecta) it is worth mentioning that some centipedes and millipedes are known to produce sounds by stridulation, and it seems likely that further work will show that these are communicative in function.

Dancing Bees: The Perfection of Invertebrate Communication

We now come to the enormous group which may be described as the apex of the invertebrates, both in regard to structural elaboration and specialisation and behavioural and communicative finesse—namely the insects. This group, which contains more species than all the rest put together, is of particular interest from our point of view. Among these, by far the best known and most important instance is provided by the dance communication of the honeybee (Apis mellifica), which was worked out by Karl von Frisch and his pupils and first announced in detail in his classic paper of 1946. The first full account in English was provided in von Frisch's book, The Dancing Bees (1954), and a summary of this with much further detail is to be found in his great book, The Dance Language and Orientation of Bees (1967a). The main outlines are so well known that they need only be summarised very briefly here.

Von Frisch found that scout bees, when they have found a rich source of nectar, return with a full load of pollen or nectar to the hive and communicate accurately the location of their find by dancing in the dark hive on the vertical combs. This communication is effected by the famous waggle dance or figure-of-eight dance. (See Figure 13.) The angle between the waggle run and the vertical is determined by the position of the sun relative to the food, and this angle changes as the sun travels across the sky. It was then shown that bees can compensate for sun movement. Then Lindauer discovered that, when swarming is imminent, scout bees communicate the location of possible new sites for the colony by dances that are the same as those used to announce food except that they last much longer, some-

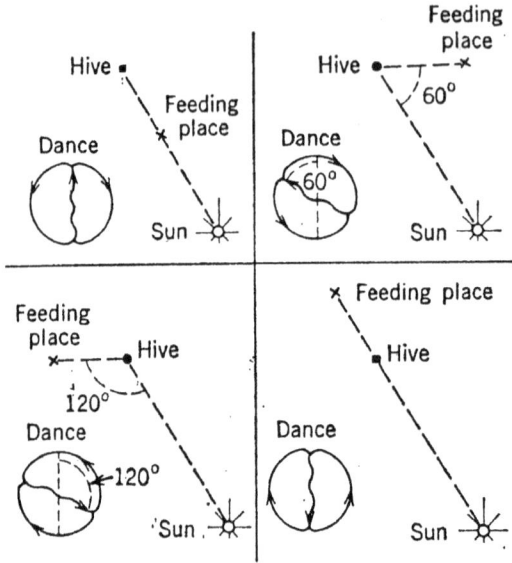

Figure 13 The waggle dance of the honeybee, performed on the vertical face of combs inside the dark hive. The direction of the waggle run across the diameter of the circle conveys the direction of the food discovery. In the hive the direction is relative to the vertical, in flight relative to the sun. Thus a following bee must transpose the angle of the dance to the vertical to an angle relative to the sun when it sets out to locate the discovery that the scout has announced. (After von Frisch, 1954.)

times several days. During the course of these dances the relative direction of the sun changes and the orientation of the dance does so too; only when very few, or no, dissenting directional votes are cast does the swarm move to the new hive site that they have thus agreed upon.

Persistent dances can also be induced by placing food inside the hives. When the scout bees dance under these circumstances, they indicate the location of the most recent discovery outside the hive. Even if the sun and sky are not visible to them before they enter the darkened hive to dance, the waggle runs continue to indicate the correct direction of the previous site. Thus the orientation of the waggle run across the comb changes through the day, shifting counterclockwise relative to the vertical.

Distance communication in the bee dance is based on the

energy expended on the outward flight to the nectar source. It can thus be rendered to some extent inaccurate by variations in the strength and direction of the wind encountered. With this limitation the rate of the waggle run is correlated with the distance to the nectar source, and this is in turn correlated with the time of each circling movement of the whole dance. At very short distances the method of signalling changes to a round dance, which communicates distance but not direction.

The complete waggle dance thus indicates both the direction and the distance of a food source, and constitutes, for the colony of bees, an extraordinarily efficient method of harvesting as rapidly as possible a new and abundant source of food. The dance is only performed when a worker has discovered, or is foraging at, a particularly rich source of supply. Each performance of the dance on the comb results in a number of other bees setting out and finding that particular food source. If the supply is still rich when the newcomers reach it, they also dance on the combs on their return, and so a numerous band of foraging workers is quickly recruited for work at a rich source of supply. As soon as the source begins to fail, the returning workers cease to dance, although they themselves continue exploiting that source as long as an appreciable yield is obtained. So the whole mechanism serves, not only to direct new foragers to food supplies that have been discovered by fellow members of the colony, but also to get them there in approximately the right numbers to exploit the food supply properly. Hockett (1960a; see Table I), has discussed these results, evaluating the performance in the light of his series of design features. He shows that this communicative device is unique amongst the invertebrates in showing semanticity (Item 7), productivity (Item 11), and also, in his view, is unique in the animal kingdom in always showing displacement (Item 10). Whether it shows a tradition (Item 12) is doubtful.

Wenner and Johnson (1967) and Wenner, Wells, and Rohlf (1967) have recently questioned the theory of dance communication as set out by von Frisch and his co-workers, arguing that the dances lack communicative importance. According to them the bees find their way to food sources by means of other cues such as odour. Their criticisms, however, appear to lack adequate foundation (see Thorpe, 1972) and, at the time of writing, von Frisch's work seems to have been finally substantiated by the paper of Gould, Henerey, and MacLeod (1970).

Although the dance language of the honeybee has, rightly, taken pride of place in this section of our discussion, nevertheless it must not be supposed that it is entirely unique amongst the insects or even amongst the Hymenoptera. There are, in fact, a number of less well-developed, but not dissimilar, methods of communication found in the bees. Those who wish to follow this line further must consult the writing of Lindauer (1961, 1967).

Ants: Chemical Signalling

Now leaving aside gestural-visual communication and audio-communication in the Hymenoptera, we must make brief mention of the extraordinary development of chemical communication systems. There is a great and rapidly accumulating literature on this subject and those interested are specially recommended to the works of new pioneers: C. G. Butler (1967) and E. O. Wilson (1968; Wilson and Bossert, 1963). Figure 14 displays diagrammatically the elaboration and diversity of communicative substances secreted by a number of those few ant species which have been investigated. These substances function either by evoking immediate behavioural responses, with what may be called releaser effects, or by means of endocrine-mediated primer effects that alter the physiology and subsequent behavioural repertoire of the receptor animal (Wilson, 1968). The sensitivity to these substances is astonishingly high. It has been estimated that in many cases no more than a few molecules strike the chemosensitive sense cells. In fact it has been shown that a single molecule can, in certain circumstances, be sufficient to fire one of the chemical sensory hairs. Pheromones, as in the bumble-

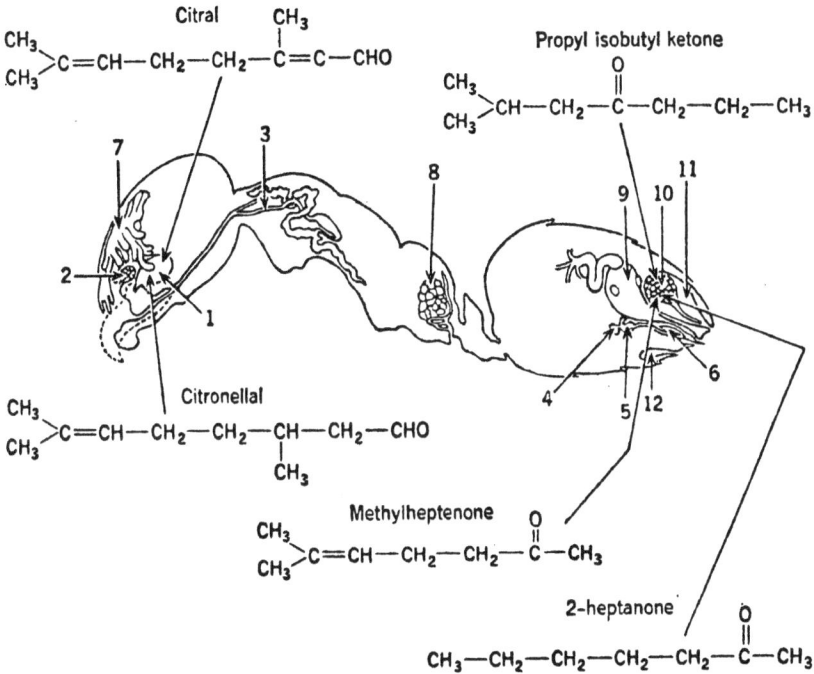

Figure 14 Some ant alarm substances which have been identified and the location of the glands which secrete them. Citral identified from *Atta rubropilosa*, citronellal from *Acanthomyops clariger*, propyl isobutyl ketone from *Tapinoma nigerrimum*, methylheptenone in *Tapinoma* and other species, and 2-heptanone from *Iridomyrmex pruinosus*. The exocrine gland system represents *Iridomyrmex humilis*. (After Wilson and Bossert, 1963, Wilson, 1963b.)

bees (*Bombus*) and innumerable ant species, can be left behind as a continuous signal after the animal has departed; so they are thus used as territorial and trail markers as well as to provide individual nest odour.

Wilson estimated that the transfer of information can be surprisingly rapid and that the potential transmission rate for spatial information in the Fire ant's (*Solenopsis saevissima*) odour trail is about one "bit" every eight seconds; a rate comparable, as he says, with that which has been computed for the waggle dance of the honeybee with respect to purely spatial information.

Bossert has argued that patterned transmission of pheromones, consisting of amplitude and frequency modulation (regular patterns in frequency of release over a given time period), is technically feasible over very short distances or in a low, steady wind. If such transmission actually occurs, Wilson estimates that it could be used to process one hundred or more "bits" of information per second—though there is, of course, no evidence that the receiving animal absorbs it at anything like this rate. The number of possible organic odorants is astronomically large, and there are, no doubt, innumerable instances yet to be discovered and studied. In ants the pheromones used for trail-forming are relatively volatile, and a natural single trail would evaporate within a minute or two to below threshold density, depending, of course, on how absorptive is the substratum. This means that a single trail-laying worker can pinpoint a food source only within a few feet of the nest, for the trail fades before other workers can follow it for greater distances.

The idea that chemical "shapes" can be perceived by insects has often been discussed, but good evidence seems yet to be lacking. Trails left by ants in the form of a drop of fluid from the tip of the abdomen often have a characteristic shape in that the fluid drop points in the ant's direction of travel; but I know of no evidence that ants which are lost refer to the shape of the marks to tell direction.

The trail substances used by ants tend to be species-specific in action, affording, so to speak, a private line for communication within a species when the foraging territories overlap. It is also evident that in many species of ants, as also in bees, individual colonies may have their own characteristic odour within their species odour. A most striking case of recruitment by insect pheromones is provided by a certain bark beetle (*Ips confusus*). When males of this species work their way into the phloem-cambial tissue of a host tree, they release a volatile substance from the hind gut that is attractive to both males and females. Other individuals, exploring in the vicinity, are drawn to the penetration gallery producing a mass attack which is only too familiar to students of forest entomology.

Besides pheromones which carry orientational or directional information, there are many examples of substances which, just as in the "Schreckstoff," or "alarm substance," in fish described by von Frisch, act as warning of danger to other members of the species. It seems that in the ants such alarm substances are not by any means always characteristic of the species—not even always characteristic of the subfamily. Wilson and Bossert (1963) have shown that in two genera of ants, *Lasius* and *Acanthomyops,* the terpenoid alcohols produced (if they are, as they appear to be, sex substances) are remarkable in that they occur in medleys—each species manufacturing a blend in which the proportions of the constituents are peculiar to the species. How far this may turn out to be a general feature is anybody's guess; but if applicable, it increases the potentialities of pheromones for information purposes very greatly indeed.

Wilson (1968) has listed the various ways in which chemical systems can be adjusted to enhance the specificity of signals or to increase the rate of information transfer. His classification is as follows:

1) Adjustment of fading time.

2) Expansion of the active space. Thus if the pheromone is expelled downwind only a relatively small amount is required, since orientation can be achieved by the following insect zigzagging upwind and so keeping in the zone of stimulation—as do many male moths flying upwind, from truly astonishing distances, to find a single female ready for mating.

3) Temporal patterning of single pheromones.

4) Use of multiple exocrine glands. (See Figure 11 above.)

5) Medleys of pheromones (the phenomenon just discussed above).

6) Change of meaning through context.

7) Variation in concentration and duration.

8) New meanings from combinations.

It is still largely guesswork which of these various categories are the more important, but it is certainly true that all are possible means of information transfer, not only in the Hymenoptera (ants, bees, wasps, etc.) but widely throughout the insects and other invertebrates.

Insects: Signalling with Sound

It remains to say a few words about auditory communication in the insects. Here again, the use of the method is widespread, although the Orthoptera (including the grasshoppers and crickets) and the Hemiptera (including the cicadas) provide the major examples. In this field, the work and summaries of R. D. Alexander provide the main door of easy access to the subject. (See Thorpe, 1972, Chap. 5. Also Frings and Frings, 1968.) Alexander (1967) arranges the acoustic signals of arthropods under nine functional headings. Omitting those which we have already dealt with under Hymenoptera, namely food and nest-site directives which are limited to social species, these are:

1) Disturbance and alarm signals (predatory repelling and conspecific alarming).

2) Calling signals (pair forming and aggregating).

3) Aggressive signals (rival separating and dominance establishing).

4) Courtship signals (insemination timing and insemination facilitating).

5) Courtship interruption signals.

6) Copulatory signals (insemination facilitating and pair maintaining).

7) Postcopulatory or intercopulatory signals (pair maintaining).

8) Recognition signals (limited to subsocial and social species and functioning as pair- and family-maintaining stimuli).

9) Aggressive mimicry signals (prey attraction by production of pair-forming signals of prey species).

In considering the sound communication of Orthoptera, we must remember that the insect auditory organ usually, and perhaps nearly always, consists of a system which is highly sensitive to amplitude modulation and to temporal spacing but normally insensitive to frequency modulation. (Michelsen [1968] has described an exception to this in the locust.) Figure 15 gives an indication of the behavioural sequences and cycles associated with sound communication in adult grasshoppers, crickets, and cicadas.

Fireflies: Signalling with Light Flashes

The special instance of visual communication provided by the fireflies, which are beetles of the family *Lampyridae,* is of peculiar interest. Lloyd (1966) describes the flash communication of fireflies in the following remarkable passage:

At the time of evening characteristic for the species, males arise from the grass and fly and flash, most of them keeping within an ecologically well-defined area such as a lawn, forest edge, stream bed, or wet corner of a pasture. Male flight paths during moments of light emission are characteristic for the species; some species can be identified by this behaviour alone (Plate 3). Females are found on the ground and on grass or other low vegetation. When a male receives a flashed answer from a female after the species-characteristic interval following his own flash, he turns and flies towards her. After a few seconds he repeats his flash pattern; if he again receives the correct flash response, he continues his approach. Flight terminates a few centimetres from the female after from 1 to 10 flash exchanges. After landing, the male usually completes the approach by walking and exchanging flashes with the female. Males mount females immediately upon contact. For complete attraction, only flash signals are necessary, and in all species tested, males were attracted to females caged in airtight glass containers. During approaches, females frequently fail to answer some of the male flashes, and when they resume answering, males continue

95

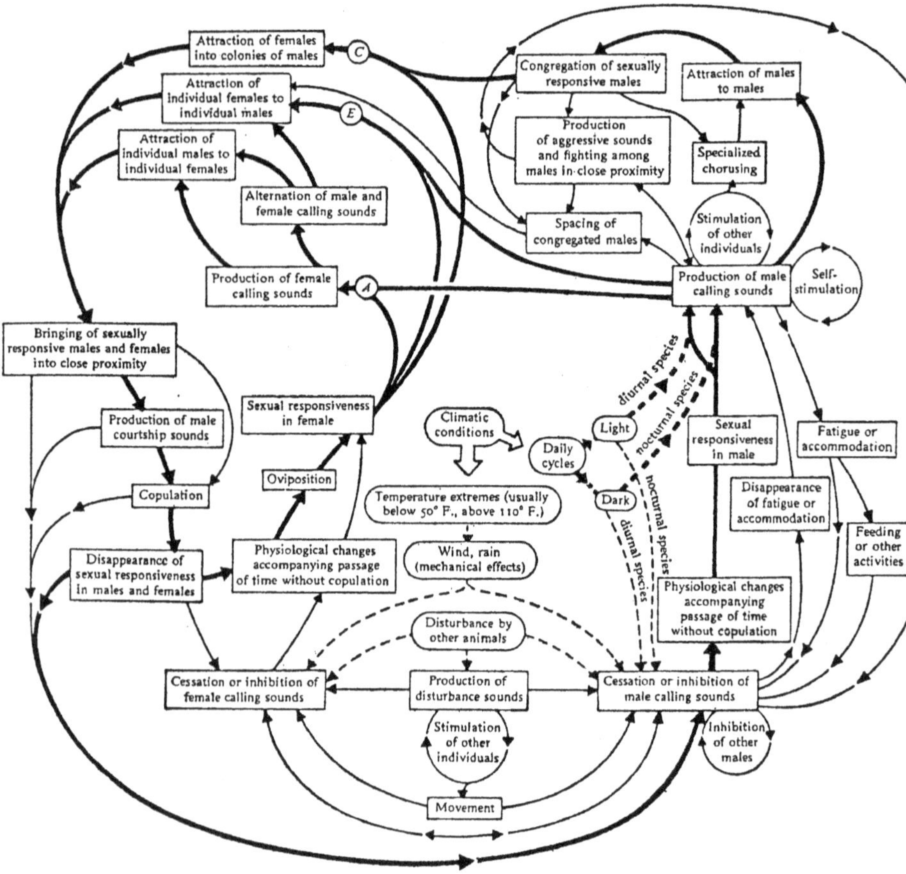

Attraction of females into colonies of males

C

Attraction of individual females to individual males

E

Attraction of individual males to individual females

Alternation of male and female calling sounds

Congregation of sexually responsive males

Attraction of males to males

Production of aggressive sounds and fighting among males in close proximity

Specialized chorusing

Spacing of congregated males

Stimulation of other individuals

Production of female calling sounds

A

Production of male calling sounds

Self-stimulation

Bringing of sexually responsive males and females into close proximity

Production of male courtship sounds

Sexual responsiveness in female

Climatic conditions

Light

Sexual responsiveness in male

Fatigue or accommodation

Daily cycles

Oviposition

Copulation

diurnal species

nocturnal species

Temperature extremes (usually below 50° F., above 110° F.)

Dark

Disappearance of fatigue or accommodation

Feeding or other activities

Disappearance of sexual responsiveness in males and females

Physiological changes accompanying passage of time without copulation

Wind, rain (mechanical effects)

nocturnal species

diurnal species

Physiological changes accompanying passage of time without copulation

Disturbance by other animals

Cessation or inhibition of female calling sounds

Production of disturbance sounds

Cessation or inhibition of male calling sounds

Stimulation of other individuals

Inhibition of other males

Movement

Figure 15 A diagrammatic representation of the behavioural sequences and cycles associated with sound communication in adult Orthoptera and Cicadidae. Heavy lines indicate more important sequences, and the symbols (C), (E), and (A) designate sequences most characteristic of the Cicadidae, Ensifera, and Acridinae, respectively. (From Alexander, 1960.)

96

their approaches. Males remain in the area of a previous response, emitting their flash pattern for several minutes after females are removed.

In most species, activity lasts for about one half-hour and then decreases slowly over the next thirty to forty minutes, until eventually only an occasional flash can be seen.

Figure 16 shows how the temporal patterning of the firefly flashes resembles the temporal patterning of the stridulatory calls produced by the Orthoptera (Figure 17) and by the very special sound-producing mechanism of the cicadas.

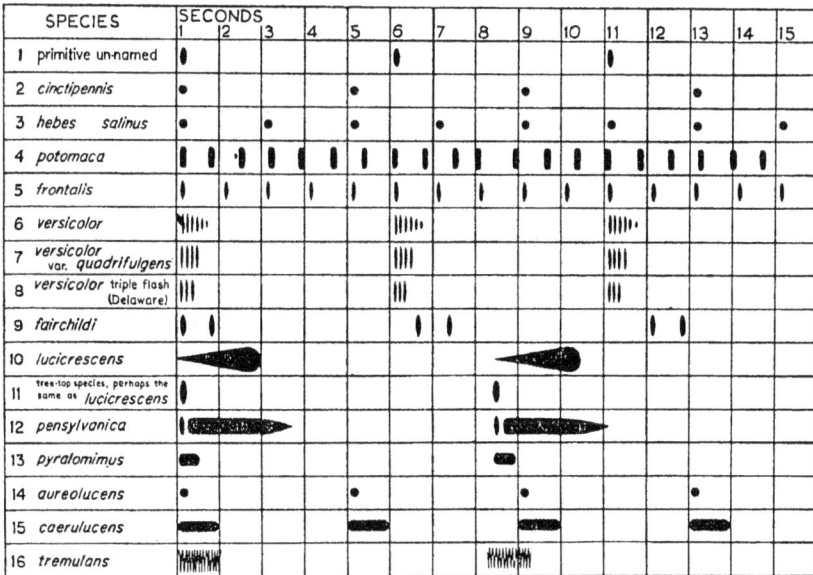

SPECIES	SECONDS 1	2	3	4	5	6	7	8	9	10	11	12	13	14	15
1 primitive un-named	❙					❙					❙				
2 *cinctipennis*	●				●				●				●		
3 *hebes salinus*	●		●		●		●		●		●		●		●
4 *potomaca*	❙ ❙	·❙ ❙	❙ ❙	❙ ❙	❙ ❙	❙ ❙	❙ ❙	❙ ❙	❙ ❙	❙ ❙	❙ ❙	❙ ❙	❙ ❙	❙	
5 *frontalis*	❙ ❙	❙	❙	❙	❙	❙	❙	❙	❙	❙	❙	❙	❙	❙	
6 *versicolor*	⦀⦀ⁱ					⦀⦀ⁱ					⦀⦀ⁱ				
7 *versicolor* var. *quadrifulgens*	⦀⦀					⦀⦀					⦀⦀				
8 *versicolor* triple flash (Delaware)	⦀					⦀					⦀				
9 *fairchildi*	❙ ❙					❙ ❙					❙ ❙				
10 *lucicrescens*		◄▬				◄▬									
11 tree-top species, perhaps the same as *lucicrescens*	❙					❙									
12 *pensylvanica*	❙▬▬►					❙▬▬►									
13 *pyralomimus*	●▬					●▬									
14 *aureolucens*	●				●				●				●		
15 *caerulucens*	▬▬				▬▬				▬▬				▬▬		
16 *tremulans*	⫼⫼⫼					⫼⫼⫼									

Figure 16 Pulse patterns during flashing in male fireflies of the genus *Photinus*. Species 2 and 14 (taken in Maryland and Minnesota respectively) have the same flash pattern but are quite different morphologically and may be allopatric. Delay times in female answers may be different between species. (From Alexander, in Sebeok, 1968.)

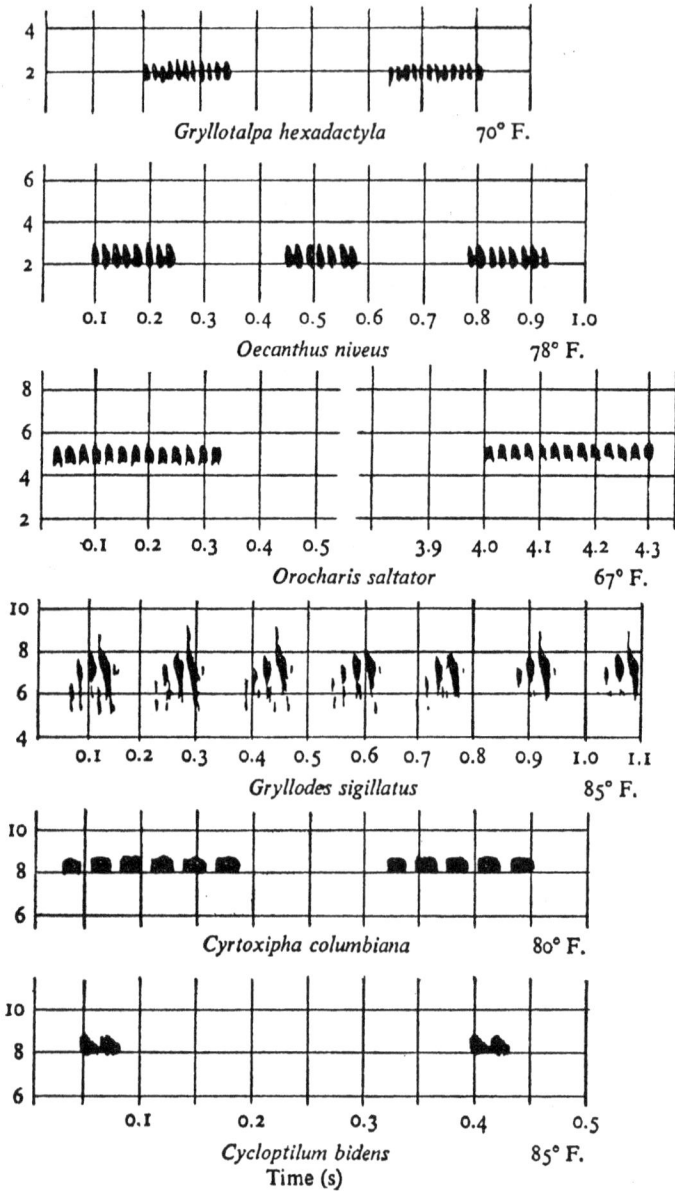

Figure 17 Chirp patterns of calling songs in six different subfamilies of crickets. Top to bottom: *Gryllotalpinae*, Champaign County, Ohio, 24 August 1954; *Oecanthinae*, Erie County, Ohio, 26 July 1955; Encopterinae, Dyar County, Tennessee, 24 September 1955; *Gryllinae*, Florida laboratory culture; *Trigonidiinae*, Lenoir, North Carolina, 2 August 1955; *Mogoplistinae*, Raleigh, North Carolina, 8 August 1955. Ordinate, kc/sec. (From Alexander, in Sebeok, 1968.)

Fishes: Communication by Chemical, Electrical, and Pressure Senses

Turning now from the invertebrates to the fishes we again have to deal with a large group of species in which form and colour are often highly distinctive both of the species themselves and, during the breeding season, of sex within the species. It is consequently not surprising that a great deal of communication is by recognition, sometimes minutely precise, of patterns of form and colour and subtle combinations of these. That many species are territorial, and many others show the elementary social behaviour of schooling, further emphasises the communication problems that must arise in this group. Moreover the fact that fishes are aquatic animals raises still further points of special interest for the biologist studying communication systems.

Although a great many fishes which live in shallow water, in clear streams, and in such situations as coral reefs are highly visual animals, there are equally an enormous number which live at great depths where light is sparse, or in water which is highly charged with concentrations of microplankton which severely limit the penetration of light and the efficacy of visual organs. The same difficulty arises with fish living in muddy fresh and coastal waters. Indeed Dietrich (1963) expresses the opinion that the range for effective vision in the marine environment is generally less than one metre, and in areas of high turbidity the effective range may be reduced to only a few centimetres. It is thus not surprising that the olfactory organs of many fishes are extraordinarily sensitive. Froloff (1925, 1928) and Bull (1928–39) were the pioneers here. These workers found that two species of *Blennius,* when offered sea-water extracts of natural food substances, were able to differentiate between concentrations of 0.000375 per cent and 0.00075 per cent weight of living food substance in sea water. Later, the work of Hasler and Wisby and also of Kleerekoper and Mogensen (reference in Hinde, ed., 1972) has further shown the extraordinary powers of fishes

99

such as trout and lampreys in detecting specific amines secreted by particular species. Von Frisch (1941) demonstrated that a minnow (*Phoxinus laevis*) that has been frightened, or is in some way under stress, produces substances in its body mucous that stimulate fright behaviour in other animals of the same species. There is little doubt that the study of fish pheromones has only just begun and is of great promise.

An outstanding landmark in the knowledge of the sensory powers of fish was the discovery by Lissmann (1951, 1958) that some fishes of tropical rivers, notably the *Mormyridae* and *Gymnotidae* of the great turbid river systems of Africa and South America respectively, use electric pulses for orientation. They detect objects by perceiving the electrical field distortion of the discharges which they produce. It is known that each species of Gymnotid fish has a characteristic resting pulse pattern of electric discharge which may be modified by particular circumstances and activities. Lissmann (1963) has recently discovered electrical receptors in other species, the function of which has not yet been fully investigated. Among fish species producing both weak and strong electrical fields, casual observations suggest that the electrical discharge may have a social function, though it remains to be seen whether such signals as have yet been described permit individual and species recognition; on general grounds, it seems highly probable.

It has been shown by Harris and van Bergeijk (1962) that the swim bladder acts as a transducer for pressure waves, transforming them into local "near-field" effects. Pure pressure waves are rapidly and effectively propagated in water but are essentially non-directional except at close range and high intensity. As Tavolga (1956) points out, there is, as yet, no evidence that fish can assess direction in a far field. He says, "In effect, fishes have but a single ear since the two inner ears are not only close together but coupled to a single swim bladder." However, whether or not fishes can localise sounds with any high degree of efficiency (and the evidence is still contradictory), much further evidence of widespread sound production amongst fishes has come to hand as a result of the development of underwater microphones. The significance of this is, as yet, not understood, but playback experiments have demonstrated that responses can be elicited by recorded sound. The grunts of male gobies (*Bathygobius soporator*) in collaboration with visual stimuli encourage female courtship, and they also elicit the approach of males.

In the satin-fin shiner (*Notropis analostraneus*), Stout (1963) has shown that territorial males produce single knocks when chasing and during courtship; rapid series of knocks during display fighting; and purring during the courtship activities of approach, circling and "male passing over nest site." Playback of the knocks tends to elicit aggressive behaviour from other males, while purring sounds favour courtship activities. There is evidence that sounds of other species fail to elicit responses in some cases but are effective in others.[10]

COMMUNICATION AMONG AMPHIBIA AND REPTILES

Having glanced at the fishes, it is extremely instructive to see the big changes that have taken place in vertebrate communicative behaviour with the transition from the marine environment to the land and all this has implied. Indeed it is almost uncanny the way in which sex recognition and the communications which signal the readiness to mate in frogs and toads parallel, one might almost say parody, in very simple form the same processes in the higher land mammals. Thus we see that the males tend to be aggressive towards one another and show this by visual displays, by vocalisations, and by pheromone secretion. A female, on the other hand, when approached by a male may have very little in the way of either structure, or behaviour, with which to identify her sex; though she may of course very frequently have specific pheromones. Female technique in these situations is to begin by remaining placid. That is to say, she does not react aggressively; neither does she run away. The effect of this is to assuage aggression and to encourage a sexual approach, and not until this is fairly far advanced does she, in many cases, begin to give specifically sexual attitudes or signals, and then only of course if she is in the hormonal or physiological state which permits her to be reproductive. We shall find this general scheme occurring again and again throughout the higher animals as the underlying basis for female signalling whatever further elaborations and developments have been erected on top.

Among the amphibia the first group to be considered is the Apoda which comprises the *Caecilians,* a group of worm-like creatures occurring throughout the tropical regions of the world and living mainly in burrows in the soil. Since the eyes are vestigial and there is no evidence of vocalisation, it can be assumed that tactile and chemical signals are the most likely means of communication. The Urodela (the tailed amphibia) comprise, for our purposes, chiefly the salamanders and the newts. Here again, chemical signals appear to be the most important. In the newts (Tinbergen, 1953), sex recognition and courtship are mediated by a series of signals, involving:

1) *Visual signals.* Most species are markedly sexually dimorphic, and the male assumes specific attitudes during courtship. Lack of movement by the female intimates to the male that he is to continue courtship.

2) *Tactile signals.* In many species a sudden leap by the male sends a strong water current to the female, sometimes even pushing her aside.

3) *Chemical signals.* Scent glands are distributed over most of the body in both sexes and appear to produce sexually stimulating secretions. The tail-waving of the male creates water currents carrying a chemical stimulant to the female. There is no evidence that sound signals of any kind play a part in communication amongst the tailed amphibia. The salamanders also communicate the identity of species and sex and the physiological readiness, or otherwise, to mate; mainly through chemical, tactile, and visual signals, probably in this descending order of importance. But

their communication signals appear more complex and varied than in the other tailed amphibia.

When we come to the frogs and toads (Anura), the situation is strikingly different in that vocal communication is of major importance. But whereas a number of non-human primates have a vocal repertoire of up to about twenty sound types, and the birds a similar number, various frogs and toads are known to produce only up to four recognisably distinct sounds.

In general, the sounds produced by the Anura can be classified under five headings, of which the first three are the only really important ones for the purposes of the present discussion. The first is *the mating call*. This covers the sounds produced by most adult frogs and toads which are commonly heard as choruses from breeding aggregations, or sometimes from isolated individuals. These mating calls are produced only by the adults, in most species only by the male, and are thought to be clear evidence of sexual maturity. When a frog or a toad approaches a member of its species in a breeding pool, one can fairly safely assume that the vocal signals have already effectively communicated species identification. There remains the question of identification of sex and of the reproductive state of the female that is clasped by a male. Hence we have the second call, *the male release call*, normally uttered at a breeding site. He clasps males or females indiscriminately, but differential behaviour in the sexes determines whether he retains his grip. If the individual seized is a male, his struggles, accompanied by sounds variously described as chirps, croaks, grunts, or clucks, usually elicit his release. By contrast a ripe female seized by a male of her own species emits no sound, remains passive, and the male retains his grasp. Bogert describes the male release call as a short explosive sound repeated at irregular intervals. This is in contrast to the often much more complex mating calls of some of the frogs, which may be repeated at regular intervals with a characteristic rhythm, are often trill-like, and sometimes have a relatively complex acoustical structure.

The third anuran type of vocalisation is *the female release*

103

call. In some species unreceptive females utter sounds similar to the release call of the male. Thus Noble and Aronson mention warning croaks in Leopard frogs (*Rana pipiens*) of both sexes. If clasped by a male, the female utters the croak except during the ovulatory period when she becomes receptive as well as silent. She is mute during sexual congress and the male's clasp does not elicit the croak until several hours after oviposition is completed. This female release call, while certainly widespread, does not appear to have anything like the biological significance of the two types of call previously discussed.

Still less important seems to be a fourth type of call, *the postoviposition male release call.* According to Lutz the Brazilian Tree frog (*Phyllomedusa guttata*), after spawning is completed, begins to cluck softly (quite a different call from that of the mating call) and then leaves the female, who remains in the same position for another thirty minutes. Fifthly there are *ambisexual release vibrations* which are not vocal in the sense that they do not depend upon the vibration of the vocal cords, but are probably produced by accentuated respiratory movements that cause a cup-shaped cartilage (the arytenoid) to vibrate— the vibrations being transmitted to the body musculature. It is supposed that the inflated lungs may then serve as resonating chambers and hence render a vibration audible to man.

The reptiles present a much less elaborate picture of vocalisations than do the amphibia. The roaring vocalisations of the American alligator (*Alligator mississippiensis*) (Evans, 1961) and the Nile crocodile (*Crocodilus niloticus*) (Cott, 1961) are, however, of much interest. In both animals it seems that calling by the males is answered by other males and is a territorial defence device; and that females are attracted by the roar of the males during the breeding season and, in addition, by the secretions of musk glands which are situated near the jaws and are primarily functional during courtship. The so far but little-studied vocalisations of turtles and tortoises seem to be employed in a similar way and are also supplemented by the use of chemical signals. Snakes are notoriously silent, but the rattling of the rattlesnake (*Crotalus* spp.) provides positive identification for an animal that is well protected by its venom apparatus. Lizards have elaborate visual displays but are, on the whole, silent creatures. However, a striking exception to this is provided by the geckos which, being nocturnal, have developed extensive vocalisations. The Leopard lizard (*Crotaphytus wislizenii*) is particularly remarkable in this respect.

II. Vocal Communications in the Higher Vertebrates, Especially Birds.

BIRDS

Birds are the most vocal animals apart from man. They use sounds to convey information between the members of a pair or a potential pair, between parent and young, between siblings, between conspecifics in a feeding or migrating or roosting flock, and often between different species within such a flock. Moreover, their vocalisations are incomparably more complex and more precisely modulated and controlled than are those of other animals; and the apparatus for achieving these results is, as far as is known, unique both in principle and in structural design.

Information Content of Songs

Before proceeding it may be well to remind the reader of the distinction between "message" and "meaning" (Smith, 1968). We often find that a given utterance by a bird contains much potential information, but that only part of this is used in a given set of circumstances. Let us take the example of the song of the robin (*Erithacus rubecula*). This is normally a proclamation announcing occupation of a territory and readiness to defend that territory against all rivals. The song itself is an elaborate succession of sounds, some of them individually quite complex. And this sequence of sounds may be in some respects distinct from one robin to another. If, when a robin has first established a territory, one plays back to it the song of another robin, or of that robin himself, he gives a violent aggressive reaction. But just as violent a reaction can be produced by playing back a very simple schema of a robin's song consisting of the alternating high and low notes at the correct time intervals but omitting all else; so in this experimental situation all the other "information" in the song is disregarded (Brémond, 1967). But we know, from work on this and many other species, that in natural circumstances a great deal of the detailed structure of the song, which in this experimental situation may be ignored, can be perceived and acted upon.

Thus it has long been realised (e.g., Thorpe, 1958) that a rival chaffinch (*Fringilla coelebs*) may recognize a given male not merely by the position of his territory but by the individuality of his voice. Since then many new instances have come to light (e.g., Falls, 1969), and as Hinde (1958; see Thorpe, 1961) proved, the territorial singer can sometimes quickly adapt to a rival by matching its song pattern to that of the intruder. As Brémond (1967) has described, the robin's instantaneous imitation of an invader's signal amounts to saying "I am talking to you, invader of the moment." (See Busnel, 1968.) All these examples, and there are many more, indicate a syntactic element, a real combination of signals. Moreover, the tropical shrikes *Laniarius aethiopicus* and *L. erythrogaster* (Thorpe, 1973) can modify the messages encoded in their male/female duets by changing the acoustic and temporal patterning of their antiphonal contributions.

In fact, a robin, in its response to intruders, responds selectively to auditory information in just the same way as it does to visual information. Many years ago Lack (1939) showed that a mere bunch of red feathers stuck on a wire in a robin's territory was sufficient to release a violent and continuing attack. Nevertheless, a robin in a different situation, for instance when it is choosing (or responding to) a potential mate, can react to very subtle differences in the colour and attitudes of the approaching robin. In this case the context of the message determines to a considerable extent what part of the message is responded to, and thus its meaning. If a recipient uses the context in responding to the message, one message can carry several meanings. The constant message, yielding different meanings in different contexts, is a simpler device than one which varies the message together with the meaning. In general, in the case of simple calls, which for instance give warning of predators, inform the other members of the flock that food has been found, or tell the parents that a chick is hungry or lost, discrete meanings cannot well be transmitted by means of a single message, for the context is not sufficiently well perceived by the recipient. But the examples of song already discussed show how important it is to distinguish between message and meaning in every instance, and how dangerous to assume that all potential information in a message is perceived or understood by the hearers and affects their behaviour appropriately.

Call Notes of Birds

Having referred to "call notes" it is now convenient to say something about the commonly made distinction between call notes and song. Call notes are usually simple in structure, consisting of one or a few bursts of sound, in contrast to the longer and more complicated sequences of song. Call notes in the main convey information which may warn of danger, help to control the movement of a flock, indicate the whereabouts of food, and so forth. Song, on the other hand, is a type of vocalisation appropriate to, and often confined to, the breeding season; it is given primarily by the male under the general physiological control of the sex hormones and, as we have seen, is often capable of a high degree of modification by imitative learning.

Call notes are often adapted to the particular function that they serve, and we may consider one example, the call notes used to warn conspecifics of the presence of predators. Such notes are specialised in their acoustic structure for the particular type of predator encountered. Figure 18 shows the type of call

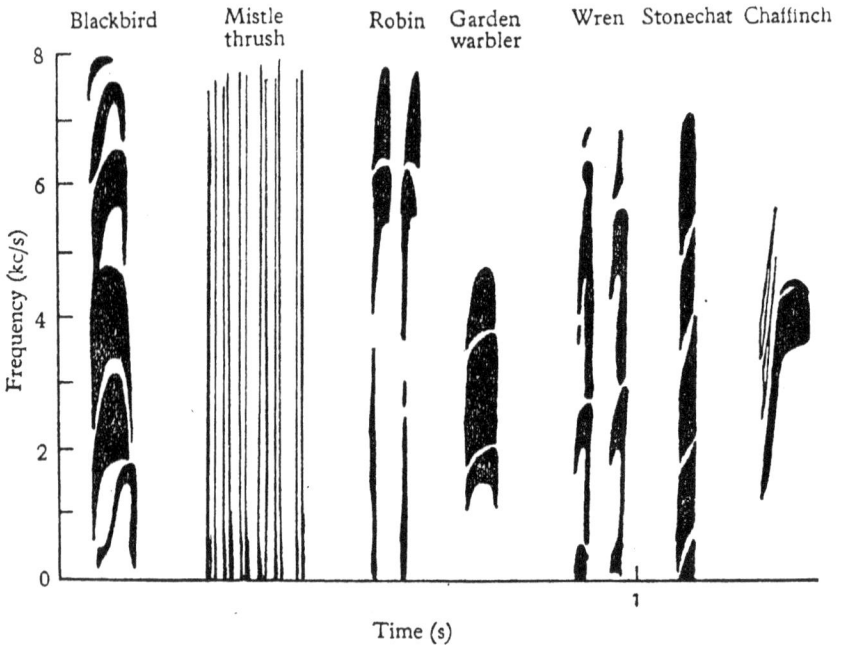

Figure 18 Calls of birds from several Passerine families given while mobbing owls. (From Thorpe, 1961, after Marler, 1959.)

given by many small birds in response to some enemy either on the ground or perched in a tree, a predator such as a hawk, an owl, or a weasel. It is clear that these sounds are all loud, repetitive, and cover a great frequency range. They are often given in a situation in which it is presumably advantageous, for the bird concerned, to draw attention to this particular danger and warn others of its exact location. An example is the mobbing response of many small birds to a perched owl: they stand around at a fairly safe distance and chatter at the enemy. The result is to attract neighbours to join in the mob; and it is to be noted that the call structure is such that it is very easily located —by a feature which our ears experience too. For loud, click-like sounds are very easily and accurately located at both the right direction and roughly the right distance by both birds and men.

Figure 19 shows an entirely different kind of call which is

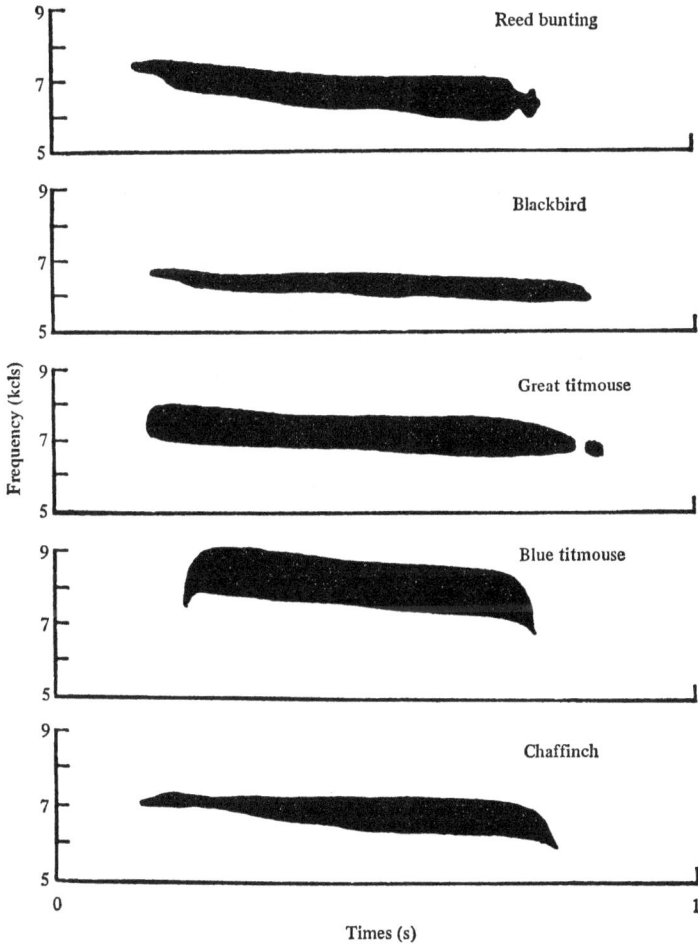

Figure 19   Calls of five different Passerine species given when a hawk flies over. (From Thorpe, 1961, after Marler, 1959.)

given when a flying predator is in the air above. If the predator is a hawk or an owl, then the threat is immediate and the danger great. So instead of mobbing, the bird dives into the nearest shelter and gives a type of call which starts and stops gradually and maintains a fairly constant pitch somewhere around 7 kHz =7 kc/s). Other birds, hearing these calls, likewise fly to shelter and repeat the same call from their hiding places. The immediate point that strikes one on hearing these calls is that they are extremely difficult to locate. This is due, in the first place, to the fact that they lack the characteristics previously mentioned which make localisation easy. But besides this there is another reason.

A bird employs the same methods as we do to locate the origin of a sound. These consist in comparisons between the sound as received by the two ears involving three different types of data: (1) phase difference, (2) intensity difference, and (3) time of arrival. Phase difference is most likely to be valuable at low frequencies; for instance, the data become ambiguous when the wavelength is much less than twice the distance between the two ears. Intensity differences are most valuable at fairly high frequencies and the differential effect is due to the "sound shadow" cast by the head of the listening bird; sound shadows only become important when the wavelength approximates the diameter of the obstruction. Differences between the time of arrival at the two ears will, of course, be more obvious the larger the distance apart of the ears. Calculation suggests that sounds of about the frequency of 7 kHz will be maximally difficult to locate for the ears of a bird of medium size—say a hawk or an owl (Marler, 1955). This frequency is too high for effective binaural comparisons of phase difference and too low for there to be enough sound shadow perceptible by the ears. Thus the "seet" call of the male chaffinch probably gives no clues as to its location, either by phase or intensity differences. This leaves only the third method, the appreciation of binaural time differences; and just because the sounds begin and end gradually or imperceptibly, no clues for time differences are supplied. This may, in fact, be the most important point of all, and Dr. Andrew has pointed out to me that the same effect may be achieved by a long, very regular trill, as used by the domestic fowl in response to a hawk, even though at a lower pitch. Finally, the wavelength is small enough to result in fairly free reflection from the trunks of small trees.

Bird Song—Signals Indicative of Species and Individual

Now let us consider song. This must serve both as a species and as an individual signal, and we may first consider the question of securing and maintaining species distinctiveness. Here we have to establish the mechanism for the maintenance of the overall specific pattern of the song from generation to generation. How much of this can be put down purely to genetic programming? If we examine young birds kept in complete isolation from conspecifics—isolated, that is, either from the egg or from the early fledgling life—we find a number of instances of birds so treated in which the vocalisations emerge little or no different from those of individuals reared normally. This certainly seems to be true of many of the call notes referred to above. It also seems to be true of some songs. Thus the song sparrow (*Melospiza melodia*) will produce an almost completely normal song even when it has been fostered from the egg by canaries and allowed to hear only canary song, which is entirely different in pattern and structure (Marler, 1967).

The same situation seems to obtain with many species, perhaps all species, of the pigeons and doves (Columbidae). The acoustic structure, which provides the basis of the tonal quality of the notes of birds of this family, is, on the whole, remarkably similar as we pass from species to species. To put it very crudely: almost all doves "coo." But though all the notes sound similar, probably no two species the world over "coo" in exactly the same rhythmical pattern or with the same accent. So it should, in principle, be possible to construct a table for identification of the doves of the world based solely upon the numbers of the notes in the song, the overall duration, the length of the individual notes, the times, the rhythm and the accent. And, in fact, one can often recognise a given species throughout an enormous geographical range solely by the temporal organisation of the song. Experiments on some of these species (Lade and Thorpe, 1964) and evidence from earlier work (Thorpe, 1968) indicate that the vocal pattern is completely resistant to cross-fostering or other means of exposure to alien song patterns during early life. Another example of this resistance to early experience is provided by the European cuckoo (*Cuculus canorus*), where the song produced by the male is entirely independent of the vocalisations of its foster parents.

As a result of such examples one is forced to the conclusion that there must develop, independently of experience of the species-characteristic song, a system which is fully competent of itself to activate and control the motor processes of the vocalisation. This has been shown to be the case in doves by Nottebohm (1970) and in the domestic fowl by Konishi (1963), who have shown that these birds can develop and maintain the normal repertoire and forms of their vocal signals even though complete deafening has been carried out operatively in the first days of life. In other words, in the call notes of the domestic fowl, just as, in all probability, with those of the doves and the song of the song sparrow, the mechanism is fully competent without the necessity for experience of the species song.

Neural Templates for Song—Innate and Acquired

In many birds, however, we find something less than this full competence in that some relatively specific auditory stimulation is required to render the mechanism fully effective and produce the specific vocal signals. In the chaffinch, this stimulation can come from the hearing of chaffinch-like songs during the bird's first autumn, some months before it starts to sing itself. As one might expect from this, the normal song structure cannot be produced if the chaffinch has been operatively deafened as an early juvenile. The overall song structure—what one might call the "sound skeleton" of the song—which constitutes the specific vocal signal, is not produced by birds so treated. (Though again, some call notes seem unaffected by this procedure of deafening: Nottebohm, 1968, 1970.) However, once the normal song structure and patterning has been allowed to establish itself in the natural manner, operative deafening at a later stage in its life does not affect its performance and maintenance. Thus the stereotyped movements of singing are independent of at least that source of feedback which, from comparisons with the difficulties which some deaf human beings experience in maintaining normal speech, we should have expected to be the most important.

Nottebohm (1970), in discussing the establishment of a song memory in *Fringilla coelebs*, points out that the imitation of a song model consists of two processes: (1) establishment of the memory as an auditory template, and (2) its conversion to a motor pattern. If the auditory template is to be matched by song development, hearing must remain intact. Adult male chaffinches, deafened after one full season of singing experience, retain their song pattern with great fidelity. By contrast, the song patterns of a year-old male, deafened when it had almost but not quite perfected its two song themes, were not retained but regressed in quality. (This suggests that there are two stages in the development and stabilisation of song—a transient memory and, later, a permanent memory retained even in the absence of auditory feedback. Whether these memories are just an efferent programme or an integration of output and proprioceptive feedback is not known.) Clearly then, the song of such species is at least very different from speech in that an innate template requires development by auditory experience which must be, in at least some respects, specific if normal bird song is to be produced, whereas a child can learn the phonetic characteristics of any language to which it is regularly and fully exposed.

But even the stimulus of a very poorly organised or almost completely disorganised vocalisation from another chaffinch can canalise song development. Hand-raised chaffinches reared in groups acoustically isolated from other members of the species produce songs more complex than those of hand-raised individuals kept alone. However, the songs are not necessarily more like the normal species song, for each such group produces its own idiosyncratic pattern. But autumn-caught birds, which have had some previous experience of the species song, do produce more normal songs if they are subsequently kept in acoustically isolated groups rather than if they are kept alone: apparently in both cases the experience of countersinging facilitates song development (Thorpe, 1958, 1961).

Song Learning by Imitation in Birds

In the chaffinch, learning of refined details of song is at its maximum early in the first spring—namely when the bird is about eight months old—and increases up to a peak at about fourteen months, after which it ceases entirely. Singing behaviour becomes fixed and unalterable after the first breeding season. By contrast, in other species such as the red-backed shrike (*Lanius collurio*) and the canary (*Serinus canaria*), a period of ability to learn new song elements may recur annually.

Thus it appears that, in the chaffinch, an innate template does exist, even though by itself, without any auditory experience, this template cannot express itself in full control of the motor pattern of vocalisation. Indeed, if there was no such template and it were all a matter of imitation, then the song of the chaffinch could hardly be as stable as it is. A good instance of this is given by the introduction of chaffinches to New Zealand in 1862 and to South Africa in 1900. After this long period of isolation, during which it can be reasonably assumed that no further introductions were carried out, the basic song structure has not drifted substantially away from that characteristic of the ancestral population in Europe. If everything were imitatively learned, it is almost inconceivable that this would be the case. But the bullfinch (*Pyrrhula pyrrhula*) is very different; a young bullfinch seems to learn songs only from its own father (Nicolai, 1959). If fostered by canaries, it will adopt canary song and ignore the songs of bullfinches even if kept in the same room.

Other cases of song learning have been analysed in various

species of finches and in some of the buntings (Marler, 1967), in addition to the chaffinch. One of the species discussed by Marler, the Arizona junco (*Junco phaeonotus*), is peculiar in that the situation found in many other species is in some degree reversed. That is to say, the birds seem to acquire the overall song pattern by imitation, but the syllabic structure of the songs seems to depend upon birds stimulating each other to invent or improvise diverse syllable types. The diversity of songs of the European blackbird (*Turdus merula*) provides another remarkable instance of vocal inventiveness (Hall-Craggs, 1962, 1969). As our knowledge extends there will probably be found an almost infinite gradation of combinations of these various factors in the song development of different species.

In some species the imitative contact necessary for effecting maintenance of the species' distinctiveness also produces or maintains group distinctiveness of vocal signals. The chaffinch, by means of the control exercised over its imitative ability, maintains the normal outline and main features of the song but fills in the structure by taking, perhaps, most of the finer details from its singing neighbours. The white-crowned sparrow (*Zonotrichia leucophrys*) provides another instance. In this way a group dialect is produced such that the birds from one locality tend to approximate to one another in the details of their song; and those from a locality say fifty or a hundred miles away tend to have a slightly different average pattern of fine detail. Sometimes such dialects are restricted by quite small barriers such as river systems. Such local dialects often seem to serve no particular function, being no more than an accidental outcome of the way in which the song matures. Perhaps (Thielcke, 1969) they help to make the song signal more effective by reducing local variability. But in certain cases they must surely help in the early stages of genetic divergence. Be this as it may, within the local dialect the individual birds can develop their own peculiarities of song so that this can now serve the additional function of individual distinctiveness. An interesting case of this is shown by songs of the bou-bou shrikes (*Laniarius aethiopicus major*) depicted in Figure 20 (Thorpe, 1966, 1972). Here, the two mem-

Figure 20 Antiphonal songs of *Laniarius aethiopicus major* from various areas in East Africa. *x* and *y* indicate the contributions of the two members of the pair, but *x* may sometimes refer to the male and sometimes to the female, and similarly with *y*. (The figure "8" above the treble clef indicates that all that follows should be read as one octave higher than would otherwise be the case, e.g., middle "C" becomes 512 Hz instead of 256 Hz scientific pitch.) (From Thorpe, 1966.)

bers of a pair learn to duet with one another and, while adopting certain phrases and rhythms which are characteristic of the locality, work out between themselves duets which are sufficiently individual to enable the bird to distinguish and keep contact with its mate by singing duets with it (or, to be more exact, singing antiphonally with it) in the dense vegetation in which they usually live. (See also Hooker and Hooker, 1969.)

In some birds, no doubt, vocal quality alone may suffice to distinguish a species, and in that case the imitative and inventive powers of the bird can be used, if necessary, to produce a completely individual vocalisation. In the wild, most birds with imitative powers restrict these to the task of copying members of their own species and do not, even in captivity, mimic other bird species—still less man himself. But, as everyone knows,

116

there are other species which mimic widely: the mockingbird (*Mimus polyglottos*) in North America, the starling (*Sturnus vulgaris*) in Europe, and the racquet-tailed drongo (*Dicrurus paradiseus*) in India are good examples. These birds are something of a puzzle since it is not at all clear what biological advantage is achieved by imitating other species. The Indian mynah (*Gracula religiosa*), however (Thorpe, 1967), shares with the parrots the peculiarity that, while supreme imitators in captivity, they have never been heard to imitate any other species in the wild. Thanks to the work of Bertram (1970) we are now beginning to understand the situation in this very puzzling case. It appears that these mynahs do, in fact, imitate—but only other mynahs. Since mynah calls are of such a wide range of patterns and of such acoustic complexity, this imitation is undetectable by man's ear without long training and close study of neighbouring individuals. When, however, these birds are hand-reared, they seem to imprint very easily and thus they imitate all sorts of noises in their own environment, particularly the noises most closely associated with human beings. Hence their fame as mimics.

Sea Birds—The Fullest Development of Individual Recognition by Voice

We now come to a problem where the emphasis is somewhat different. Successful social organisation in animals often requires a capacity for mutual recognition, at some distance, between mates and also between parents and offspring. That is to say, it is often necessary not only for adults to recognise specific characters of their young and vice versa, but also for them to recognise one another individually, so that parental care and familial organisation and cohesion can operate. So far I have been discussing birds in which the young must be cared for, or maintained in a nest, by the parents, where individual recognition of parents by young, or vice versa, is usually unimportant. With nidifugous species, where the young move about and may scatter soon after hatching, individual recognition is often crucial. This implies both individual distinctiveness and the ability to learn and respond appropriately to individual differences. Indeed, when we consider the problem of reproduction and survival faced by birds such as many species of gulls, terns, gannets, penguins and so on—birds which nest in very dense colonies and obtain their food during the nesting period in rather restricted areas of sea or coastline near their colony—we can at once see a number of ways in which such abilities for individual recognition could be advantageous. Without individual recognition, the feeding of the young, at least as soon as they become mobile, could be a very wasteful process. Hordes of young would be competing for food from each individual adult as it returned to the colony, with the result that the strongest, the most fortunate, the most mature or the quickest would obtain ample food and many others would starve. And those which did survive would be no better fitted to take their place as members of a colony-nesting species. In the circumstances of colony-nesting, the eugenic need is for selection to operate so that adults which ensure that their own young are fed are at a selective advantage without, thereby, decreasing the chances of other young in the assemblage. This is the *sine qua non* of social life.

Again, it is important that the parent should bring food—for example, fish—of the right size for young of a given age: a fish three inches long may be too large for a small chick to swallow, whereas occasional meals of fish 0.25 inches long would result in undernourishment of the larger chicks. Similarly, it is often apparent that the smaller young receive a different kind of food from that brought to the larger ones. So both size and quality may vary with age. The same problem arises in the brooding of the young birds, especially during bad weather. If all were haphazard, some young would get too little brooding and some too much, which would presumably result in disastrous mortality.

Later still in the life cycle, when the young are nearly ready to fly or are first flying, it may be necessary for them to follow a particular parent rather than to accompany anonymously a flock of adults. Following an individual parent will give the young bird a much better opportunity to learn by example and experience how to find places where the right food can be obtained in quantity, and how to learn the best way of catching and eating it. Furthermore, as is usual in mammals, parental care is of immense importance in protecting against predator attack and learning how to avoid it.

That fidelity to nest site and mate is probably widespread in birds and is, indeed, of adaptive value in enhancing breeding success has been demonstrated by the work of Coulson (1966a, b) on the kittiwake (*Rissa tridactyla*). Coulson found that a female which retained her mate from her previous breeding season bred earlier, laid more eggs, and had a greater breeding success than one which paired with a new male. More recently it has been shown (Ashmole and Humbertotova, 1968) that parental care in sea birds may be much more prolonged than has hitherto been thought; and, of course, parental care at sea can only be achieved if there is mutual recognition.

Now if the visual powers are sufficiently well developed, vision will probably provide a larger number and greater variety of cues for recognition than any other sense. But it also seems certain that in birds, just as in primates, because of the greatly varying conditions of visibility, lighting, apparent size, and angle of approach, the difficulty of instantly recognising a complex visual pattern must be very great indeed. In fact, the visual responses of sea birds must constantly be at the mercy of sudden unpredictable changes—dazzle, fog, cloud, and, of course, darkness (Thorpe, 1968).

Consequently, if a sense that does not involve such great difficulties over perceptual constancy could be used for recognition, either in addition to or in place of vision, there would be great selective advantage in doing so. So the questions arise. How far can the auditory sense serve this purpose? Is the acuity and complexity of auditory perception great enough? And is the sound production of each bird sufficiently constant to that individual and sufficiently distinct from other individuals to allow for such a system to operate?

Now it is likely that, if sounds can be used, the message they carry is far less liable to distortion and interference than the visual patterns perceived by the eye from a distance. The only important advantage which vision seems to possess is the precise directional adjustment of the focussing power of the eye whereby the gaze can locate and track the object and so maintain fixation. But studies of the so-called "cocktail party" phenomenon indicate that, with the human ears at least, the capacity of hearing is able to overcome these obstacles created by loud and continuous random noise and so maintain contact with a preferred sound signal in very much the same way as the eye can locate and track an object. So it is not too much to expect that the roar of wind and sea and the hubbub of the colony may be similarly overcome by the hearing of colonially nesting sea birds.

As to the parameters which are available for recognition of a complex sound, they are much greater than might at first be expected. Meaningfully patterned sounds vary in more elaborate ways than simply pitch, loudness, and duration. To quote Gibson (1968), such sounds:

> . . . instead of being of simple duration vary in abruptness of beginning and ending, in repetitiveness, rate, rhythm, and in other subtleties of sequence. Instead of simple pitch, they vary in timbre or tone quality, in vowel quality, in approximation to noise, in noise quality and in changes of all these in time. Instead of simple loudness they vary in the dimensions of loudness, the rate of change of loudness and the rate of change of change of loudness. In meaningful sounds these factors can be combined to yield higher order variables of staggering complexity. But these mathematical complexities seem, nevertheless, to be the simplicities of all auditory information, and it is just these variables that are distinguished naturally by an auditory system.

To come now to colony-nesting birds, Tschanz (1968, summarising nearly ten years of work) was a pioneer in his demonstration that young guillemots (*Uria aalge*) learn to react selectively to the calls of their parents and that, during the first few days of life, the parents similarly recognise their own young. Indeed, there is some evidence that the young, while still within the egg, may learn to recognise some aspects of the sounds produced by the adults. In this species, however, the biological necessity for these powers of recognition is not at all clear.

There has long been considerable reason for suspecting that in some terns and gulls, also, the adults can recognise their mates and young, and the young their parents, by call alone (Thorpe, 1968). Recently some further progress in this field, with relation to the terns and, rather surprisingly, the gannets, has been made. Hutchison, Stevenson, and Thorpe (1968) found that, with the Sandwich tern (*Sterna sandvicensis*), the so-called "fish call," uttered by the parent when returning to its young with food, has just the kind of structure required to provide auditory data for individual recognition. In the forty different individuals with which it was possible to obtain a series of samples of the "fish call," each bird had a call measurably distinct from all the others, and the successive calls given by any one bird were extraordinarily similar. Plate 4 shows the sound spectrograms of typical recordings of two consecutive calls of three different individuals of the Sandwich tern. Table III gives correlations between certain measures of successive calls for twenty individuals.

Having provided this evidence that each Sandwich tern has its own individual "fish call," we may ask the question: If other birds of the same species were to identify an individual's call, which features might they use? If the variation of a particular characteristic were large, it would presumably be easier to discriminate differences between the birds than if the variation were very small. Furthermore, if two measures of a particular characteristic have about equal variation, and the mean of one measure is smaller than the mean of the other, the data from human subjects suggests that it might be easier to discriminate differences over the low absolute values. For example, if the

**Table III.   Correlations between two successive calls of
the same individuals. Total sample twenty individuals.**

Measure	Correlation coefficient
Total duration	0.98
Duration of segment *a*	0.92
No. of vertical bars in segment *a*	0.82
Duration of segment *b*	0.94
Lowest frequency in segment *b*	0.95
Duration of segment *c*	0.98
No. of vertical bars in segment *c*	0.98*

*These are all significant at less than the 0.01 level.

standard deviation were 1s., it would be easier to discriminate
difference from a mean of only 1s. than from a mean of 100ss.
Thus, the standard deviation divided by the mean value of a
series of measures should give a ratio for which low values indicate small variation and/or a large mean, or a difficult series
of measures to discriminate; and high values indicate an easier
one. If we assume that a similar rule can be applied to the Sandwich tern, then those measures which have the largest values of
the ratio *standard deviation/mean*, with respect to a particular
characteristic (for example, duration), would be most likely to
yield sources of discriminable, inter-individual differences. It
could be argued also that the measure having the smallest
values of this ratio might indicate the features which identify
a call as that of *Sterna sandvicensis*.

This ratio was obtained for each measure (Table IV). Because
the duration of segment *c* has a higher ratio than the other three
duration measures, and because the number of vertical bars in
segment *c* has a higher ratio than the number of bars in segment
a, it is more likely that both duration and number of bars in
segment *c* are used to identify the individual's call than are

Table IV. Ratios of standard deviation over mean for forty individuals.

Measure	Ratio
Duration of segment *c*	5.85
No. of vertical bars in segment *c*	3.62
Lowest frequency of fundamental of segment *b*	3.09
Duration of segment *b*	1.81
Total duration	1.74
Duration of segment *a*	1.55
No. of bars of segment *a*	0.52

those measures in other segments. Finally, the lowest frequency of the fundamental of segment *b* has a high ratio, and if terns are more or less equally sensitive to changes in the frequency as they are to changes in duration, then this, too, might contribute to the discrimination of calls of different individuals. All this seems to amount to an interesting confirmation of Marler's (1960) suggestion (also supported by Falls, 1969) that the two functions of species recognition and individual recognition will often be relegated to different parameters of a song.

In summary we can say that, while the extent to which these separate individual characteristics in the Sandwich tern are recognised as distinctive by the birds themselves has not been investigated, it is clear that if the "fish call" is used (as it seems to be) as an effective means for individual recognition in a large colony of two thousand or more pairs, patterning of the call could play an important part.

With the common tern (*Sterna hirundo*), Stevenson et al. (1970) have demonstrated that the young bird, at four days of age, while quite unresponsive to the playback of calls of other members of the colony, responds immediately on being played the returning call of one of its own parents; its response being a sudden, alert "cheeping," turning, and walking towards the loudspeaker. It seems then that the returning call of the parent common tern carrying food is quickly learnt and responded to by the individual young concerned. To put this in anthropocentric terms, with both the Sandwich tern and the common tern it appears that this call is in effect saying, "Here is Mum (or Dad) with food."

The individual recognition of voice in the gannet (*Sula bassana*) raises rather different problems, some of them more difficult, and it will hardly be necessary to enter here into all the details. (These can be found summarised in Chapter 6 of *Nonverbal Communication*, edited by R. A. Hinde, Cambridge University Press, 1972.) Here it is sufficient to say that the gannets while very silent at sea are extremely noisy on their nest sites. The young are never left untended except towards the very end of the fledgling period, one of the parents always staying at the nest to brood or guard them. The other member of the pair returning with food has a landing call of a series of eight or ten consecutive squawks and it appears clear from our observations that the adult on the nest recognises her mate amidst the general hubbub by some individual peculiarity of these squawks just as efficiently as do the terns. In the case of the gannet the sound spectrograms give no indication whatever of an individual voice pattern; but when we come to study the fluctuations in amplitude with time, again we find individual peculiarities observable in the graphs, and again these constant individual differences are shown at the beginning of each squawk whereas the end of the squawk is much less individually characteristic. Also, in the gannet as with the tern, it seems reasonable that the identifying part of a call should be at the beginning (after comparatively long periods of silence) so that sitting individuals, who probably pay low-level attention to all sounds coming from the proper direction, can receive individual information efficiently.

But here we must remember the peculiar environment to which the sitting gannet is exposed. A dense breeding colony of gannets packed on every available ledge of cliff is a place of indescribable hubbub. Most of the noise is coming from the birds in flight. Given such conditions of movement and noise, what then ought to be the most effective type of signal? The probability is that intermittent signals such as those given by the gannet may be very easy to locate. The sitting birds do not appear to be searching visually for their absent mates. The incoming birds tend to approach the colony upwind, diverging towards their particular nests only when they are some yards away. It can be argued that the acoustic structure at the beginning of each call probably facilitates accurate localisation, and by tracking approaching sources of sound, a sitting bird might quickly detect one which was approaching its nest and at the same time gain further information as to its identity from these individual features. It is something of a surprise to find species where amplitude fluctuations seem to provide the key to recognition, for it has usually been assumed that the bird ear, like the human ear which it so much resembles, is comparatively insensitive to these relatively small and rapid changes in loudness but is very sensitive to changes in patterns of pitch and timing.

There is another aspect of this ability of the gannets which is puzzling in that we could never find any evidence that the young bird responded to the individual parent calls at all. They were generally stuffed full of food and always guarded by a parent and so never endangered themselves by wandering about the colony from one nest to another. Thus the situation is very different from the crowded colonies of many terns where the young are highly mobile. It is possible that the answer is to be found simply in the conclusion that recognition of individual vocalisation in the gannet is a means of securing that, after the long period out at sea during the winter, the two members of a pair can recognise one another again when they return to the nesting cliffs. We have seen that there is a definite selective advantage (for some sea birds at least) in remaining paired from season to season, and it seems very unlikely, from what we know, that the adults keep together as a pair during their winter ocean wanderings. This may indeed be an explanation which applies to the above-mentioned work on the guillemots, though in that case it is certain that the young do recognise their parents. Perhaps in the guillemots it is necessary for the young to be fed out at sea for a longish period after fledging, a situation which does not apply to the gannet.

The Aural Sense in Birds—Its Perfection and Complexity as Compared with That of Man

While those few birds which have been investigated certainly have a finer temporal sense than do human beings, their frequency (pitch) perception is of the same order as that of the human ear. How well they perceive amplitude (loudness) is not known. It is perhaps worth speculating that perception of amplitude fluctuations could be a way of accommodating for changes resulting from movement (White et al., 1970). There are changes in the temporal structure of a sound in proportion to the rate of movement of its source (the Doppler effect). It follows that all sound frequencies received are also changed. This would mean that the frequency and time structure of an approaching bird's call would be heard with a more or less constant shift from their true values, the shift depending on the caller's speed of approach. Amplitude would, however, change only gradually as the bird came nearer.

Until recently, the most extensive work on the individuality of sounds has dealt with humans. A great many experiments suggest that amplitude fluctuations of speech are relatively unimportant and, indeed, may be removed electronically without seriously affecting intelligibility. Computer recognition of individual speech shows that frequency/time parameters are more useful than amplitude characteristics (White et al., 1970). In the gannet, amplitude changes are highly constant to the individual, though whether the birds themselves use this characteristic, or some other feature not yet detected, has not yet been unequivocally proved.

It has, however, been shown (White, 1971) that when landing calls of known individual gannets were recorded and subsequently played back to their sitting mates, the filmed responses of the mate and the rest of the colony gave strong evidence that the calls of both males and females were recognised individually by their respective mates. There was, however, no evidence for similar recognition of neighbours.

Imitative Ability in the Indian Hill Mynah

But let us return to the question of imitative ability. It is clear that a capacity for vocal imitation must be widespread in birds, to account for the way in which they use their vocalisations for communication and for the production of local dialects. In some species, such as the Indian hill mynah, this ability is very large indeed; in others it is very slight or perhaps absent. Such ability as there may be in the terns discussed above (and it must be very small indeed) must be under strict control, as otherwise the individual terns in the colony would not have the idiosyncrasy of voice that we find. In other words, the problem here is to inhibit or control the imitative powers in certain circumstances in order to maximise the tendency to produce individual peculiarities of voice. This suggests that the motor learning involved in the production of sound signals is a different process from the perceptual learning involved in recognising those signals; and, in certain species, the two must be kept very strictly apart. Moreover, this work on the vocal communication system of sea birds emphasises the importance of auditory powers as the perceptual basis for group organisation. Clearly, the young must have an extremely high ability for learning the individuality of their parents' calls, and the adults the same ability for learning the individuality of their mate's calls. But they *must not* imitate them slavishly. If they imitate at all, they must imitate the component parts and then randomise them. But perhaps for this task "pure inventiveness" would be better!

Summary of Vocal-auditory Communication in Birds

To summarize, the variability of the "songs" of birds are adapted primarily by genetic programming and secondarily by imitative adjustment, to distinguish the species from every other species, and to distinguish one individual more or less certainly from all others in a population.

These ends may be accomplished in different species by differences in the degree of competence of the innate neural template for song structure. Thus the degree of individual experience necessary to develop the full song by addition to, and adjustment of, the innate template may range from nil or minimal on the one hand to something near totality on the other. The song of some species (for example, the chaffinch) can be so precisely controlled and adjusted by limited use of the imitative faculty that the song can serve both functions at the same time, and local dialects may arise as a by-product of the mechanism of development, though it is easy to think of various ways in which they might be adaptive. In species such as the sea birds which nest in dense colonies, individual recognition is combined with specific recognition, but there seems to be little group distinctiveness. The considerable advantage which recognition based on acoustic signals offers as against visual recognition, especially under the difficult conditions imposed by life in dense colonies on the seashore, seems clear. But more interesting still, to my mind, is the possibility hereby raised (it is as yet no more than a possibility) that the great breeding assemblages may be social units to a degree hitherto unrealised. Moreover, I think it can be said that as this kind of work proceeds, we find ourselves viewing with an ever-increasing respect the auditory capabilities of birds, for they possess ears which are in some respects inferior to ours and in others markedly superior but in either case showing a capacity for organising their auditory perception and their vocalisations with the precision exceeded only by man, and possibly by bats, but seldom even approached by other mammals.

Bird Language and Human Speech

In man, language is, of course, the prime vehicle for the transfer of social information. There has, perhaps, in the past been too much readiness to use the term "language" for the vocal-auditory transmission of information amongst animals. Nevertheless, in spite of the dangers of this nativistic view—dangers which are well exemplified by Table I—such usage has recently been supported by well-known students of human language (Chomsky, 1967; Teuber, 1967), where language is defined as "specific sound–meaning correspondence." Chomsky (1968) considered the matter further and retreated somewhat from his first position. But his difficulties have in fact now been dissolved by the work on primates, to be described later. As a result of studies by many workers, Teuber (1967) said, "It has become clear . . . that linguists are ethologists, working with man as their species for study, and ethologists linguists, working with non-verbalizing species."

I sometimes amuse myself by imagining an intelligent visitor from another planet arriving on this earth just before the differentiation of the human stock—say somewhere about one million years ago. If such a visitor had been asked by an all-seeing Creator which group of animals he supposed would the most easily be able to achieve a true language, I feel little doubt that he would have said unhesitatingly, "Why, of course, the birds." And indeed, if we now look at the birds together with all the mammals other than man, we have little hesitation in saying that the birds are by far the most advanced both in their control of their vocalisations and by the way in which they can adapt them collectively and individually to function as a most powerful communication system.

But having said this, I am sure that the recent studies on the ability of chimpanzees to learn sign language (which will be discussed in a later chapter) must give us cause for hesitation.

Perhaps it is the human capacity for conceptualisation that is the key to the riddle, although, even here, it is not certain that the conceptual powers of birds are less sophisticated and effective than any of the subprimate mammals. But if powers of conceptualisation are the answer, it is clear that they must have come *before* the evolution of language, as we now know it, in the human stock. On the other hand, it is also clear that we must not run the risk of being too simple-minded about human language. It is unique particularly in the possession of numbers 14–16 of the design features listed in Table I. Yet human language is made up of many features which are found in the various communicative systems of animals—fish, insects, mammals, and birds. Birds certainly have more of these features together than does any other group. But perhaps it will turn out that these three key abilities— numbers 14–16—can only be fully possessed by animals with a large mammalian-type brain, although there is, as far as I know, no neurological evidence to explain why this should be so. Perhaps birds, with the brain they have, cannot get any further on the road to true language, and indeed perhaps none of the existing mammalian stock, not even the primates, can do so either. This in any case brings us to the question of there being some special type of *mental* organisation necessary for the production of human language, as Chomsky has maintained. If we grant this for human language, why should we not admit the possibility also for certain systems of animal communication? If we look closely at the more advanced vocalisations of birds, and if we consider the recent experiments on gestural language in chimpanzees, one begins to wonder about this. We certainly cannot rule out this possibility on neurological grounds; and it is part of the basic assumptions of the physiologist that there must be in the brain neural structures or adaptations appropriate to the exercise of all the mental capacities possessed by the organisms in question.

We may never come to know how this great gap between the highest animal "language" and the language of man was bridged by the human ancestral stock. No anthropologist nowadays ever hopes to find a language which is primitive in the sense of forming a link between the language of man and the communication systems of animals. The search for a primitive language was abandoned by sociologists and anthropologists fifty or more years ago. And this recognition of the uniqueness of the human language and, still more, the understanding of those respects in which it is unique constitute a great step forward in comprehension of the relationship or lack of relationship between man and the animals. But if we are ever to find out how such a gap might possibly have been bridged, it seems, to some of us at least, that the fullest possible study of bird language is an essential preliminary.

THE HIGHER VERTEBRATES

The Song of the Humpbacked Whale

As was stated earlier in this chapter, birds are the most vocal animals apart from man. Therefore, in a general survey such as the present, we reach a better understanding of the significance of animal vocalisation by concentrating our attention on the birds. Nevertheless I do not wish to give the impression that there are not other extremely interesting examples at hand, and I feel I must allude to two or three of them. As an example taken from amongst the Ungulates, it is of great interest that the reindeer appears to be able to recognise by voice alone many other members of its herd. Then there are the whales. I might introduce this by asking a riddle: "In what way does the Humpbacked whale resemble the Common wren?" The answer is that they both have similar songs! The admirable work of Dr. Payne in the Bermudas studying the underwater sounds produced by the humpbacked whale (*Megaptera novaeangliae*), during its period of migration towards the breeding ground off Nova Scotia, has shown that the whale of this species has a definite song, similar to that of the wren, in that it contains about 200 notes, but it takes ten minutes to sing and not three seconds as does that of the wren. It has relatively about the same range as the wren, including high-pitched "bleeps" and squeaks and low thunderous roars. It is also, of course, extremely loud.

There seems little doubt that it is in fact a specific signal peculiar to that species and identifying its presence to all the other whales within hearing distance. And the hearing distance is colossal. Because of the particular oceanographical conditions between depths of about 1,000 and 2,500 feet which ensure that the sound is conducted with extremely little attenuation through this band, there is every reason to believe that the whales could, in theory, communicate over perhaps about 2,000 or 3,000 miles of ocean by the transmission of this song through the water. That is to say the whale in the Arctic *could* communicate with a whale in the Antarctic! Indeed, were it not for the continents it is conceivable that the song of a whale could be heard round the world.

There is further evidence, at present very slight, that different populations of whales, and perhaps different individual whales, may show characteristic differences in their song patterns. This is surely one of the most remarkable discoveries concerning animal communication in recent times and we shall wait impatiently for further details. There is bitter tragedy in the thought that one of the most outstanding songsters in the world is threatened with extinction by the insensitive greed of man, who continues to kill whales for a return of raw materials which is quite negligible compared to world resources and materials which can be obtained more easily and with little, or no, cruelty from domestic animals and from plants.

Audio-perception in Bats

Finally, to jump from the largest mammals to some of the smallest, we may conclude by mentioning the bats whose powers of echo location have also been unravelled by recent work, particularly that of Donald Griffin and his colleagues (1958). Not only do the bats guide themselves and find their prey in darkness by this means, it now seems likely that bats go far beyond the immediate necessities of their echo-location systems and indeed exploit all the information parameters theoretically available in the ultrasonic spectrum. Here again a totally unsuspected wealth of interest and behavioural adaptability is being revealed (Adler, 1971).

Chapter 4

INNATE BEHAVIOUR VERSUS ACQUIRED BEHAVIOUR

The aim of this chapter is to deal with what in ordinary language is often referred to as "the problem of instinct." The idea of the antithesis "instinct *versus* learning" has been inherent in the discussion of "instinct" for well over thirty years; while this question is still of interest, it has recently become clearer than ever before that to fasten on the characteristics of these two words as rigid alternatives may well lead us astray into rather sterile country. So I intend now to look again at the old "instinct-learning" problem in a somewhat new light. It is necessary to do this because the question as to how far human behaviour is "instinctive" is often asked and has, if one takes the trouble to analyse it thoroughly, a real and important meaning. But we can easily go completely astray if we do not understand the present position which has resulted from the work of ethologists, neurophysiologists, and endocrinologists during the past thirty years.

THE HISTORY OF THE INSTINCT CONCEPT

The word instinct originally meant "driven from within," and since it was used primarily in relation to human behaviour, it is still loosely employed to refer particularly to the more compelling and little understood springs of human action. From that point of view it was obviously regarded as having a very high emotional correlate; and this was expressed by an early twentieth-century psychologist in the phrase "Emotion is the boiling over of a heated instinct." The naturalists of the second half of the nineteenth century tended to use the term in an extremely vague manner. Because they were primarily interested in animals in the field, rather than animals in the laboratory or dissecting room, and because they were particularly involved with systematics, life history, geographical distribution, etc., they contributed relatively little to what we should now consider the scientific study of animal behaviour. Of course their life-history studies did involve a great deal of description of instinctive behaviour, much of it admirable. This applies particularly to the entomologists of the period—people such as the Peckhams in America, Adlerz in Sweden, studying hunting wasps, and Jean Henri Fabre in France, although the latter was sometimes hasty and inaccurate in his conclusions and careless about his identifications. He was however a superb writer and his books on insect life histories were for that reason deservedly regarded as classics. At that time instinctive behaviour in animals was regarded as having four main characteristics. A: it follows a recognisable and predictable pattern in almost all members of a species or at least all members of one sex of a species, that is to say it is heritable. B: it is not a simple response to a simple stimulus but a sequence of behaviour that usually runs a predictable course; that is to say it shows a patterned sequence in time. C: its consequences, or at least some of them, are of obvious value in contributing to the preservation of an individual or the continuity of a species, that is to say, it is adaptive. D: instinctive behaviour often develops when all the ordinary opportunities of learning and practising elaborate behaviour patterns are absent, that is to say, it is spontaneous or endogenous. Indeed in many cases the elaborate instincts of insects, whereby, for instance, a caterpillar spins its cocoon, are performed only once in the lifetime, and an almost perfect performance of them is necessary for survival.

So the studies of the naturalists of those days did not provide very much evidence for a real understanding of the nature of instinctive behaviour. Unfortunately the work of the physiologists and psychologists was almost equally useless. The physiologists had of course for a long time been employing the concept of reflex action, by which they denoted the simple and almost invariable response of a simple organ-system (ideally a single muscle) to a simple stimulus. The term used in this way need not of course imply any particular underlying physiological mechanism.

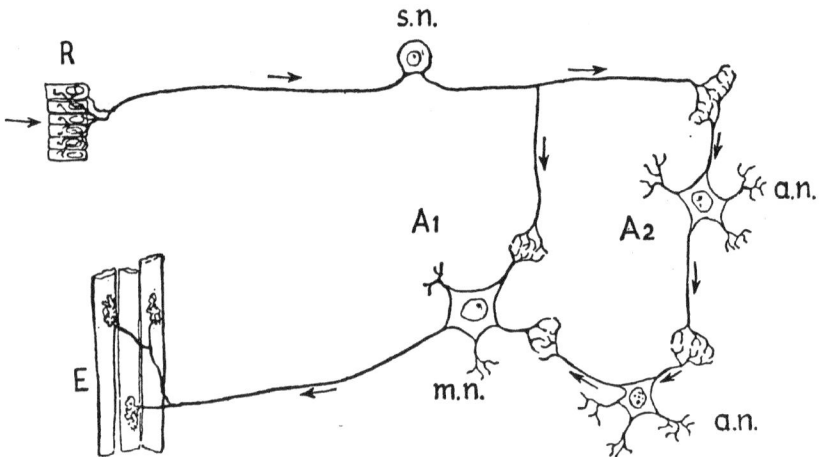

Figure 21 A diagram of a reflex arc, showing the simplest type of reflex arc in which the adjustor (A1) consists of only two neurones, a sensory (S.N.) and a motor (M.N.); and a more complicated type in which the adjustor includes (A2) association neurones (A.N.) interposed between the sensory and the motor neurone. R, Receptor; E, Effector.

But in practice it was always assumed that the mechanism was what was known as the "reflex arc" and every elementary textbook contained a diagram showing this supposed mechanism. In practically all animals above the protozoa and lower metazoa, different parts of the body are specialised for different functions. Thus a cell in one part of the body will be specialised as a sense cell for receiving particular stimuli and another cell in another part of the body will be specialised for causing movement as a muscle cell—so then another mechanism in the form of a nerve cell or cells has to be produced to relate the activities of the sensory cell or *receptor* with those of the muscle cell or *effector*. Thus we arrive at the concept of the elementary reflex. So towards the end of the nineteenth century the physiological view of animal behaviour was primarily that of the co-ordination of a very large number of simple, quick, muscular movements executed in an immediate response to simple environmental stimuli and to combinations of such stimuli in varying degrees of complexity. It was thus fashionable to suppose that this was the basic element of behaviour and that all the more complex behaviour patterns could be regarded as chain reflexes—motions such as those of walking, swallowing, and so forth constituting one reflex setting off another and another, and so producing complex, fairly stereotyped, and highly co-ordinated movements. So the physiologists of the time would have said that instinctive actions are simply elaborate chain reflexes.

In fact those physiologists were often completely wrong as is shown by modern studies of the act of swallowing in a mammal such as the dog. In this animal Doty et al. (1956–68; refs. in Hinde, 1970) have shown that this very elaborate movement, involving in all about twenty different muscles (see Figure 22), once it is set in motion (as it can be by a wide variety of stimuli), proceeds inexorably according to an immensely complicated programme of internal control mechanisms which are situated in the nervous tissue of the brain and brain stem. The modern view is that this type of organisation is almost always the basis of instinctive acts, though there is in many cases much more modification and control exerted on the course of the action by "feedback" from the muscles and from organs of special sense than is evident in the act of swallowing (Hinde, 1970).

Moreover it has now been shown that even many of the simple multicellular animals, having, compared to the vertebrates, nervous systems of the simplest (sea anemones) or relatively simple (Crustacea) kind, are nevertheless capable of remarkably com-

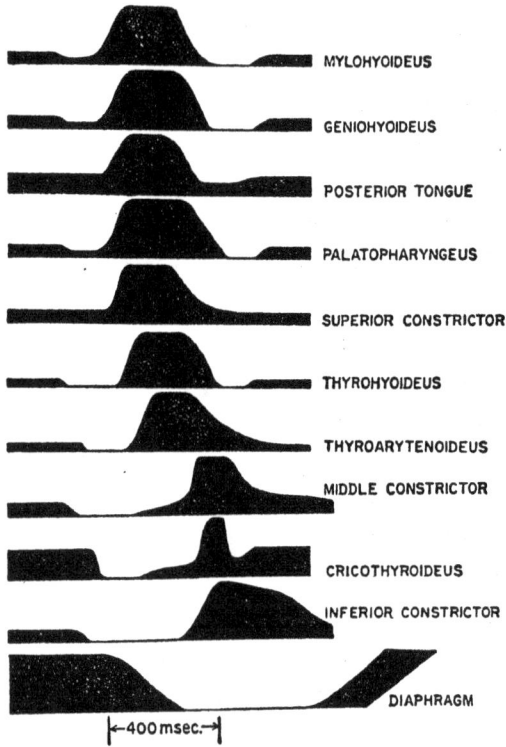

Figure 22 Schematic summary of the activity (shown by the electromyograph) of various muscles used by the dog in the act of swallowing. Height of line indicates intensity of action in each muscle. (From Doty and Bosma, 1956.)

plex patterned sequences of instinctive actions, actions which are endogenous in that they are not guided step by step by external stimulation. Nevertheless in many of these examples it appears certain that a chain-reflex concept cannot apply. Thus Figure 23

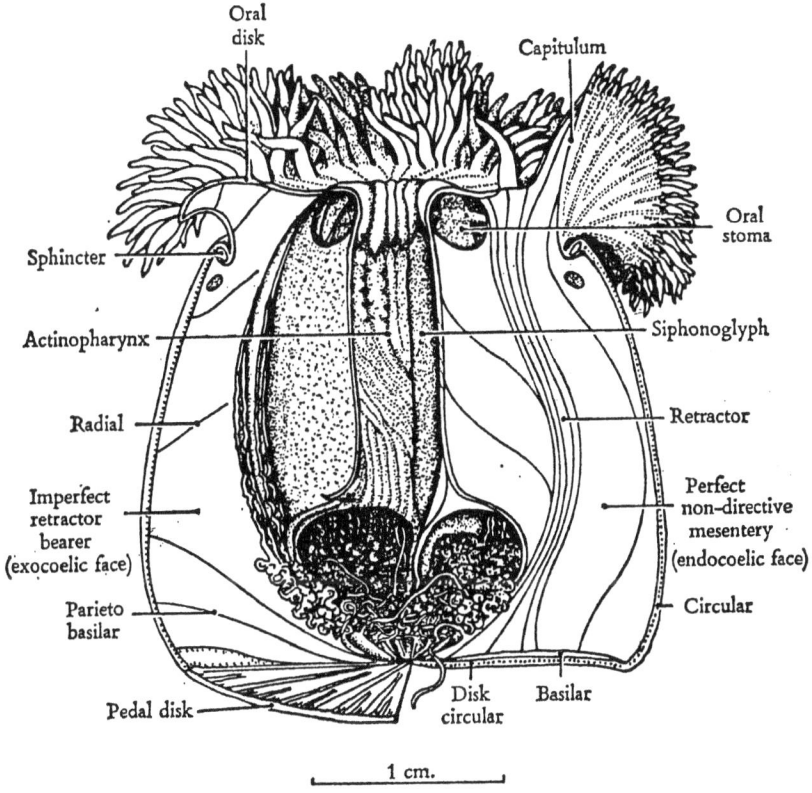

Figure 23 Diagram of the general muscular organisation and anatomical structure of the sea anemone *Metridium*. (From Pantin, 1968, after Batham and Pantin, 1951.)

shows the basic structure of the sea anemone *Metridium* as essentially a tubular sac with a double wall composed of radial and longitudinal muscles. This structure is innervated by nothing more complex than a thinly stretched nerve net and, instead of any ganglion or brain, a simple ring of nervous tissue around

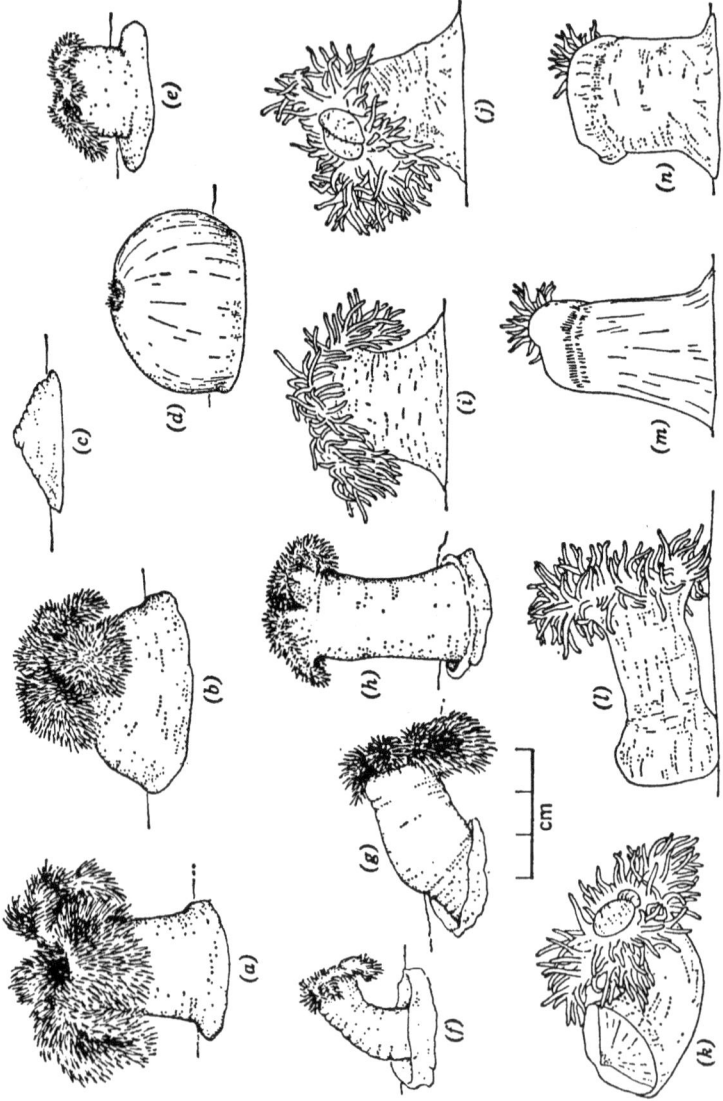

Figure 24 Diverse actions characterise even simple organisms. The sea anemone *Metridium senile* (a–h) may (a) expand, (b) move (here to the left), (c) and (e) contract, (d) enlarge after feeding, or (f–h) "shrivel." Another species, *Stomphia coccinea* (i–n) holds a (i) normal posture, (j) bends, (k) swims, (l) rests after swimming, (m) extends after contracting, and (n) responds to a starfish. (From Marler and Hamilton, 1966, after Batham and Pantin, 1950a; Sund, 1958.)

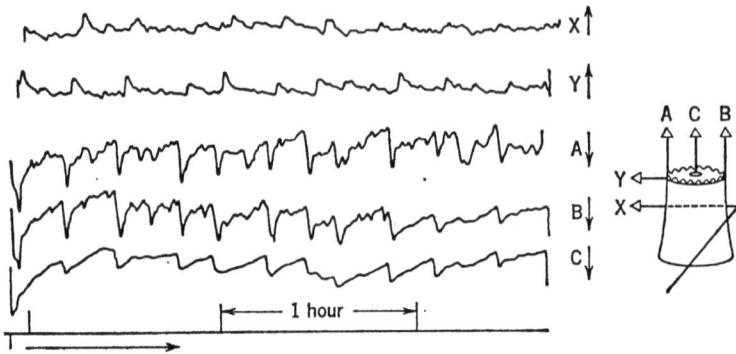

Figure 25 Short-term rhythm of muscular action of *Metridium senile*. Arrows indicate the direction of contraction. The activity records are direct kymograph tracings. (From Marler and Hamilton, 1966, after Batham and Pantin, 1950a, 1950b.)

the mouth region. In theory such an organism should be capable of little more than simple contraction and expansion. Yet lapse-rate photography and other methods have revealed an astonishingly well-organised series of movement patterns appropriate to the various exigencies of the animal's existence (Figure 24), coupled with short-term rhythms of muscular activity (Figure 25).

In the Crustacea, creatures complex in nervous structure, to be sure, but still far below the vertebrates in this respect, we can find highly elaborate "gestures" precisely timed and exactly controlled in every detail—which again are certainly not chain reflexes and nothing more.

Figures 26 and 27 show the displays of males of seven different kinds of fiddler crabs (*Uca* spp.). There are about 40 species of this genus living on the tropical beaches of the oceans of the world. They have adopted a striking means of signalling to other members of the species by the use of a single enlarged claw which had been especially developed, in the course of evolution, for sexual and aggressive displays. The claw is waved in a ritualistic way so as to provide a gesture absolutely characteristic of the species so that there can be no mistake in identity. As the

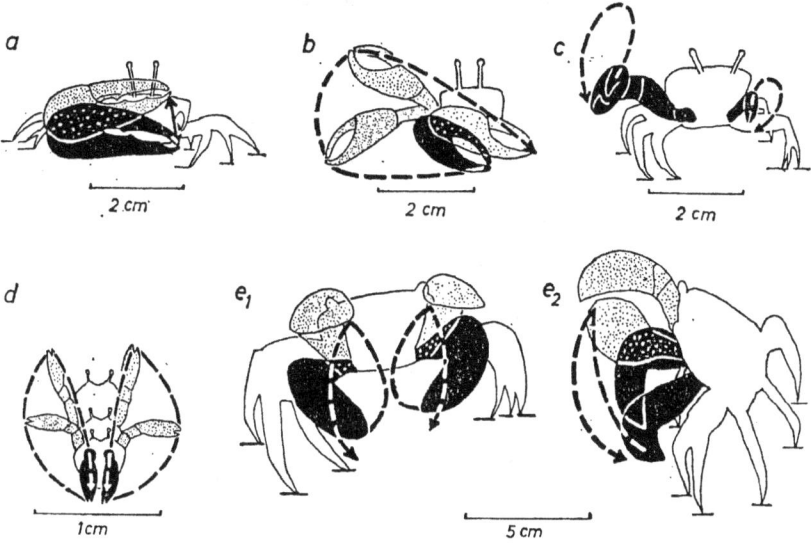

Figure 26 Various types of claw waving in crabs; (a) *Uca rhizophorae* (vertical waving); (b) *Uca annulipes* (waving sideways); (c) *Uca pugilator* (waving type with the claw stretched far out); (d) *Dotilla blanfordi*, (e) *Goniopsis cruentata*. (After H. Schöne and H. Schöne, 1963.)

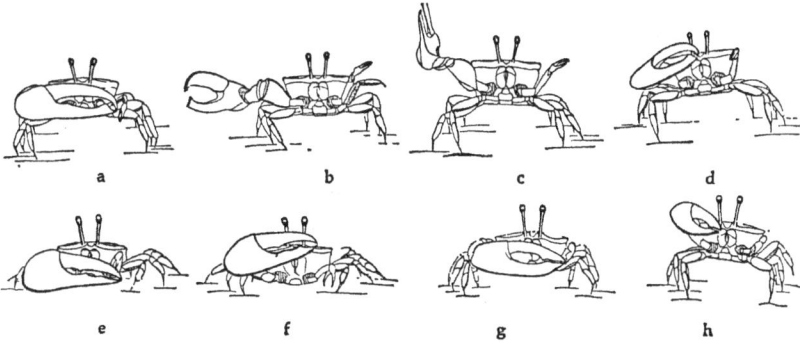

Figure 27 Various types of claw waving in the genus (*Uca*); Top: *Uca lactea* (Fiji Islands), lateral waving type. The claw, which is initially pulled in (a), is stretched out in a sideways movement (b); then it is raised (c) and returned in an arc into the original position. e–h, Examples of vertical waving; e and f, *U. rhizophorae* (Malaya); g and h, *U. signata* (Philippines). (After J. Crane, 1957.)

143

figures show, the timing and form of the movement—as also the particular attitude which the claw takes up in the course of signalling—are all so constant that by this alone an expert can distinguish the species of crab whether it comes from the shores of Panama, Tahiti, or Bali. There must obviously be some very precise mechanism, presumably some integration of nervous and hormonal controls, which ensures that the individual always performs these gestures exactly at the right speed, amplitude, and intensity, for otherwise the whole system would break down.

Innumerable similar examples could be described from amongst the display movements of many other groups in the animal kingdom, e.g., insects, fish, and birds. In all cases, since such movements are mostly communication mechanisms, the visual apparatus and perceptual abilities must be equally exactly adjusted to recognise, and distinguish from all other visual stimuli to which the animal may be exposed, the significant movements which indicate the right sex and the right species in the right phase of the breeding cycle.

The nineteenth-century psychologists were hardly of more help than were the physiologists. The whole outlook of the psychologists was involved with human beings, and their efforts were centred upon the problems of the human mind, its feelings and emotions. It is obvious that this approach could not provide the tools required for the scientific study of animal behaviour. But in due course, psychologists became imbued with the concept of association, and the study of the association of ideas, as shown in the human learning of nonsense syllables, began to reveal in human behaviour something very similar to the observations which were at a later date to come from Pavlov in regard to the conditioning of the reflexes of dogs. Ebbinghaus, in late nineteenth-century Germany, had been the pioneer amongst psychologists in the scientific and objective study of human behaviour. In 1898 Thorndike, in America, published the first results of similar studies with animals. In these experiments cats and dogs were confined in puzzle boxes, and the way in which they learnt the trick of releasing the catch so that they could get out and reach food was observed and recorded. This work resulted, as did the work of Lloyd Morgan in England about the same time, in an associative theory of animal learning described by him as "trial and error."

Such ideas were developed by J. B. Watson as a general theory of behaviour, fundamentally associationist in outlook, which became known as "Behaviourism." This school prided itself on being purely objective, inclining to a rigid, mechanistic outlook and dispensing with any vague and unnecessary concepts involving mind. In short it implied that it was a physiological rather than a psychological system. Behaviourism received a great impetus from the fact that in its early days the work of Pavlov for the first time became known outside Russia, and so there seemed at last to be a physiological system that could be related in detail to the superficially physiological ideas behind behaviouristic psychology. And indeed the experiments of Pavlov on conditioning of reflexes such as the attachment of fairly stereotyped responses like salivation to new stimuli, such as the ringing of a bell, provided what seemed a neat and a scientific way of accounting for the basis of learning. And there is no doubt that this new knowledge from Russia gave a great impetus to, and was seen as supplying strong evidence for, the views of the Behaviourists. Indeed the only alternative at that time to the views of the Behaviourist-reflex-physiology school on instinctive behaviour was that held by some of the more vitalistic naturalists and psychologists of Central Europe. They held that instinct was something basic to the very idea of animal life, some design built into nature, and that these designed entities, these ultimate elements of behaviour, could not be further broken down. Indeed some felt that it was improper or indecent to enquire further into them. So the whole concept of instinct came to be regarded as scientifically useless and indeed rather disreputable.

The obvious deficiencies of the existing mechanistic-physiological approach to the study of animal behaviour first became apparent to those workers who were studying the more highly developed perception of animals and men; and so it was that Wertheimer (1912), working on the visual perception of movement, and later his disciples Wolfgang Köhler and Kurt Koffka were led to propound the concepts and theories which in due course came to be known as the Gestalt Psychology. These in their turn had a far-reaching influence upon our ideas of animal behaviour and, through a quarter of a century of debate, had (in the form of various field theories) a great influence on the development and fate of Behaviourism itself.

The Influence of Darwin

But the conclusions of the work of the visual physiologists were rather remote from those of the ordinary naturalists and did not impinge much upon their studies. So it came about that it was only the laboratory workers, the physiologists and comparative psychologists, who were thought of as being "real scientists." But in fact 95 per cent of the work of physiologists was done with dogs and cats, and 99 per cent of that of the comparative psychologists with the white rat. This being so it was hardly surprising that a distorted and incomplete picture of animal nature and behaviour emerged. What then had happened to the naturalists? Darwin of course was a field naturalist and indeed his work inspired scientific natural history studies of great moment in the field of marine biology. But apart from this, it is a curious fact that Darwin's promulgation of the natural selection theory also had the extraordinary result of sending students of terrestrial animals (as well as many who were concerned with marine life) indoors for fifty or more years, where, as embryologists, comparative anatomists, and at length comparative physiologists, they attempted to work out, with techniques which were then new and exciting, the full implications of Darwin's tremendous generalisation. So as a result of the activities of a field naturalist a large part of natural history suffered much neglect.

But new ideas about animal behaviour were astir and these were in part due to another book of Darwin's, *The Expression of the Emotions in Man and Animals* (1872), which in some respects behaved like a time bomb, the full effects of which were not felt until fifty years later. These new ideas about animal behaviour, and the new attitude accompanying them, arose inde-

146

pendently with different workers in various parts of the world. Edmund Selous, Eliot Howard, and Julian Huxley in Great Britain; Wallace Craig, C. O. Whitman, and Karl Lashley in America; O. Heinroth and J. von Uexküll in Germany; and last, but not least, Konrad Lorenz in Austria. And it was Lorenz who welded these new ideas together into a workable system, one which codified existing knowledge and integrated many new avenues of research and which eventually came to be known as ethology.

The Rise of Ethology

The term ethology is of interest because it was by no means new; in fact it was in general use in the late eighteenth and early nineteenth century, to signify "the interpretation of character by the study of gesture." This was soon extended to cover "the art of mime." This use of the word was in fact extraordinarily appropriate because the new school of animal-behaviour study, with its new approach, concluded that the first and most essential step in the scientific study of the behaviour of any species was to carry out a strictly objective study, or inventory, of the movements or motor patterns in their subject's repertoire. Thus when the term ethology first came into its new use amongst zoologists, it carried a relatively restricted meaning, signifying the comparative study and analysis of the instinctive or stereotyped movements of animals. So, for the twentieth-century pioneers, the word "ethology" eventually meant the comparative anatomy of gestures; only now it was the gestures of animals, and not the gestures of human beings (or indeed the gestures of actors), which were to be studied and which it was hoped would reveal the true characters of the animals—in the same way as the study of human gestures can reveal the characters of men.

The Characteristics of Instinct

Let us now consider in a little more detail the four traditionally assumed characteristics of instinct enumerated above. First to take *characteristic A:* It is now abundantly clear that many of the movements of every species of animal that has ever been carefully investigated are sufficiently constant and predictable to serve as specific characters—in just the same way, and often to the same degree, as are the bodily structures themselves. This is true whether we are dealing with the display movements of birds (Plate 5), the web-spinning movements of spiders, the burrowing habits of marine worms or the prey-catching techniques of weasels or wolves, the food-hoarding movements of squirrels or the browsing methods of antelopes. And in the higher animals this is particularly true of those habits which lead to choice of a mate and successful copulation. In fact "instinctive behaviour" of this specific kind is found in relation to: (1) *Sex,* including aggressive and submissive behaviour and fighting of various kinds (including territorial behaviour); (2) *Nutrition,* including the way of obtaining and eating the food; (3) *Care of the body surface,* including preening, grooming, and scratching; (4) *Escape from predators,* including methods of concealment, threat (see Plates 7, 8), freezing, "shamming dead" (better called "thanatosis"), and taking flight; (5) *Social behaviour,* including methods of responding to other members of the social group irrespective of whether or not they are of the other sex (see Figure 31); and indeed (6) *Sleep* itself, including the rhythms of rest and wakefulness, positions assumed in sleep, and so on.

So we can see that there is a very strong a priori reason for assuming that these fixed and species-characteristic types of behaviour must be *primarily inherited* (*characteristic A* above) and are relatively little influenced by the *individual* experiences of the particular animal being investigated. But we must of course beware of assuming that all behaviour which is primarily inherited is also rigid. For instance it may well be that many animals have a tendency to play, a tendency to explore their environment, in which the hereditary make-up may play a large part but in which the form of the action may vary greatly according to the individual experiences previously encountered. Next to take *characteristic B* (*Patterned*): It is so obvious as to need no emphasis that many of these actions are far from simple or

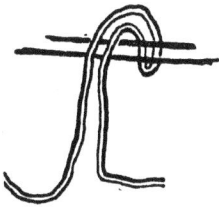

LOOP TUCK

SIMPLE LOOP

INTERLOCKING
LOOPS

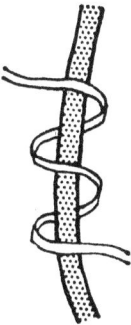

SPIRAL COIL

SIMPLE WEAVE

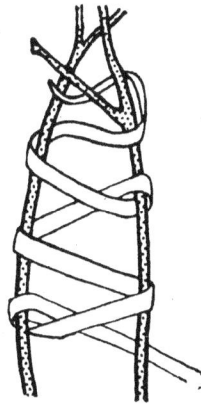

ALTERNATELY
REVERSED WINDING

HALF HITCH

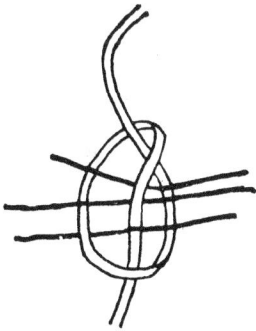

OVERHAND KNOT

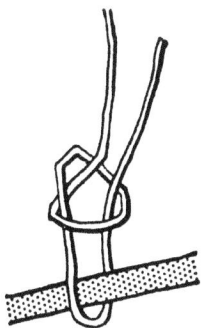

SLIP KNOT

Figure 28 Types of stitches and fastenings used by different weaverbirds (Ploceinae). (From Collias and Collias, 1964.)

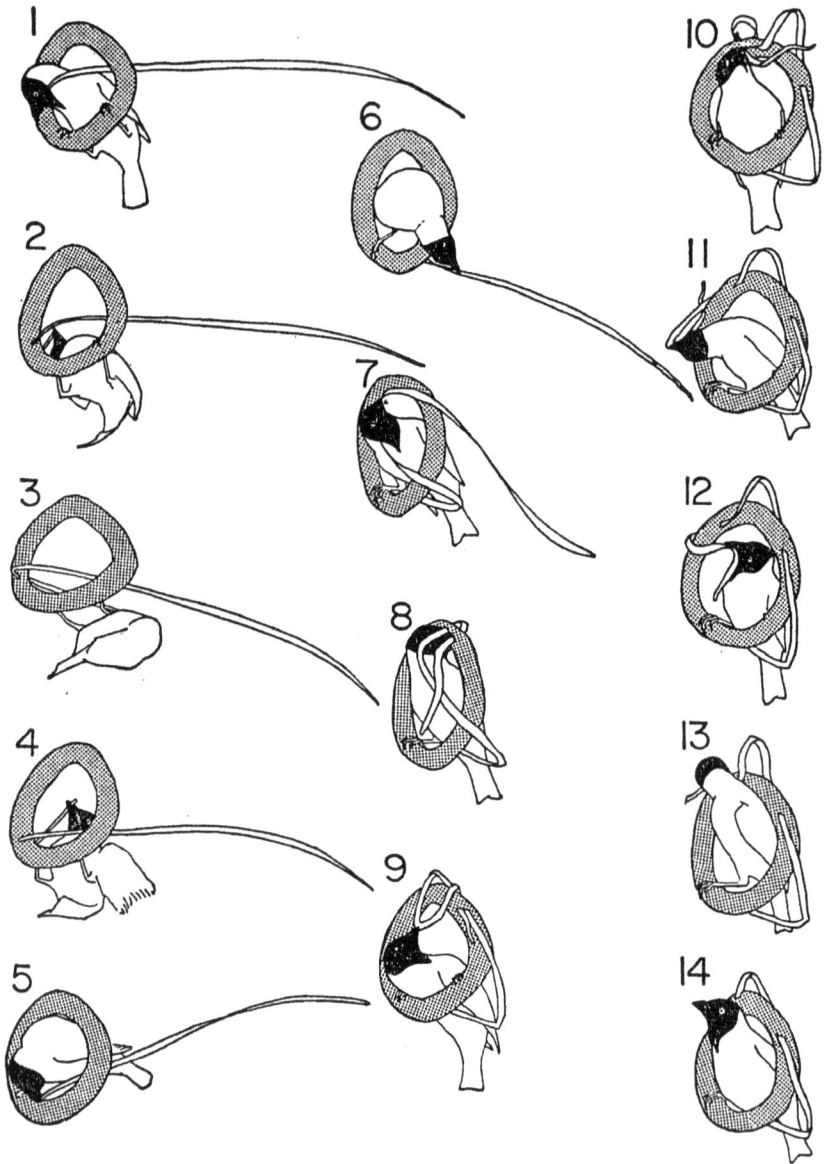

Figure 29 A typical sequence of movements by a male village weaverbird as he weaves into his ring a single strip, torn from a leaf blade of elephant grass. (From Collias and Collias, 1962.)

brief and in fact show extraordinary elaboration, perhaps complete in seconds, perhaps not even complete in minutes, hours, or
days. *Characteristic C (Adaptive)*: Again and again it is clear
that without having these actions to some extent performed, the
animal's chances of successful survival to maturity and eventual
breeding would be virtually nil. The outstanding example provided by the nest-building of the weaverbirds is illuminating in
regard to all the above three characteristics. (See Plate 6 and
Figures 28, 29, 30.) *Characteristic D (Endogenous)* is also very
important, for it leads to one of the types of experiments which
has been found most useful, namely the rearing of an animal in
a highly simplified environment, perhaps in isolation from all
members of its kind—as when a songbird is reared in a soundproof
chamber. From such an experiment one can often deduce the
extent to which the behaviour in question is guided, governed, or
in any way triggered off by external circumstances.

It was for these reasons that the tendency arose to make a
sharp distinction between, on the one hand, behaviour which
was innate and, on the other, behaviour which was acquired by
individual experience, such as learning or other similar processes.

The Relation Between Environmentally Stable
and Environmentally Labile Behaviour

We now know that such a sharp division can lead to erroneous
conclusions and to fruitless argument. For it is obvious that a
great deal of behaviour that is governed to a large extent by the
genetic make-up of an animal may also be greatly affected by
experience. So we come to the view that it is often more useful to
consider whether a given item of behaviour is *environmentally
stable* on the one hand or *environmentally labile* on the other.
And indeed items of behaviour may vary greatly in this respect
within a single species—some of them clearly falling into one
category, others into another. Thus the nesting behaviour of birds
may be extraordinarily constant under greatly varying conditions, as may be the call notes by which the movements of a

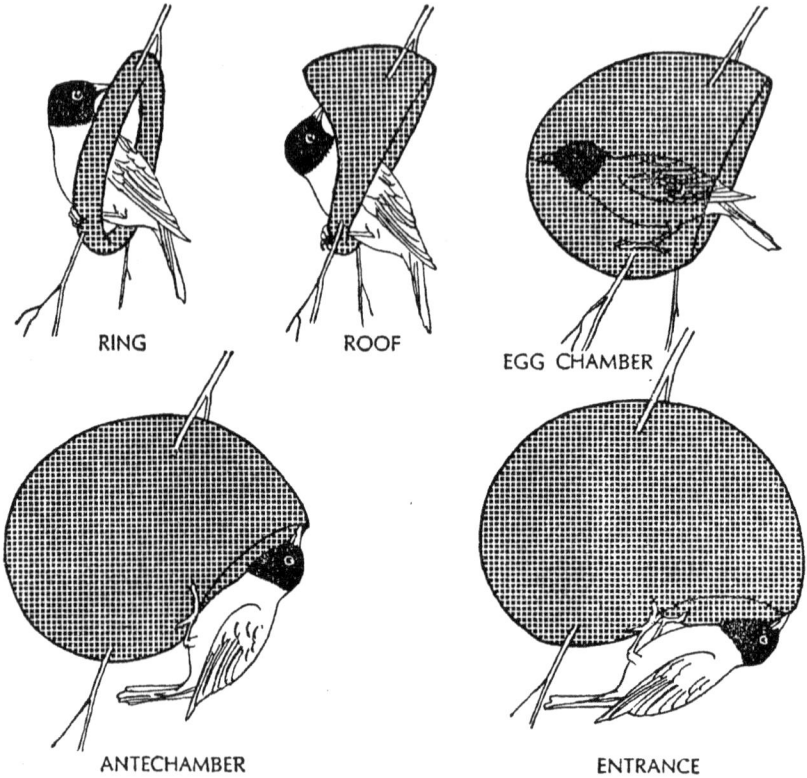

RING   ROOF   EGG CHAMBER

ANTECHAMBER   ENTRANCE

Figure 30 Normal stages in nest-building by a male village weaverbird. The diagrams show successively the building of the ring and roof, the completion of the egg chamber, and the building of the antechamber and entrance. Notice how the male perches in the same place while building throughout. (From Collias and Collias, 1962.)

flock are co-ordinated or the alarm to various kinds of predators given. On the other hand feeding habits may be extremely labile, and so we may get groups of individuals of the same species in different situations or different parts of its range which have very different feeding habits. For example, the swallowtail butterflies (*Papilio machaon*) of England always lay their eggs on the marsh carrot, *Peucedanum palustre,* while on the continent of Europe they are found breeding on a great variety of related plants.

152

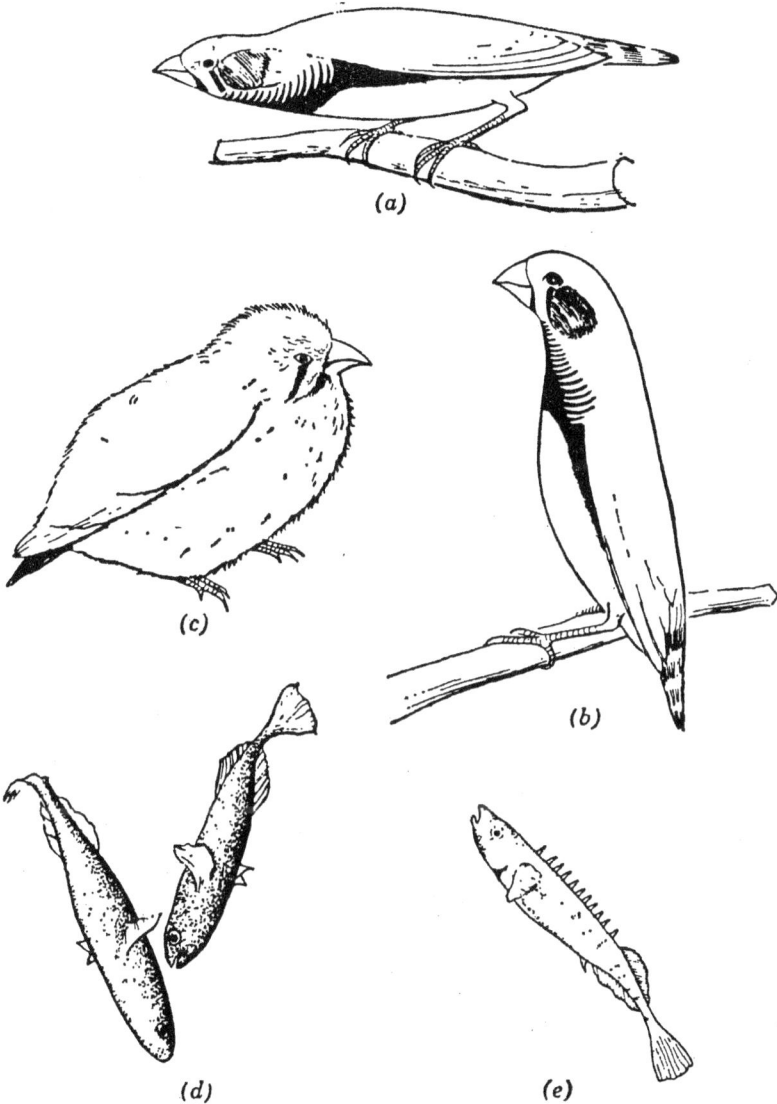

Figure 31 The submissive behaviour of many animals is the "antithesis" of aggressive postures. In the zebra finch, *Poephila guttata*, the intensely aggressive posture (a) with plumage sleeked, which a male takes when facing a rival, contrasts with the submissive posture of the hunched female (c) with plumage fluffed out. In (b) a male stands in another less aggressive posture. In (d) two male ten-spined sticklebacks, *Pygosteus pungitius*, assume aggressive posture, accompanied by dark coloration. A submissive individual (e) blanches and assumes a head-up instead of a head-down position. (After Morris, 1954, 1958.)

153

The Two Natural Divisions of a Life History

But while it is true enough that the animal, even in the egg or in the womb, is exposed to variations of environmental conditions just as it is after it is hatched or born, nevertheless there is no sharper distinction between the phases of a life history than between the first phase which is in the egg or the uterus and the second phase which is free living, when all the creature's senses are active and are being exposed to environmental stimuli of every conceivable kind.

Fixed-action Pattern, Consummatory Acts, and Consummatory Stimuli

A central argument of what may be called the classical school of ethology was that in each example of true instinctive behaviour there is a hard core of absolutely fixed and relatively complex automatism—an inborn movement form. This, so it was argued, is the essence of the instinct itself. The original name used by Konrad Lorenz, *"Erbkoordination,"* is usually translated as *"fixed-action pattern";* and it is examples of such fixed-action patterns that we have just been discussing. Where, as is so often the case, such fixed-action patterns constitute an end point, or climax, of either a major or minor chain of instinctive behaviour, they have come to be known as "consummatory acts"—a term which in fact had its counterpart, if not its origin, in much earlier writing both of physiologists and psychologists. The most obvious cases of such consummatory acts, in the original sense, are to be found in those behavioural contexts which are most intimately and directly concerned with survival and reproduction. The acts of copulation and of the ingestion of food, for instance, are acts which most obviously bring to conclusion, at least for a while, the elaborate chains of instinctive behaviour which have preceded them. Now while in both these instances the immediate physiological effects, such as the discharge of semen or replenishment of the food reserves of the body, are obviously partly responsible for the satiety which follows, it is by no means always or entirely the case. Thus the acts of picking up food, chewing, and swallowing, all contribute to the assuagement of appetite; and if the stomach or crop be artificially distended at the same time, or if by some other means it is ensured that the animal receives no nutriment whatever, nevertheless the consummatory result is still maintained.

But examples such as this raise another aspect of the problem: the consummatory acts affect the animal that performs them by means of sensory feedback. And so perhaps in such cases we are just as correct in speaking of *consummatory stimuli* or *consummatory sensations* as we are in speaking of consummatory acts. In experiments in which puppies are deprived of sucking experience, though adequately fed, during the first ten days of life, it has been shown that the sucking reflex is independent of hunger and food intake. The puppy still sucks even though its stomach is filled with milk. And there is similar evidence which suggests that the act of sucking, and the stimulus situation associated with it, are consummatory in young animals as distantly related as the bottle-nosed dolphin (*Tursiops truncatus*), the dormouse (*Muscardinus avellanarius*), the domestic cat, and man himself (reference in Thorpe, 1963, p. 448).

Nesting Behaviour

No doubt these conclusions apply to the outstanding example of the nest-building of the weaverbirds alluded to above, though they have not been fully analysed in that case.

Similar analysis has however been made in regard to birds which build the usual and much simpler type of cup-shaped nest. In such cases, after the female bird in breeding condition has found a nest site, it starts by fetching material of a particular kind—sticks or twigs or pieces of grass—and placing it on the chosen site. A jackdaw or rook, standing on the potential nest locality with the twigs held in its beak, performs a downward and sideways sweeping movement, which brings the material into contact with the ledge or the branches on which the nest is to be built. The moment the twig or branch carried by the bird meets a resistance, the sideways movements are strengthened and transformed into a series of quick trembling thrusts. When these thrusts successfully wedge the twig in position so that it offers an increased resistance, the movement gains in intensity till, sooner or later, the twig sticks really fast. After this "consummatory act-consummatory stimulus," the bird loses interest for the time being. To start with, the inexperienced jackdaw shows no sign of having any "conception" of what appropriate nesting material should be like. It will try with any objects that come to hand and are small enough to be handled, including such surprising but handy objects as pieces of ice and seatings of small electric bulbs. None of these things ever gets so firmly lodged by the movement (which Konrad Lorenz calls "tremble-shoving") as to result in a stimulus sufficiently consummatory to ensure successful nest-building. Such a failure quickly extinguishes the individual's response to inadequate objects, while an equally quick positive conditioning is effected by adequate ones. Lorenz says, "In fact, the birds become 'connoisseurs' of that kind of twig that is just flexible enough to be shoved into crevices, just twisted enough to stick well, and so forth. Hence very often most of the material used in all the nests of a jackdaw colony comes from one species of tree." (See Lorenz, 1969, pp. 49–50.)

In contrast to a jackdaw, many small songbirds do apparently have an inborn recognition of the kind of material that should be sought for in the different periods of nest construction. Such a bird has first to gather nest material, then it must carry the material to a nest site and, sitting in the partly formed nest cup, build it into the structure. Just as in the jackdaw, building involves a small number of characteristically stereotyped building movements. So we have behaviour which may be called a "gathering and carrying" followed by "sitting-building." The course of the building behaviour is obviously much influenced by stimuli received as the result of building; and the bird becomes more sensitive to these as the nest-building proceeds. The fact of this innate recognition of suitable bents and grass stems as appropriate for building can be shown very dramatically if one rears canaries, as it is quite easy to do, in artificial nests made of felt, so that the young birds have never encountered anything whatever which is long and flexible. When such female birds themselves come to the stage of nest-building they can of course do nothing unless some material is provided. But the instant pieces of grass or little bits of string, or any long and flexible objects, are placed in the cage they display interest; and in seconds, or less, are carrying them to the nest place and starting the weaving movements. When the nest has reached a certain structure, feathers are then required for lining. Again, if no feathers or similar soft materials are provided, the activity will cease. But the innate capacity to recognise feathers as the kind of stuff with which nests "should be lined" is dramatically illustrated by the way in which birds may pluck their own feathers in order to line the nest. Still more remarkable was an instance which occurred in one of Professor Hinde's experiments in which a deprived female canary took hold of one of its own feathers with its beak, flew to the nest site in the cage without pulling the feather out, went through the motions of lining the nest with it, then flew back to the original point in the cage from which it started only to repeat the same performance again and again as if it were building an effective nest.

It is interesting to compare the nesting behaviour of a brown rat under similar circumstances (Eibl-Eibesfeldt, 1963, quoted by Lorenz, 1969). The brown rat possesses three motor patterns which achieve the collection and general arrangement of nesting material. Having decided on a potential nest site, the first item of behaviour to take place is running out, grabbing nest material, carrying it back, and dropping it at the point of departure. (It is interesting that inexperienced rats if deprived of all material do exactly the same with their own tails, behaving *pari passu* in just the same way as did the feather-deprived canary.) The rat's nesting pattern No. 2 consists in sitting in the nest, turning from side to side, and heaping up with its forepaws a more or less circular wall of nesting material. Pattern No. 3 involves patting the inside of the wall with the forepaws so as to tamp down and smooth the inner surface of the nest cavity. It is very interesting to note that an inexperienced rat, offered paper strips or other soft material for the first time, will get into a frenzy of all three of these activities, each of which is performed to complete perfection not differing even on analysis by slow-motion pictures from those of an experienced rat. However, the naïve rat does something the inexperienced one never does—after having carried two or three paper strips which are lying flat on the ground, it will perform heaping up movements in the empty air above them, even to the patting movements, tamping down the nest wall not yet in existence. Konrad Lorenz (1969) argues that it is the failure to get the "rewarding reaffirmation that teaches the rat not to do the heaping up movements before enough material has been carried in; similarly not to perform the patting movements before a sufficiently high nest wall has been heaped up."

The Analysis of Bird Songs

Another example of the sensory localisation of the innate information required to ensure the correct running off of a behaviour pattern comes from study of the vocalisations of songbirds. Here the warning calls (see Chapter 3 above), flight calls, and so on, which are brief and basically very simple utterances, are indeed inherited as simple fixed motor patterns just as are the calls in ducks, chickens, and so forth. The song of many passerines, however, as distinct from the call notes, is not based on any inherited motor patterns even in species in which a bird reared in the isolation of a soundproof room develops a recognisable species-specific song. But it has been demonstrated that birds that were deafened before a certain age develop nothing but an absolutely amorphous twittering. "Innate information" about how the specific song ought to sound is situated in a template that lies exclusively on the sensory, or receptor, side of the neural mechanisms involved in the whole behaviour pattern. The young bird, which, in the so-called subsong, utters a wide range of sound combinations much as the human baby does, matches fortuitously produced utterances with its auditory template and retains those that match best (Konishi, 1965, 1966; see Lorenz, 1969, p. 51).

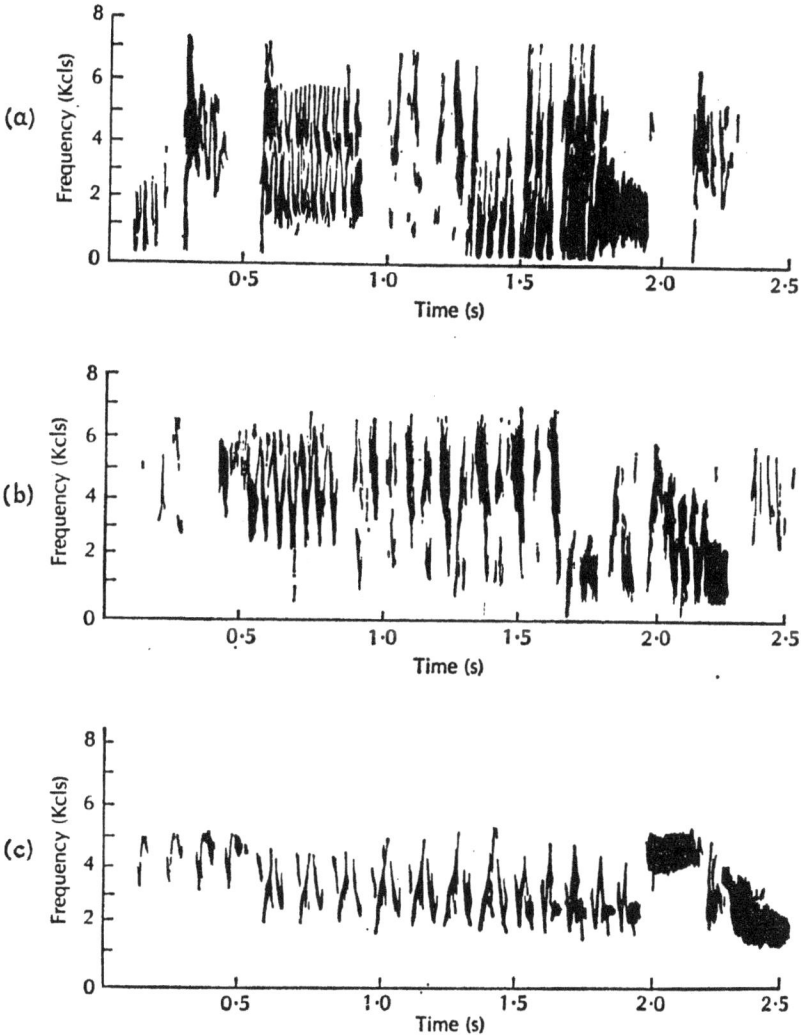

Figure 32 Sound spectrograms showing three stages in the subsong of the chaffinch. The full song of same individual is shown in the upper diagram of Figure 24. (After Thorpe, 1961b.) (a) Chirps and rattles having a large range of frequencies; (b) transition to full song; (c) spring song, still looser and longer than normal full song.

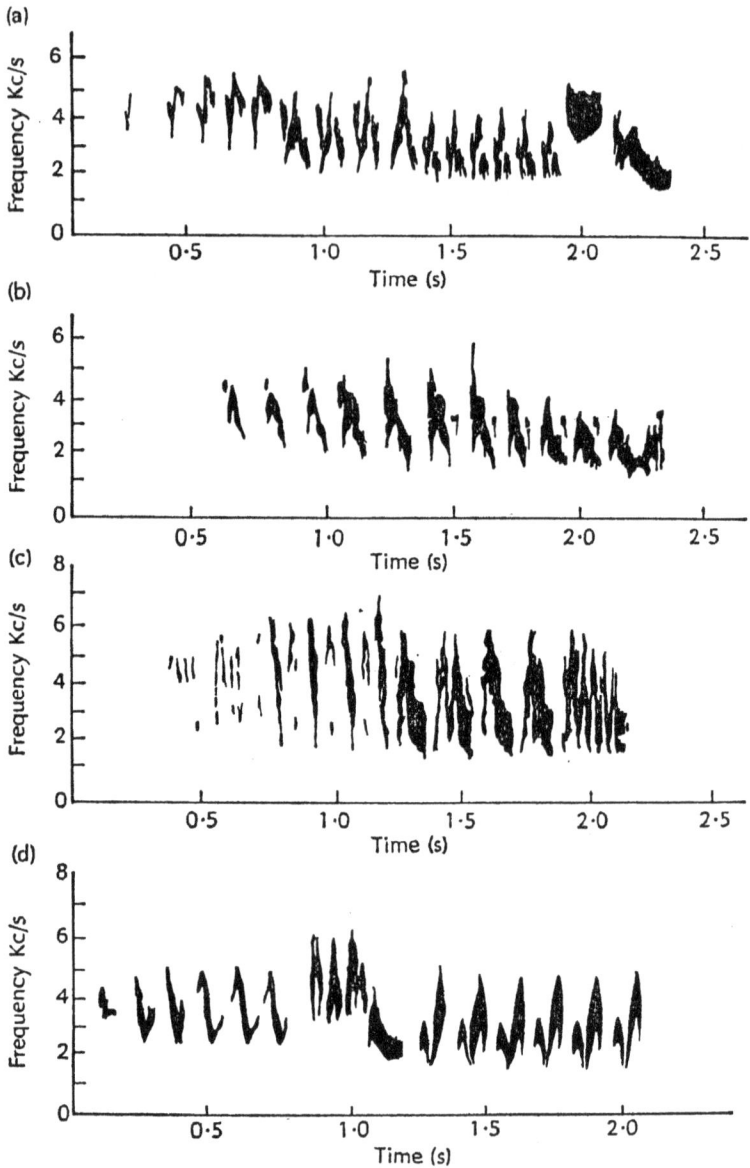

Figure 33 Chaffinch song. (After Thorpe, 1961b.) (a) Characteristic normal song; (b) song of an individual reared in isolation; (c) song of an individual from a group reared in isolation; (d) song produced by a bird reared in isolation, after tutoring with a rearticulated chaffinch song with the ending in the middle.

One could continue to give examples of this kind of behaviour, each of them having some particular interest or stressing some particular aspect of instinctive organisation. It is very noteworthy, for instance, that one can see just the same behaviour-stimulus situation in the process of shell collection by hermit crabs (E. S. Reese, 1963, referred to in Hinde, 1970).

Drives

The examples I have just given display quite dramatically the evidence for intense concentration and urgency behind these instinctive behaviour patterns which can lead, both in the rat and the canary and in innumerable other animals besides, to an actual break-out of the behaviour pattern so to speak *in vacuo*, as was shown by both the rat and the canary. And so watching animals in these situations we often receive the impression (an impression we are familiar with from our own behaviour) of an emotional tension behind the exercise of the instinctive act. Psychologists have for long expressed this concept with the terms drive, motivation, and so forth. The term drive in its widest sense can be defined as "the complex of internal and external states and stimuli leading to a given behaviour" (Thorpe, 1951). But such a definition is too wide and all inclusive for many purposes and it is at least convenient to narrow it by omitting, for example, the words "and external" in the above definition. And so this idea of an internal drive is much nearer to the sense in which the word drive is normally used by psychologists and students of behaviour. Certainly its earliest usage in behaviour literature implied little, if anything, more than a state of internal activity or disequilibrium either of the central nervous system, or of glands or viscera in turn stimulating the nervous system. This activity could be conceived of as either actual or potential, e.g., some sort of state of tension or loading ready to activate the animal. This effect is sometimes termed "mood" or in German "*Stimmung*." In fact with the enormous increase in knowledge and understanding

161

of the action of hormones—both as an intermediary, a two-way interaction, between the central nervous system and the other organs of the body—we can now see how virtually all behaviour may be controlled with the greatest precision by these two systems acting together.

Hormones and Motivation

At the time when the ethologists first enunciated their "system of instincts" there was great reluctance amongst the neurophysiologists to admit that the nervous system could be effecting anything like the very precise determination and direction of movements which the theory required. Now, however, all that is changed, and the views of modern neurophysiologists stress rather the ubiquitous nature of central patterning. Indeed T. H. Bullock (1961, 1966) stresses that "the output of single neurones and groups of neurones is normally probably always patterned." And again he says, "A whole world lies before us, of integrating units that receive converging inputs, process information according to weighting factors, transfer functions, and network connexions, to achieve an abstraction of certain qualities from the arriving messages; in other words 'recognition on predetermined criteria.' The types of units in the optic nerve of the frog are not the same as those so far described in goldfish; they are similar to, but not identical with, those in the pigeon; they are quite different from those in the cat, which in turn differ from units in the rabbit." But it is not only the nervous system which is now seen as a much more effective instrument in controlling these fine details of instinctive behaviour; similar advances in the study of the effect of hormones show how precise and finely adjusted the hormone changes are and how quickly and delicately they control behaviour. An outstandingly good example of this is shown by the work of Hinde on the breeding behaviour of canaries (Figure 34).

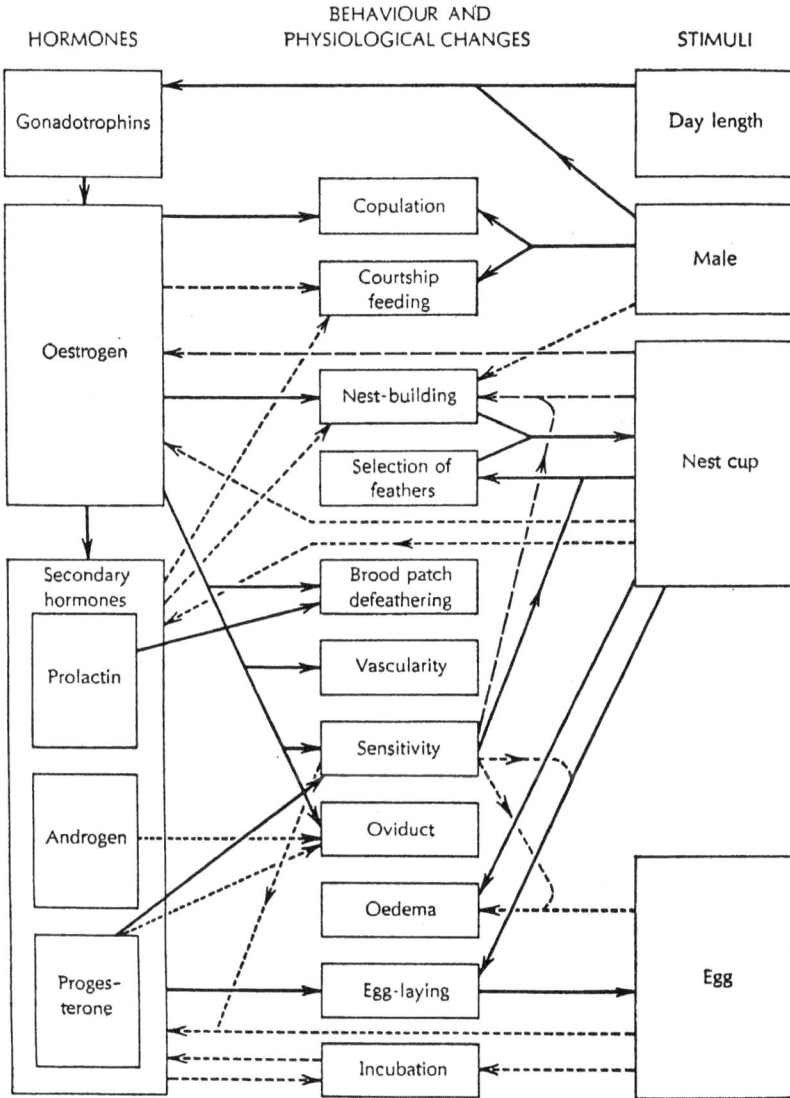

Figure 34 Relations between external stimuli, internal hormonal conditions, and reproductive development and behaviour of female canaries. Continuous lines, experimentally established positive effects; discontinuous lines, negative effects; short dashed lines, probable relationships not yet established with certainty. Where the extent to which an effect may be indirect has not yet been established, only the direct effect is shown. (Modified after Hinde, 1965.)

163

There has been much argument in the past as to whether, and to what extent, drives can be usefully classified as either special or general. It is quite obvious, from what has already been said, that there is a great deal of motivation which expresses itself in the activation of particular patterns of behaviour (or at least in the activation of groups of behaviour patterns) which are functionally related in one way or another. If this is conceded, as it must be, the question can then be asked whether we should classify drives by their apparent objects and results and, if so, to what extent. Obviously there seem to be what may be called sex drives and hunger drives. Used incautiously such assumptions, particularly expressed as they were at one time under the title of "determining tendencies," can lead us to the supposition that almost every activity of which an animal is capable has a special drive behind it. This has led in the past to fantastic multiplication of drive states—including such absurdities as social drives, pain-avoiding drives, respiratory drives, comfort drives, self-preservatory drives, excretory drives, and so on *ad infinitum* in absurd confusion.

The Effects of Specific and Non-specific Stimuli

So we have to look not merely at the kind of action which a drive produces but also at its mechanism. And if we do this, we find that while some drives are obviously specialised in their effects, it is nevertheless quite hard to find a drive, particularly if hormone secretion plays a substantial part in its make-up, which is confined in its effects to a single type of activity.

It has proved extraordinarily difficult to devise experimental situations which show exactly how specific drive is. But as Hinde says, "On present evidence the reasonable assumption is that, within limits, the intensity of any one type of behaviour *depends only on motivational factors more or less specific to it* (my italics) and that others are of relatively minor importance." On the other hand there is a great deal of evidence for a more general effect of drive. Thus various carnivores (Beach, 1947), many birds, amongst them gulls (Armstrong, 1950), and monkeys (Hinde, 1970) (all references in Hinde, 1970) are especially likely to show sexual behaviour after a mild disturbance; and painful stimulation, such as that arising from an electric shock to the foot, can elicit fighting (Ulrich et al., 1964) or copulation (Barfield and Sachs, 1968) (refs. in Hinde, 1970) in a considerable number of mammalian species. And of course there are factors of a general nature such as changes in temperature which, at least in animals such as insects, govern the general range and intensity of response. Ants, for instance, walk slowly and go about their other activities in a lethargic manner if the temperature is too low and may be speeded up if the temperature is slightly above the normal. So some sort of general drive supposition is a necessity.

But as Fentress (1968; ref. in Hinde, 1970) shows, to prove the extreme form of the general drive hypothesis it would be necessary to show that each motivational factor influenced all responses to some extent. But an animal can do only a limited number of things at a time, and so a supposedly non-specific effect could only be proved by observations of all specific activities, each in a situation appropriate to it; and, as Hinde (1970) points out, it is rare that proponents of a general drive theory have observed even two different activities in the same experiment. It follows that a distinction between specific and non-specific effects of a stimulus change is often extremely difficult to draw; and I agree with Hinde when he says that the question is more profitably phrased in terms of how specific or how general the effects of each factor may be. While all the components of a drive can, of course, be directive—in the sense in which I employ it here, of a mechanism adapted to achieve a particular goal—it would seem that only the central nervous system component can have the necessary complexities of structure to enable it to originate or provide anything that appears to go beyond the limits of mere directiveness and to approach even the appearance of true purposiveness. When we see how intimately interlocked are visceral, hormonal, and central nervous system factors in internal drive, we see at once that such internal drives are something much more complicated, at least in most cases, than mere visceral stimulation; and so the present picture is one of an internal drive in the form of patterns of activity in the central nervous system which can be either the result of visceral stimulation or the result of hormonal stimulation or can be truly endogenous in the sense of originating within the nervous system itself (Adrian, 1950).

T. H. Bullock (1961, 1966) shows how such a variety of examples of nervous organisation for controlling behaviour are now neurophysiologically established, mainly in the invertebrates, that we have ample factual evidence for the existence of neuronal devices which, singly and in co-operation, can account for all postulated types of organisation of behaviour: from behaviour of the highest degree of fixity on the one hand, to extreme flexibility on the other, and from systems exhibiting complete peripheral initiation and control to those where this control is exclusively central.

The Relation to Genetic Factors

Since the development of modern macromolecular biology with its implication, already referred to, that the DNA of the nucleus amounts in effect to an instruction book for the building of the organism, it is tempting to look upon the truly innate components of an animal's structure and behaviour as those which are coded in the DNA of the germ plasm. Then we can assume that the acquired part is that which comes either through the mediation of the sense organs of the animal or through the direct effect of influences such as illumination, temperature, and chemical substances. Now of course it will have been obvious, from what I have said above, that no one in their senses would assume that there is no interaction between external factors and internal ones; between hereditary information and acquired information. No one, not even the most rabid exponents of the instinct versus learning argument, ever supposed any such thing! It follows that the argument of Hebb (1953) that to ask how much a given piece of behaviour depends upon genetic factors and how much on environmental is as meaningless as to ask how much the area of a field depends on its length and how much on its width is absurd—because if the field had no length or no width, it would have no area. And of course an organism can neither be without a genome nor can it be without an environment. But the field can have an area (although we shouldn't call it a field) if it is 1 millimetre wide and 20 miles long, and it can well be that in an organism an overwhelming proportion of the instructions which determine its make-up and its activity comes from one source and a minuscule amount from another. In a highly impervious cyst or arthropod egg, the effective influence from the environment during the egg or cystic stage may be effectively only that of temperature and oxygen supply. And indeed the structure of the cyst wall or the eggshell (chorion) seems often specifically designed to eliminate external influences to the utmost possible degree. It would be a mistake of course not to recognise that the DNA in the egg cell has an internal environment which itself may contain a great deal of DNA; and there is no doubt whatever that there is interaction between the DNA and the rest of the system. But let us suppose for the sake of argument that, as in the development of a nematode worm, or of a springtail (Collembolan), the form and capacity of the hatching organism is little different from that of the same organism when it is ready to reproduce. In this case it seems entirely reasonable to assume that the features of the organism are mainly determined by its hereditary constitution and extremely little, and only in a very general way, influenced by abnormalities of the environment or changes in it. So we come to the question as to whether it is possible to give any estimate of the information content of an organism which is sufficiently accurate to be useful.

Instinct and Information

The task is certainly one of formidable difficulty and it must be at once admitted that the resulting calculations are only the roughest approximations and perhaps often little more than plausible guesses. Nevertheless such calculations do enable us to gain some idea of how complex a system really is; and so it may give us a clue as to whether a given hypothesis for a particular biological process or event is reasonable or totally unreasonable. Information theory in fact does not tell us how to do something, but rather how difficult it is to do. I think therefore the whole problem has to be looked at as a question of the complexity of a system. Some writers seem to assume that such a use of information theory is invalid; so they would argue there is no sense in speaking of information content except in relation to a communication channel of some kind. Thus once a system has been ordered, the attempt to describe that order by information theory is inadmissible; information only makes sense when instructions are being conveyed from one system to another.

That this criticism is in fact invalid, I think, is apparent from the work of one of the leaders in this field, namely L. Brillouin (1962) who uses the term information to cover the degree of organisation of a static system. It is of course true that the amount of information required to specify a system cannot be dealt with *in vacuo*. Hinde (1970) argues that in order to measure the information required to describe a given state or a given pattern of behaviour, we must know the number of states or patterns of behaviour possible. In the ordinary case of transmission of information the scale or grid is given by the conditions of the communication channel and the speed with which they can work. When one speaks of the information content of a system without specifying a grid or channel, then one is doing so in relation to a fully randomised state, and one is then using one's estimate as an estimate, however approximate, of the degree of order or disorder of the system. Now of course there is a very considerable order in the system quite apart from the order in the DNA. It is possible to make allowances for and very rough estimates of the amount of order in the non-DNA part of the system. In that case we are making some estimate of the order already present and calculating the degree of order to be further added to give an observed result. As Sydney Smith says (1960), "The biologist and communication engineer would both argue that there is little more information in two identical cells than there is already present in one." I think it follows that the question of the information content of a cell or an organism and the sources from which it comes is not a pseudoproblem but a real one, however blunt an instrument present information theory may prove itself to be. It follows that it is worthwhile attempting to estimate, however great the difficulties may be, the relative contributions of genome and environment to the organisation of a fully grown animal. As I see it the problem is very much that posed by an enzyme and its substrate. I think biochemists would unhesitatingly say that if we are considering the activities of the enzyme, then a vastly greater proportion of information resides in it and a relatively small proportion within the substrate. Again we have great complexity in the one and much less complexity in the other.

Preliminary Statement on Learning

To sum up then, we certainly have at last escaped from the innate-learned controversy in its original and sterile form. But to shut our eyes to the reality of the difference between innately coded information and information which arises elsewhere seems to me to be misguided and to deny that living beings are more highly organised than the non-living world. It is all very well to say that development involves, as indeed it does, "a nexus of causal relations." And it is true that the more we study living beings the more complex we find this nexus of causal relations to be. And if it is so complex, we are tempted to assume that there is no possibility of analysing it into manageable parts and proportions. But, if so, we are thereby abandoning all attempts to explain the difference between one organism and another and how that difference is maintained. In fact this seems to me very similar to a return to the old idea of the nineteenth and early twentieth centuries that instinct has to be accepted as something

given and that it is useless if not impious to attempt to understand it. This is rather a similar point to that made by some
exponents of genetics who argue that genetics is the study of
differences. It is of course true that genetics progresses by the
study of differences in that the study of differences enables the
geneticist to isolate and manipulate small elements in the genetic
make-up. But if that was all there was to it, genetics would soon
dwindle and die. For what genetics really does is to investigate
the hereditary make-up of animals and to find out how it is
that certain characteristics are handed on from one generation
to the next, and handed on under very great differences of environmental conditions. So I would agree with Hinde (1969)
that we do not wish to return to the old dichotomy of learning
versus instinct, but we do wish to enquire into the degree of
complexity of the organism and to make estimates of the stability
or lability of its structure and behaviour under different environmental influences. So the problem is not innate versus
learned, but is better expressed by the words linked with two
arrows in opposite directions, thus innate ⇌ learned.

Later we shall consider in more detail the significance of learning and the way in which it adjusts, and is itself controlled by,
the instinctive or innate organisation of the animal. In doing
this it will be very necessary to make a distinction, which I myself have not always made in the past, between "adaptive change
in behaviour as a result of individual sensory (or perceptual)
experience"—which is learning in the true sense, and a very
different matter, "change in behaviour as a result of individually
experienced environmental influences which are not mediated
by the perceptual systems of the animal." And in the same way
it is becoming more and more important to make a distinction
between experience which is, as in true learning, the result of
the active or actively organised process of perception and on the
other hand the result of entirely passive receipt of environmental
influences.

Finally I would like to emphasise at this stage that I have
said nothing about an important form of learning which relates

especially to the problem of instinct, and that is "imprinting." The reason why I have not discussed this here is because it is of such great importance in relation to the behaviour of the higher animals and of man himself that it can be considered more appropriately in the second part of the book.

Chapter 5

ANIMAL PERCEPTION

In the last chapter we, so to speak, set the scene for considering learning abilities in animals and man. Now we come to consider learning with particular regard to the perceptual powers of the organism.

The Types of Learning Relevant to Perception and Perceptual Organisation

In relation to this problem of perception there are two types of learning which are particularly relevant and which imply something more than (i) "latent learning" which is the associative conditioning caused by an immediate reinforcement or reward for food; or (ii) simple "learning not to respond" which we know as habituation. Latent learning is conveniently defined as *"the association of indifferent stimuli or situations without patent reward."* This phenomenon was originally established by separating a litter of young rats into two equal groups and giving the first group the opportunity of running about in a maze without any reward in the food box at the end, for, say, half an hour a day for about ten days. This group was then tested for rate of learning the maze (according to the usual methods) as compared with the other half of the litter which had lacked previous experience of the apparatus. It was found that those rats that had the chance to explore the maze without finding any food or reward of any other kind in it had nevertheless learned a very great deal about its layout; so that, in some experiments, once they had found food in one part of the maze, they were thereafter immediately able to go straight to that point from whatever part of the maze they were first put down in. They thus showed significantly shorter times in their complete learning of the maze as compared with the non-experienced rats. In fact the result of this treatment was to show that learning had been going on from the first experience in the empty maze, but was in fact "latent" until the opportunity to reveal itself was made "patent" by the insertion of a reward.

To express this in more sophisticated language, one may say that the first group of rats in their rewarded experience of the maze were in fact learning conditional probabilities of association between the stimuli coming from various parts of the maze. These stimuli of course were primarily spatial ones since others were pretty much excluded by the methods of the experiment. This type of learning is of great importance when we come to consider the normal behaviour of higher animals in the wild. It is in fact not a hard-and-fast category in itself since in some respects it is very close to "trial-and-error learning," and some trial-and-error learning can take place in the apparent absence of reward. But the importance of it is that the concept of reward or reinforcement now becomes extremely tenuous. So with latent learning, and still more with the concept of insight and insight learning which we discuss next, we become deeply involved in the consideration of the processes of sensory perception.

INSIGHT, OR EXPLORATORY LEARNING

The concept of insight has been the subject of experiment and debate amongst psychologists ever since the term was brought into use by Wolfgang Köhler (1921), and its use still gives rise to difficulties, although much progress has been made. Evidence for the occurrence of insight was first provided by a famous experiment with captive chimpanzees. The animals were kept in a large hall where there was food (usually a bunch of bananas) hanging from the ceiling well out of reach. On the floor of the room there were a number of wooden boxes or packing cases lying haphazardly around. As soon as the chimps saw the food they would of course try to reach it, usually by jumping for it persistently. After a number of attempts without success, they would become discouraged and sit rather glumly about. Then suddenly one chimpanzee would be observed to hit on the scheme of dragging a box under the food. Standing on this box he was certainly nearer to the bananas but not yet able to reach them. He might then be seen looking from the box first moved to other boxes in the room and, after a few minutes apparently engaged in sizing up the situation, would get a second box and drag it on top of the first. This too might not be high enough and eventually a third box had to be fetched, and by this means a precarious sort of ladder was constructed, very liable to tumble when the apes climbed up but nevertheless sufficiently stable to enable them to snatch the food. Köhler concluded that the apes had succeeded in realising the potentiality of the boxes, and, once this had been done, were able to proceed to the intelligent solution of the problem. The ability to achieve this solution obviously depended on a new organisation of the animals' perceptions—visual, tactile, and spatial— so that they were able to embark on a new course of action appropriate to the situation without showing overt trial-and-error behaviour, but perhaps, as some psychologists have expressed it, implying a mental trial and error amongst ideas.

On the basis of such experiments, insight learning can be defined as *"the sudden production of a new adaptive response not arrived at by a random sequence of haphazard attempts."* Alternatively we may define insight learning as the *"solution of a problem by the sudden adaptive reorganisation of experience."*

Thus both latent learning and insight learning appear to involve a basic faculty, which Köhler called insight, but which we can describe as a form of perceptual synthesis. This synthesis enables the animal to, so to speak, build together perceptions which are not in the first place of any significance to it or its needs. It is obviously very closely related to the ability to learn rapidly to recognise patterns. The fact that psychologists were very reluctant to accept this idea of latent learning, and the numerous demonstrations of it that have been supplied by zoologists in their studies of the way in which animals find their way about, is very remarkable. For when we consider that latent learning, or something like it, is found in all groups of animals from bees and hunting dogs up to man himself, it seems rather odd that psychologists should not have noticed it when they have argued for years about what the rats could or could not do in their mazes.

This problem is exemplified beautifully by the hunting wasp (*Ammophila*) which makes a burrow in sandy soil, then finds a caterpillar which it immobilises, but does not kill, with its sting. The wasp then puts the caterpillar down the burrow as provision for the eggs that it will later lay and goes out to find another caterpillar. The wasps search for the caterpillars while in flight. But when they have caught and stung a caterpillar, they have to drag it back to the burrow along the ground since the weight is too great for aerial transport. A great many experiments have shown that the wasp returns to its burrow (even though in most species the entrance has been closed by the wasp before it leaves) without any difficulty. It does this by observing the position of familiar objects like pine cones or stones or trees or small bushes in the neighbourhood. In fact the wasps learn the details of the "landscape" in the region of their burrow with extraordinary exactness. If, while a wasp is away hunting, one removes one or two apparently obvious landmarks in the neighbourhood of the entrance, the animal will still nevertheless find the hole by using other landmarks which the experimenter had not yet thought of. In fact the wasp's visual perception is organised in a very highly detailed manner so that in order to confuse it on its return you have to do quite a lot of "landscape gardening"!

This perceptual synthesis can be accomplished by many of the higher Hymenoptera but particularly the hunting wasps and the colony-forming bees. Every experienced beekeeper knows that if you move the hive from one site to another, those bees which are out foraging at the time that the hive is moved of course return

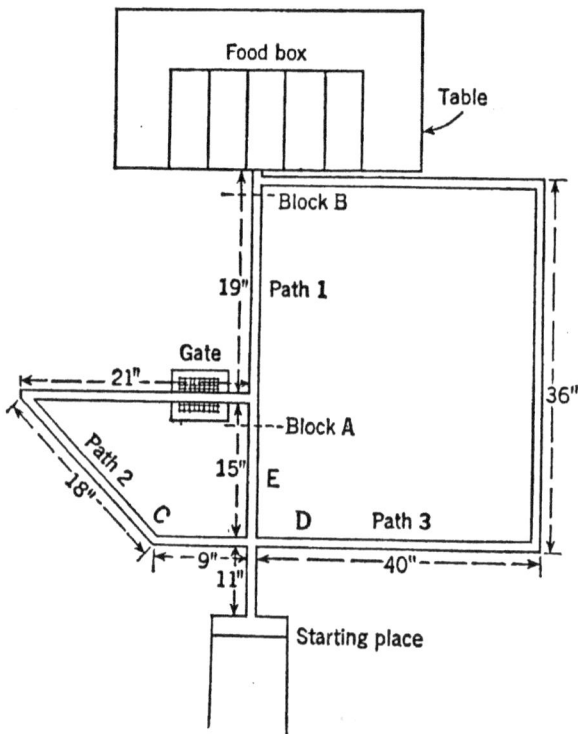

Figure 35 Tolman and Honzik's apparatus to test for learning by insight in the rat. The pathway is elevated. Preliminary training taught the rat that, after finding path 1 blocked at A, he could reach the food box via either paths 2 or 3. Evidence of "insight" occurs when, finding path 1 blocked at B, the animal selected path 3 (which was not preferred under ordinary circumstances) instead of path 2, which was not as inadequate as path 1 to take him to the food box. (After Tolman and Honzik, 1930a.)

to the old place and are very unlikely to be able to find the hive in its new location unless it is very near. If however you move the hive at night or before opening it in the morning while all the bees are inside, one notices that the foragers, instead of leaping out of the entrance and flying straight off as they normally do, will now hesitate and then perhaps circle around the hive for a few seconds or minutes, clearly learning the new landmarks, by what one may call a "survey flight," before they go off. From what we have already said about bees it is clear that their perceptual and communicative abilities are very highly organised indeed. But one can find essentially the same thing much lower in the animal kingdom. It can be found in a very elementary form in limpets and many other molluscs and in many fish; in fact this phenomenon occurs in virtually every kind of animal which has a nest or home or shelter which is important for it to be able to return to.

This phenomenon of latent learning or insight learning can be investigated quantitatively by means of a special type of maze (Figure 35) which provides both a long way and a short way to the food box at the top from the starting place. In this case preliminary training teaches the rat that after finding path 1 closed, it can reach the box by either paths 2 or 3. It is evident that insight occurs when the path is blocked "D" and the animal, in this case a rat, selects path 3, which was not preferred in ordinary circumstances, instead of path 2 because of the inadequacy of that path to take him to the food box.

Recognition of Pattern

Clearly this ability can largely be equated to a "recognition of pattern." We find that, right through the animal kingdom, as soon as the eyes have reached the stage at which they are able to relate the position of objects in the visual field, animals are liable to pay particular attention to certain types of patterns. A pattern which is particularly important and very easily recognised in the life of many animals is a circle; and many of my readers will

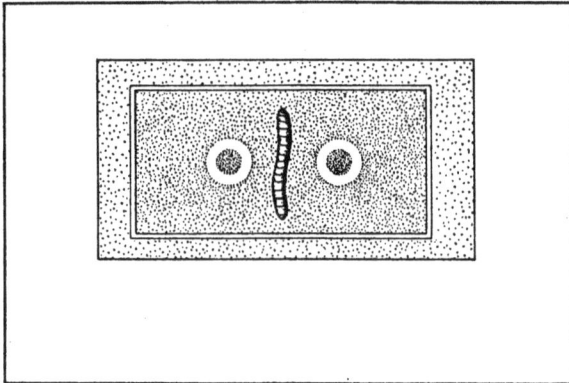

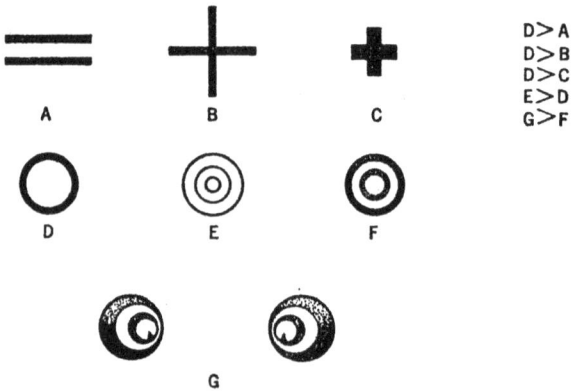

Figure 36 The arrangement used by Blest (1957a) to test the response of birds to eye-spot patterns such as those on the wings of a butterfly *Precis almana* given here. A model is projected onto a screen behind a meal worm placed on a slide where the bird has been trained to take food. The relative effectiveness of the models in alarming the birds is shown below. (After Blest, 1957b.)

have noticed how commonly circular patterns are to be found on the wings of butterflies and moths and other insects and as part of the plumage patterns of birds. Very often we find (Plate 9, Figure 36) that the circles are normally covered but can be suddenly exposed by a movement of the wings with very startling effects. There is ample evidence that this sudden display of a circle is a deterrent to a potential predator. Figure 36 shows a simple but ingenious method used in my laboratory to test the response of birds to eye-spot patterns such as those on the wings of a butterfly. The patterns are projected on a screen behind a meal worm placed on a tray where the bird has already been accustomed to taking food. The figure shows the relative effectiveness of the model in alarming the bird. Thus D is more effective than either A, B, or C. E is more effective than D, and G more effective than F. Particular interest of this experiment is that the model most effective in frightening the bird is that which looks most like a real eye—it has, so to speak, a sort of "glance" in the eye. So it seems that realistic eye-spot patterns have been developed by natural selection as a safeguard against attack by predators. Indeed it is clear that the recognition of a circular pattern or an eye spot as something suggesting an eye is very deeply ingrained in many animals. Figure 37 shows an experiment in which goldfish were trained to distinguish between shapes, and indeed there are many other ways in which these perceptual abilities of animals can be tested in the laboratory.

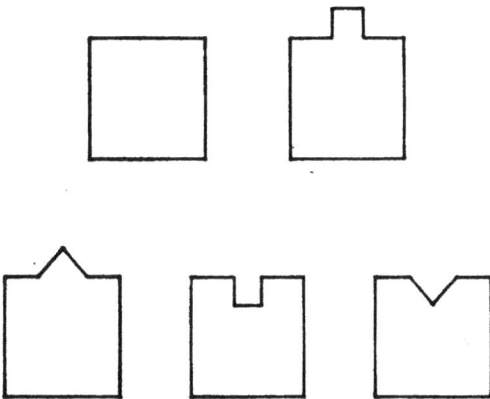

Figure 37 Goldfish were trained to discriminate between the top two shapes. The other three shapes were treated as similar to the right-hand training shape.

179

Rate of Perceptual Development—Laboratory Animals versus Those in Their Natural Habitats

Now let us turn to more natural situations. One of the most re-markable examples of exploratory learning, as it is often con-venient to term this process involving perceptual synthesis, is provided by the Gobiid fish, *Bathygobius soporator*, a species which inhabits tidal pools in the Bahamas and other tropical shores. Aronson (summarised in Thorpe, 1963) finds that the fish are so well orientated that they are able to jump from pool to pool at low tide without running any significant risk of finding themselves on dry land. That is to say, at low tide it is obvious that they know the layout of the pool sufficiently well to enable the fish to leap correctly, even though it is perfectly clear that they cannot see one pool while they are swimming in another. Subsequent work has confirmed the conclusion that these gobies swim over the rock depressions at high tide and thereby acquire an effective memory of the general features and topography of the limited area around the home pool, a memory which they are able to utilise at low tide when restricted to the pool. Figure 38 shows schematically the pools, paths, and jumps studied in a particular location. This makes abundantly clear the remarkable precision of perceptual knowledge which the fishes have acquired.

Even more remarkable are the perceptual achievements dur-ing the migratory and homing performances of fish such as salmon, trout, white bass, etc. Most fish migrations consist of (a) a dispersal of eggs, or larvae, or young fishes, either by drifting passively with the current or by an active search for normal habitats; (b) return journey—an active movement usually against the current to the spawning grounds; and (c) a dispersal of the "spent" fishes, a process which may again be either passive with the current, or active, in search of fresh feeding grounds. Little can be said as to the means of maintenance of ordinary periodic migration movements. In some cases it is impossible that learning of the topography can play any part in this, and there seems to

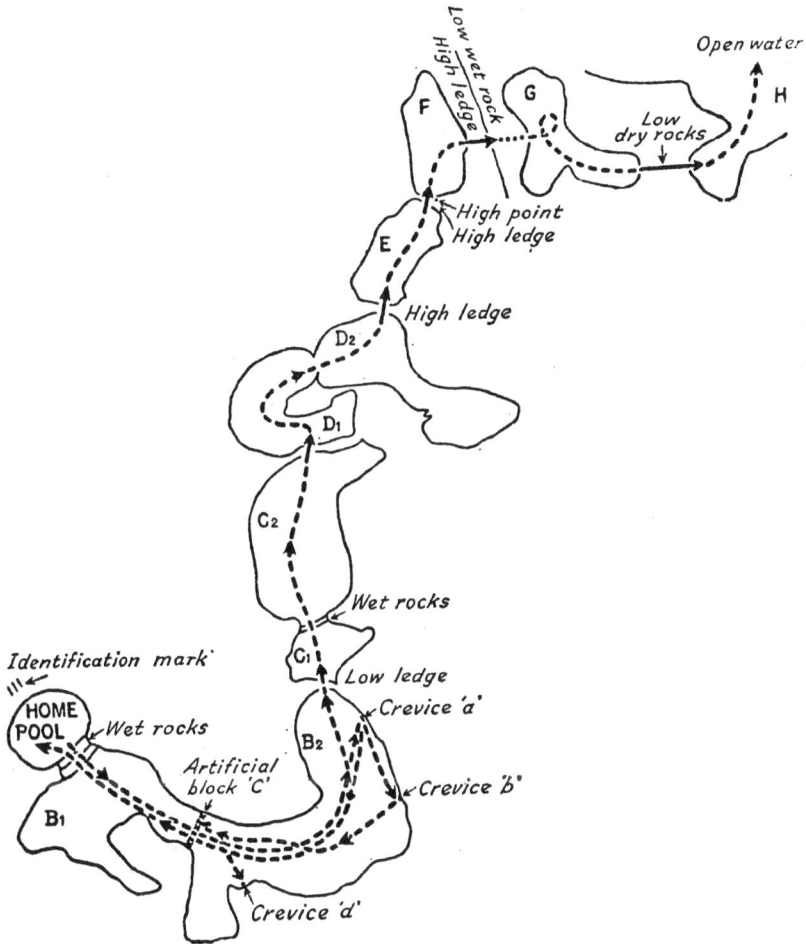

Figure 38 Schematic outline of the pools, paths, and jumps in a partic-ular experiment of the orientation behaviour of the Gobiid fish *Bathygobius soporator*. The heavy broken lines represent the paths taken by the fish while swimming; the heavy plain lines indicate the jumps; the heavy dotted lines represent climbing or skipping over wet rocks. (After Aronson, 1951.)

be a general lack of evidence that schools of young fish follow, or are in any way led by, experienced adults. So it must appear that the regularity and consistency of the main migration routes of fish is a product of the innate organisation of the fish, together with a sensitivity to current, water temperature, food supply, and other characteristics of the environment.

181

As soon as fish-marking techniques were sufficiently well developed to yield results, evidence began to come in showing that some species of fish, particularly of the genera *Salmo* and *Oncorhynchus*, were returning to spawn, not merely in the geographical area in which they were hatched, but actually in the same stream and even identical portions of the stream, which they had inhabited in their earliest youth. There is now clear evidence that a high proportion of some species of salmon and trout succeed in returning to the stream in which they had emerged as youngsters, and that very few individuals of these species enter streams a hundred or so miles away from the streams in which they were reared. Transplantation experiments carried out on Chinook salmon (*Oncorhynchus tschawytcha*) showed that all the fish from transplanted eggs which were recovered were found in the river in which they were brought up and not in the river in which they were spawned. Again it was found that over four years of experiments, 97.9 per cent of steelhead trout (*Salmo gairdneri*) returned to the home stream and only 2.1 per cent were seen four miles distant. Similar figures for silver salmon (*Oncorhynchus milktschitsch*) in the same streams were obtained.

It is now quite clear that the return is not to be explained on the assumption that the intervening period has been spent in the near neighbourhood of the native stream. In fact quite the contrary, as accompanying Figure 39 shows, for the Chinook salmon. It is now evident that one species (*O. nerka*) normally travels approximately 100 miles a day when the urge to return is upon it; and there is a record of a salmon (*S. salar*) which travelled at the rate of 60 miles a day for twelve days.

The next problem concerns the sensory stimuli which serve as guides or reference points during these astounding homing performances. There are certainly a large number of possible stimuli to be considered, of which water currents are amongst the most important. However, fish will very rapidly learn to keep a particular course and direction, employing orientation by the sun as a basis and using many different clues for keeping steadily on course. But it seems clear that, in many cases, accurate return

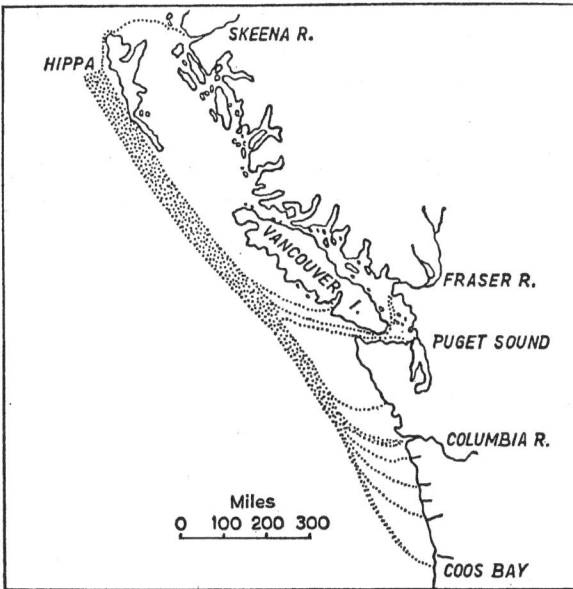

Figure 39 Distribution of Chinook salmon tagged in the sea, Hippa Island, British Columbia, 1925. (From Scheer, 1939, after Williamson, 1927.)

cannot be the result of visual memory of the home or the route therefrom. The young salmon descending for the first time proceed slowly, "playing about" along near the shore, probably drifting passively for large stretches of the route. The returning adult swims strenuously in deeper water of the same river, and the two pathways must then often be separated by a distance greater than the visual range. So we have to fall back on the assumption that it is the ability of the salmon to perceive and remember the chemical characteristics of the water of the stream bed which enables it to achieve the apparent *tour de force* of returning to the stream of its nativity, anything from two to six years after having left it. It has been shown that the organs of chemical sense can appreciate small, but probably constant, differences in the characteristics of water from different streams and currents, including, of course, differences in salinity. Moreover a learned olfactory preference for the waters of the home creek has been demonstrated experimentally. Then there are also differences in temperature, hydrogen-ion concentration, proportion of dissolved gases, temperature and density stratification, and the general turbulence. Added to this there might be recognition of the characteristic sounds made by waterfalls and rapids, the memory of the general nature of the river bottom (which of course might be partly visual), and perhaps the memory of the type of food to be obtained there. Finally, as regards the route in deeper waters of the sea, we must not forget the possibility that many fishes produce noises which may make possible echo sounding from the sea bed. Or, in the absence of noise produced by the species itself, there is the possibility of the perception of the resonance effect of the surface wave noise on the bottom.

Taking into account all these sources of stimuli for orientation, let us consider what the homing performance of *Salmo* entails. Translated into laboratory terms, it is very like learning to run a gigantic and complex maze in reverse as a result of one experience of that maze two to six years before! It is not, of course, necessary to assume that the fish remembers every detail of the hundreds of miles which its journey may cover; but one must suppose it remembers the characteristics of the different sections and particularly the features of the various "choice points" constituted by the junctions of the tributaries of the main rivers. It may of course be that many of these junctions do not offer as free a choice as may appear at first sight. Yet however much we

Figure 40 Apparatus with real "cliff" which can only be experienced visually. Right, chequer-board pattern immediately below the glass; left, some distance below. (From a drawing by Yvette-Spencer-Booth.)

Figure 41 A kitten at the edge of a "visual cliff"; i.e., the "cliff" is only a perspective drawing. A glass pane covers the apparent chasm. (After a photograph in Tinbergen, 1963.)

try in our imagination to simplify the problem posed to the returning fish, it remains a most astonishing performance.

Now to contrast a situation shown by young birds and mammals when faced by a real or apparent declivity. Figures 40 and 41

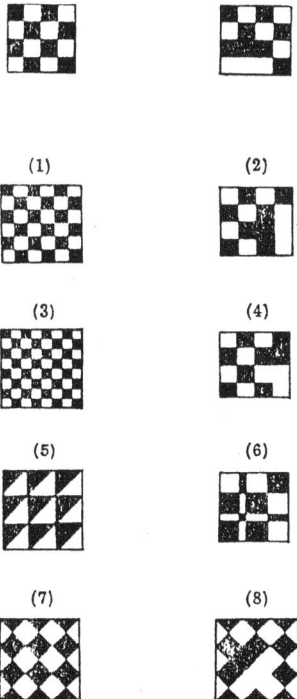

(1)

(2)

(3)

(4)

(5)

(6)

(7)

(8)

Figure 42 Rats were trained to discriminate between the top two patterns. Below each of these patterns are shown examples of other shapes treated as similar to it.

185

show the response of a chick and a kitten to what is described as a "visual cliff." That is to say a perspective cliff as in this figure. Now the young animal, the first time it sees this alarming visual pattern, pauses and investigates very carefully the apparent edge. So we must assume that a peculiar readiness to perceive this kind of danger must be programmed precisely in the brain and visual organs by the hereditary make-up, an innate programming which then later can be developed and refined by visual experience.

Plate 10 shows what might be called a "random pattern." In Figure 42 we can see that the patterns change as we proceed from one to the next but that they are treated all as equal and so one can test, in this kind of situation (Figures 43 and 44), what might be called the effective powers of the various animals when presented with choices of this kind. It is clear that the power to distinguish elaborate patterns of stimulation, as for example the visual recognition of figures whether simple or elaborate, involves the response to relations in the visual field: the essence of a pattern is the relations and proportions between its different parts. Indeed it is hard to avoid the conclusion that even the simplest stimulus is in some sense a relational one, so that, if this is true, perception in the strict sense always involves relational properties. So we may say *"perceptual learning may be defined as the ability of an organism to improve its response to variables of physical stimulation as a result of continued or repeated exposure to them."* It can certainly occur independently of conventional reward.

Thus although rats reared in darkness up to ninety-six days of age can learn to discriminate between a circle and a triangle, early experience of the forms without differential reinforcement appears to increase the ease with which learning occurs. We see that this effect is very dependent on the experimental conditions. Thus experience of forms made from metal cutouts is effective, but when the same forms are merely painted on a rectangular background, early experience may have little influence on subsequent discrimination learning. It has been suggested that the difference lies in the "attention getting" properties of the stimulus,

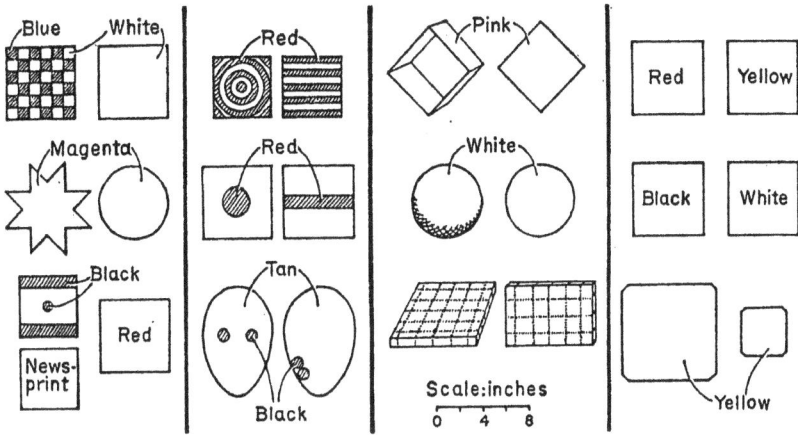

Figure 43 Pairs of targets used in different fixation tests of infant rhesus monkeys. The four sections represent the four categories of stimulus variation.

Left to right: Patterned versus plain, centred versus uncentred, solid versus plain, non-configurational variables. (After Fantz, 1965.)

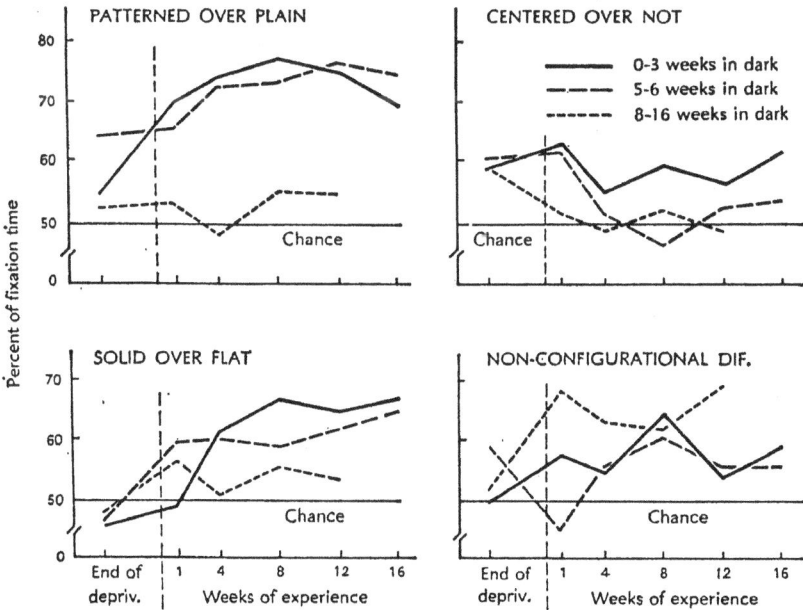

Figure 44 Post-deprivation changes in the visual preferences of infant rhesus monkeys for the stimulus variables shown in Figure 43. (After Fantz, 1965.)

187

the cutouts showing depth at their edges. The ability to abstract certain properties of a stimulus has been studied with rats required to discriminate the magnitude (successively, but in varying order of brightness, area, and height) and form of different stimuli. Animals reared in the dark, and given visual experience only during testing, showed a gradual improvement on the magnitude problem but were inferior to the light-reared animals in all tests. Improvement in the magnitude problems, each of which is essentially novel, was interpreted as indicating that the animals responded not simply to a brightness, size, or light difference but in differences in stimulus magnitude as such. Further experiments with rats have indicated the animal must first learn to differentiate the stimuli, *qua* stimuli, that is, differentiate tactual and visual clues relating to the edges and angles of the forms. They must then learn which of the objects were associated with food and which were not.

There is much evidence that the development of the correct visual response is greatly stimulated if movement relative to the pattern is produced by active movement of *the animal*. It is immensely important for most animals to learn about the environment, to learn how to use their eyes properly, for instance, and then they must be active during the process of learning; this means they must walk about and explore the environment rather than be passively exposed to it. Figure 45 shows a beautiful experiment carried out by Held and Hein (1963) at the Massachusetts Institute of Technology. In this case two kittens from the same litter were kept with their mother in the dark and put into the apparatus as shown. One, as we see, is walking; the other kitten is in what might be described as a "kitty car" and is being carried around. The apparatus is so designed that the kitten in the car is carried over exactly the same course with exactly the same movement relative to the environment as the walking kitten experiences, but of course completely passively. So the visual experience of the two animals is identical. But when they are tested to see what they have learned about their environment, it is clear that the walking kitten has learned a

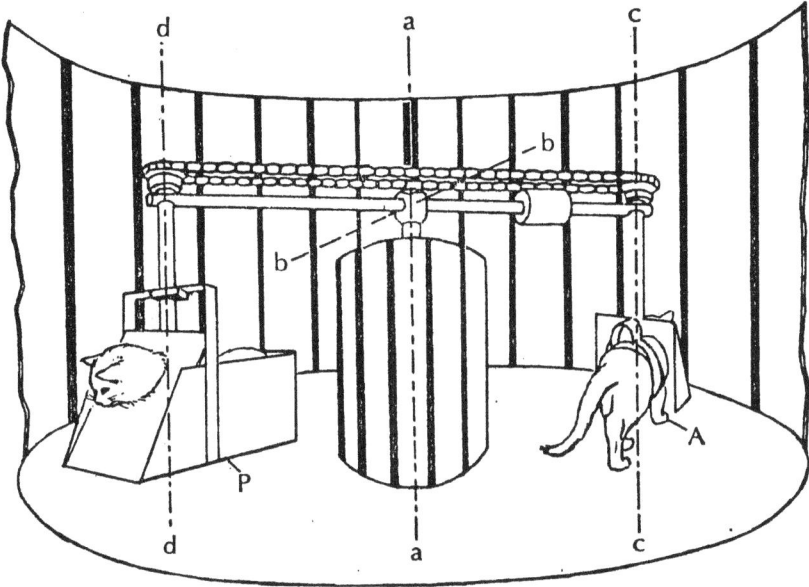

Figure 45 Apparatus for equating motion and the consequent visual feedback for A, an actively moving kitten; and P, a passively moved kitten. (After Held and Hein, 1963.)

great deal and the other has learned nothing at all. Thus being carried passively around has not provided the stimuli for effective learning of the visual world. This is very generally true of the higher animals—they must have this tendency to explore and their perceptual synthesis is achieved by this process of exploring the environment.

Finally, in this particular connection it is instructive to consider the work of Herrnstein and Loveland in Harvard (1964) who trained pigeons to respond to the presence or absence of human beings in photographs. People in the pictures might be anywhere on the photograph; they might be clothed or nude; adult or children in various postures; black, white, or yellow; in fact so varied that simple stimulus characterisation seems impossible. The results were statistically significant and suggest remarkable powers of conceptualisation by pigeons as to what is "human." Similarly monkeys have been trained to select three different pictures of insects from amongst pictures of leaves, fruit, branches, etc., of similar area and colour (Lehr, 1967). In later tests the monkeys showed significant preferences for insect pictures over those of other natural objects. Similar results could be obtained by training on flower pictures as compared with other parts of plants. However, in this case, generalisation appeared to depend on a few criteria common to all flower patterns, so it may be justly queried whether this really merits the label of "conceptualisation."

In conclusion of this particular topic it is interesting to consider what is known as the "searching image," evidence for which is displayed by many birds. Thus it has been shown that adult jays (*Garrulus glandarius*) when tested in an aviary containing bushes and trees, among which "stick caterpillars" (caterpillars which have evolved camouflage such that they look like sticks) have been placed, do not peck at these caterpillars which are nevertheless of course very good food. If they find one by accident, they will peck at all similar objects; and so if there are enough stick caterpillars in the aviary to reward them sufficiently often, they will in due course find most of them. However if the stick caterpillars are removed, the jays in time become discouraged by finding only sticks and give up looking at them. So the original situation is restored.

Particularly interesting in this connexion are some recent studies made in the field with carrion crows (*Corvus corone*). Dr. H. Croze (1970) has shown how when the regular feeding ground of a population of wild carrion crows is baited with some new food object, such as a well-camouflaged egg of a kind not previously encountered, or some other unfamiliar thing equally camouflaged, the first finding of one of these objects, together with the appreciation that it has food value, is sufficient at once to start the bird seeking similar objects in the locality. Both wild and hand-reared crows form their searching image faster than any animal in a psychological laboratory ever learnt its "choice from sample." The rapidity and ease with which the crow can generalise and compare is indeed astonishing. Results of this kind suggest that even the most undisturbed wild animals in their natural environment achieve swiftly, and easily, tasks which a laboratory rat or pigeon might take thousands of trials to master in an artificially contrived apparatus.

These results and others of their kind show dramatically, as indeed do the studies of homing salmon, how essential it is, if one is fully to appreciate the complexity and flexibility of animal behaviour, to study it in the wild, with proper experimental techniques, as well as in the laboratory. In many fields the experimental psychologists have in fact lagged years behind their ethological colleagues in understanding animal behaviour, merely because of a simple failure to investigate and understand the animal in its natural habitat. And even when telemetric methods with computerised analysis are employed, the results can be totally misleading because until one knows the behavioural repertoire of the animal in the wild one does not know what particular actions or particular types of behaviour are relevant for analysis. One cannot observe everything at once even with the most modern technique; and so one may set one's apparatus to observe certain actions which one thinks may be important and of course see nothing whatever of other movements which may later turn out to be far more significant.

Perceptual Achievements of Birds
During Migration and Homing

I now wish to discuss another facet of bird behaviour which illustrates even more dramatically the astounding powers of perceptual organisation which many of these creatures possess. Everyone of course knows that some birds migrate and that in the Northern Hemisphere they tend to go southwest in autumn and northeast in spring. They do this by maintaining a particular direction relative to the sun, allowing for the sun movement during the daylight hours. It goes without saying that in any species where the young birds migrate to winter quarters before the adults, the former must possess the ability to fly in a constant direction. It has now been well established that as a result of experiments in "orientation cages," with birds under the hormonally controlled urge to migrate, many birds will flutter in that compass direction in which they "should" be flying at that time of year. Under these conditions, some birds such as starlings (*Sturnus vulgaris*) remain orientated, that is, flutter in the correct direction, only so long as they can see the sky and the sun is not obscured. If the apparent direction of the sun is changed by mirrors, the orientation of the birds changes accordingly.

The direction of the sun, of course, changes with the time of day, but the migration direction does not. The bird must therefore be able to correct for the movement of the sun; i.e., it must have some sort of internal clock mechanism. The existence of this clock or chronometer, which depends on the light-dark cycle and can be upset by providing an artificial cycle out of phase with the natural one, has been well established by experiments. The exact method by which the sun is used however is still somewhat doubtful. It seems that some species such as starlings can orient by using the azimuthal direction alone, while others may be able to extrapolate the sun's observed path to find the highest point, which in the Northern Hemisphere is always due south and so can serve as a fixed reference point. Nocturnal migrants of course face other problems. Various warblers are able, when migrating in autumn, to maintain correct direction even when they can only see the central part of the sky. However they become disoriented when the stars are hidden by cloud. In these cases it seems fairly clear, though perhaps not certainly proved, that the birds are responding to the form, or "*Gestalt*," of stimuli provided by the star pattern, especially those in the neighbourhood of the North Star. Even the relatively simple task of maintaining a direction on a migratory flight involves formidable sensory and perceptual problems which are not yet fully understood.

Birds can succeed in far more complex orientational tasks than this. It has long been known that birds forcibly removed from the nesting areas during the breeding season, and transported long distances before release, are often able to return to the nest with such speed and reliability that random search for familiar landmarks cannot possibly be the sole explanation. A few instances will show this. Experiments with oceanic birds provide the most telling examples. Thus the Manx shearwater (*Procellaria puffinus*) was the first species used in critical experiments (Matthews, 1968). Shearwaters, taken from their breeding burrows on the island of Skokholm off Pembrokeshire, transported in blacked-out boxes to Cambridge and there released, covered the return journey to Skokholm (approximately 290 miles), in some cases, in no more than six hours. Since this species never normally flies overland, almost the whole of this route must have been completely unfamiliar. Even more remarkable was a bird of the same species which, taken by air to Boston Harbour in the United States and then released, returned to its Skokholm burrow in thirteen days, having covered the journey of 3,050 miles at an average speed, assuming daylight flight only, of over 20 m.p.h. In this case again, the bird can never have been familiar with the East coast of North America and the western Atlantic since this area is beyond its normal geographical range.

One other case, and a very striking one, among oceanic birds may be given, namely that of the Laysan albatross (*Diomedia immutabilis*). In a number of experiments the longest homing flight was from the Philippines to Midway Island—4,120 statute miles covered in thirty-two days. The fastest flight by this species was from Whidbey Island, Washington—3,200 statute miles in 10.1 days, which equals 317 miles per day, though the performance of the Leach's petrel, which covered nearly 3,000 miles at an average of 217 miles per day (Billings, 1968), is in some respects even more astonishing. Again with some of these birds, releases were outside the normal range of the species. In a significant majority of these cases, the birds on release immediately set out in approximately the correct direction for home. This implies that the bird released from an unknown point is already goal oriented and that it can perform the equivalent of fixing its present position on a grid of at least two co-ordinates, calculating the course to steer to regain the co-ordinates characteristic of home, and steering it. This does not mean of course that the bird goes through the sequences of calculations necessary for the human navigator who uses, say, a wireless position line, a sextant observation of the sun, nautical almanac, chart, a ruler and protractor, and so on. The knowledge of how this is achieved is still so incomplete that we are unable to say what measurements the bird takes to fix its position on release. It is however established that it is not responding to forces resulting from the earth's magnetic field and is not likely to be responding to forces relative to the earth's rotation (Coriolis force).*

Observation of the sky seems to be important, for many species are disoriented when the sky is overcast, and they home less well if confined where they cannot see the horizon from the point of release than they do if the whole sky is visible. The latest observations on the homing of the Laysan albatross (Fisher, 1971) suggest strongly that sky observation (i.e., celestial cues) is extremely important in this species. Like the Dove Prion (*Pachyptila desolata*) of the Antarctic (Tickell, 1962), which burrows through the snow to the exact site of its old nest, even though the topography of the whole area is obliterated by fresh snowdrifts, the albatross can also pinpoint a nest site, a territory, or a food-storage place with amazing exactitude. When returning they alight and then zigzag to their former nest sites, frequently pausing to look at the sky. After each pause they may change or correct directions until finally they land up at the exact spot. As Fisher says, "To suggest the use of celestial cues to pinpoint a territory or nest site seems preposterous. . . ." Yet the behaviour appears strongly suggestive of just this! Perhaps our knowledge is still far too meagre to warrant any speculation over such an extreme case.

Matthews (1955, 1968) suggested that diurnal birds obtain the necessary information from observation of the sun's arc, providing they can "remember" the characteristics of the sun's arc at home. Figures 46 and 47 illustrate this diagrammatically. For this system to suffice, the following "automatic" measurements and comparisons will be required: (1) The observation of the

* At the time of writing, some evidence is being produced that under certain conditions some species of birds may be able to detect magnetic forces sufficiently exactly, to render possible their use in orientation.

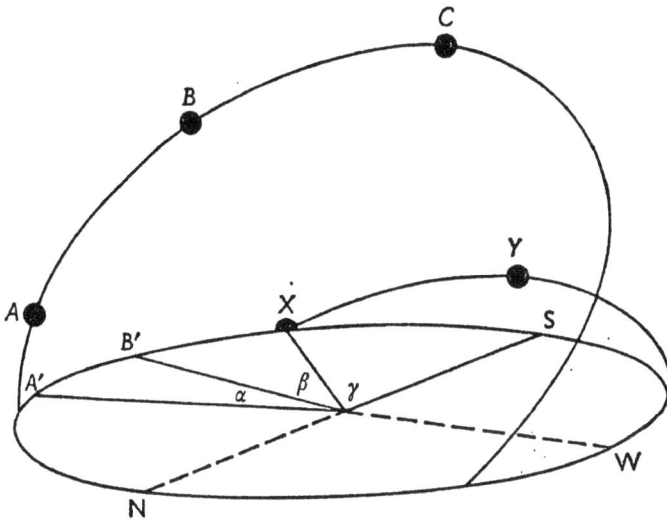

Figure 46 Perspective diagram of the sun arc in summer (upper) and winter (lower) solstices for 51° N. The sun takes the same time to move from A to B as from B to C, but its downward projection moves round the horizon at very different rates from A′ to B′ and B′ to S. Again, BC and XY are the same length of sun arc traversed in the same time, but the equivalent movement round the horizon (azimuth change) B′ to S and X to S is very different. (After Matthews, 1953.)

sun's movements over a small part of this arc, and, by extrapolation, the determination of the highest part of the arc. This will give the geographical south and local noon. (2) Comparison of the remembered noon altitude at home with the observed noon altitude. This will give the difference in latitude. (3) Comparison with home positions azimuth at local noon. This will give the difference in longitude which alternatively might be appreciated as a direct time difference which, on present evidence, seems more probable. Generally some kind of internal clock is necessary and the existence of such a clock is now fairly well established. Astonishing though these conclusions are, they seem to be inescapable on present information, and in fact this theory is simpler than many other hypotheses which have been advanced. The honeybee (and a great many other invertebrates), as is well known, has the ability to detect the polarisation pattern

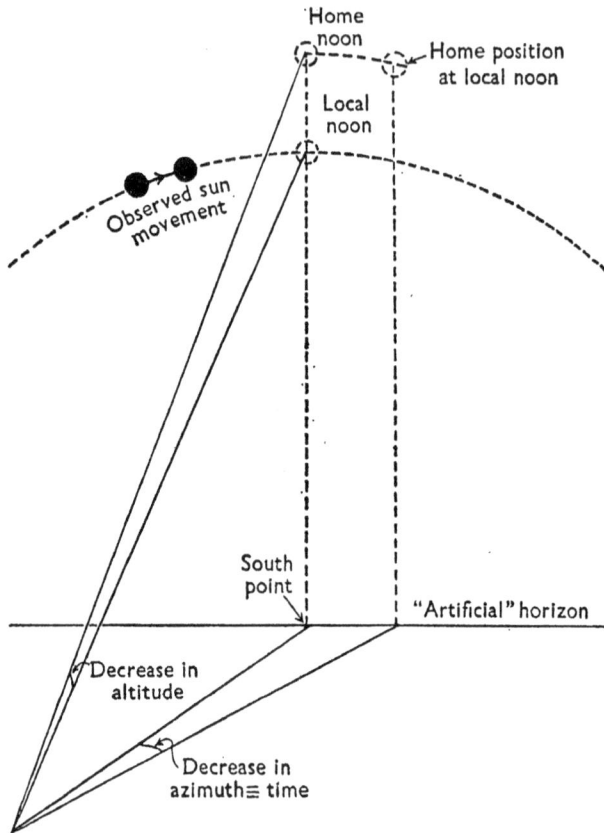

Figure 47 Diagram illustrating the hypotheses of sun navigation. Release to north and west of home (not to south). (After Matthews, 1953.)

of light reflected from the blue sky to aid it in its orientation flights; but birds have no such abilities.

The Matthews' hypothesis just outlined has been criticised by a few workers on the grounds of the improbability of the bird being able to make measurements of the required accuracy. Moreover initial orientation sometimes appears to have occurred before the sun has moved any appreciable distance along its arc. However it seems that a number of these objections are irrelevant, for Matthews has shown that some species of birds have a tendency to orient in a particular direction, usually characteristic of a stock or population, for a short while after release, and indeed it has been shown that pigeons can detect a movement as slow as

PLATE 1:   Sea anemones on the shell of a hermit crab. (From Borradaile, 1923.)

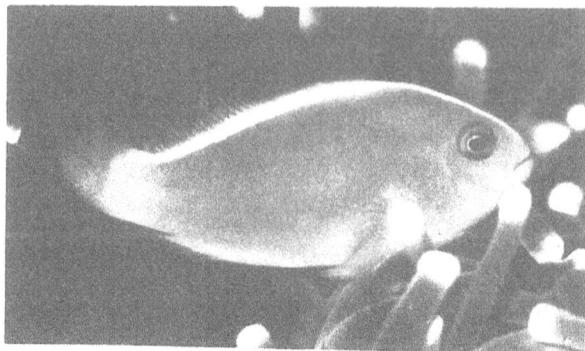

PLATE 2: The Anemone Fish (*Amphiprion skallopisus*) between the tentacles of a Radianthus Anemone. (From Eibl-Eibesfeldt, 1967.)

PLATE 3: Pulse (flash) patterns and flight during flashing in male fireflies of the genus *Photinus* as they would appear in a time-lapse photograph. (Modified from Lloyd, 1966.) The species illustrated are not all sympatric. Small triangles near numbers designating species indicate direction of flight: (1) *consimilis* (slow pulse), (2) *brimleyi*, (3) *consimilis* (fast pulse) and *carolinus*, (4) *collustrans*, (5) *marginellus*, (6) *consanguineus*, (7) *ignitus*, (8) *pyralis*, and (9) *granulatus*. (After Alexander, in Sebeok, 1968.)

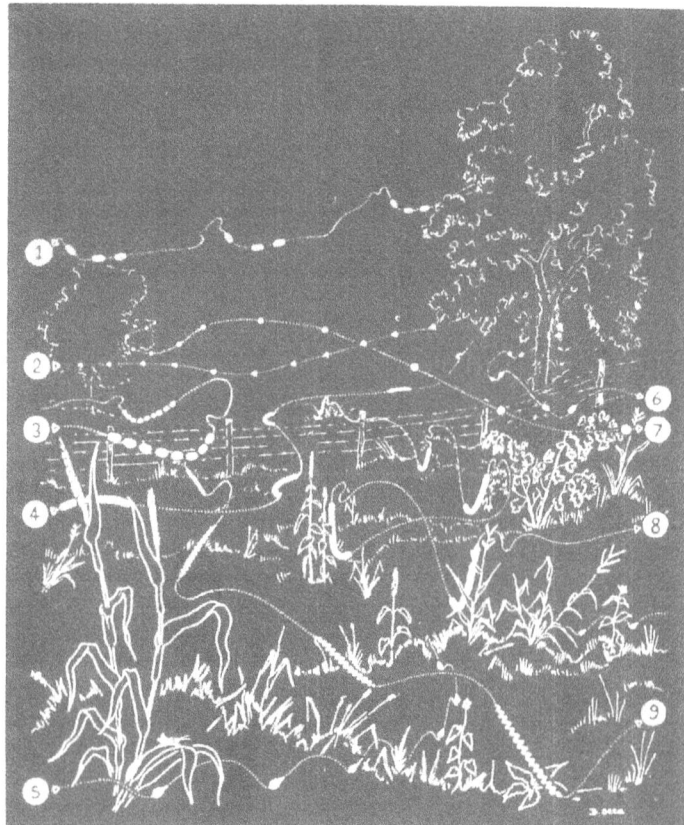

that of the sun—as can crabs! (See Hinde, 1970, p. 191.) There can now be little doubt that sun navigation occurs widely. Exactly what is measured, and in what degree of precision, is still in dispute. It has been suggested that the bird may measure the sun's altitude and rate of change of altitude. This, it is claimed, would overcome the major difficulty of the sun-arc hypothesis since the accuracy of observation required is much less. However, so far, critical evidence discriminating the two hypotheses is lacking; theoretically, the birds could home successfully merely by attempting to restore the sun's altitude to the approximate home value at the time, according to its internal chronometer. In this event, the path followed would be the type shown in Figure 48. But there is no evidence that the birds do fly such a pecul-

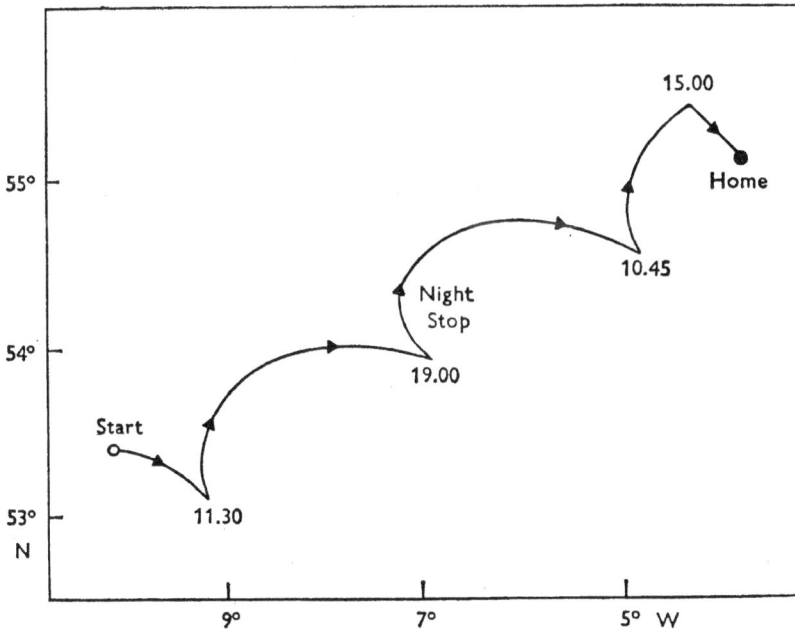

Figure 48 The curved path a bird would follow if it homed by attempting only to restore the sun altitude to the appropriate value for the time according to its internal "chronometer." In this example a pigeon released 280 miles from home and flying at 19 m.p.h. would take two days to home. The final sharp turn is where it enters the area of known landmarks. (After Tunmore, 1960.)

iar course when homing; and to do so would extend the distance flown so greatly that on this basis, if no other, it seems highly improbable. However such a theory could account for some of the slow returns observed in other species. But however satisfactory the sun-orientation hypothesis may be, it does not account for the ability of many species which orient at night. Although it is clear that birds can orient in a given direction in the night sky, there is no certain evidence that they can navigate by this method; there is however some rather doubtful indications from Planetarium experiments that they may be able to do so.

The question of the actual path followed by birds on homing flights has been much illuminated by the development, in recent years, of radio transmitters sufficiently minute to be attached to migrating birds without interfering with flight abilities. When this is done, it often transpires that the tracks are much straighter than we previously had any reason to suspect. Figure

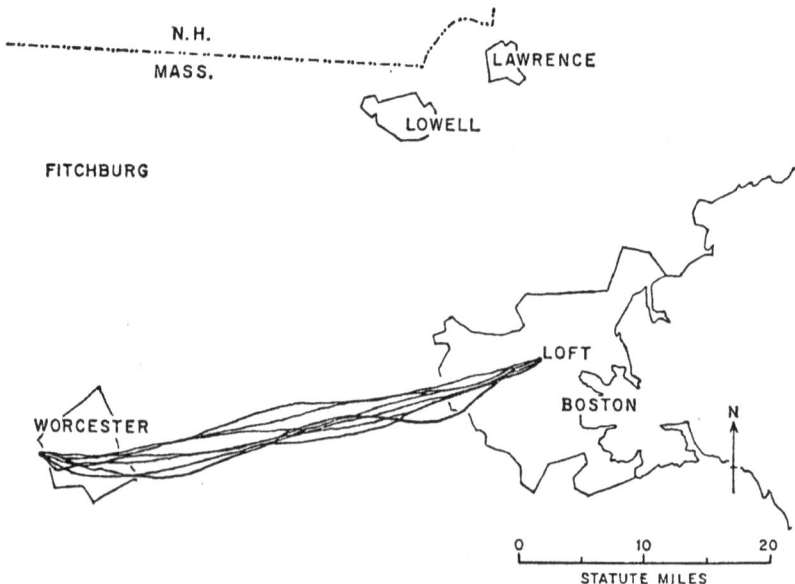

Figure 49 The control tracks of several pigeons from Worcester, showing the typical straightness of tracks found with the new tracking procedure. (From Walcott and Michener, 1967.)

49 shows the course taken by several homing pigeons from Worcester, Massachusetts, as detected by the new tracking procedure. Still more extraordinary are some of the flight paths of nocturnal spring migrants carrying radio transmitters weighing only 3 grams. Figure 50 shows some remarkable performances in the Wisconsin area. Thus a Swainson's thrush (*Hylocichla ustulata*) took off on its spring migration at 20.00 hours and was shad-

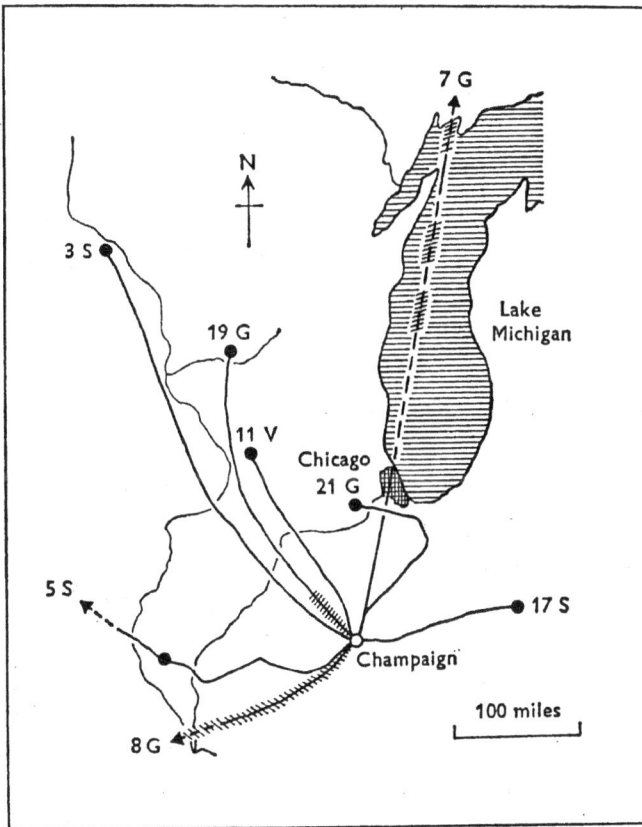

Figure 50 Flight paths of nocturnal spring migrants carrying miniature radio transmitters from Champaign, Illinois. Flights under open skies except where paths are double shaded. A dot indicates that the bird landed, an arrowhead that it was still flying when contact was lost. Major rivers, as well as Lake Michigan, are indicated. G=Grey-cheeked Thrush, S=Swainson's Thrush, V=Veery. Numbers are flight references. (After Cochran et al., 1967.)

owed through the night until it landed, eight hours later, 450 miles northwest, achieving a performance even more remarkable than appears at first sight. For the actual track flown measured only 453 miles. Even if the bird was flying a compass course and not homing to its breeding quarters, such accuracy, as Matthews remarked, is the envy of the human navigator. In another case, a grey-cheeked thrush (*Hylocichla minima*) was tracked for 400 miles (Figure 50). It took off at 19.55 hours under a clear sky and flew NNE at 20 m.p.h., helped by a tail wind of 22 m.p.h. After 140 miles its course took it over Lake Michigan, while the plane which was following it had to take the overland route for safety. However, contact with this particular bird was renewed in Wisconsin at 02.48 hours, but then the plane had to turn back because of a thunderstorm! It must be accepted of course that the bird had an initial innate ability to perceive and co-ordinate information from various stimuli in the environment such as rate of movement and altitude of the sun and possibly also of the stars.

In the case of the thrushes just discussed, it is to be presumed that they have some visual knowledge of the environment and may have flown something like this course before, at least in the opposite direction, a few months previously. But with night fliers it is extremely doubtful whether visual aids would be much help, particularly in the case of the monumental flight in a thunderstorm over Lake Michigan! And with the homing experiments, quite clearly the bird can have nothing in the way of a plan or map (based on previous experience) in its head to guide it. With homing birds, we can say with conviction that they have compass orientation to start with and landmarks nearer home towards the end of the flight to guide them; between these, all must, so it seems, be accomplished by true navigation. With night fliers, and indeed often with day fliers, celestial cues, whether from stars or sun, will often be lacking. And even when it would seem possible that nocturnal migrants might be orienting by recognisable and known landmarks, a bird may often in practice seem to disregard landmark features as navigational aids. Thus birds migrating over the Gulf of Mexico do sometimes appear to alter their direction on the basis of topographical cues, though, when inland, large rivers do not seem to be employed as guides. No doubt birds recognise many characteristics of the winds. Generally they select winds which are favourable for their goal; when forced to use unfavourable winds they correct to a high degree for lateral drift. Migrants appear to select for wind speeds within their flight capabilities—waterfowl for wind speeds above 30 knots, and passerine birds for wind speeds below 10 knots (Belrose, quoted in Matthews, 1968). Since the birds appear to be able to determine the direction and strength of the wind, it seems plausible to suggest that the wind can be used as an orientation reference. It is known that winds blowing across a terrain develop a "gust structure" which migrating birds might, at least theoretically, be able to detect. It may well be that the turbulent structure of winds serves as an additional means of orientation when on migration.

It is also important to consider other possibilities. We need to know more not only about the sensory physiology of birds but also about the atmospheric ecology of migration when neither sky nor ground is visible. It has already been said that orientation to the earth's magnetic field, while possible, still seems improbable. Similarly, inertial navigation has been discussed; but here the doubts and difficulties seem even greater, and it is hard to suppose that inertial navigation in anything like the form employed in aircraft could be involved. Indeed, biologists appear to be grasping at straws. It is possible that birds communicating with one another by flight calls might detect differential wind-drift experiences by upper and lower members of a flock and thus determine the direction of the shear. Also there are many meteorological conditions—including such patterns of air movement as roll vortices or internal gravity waves—which may produce detectable updraughts, providing both useful lift and information about the direction of wind or wind shear (Griffin, 1969). Over the oceans it is quite conceivable that birds are able to detect local characteristics of air temperature, circulation, or cloud formation, and of wave pattern due to persistence of regular winds. Similarly, landfall on islands may be easier than the ordinary landsman supposes, owing to the fact that the oceanic islands often have a characteristic cloud formation above them, visible for one hundred or more miles away. Moreover, oceanic islands in areas of steady winds may produce "wave shadows" on the sea surface which at least in theory could be an aid to landfall and to navigation.

It has been shown by Keeton (ref. Griffin, 1969) that some homing pigeons can select approximately the homeward direction within a few minutes after release in unfamiliar territory. In this case there is convincing evidence that the bird could not have seen the sun through holes in the cloud layer. If there is precise sensibility to atmospheric pressure, this again could help in allowing birds to judge their altitude and could be a means whereby they are able to determine the presence of updraughts or downdraughts—whether to obtain a lift from the former or to use patterns of vertical air movements to obtain directional guidance. Finally, there is a comb-like structure in the avian eye (the pecten) which forms a large blind spot located in that part of the visual field that usually views the sky. This is possibly useful for viewing the sun and perhaps for determining the altitude above the horizon. It is heavily pigmented and so would help to absorb the intense light of the sun's image, and its rich blood flow may distribute the resultant heat and so avoid a damage to the adjacent retina.

Here, at the present time, we are well into the regions of speculation. But there is one thing we can say without fear of contradiction: it is that the performance of birds of migratory and homing flights, when considered in terms of laboratory experiments on latent learning, pattern recognition, perceptual organisation, and exploratory learning, far surpasses anything hitherto envisaged as possible. It is indeed true that by simplifying the circumstances to which an animal is exposed in the laboratory beyond a certain point, we make it impossible for that animal to show the real extent of its capabilities. To confine a highly organised animal may result in creating a moron. The principle of "Occam's Razor," according to which the simplest explanation available is regarded as the most likely to be true, *can* be utterly misleading. Organisms often, perhaps one should say nearly always, turn out to be more complex than at first supposed.

FORM AND PATTERN IN EVOLUTION

The Evolution of Beauty

Finally, to end this chapter, I want to deal briefly with the question of the origin and meaning of the form and pattern of animals in evolution. Everyone knows that the vast majority of butterflies and moths strike the human observer as extraordinarily beautiful, showing exquisite patterns on the wing; and it is difficult to believe that this is in any sense an accident. These patterns must be perceived either by other moths or by some animal responding to them. Then we encounter the problem of appreciation of form and beauty in evolution. Birds of paradise are perhaps the most extraordinary examples of this. These birds of paradise first became known in Europe in the sixteenth century. They were imported from native collectors in the East Indies to the "plume marts" of Paris and sold for human adornment. Their beauty was so astounding that it was seriously thought that the birds were wanderers from paradise—hence their name! It was the habit of the native collectors to cut off the feet before preparing the plumes for export, and one species, the first of the group to be named by Linnaeus, was called *Paradisea apoda* and that is still its scientific name today—the only evidence, so far as I am aware, that that rather pompous and intense genius Linnaeus had a sense of humour. But it was not until the work of Alfred Russell Wallace, about 1857, that we came to have some comprehension of these extraordinary animals. So extraordinary are they that when, about the turn of the century, a particularly marvellous and bizarre species appeared in Paris and was shown to Dr. Bowdler Sharpe, who was keeper of the birds in the British Museum, he first refused to believe that it was not a human artifact! There again one has to assume that the extraordinary beauty of form and plumage must be appreciated in some degree by other members of the species and that it was in some way appreciation of its beauty that was responsible for its evolution.

The bowerbirds are hardly less remarkable (Gilliard, 1969); they seem to have an artistic colour sense and moreover they have great skill as architects. The bowers which they build are used for their courtship display. So remarkable are they that early naturalists coming across a particularly large and well-constructed type, produced by a New Guinea species, actually believed it to be a house constructed by man! Other early naturalists were so astounded by these discoveries that they declared birds should be divided into two groups—bowerbirds in one and all the rest in the other. These birds still pose many mysteries, and I personally find the fantastic development of beautiful and complex patterning of the male birds of paradise and the astounding behavioural complexities of the bowerbirds very hard to account for as simply one of those "accidental" isolation mechanisms which keep one species separate from another. They seem to have gone too far in developing the fantastic and the beautiful; they seem also to have acquired a momentum of their own which on ordinary selection principles still seems to be inexplicable. Indeed Professor G. Evelyn Hutchison of Yale wrote not long ago that the behaviour of bowerbirds "in complexity and refinement is unique in the non-human parts of the animal kingdom." Can we then assume, as most people becoming aware of them for the first time assume, that there is something of true aesthetic appreciation in the organisms which have produced them?

Beauty in Bird Song

Finally there is the question of beauty in bird song. E. A. Armstrong and J. Hall-Craggs have discussed with great sensitivity and perception the aesthetic impact of bird songs on human beings from the earliest recorded time. (See Hinde, 1969.) Hall-Craggs has paid particular attention to the blackbird's (*Turdus merula*) song, and her work on this has also been substantiated in other species to some degree. She finds (Hall-Craggs, 1962) that if a blackbird is singing well—that is to say singing well from our aesthetic point of view—and a neighbouring blackbird approaches its territory, the singer may sing more vigorously, but certainly not more musically, in order to intimidate the intruder; in fact, on the contrary, it becomes a little upset and the song becomes temporarily loose and disjointed. Phrases are left unfinished and the pauses in between the phrases become even longer than normal; so it looks as if the bird has to attend to the form of its song in order to be able to sing well by our standards. Now this principle may be applied in a broader context, for if one records the song of a particular blackbird daily, throughout its singing season, some changes of apparently aesthetic significance are detected. During the reproductive period the song is highly functional and the bird is competing with others in its task of securing a territory and attracting a mate and then maintaining its territory during the breeding period. Later in the season, when these needs have been fulfilled, the song becomes further organised, and in a manner so closely resembling our own ideas of musical form that it is difficult to deny that it is musically improved. So we appear to be moving towards the type which we call "art music" where our experience of musical scores enables us to guess what kind of change is about to happen next. And this sense of musical form seems to fit a number of bird songs in a most extraordinary way. These and many other similar observations do, I think, amount to a quite serious argument for something like musical appreciation, albeit on an elementary scale, existing in a good many birds.

Very striking confirmation of this conclusion has come from the recent work of Hall-Craggs (1972) and Thorpe (1972) on the antiphonal singing of a particular, compulsively duetting, species of African shrike, the tropical bou-bou or Bell shrike (*Laniarius aethiopicus*). Hall-Craggs points out that in examining the "musicality" of bird vocalisations we have first to consider the bird ear as an analyser comparable to the human ear. Music requires definition in respect of (1) the unit and (2) the form. Music primarily consists of melodic motion and "melodic motion is change of pitch in time" (Helmholtz). In this case two methods of analysis were employed: (1) physical measurement of tones and intervals and (2) aural determination of intervals. (1) was employed on the vocalisations of 10 pairs and a discrete population of *L. aethiopicus major*. In (2) a large number of intervals came from race *major* and a few intervals came from the duets of several species and races of *Laniarius*.

Because in *L. aethiopicus major* the notes of the duet (polyphonic singing) often coincide to form harmonic intervals, it is suggested that in polyphonic singing the beats, arising from the coincidence of fundamentals in small intervals (seconds) and between the harmonies of wider intervals, lead the birds to approach as nearly as possible the exact ratios of justly intoned consonant intervals—which is what we find: namely that *consonances are preferred to dissonances*. In fact there are reasons for supposing that consonant harmonic intervals are likely to be more effective for communication than dissonant harmonic intervals. Thus both explanations, (1) and (2) above, may be combined as leading to more efficient communication.

Comparisons were also made between "primitive," "classical," and contemporary human music and the shrike songs. Man's early attempts at polyphony usually involved consonant intervals; and it may be precisely because *L. aethiopicus* uses a rudimentary form of polyphonic music that the resultant intervals are predominantly consonant.

In conclusion I believe that among the many facts mentioned and discussed in this chapter the reader will find much evidence that many of the higher animals display abilities which approach, and even exceed, those of which man is capable. My own experience is that the longer I continue with this kind of work the greater my respect for the animal kingdom becomes. The more one investigates, the more elaborate, more organised, and the more highly adjusted the sensory powers of these animals are found to be. This leads me to an ever-new sense of wonder and an increasing appreciation of the value and significance, indeed the "worthwhileness," of study of the animal kingdom.

PART TWO

HUMAN NATURE

The distinction between man and animals is in one sense only a difference in degree. But the extent of the degree makes all the difference. The Rubicon has been crossed.

ALFRED NORTH WHITEHEAD,
from *Modes of Thought,* 1938.

Chapter 6

THE DEVELOPMENT OF
HUMAN BEHAVIOUR

My aim in this second part is to discuss a number of the main characteristics of human nature in relation to the behaviour of animals, especially the primates. In a sense, all the topics raised in the first part are relevant to the second also, and the reader will find continual cross reference helpful.

We should at this stage consider a little more closely the use of the phrase "human nature." Professor René Dubos (1970) has discussed this problem with admirable insight. People often speak of human nature with the implication that they are referring chiefly, or perhaps exclusively, to the moral and psychological side of man's nature. But, as biologists, we must adopt a wider definition than this and include both the anatomical structures and physiological mechanisms of the human body, both those which are inherited and those which are acquired or changed by experience.

THE NATURE *VERSUS* NURTURE CONTROVERSY

The controversy over how far man is a product of his environment and how far of his genetic make-up has in various forms engaged the mind of man since classical times. This resulted in the rather sterile and now outmoded "nature *versus* nurture" controversy. Those who advocated the nurture theory of human experience (Hippocrates, John Locke, and Jean Jacques Rousseau) all regarded the newborn child as like a blank page, a *tabula rasa*, on which is inscribed during life, as a result of learning and other interaction with the environment, the essential nature of the human being. This led to the belief that schools and universities could, if they fulfilled their function perfectly, produce at will any type of genius whether Aquinas or Dante, Shakespeare or Newton.

Those who took the "nature" view, particularly Thomas Hobbes and Herbert Spencer and of course many since the days of Darwin who believed that they were interpreting the modern scientific view of heredity and evolution, held that the genetic make-up determines to a very large extent the essential nature of a person. Francis Galton even concluded that the genetic view would account satisfactorily for the social stratification of society. He implied that judges begot judges, whereas workmen, artisans, and even businessmen were not likely to be born with the innate mental ability required for successful performance in the intellectual world! Professor Dubos shows that the same conflict can be found expressed in the views of Freud on the one hand and of Jung on the other.

Dubos rightly points out that this nature *versus* nurture controversy was often a false one to the extent that genes do not actually determine the characteristics by which we know a person; they merely govern the responses to experience from which the personality is built. Much light has recently been thrown on the mechanisms through which environmental stimuli determine which parts of the genetic repertoire are repressed and which parts are allowed free range. It is now thought by geneticists that at any given time in any specialised cell only about 10 or 15 per cent of the total genes in the organism are active. And this is true of nerve cells as well as of any other type. Moreover we now know that there are many mechanisms by which genes can be activated or depressed, and it is natural to assume that the activity of genes is not only governed by substances such as hormones but by many other influences present in the cellular fluid, activating or repressing in their effects.

As much of the work discussed in this chapter will make clear, early influences certainly play an important role in converting the genetic potentialities into physical and mental attributes; but it is also obvious that although there are sensitive periods when these influences are at their most potent, the human organism is undoubtedly changing continually through life. Leaving aside the result of the ageing process it is also clear that, much more important than ageing, physical and mental attributes are constantly being acted on and so changed by stimuli from the environment. Almost everything we do, almost every response we make, results in the acquisition of memories that will alter our subsequent responses to the same stimulus. The brain is able to register and store experiences until the time of death; and other parts of the nervous system, notably the reticulo-endothelial system, provide the mechanism for a kind of biological memory. And mechanisms of this kind will govern many of our physiological responses such as our allergic sensitisation to particular toxins, for instance those from poison oak or poison ivy, or, alternatively, provide us with antitoxic immunity to such diseases as tetanus and smallpox. So each person's constitution is made up of the evolutionary past embodied in the genetic apparatus and of the experiential past incorporated in the various forms of mental and biological memory. Yet above and beyond all this interplay of genetic make-up and individual experience affecting our physiological constitution, we have in addition, as is discussed elsewhere in this book, the real freedom to make decisions, to choose, to organise, to reject, and to create. To this extent then, and it is to a very great extent, man has the power and the responsibility of guiding his own development, and in highly organised societies, of affecting the future not only of his own individual life but of the race.

THE DEVELOPMENT OF HUMAN BEHAVIOUR

In discussing the development of human behaviour it is far from easy to know where to start. Coleridge (1772–1834) says: "The history of a man for the nine months preceding his birth would probably be far more interesting and contain events of greater moment, than all the three-score and ten years that follow it!" (Quotation from Leonard Carmichael, 1970.) A similar idea was expressed by Oliver Wendell Holmes who burst into verse as follows:

> So the stout foetus, kicking and alive,
> leaps from the fundus for his final dive.
> Tired of the prison where his legs were curled,
> he pants, like Rasselas, for a wider world.
> No more to him their wonted joys afford
> the fringed placenta and the knotted cord.

But what hard facts are there to support these poetical, albeit illuminating, sentiments? There is in fact a great deal of information about the behaviour of the mammalian foetus both from experimental studies of animal foetuses as well as from a great body of material derived from the study of human foetuses operatively removed, while still alive, from the mother's body. Investigations of very young foetuses (less than nine weeks) are of limited interest for our purposes. Their behaviour mostly consists of somewhat random movements, dependent upon which muscles first reach their functional state. Of more interest is the fact that at about fourteen weeks quite complex and apparently co-ordinated movements of the legs can result from stroking the sole of the foot with a hair. These complex movements include bending of the big toe, fanning of the other toes, slight bending of the sole of the foot, as well as traction higher up the limb. The only point here that seems worth noting is that, although these are responses which are often regarded as "reflex," they are far more elaborate than we should include under that term if it were strictly applied. Essentially a reflex is a quick and automatic response of a single structure, ideally a single muscle, to a "simple" stimulus. In the case that I have just mentioned, we know from a great deal of other work that even stroking of the skin is in fact quite a complex stimulus, and obviously the responses I have described are complex too. Even at fourteen weeks there is an elaborate neuromuscular co-ordination. It is however still questionable to conclude, as some have done, that before birth the organism reacts as a whole. There is undoubtedly a great deal of progress in the co-ordination of movement during foetal life, but I think it would be unwise (Carmichael, 1970, p. 515) to go further than this.

Perception During Foetal Life

The study of the development of perception in the foetus is however more relevant to our present interests. Bishop Berkeley, in 1709, put forward the view that perception (such as that of visual space) is dependent not only on the eyes but also on touch. Berkeley's argument was as follows (Pastore, 1965): "Consider, for example, a globe as the first object within reach of an infant. The visual sensation is a certain gradation of colours in the same plane. . . . in conjunction with that sensation, the infant extends his arms and feels the rotundity of the globe. After many trials, the visual sensation serves as a sign for (or suggests) the tactual idea of palpation of the globe. . . . the infant will thus have the perception of solidity even when touch . . . is prevented."

This was known as the empiricist, or learning, theory of the visual perception of space and it has had a great many supporters. But in fact it was essentially disproved more than a century ago by Samuel Bailey (1842) who pointed out that the behaviour of newborn mammals offers a better test of Berkeley's theory than does a study of the newborn human infant. As was shown earlier, a great deal of observation has been made on the be-

216

haviour of newborn mammals, and it is abundantly clear that a great many young mammals, probably the vast majority, are able, for instance, to discriminate depth as soon as locomotion is adequate, even when locomotion begins at birth (Gibson, 1958). The experiments on response to the visual cliff are a particular example of this. (See pp. 184, 185.)

Now it is quite obvious that the human infant comes into the world incomparably less well prepared to cope with the changes and chances of its visual environment than does, say, a rat, a kitten, or a giraffe. But nevertheless it seems safe to say that the human foetus at birth is not totally unprepared for its forthcoming independent life. It is, in fact, all a matter of degree. Many conclusions on this problem are very speculative, but quite a number of competent physiologists and clinicians express the view that the child comes into the world with a dim perception of an outer world, conditioned by perhaps quite elaborate sensory experiences within the womb. To quote Peterson and Rainey (1910): "The newborn comes into the world with a small store of experience and associated feelings and a shadowy consciousness."

More convincing and for our purposes more relevant conclusions than this concern the nature/nurture controversy dealt with in Chapter 4 above. There seems in fact little doubt (as Carmichael, 1970, says, p. 535) that in all mammals, including man, early behaviour is a result of the activation of structures that are as they are largely as a result of genetic endowment. There is no reasonable doubt that whatever behaviour the newborn infant displays, what we may call "the standard prenatal reactions" are as surely hereditary as are hair colour, tooth pattern, or skeletal make-up. This amounts to saying (Hirsch, 1962, that the behaviour of the human organism cannot be fully understood if we disregard the fact that it is an integrated and co-ordinated system with a behaviour, in some respects at least, adapted to its environment; and it is also a member of a population with a unique evolutionary history adapting it to the niche it presently occupies.

Let us now look at the evidences for characteristically animal-type responses in the young infant—but always, before we start, bearing in mind that for "instinct" we can read environmentally stable behaviour, as in contrast to environmentally labile behaviour.

One other important question arises concerning the behaviour of the foetus, that is, "Does the foetus display characteristic responses to pleasant and unpleasant stimuli while still in the womb?" and, if it does, "Do these responses give plausibility to what psychologists normally call the concept of 'drive'?" The answer seems to be in the affirmative, for there is evidence that facial expression can begin in the foetus in the relatively early weeks of its life; so at any rate the expressive pattern of the facial muscles, which is of so much significance in pleasant and unpleasant situations in later life, has certainly had ample opportunity for exercise during the prenatal period (Carmichael, 1970, p. 526). Certainly the foetus can respond to stimuli such as contact stimulation, loud sound, possibly olfactory stimulation, etc., which in its later life are likely to have an affective component and to be the basis of pleasantness and unpleasantness—so it may well be that there is something, which we should be justified in calling "drive," activating the unborn foetus. I expect many, probably most, mothers, having experienced the onslaught from within of the "little kicker in the dark," would be predisposed to agree with this view!

Next let us consider the evidence for those facets of "instinctive behaviour" to which we give the names "fixed-action patterns," "vacuum activities," "consummatory acts," and "consummatory situations."

Fixed-action Patterns in the Infant

As we have seen, this behaviour facet is a structured pattern of movement which, though different examples differ in their degree of complexity, is not altogether unlike a reflex. In one respect, however, a fixed-action pattern differs radically from a reflex in that whereas the threshold of activation of a reflex is, on the whole, highly constant, the threshold of activation of fixed-action pattern varies according to the state of the organism. Fixed-action patterns can vary in complexity from the simplest loco-motory and orientational movements to behaviour such as swallowing, yawning, and sneezing (previously regarded as reflex but now known, as a result of work in recent years in the case of the action of swallowing, to be of immense complication (see Chapter 4 above) to, at the other extreme, certain special displays in birds, such as are to be seen in many excellent modern documentary films of bird life (e.g., N. Tinbergen's *Signals for Survival*), which give the impression of an elaborate ritual.

In comparison with birds, the higher primates, particularly man himself, are poorly equipped with fixed-action patterns. But to the student of human behaviour, these patterns are of special interest because of the important roles they play throughout life in controlling facial expression. (Tomkins, 1962–63, quoted by Bowlby, 1969, p. 66.) This is especially so during infancy, before any systems responsible for more sophisticated types of behaviour become available. The most striking fixed-action pattern of the newborn infant is head turning and sucking. The head turning consists of an alternating side-to-side movement which in itself can be regarded as a fixed-action pattern. It can be evoked by tactile stimuli of many sorts when applied anywhere within a large zone surrounding the mouth; though (Prechtl, 1958) the movement varies in frequency and amplitude, it is stereotyped in form and usually appears immediately a hungry baby makes contact with the breast.

The side-to-side fixed-action pattern can easily be produced in premature babies of twenty-eight weeks and over, but at that stage no further action appears. But in a normal newborn, there is a directed head turning movement which is organised on much more complex lines than is the side-to-side movement. When a tactile stimulus is given on the skin immediately adjacent to the lips, the head turns in the direction from which the stimulus is coming. If the stimulus is kept constant for a while, then moved around, the head follows. This shows not only that the movement is elicited by tactile stimuli, but that its form and direction are continuously regulated by the precise location of those stimuli. (N.B. Even at full term only about two thirds of babies show directed head turning.)

The outcome of these items of behaviour, organised as a chain, is as follows (Prechtl, 1958): (1) The movement of the head leads the baby's mouth to come into contact with the mother's nipple. (2) A tactile stimulus occurring on his lips or the immediately adjacent area leads a baby's mouth to open and his lips to grasp the nipple. (3) A tactile stimulation anywhere in his mouth area and probably especially on his hard palate (Gunther, 1961) elicits sucking movements. (4) Presence of milk in the mouth elicits swallowing. Now it is quite certain that the ordinary idea that a baby feeds merely because it is hungry is not accurate. If given an empty bottle immediately after birth, the baby is driven to try to feed. There have been a number of careful experiments on the shape of objects and the texture of objects in the mouth which elicit the sucking behaviour. One of the results of this kind of work, of great interest to the ethologist, is that the human infant (and this is equally true of puppies and kittens) gives clear evidence of a "need" to suck for a period of two and one half hours each day (considerably longer than that necessary to achieve the normal milk intake), quite largely independent of the nutritional state and the nutritional needs. Indeed Bridger (1962) found that human newborns sucked more when satiated and experimentally aroused than when food-deprived. (See also Eibl-Eibesfeldt, 1967.)

We can summarise all this by saying that there seems to be no essential difference between the early feeding behaviour and orientation of babies and the similar fixed-action patterns of many of the higher animals.

Innate Behaviour in Infants

A baby's smile is one of the most endearing things about it. It has more than once been suggested (e.g., Konrad Lorenz)

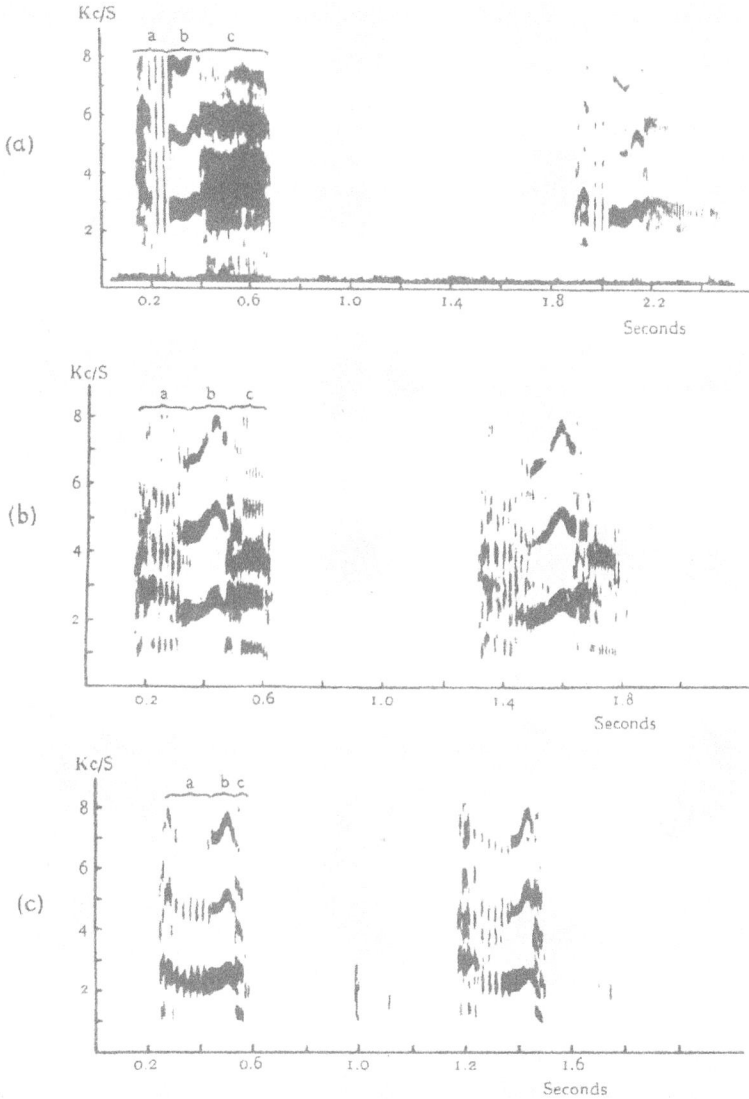

Sound spectrograms of typical recordings of two consecutive calls of individual Sandwich terns. Note that each call is divided into three segments, *a*, *b*, and *c*. Segment *a* contains anything from 7 to 15 vertical bars which indicate brief pulses of sound of great frequency range. Segment *b* shows the fundamental and usually two harmonics rising and falling during the duration of the phrase of 0.07 to 0.15 s to give an inverted "v" or inverted "u" pattern. Segment *c*, of duration between 0.01 and 0.28 s, again shows vertical bars varying in number from 3 to 28 and showing peaks of intensity at particular frequencies rather than the very wide and uniformly distributed frequency range displayed by the bars in segment *a*. (From Hutchison *et al.*, 1968.)

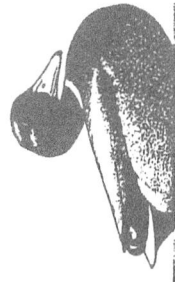

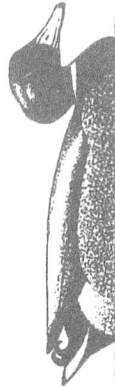

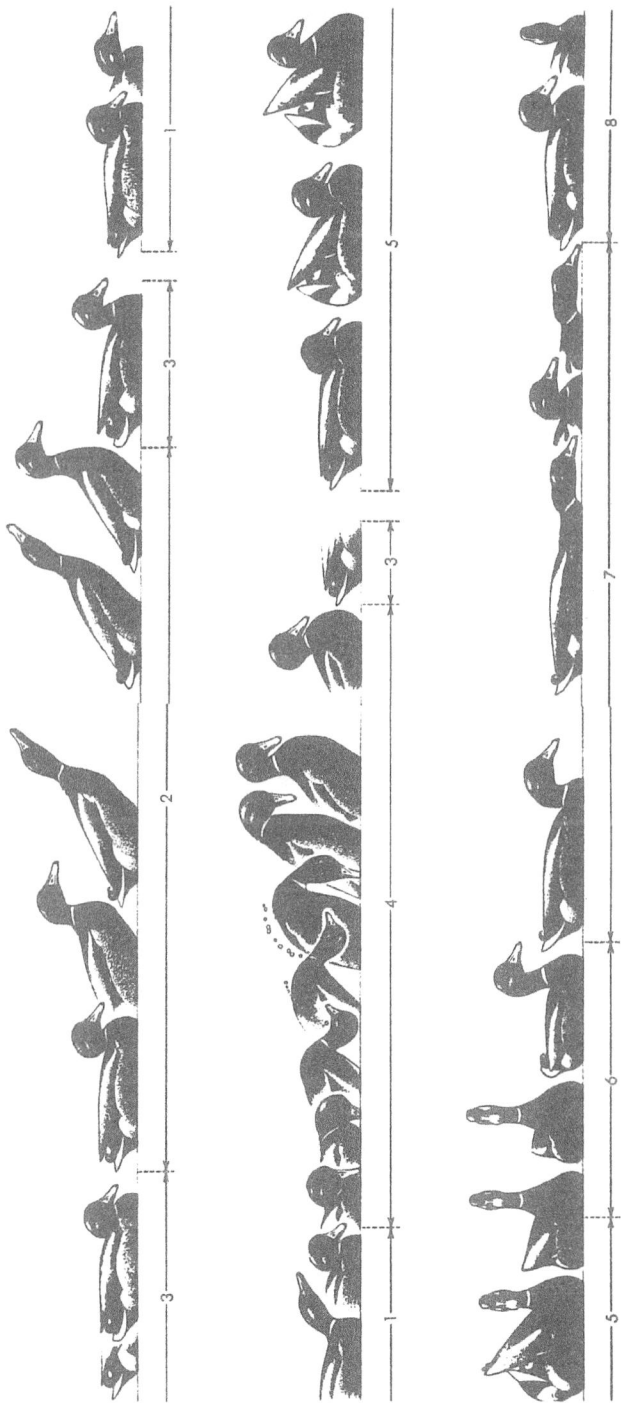

PLATE 5: Courtship movements belonging to the common genetic heritage of surface-feeding ducks as shown in the Mallard Drake. Top: the basic movements of courtship: (1) bill shake, (2) shake and stretch, (3) tail shake, (4) grunt whistle, (5) head-up, tail-up, (6) looking toward the female, (7) nod swimming, (8) showing the back of the head, (9) pull up, (10) up-down movement. The movement patterns 1–4 and 10 appear during group courtship of the drakes; 5–9, on the other hand, appear during the sexual courtship before the female in a coupled sequence from 5 up. In the lower three rows complete movement protocols are represented. (After Lorenz, 1958.)

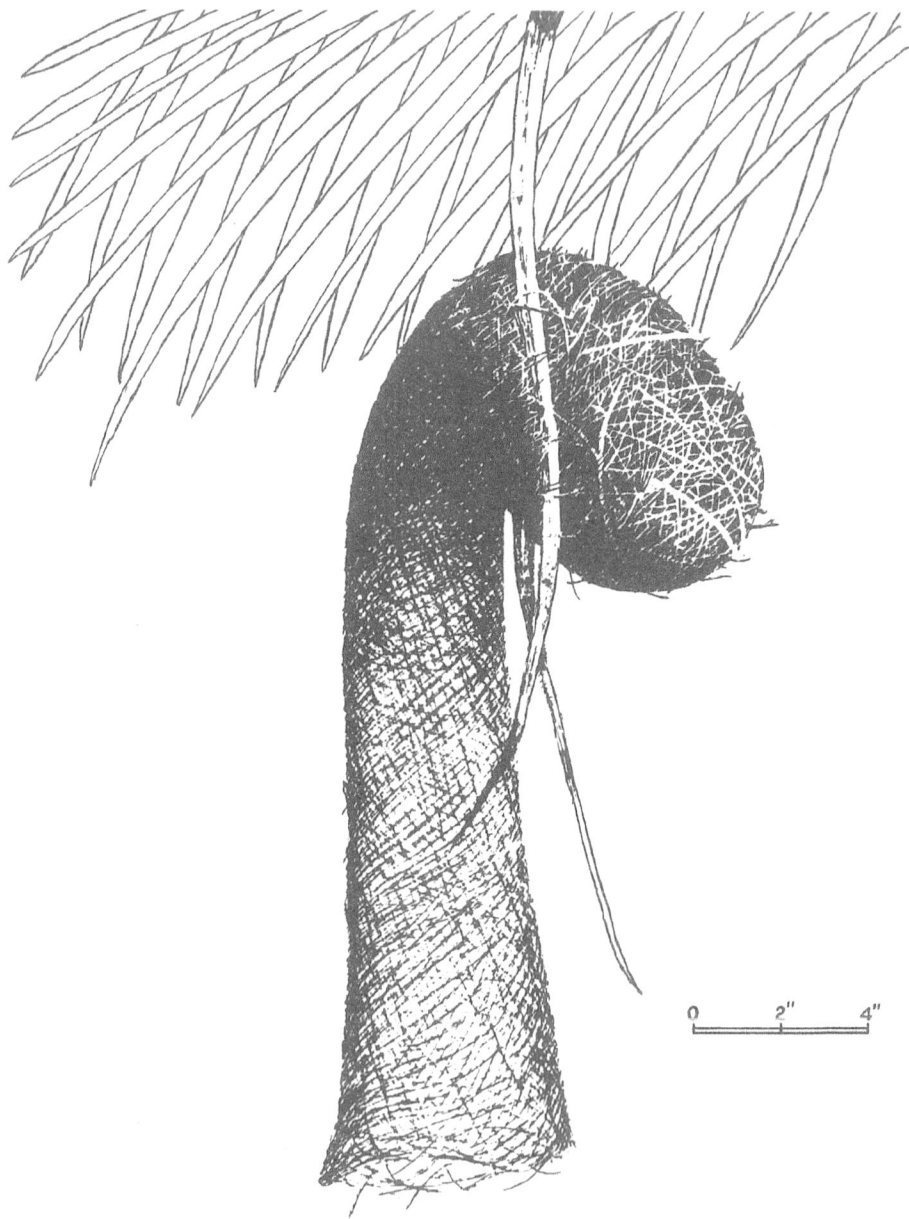

PLATE 6: Nest of a Weaverbird (*Malimbus scutatus*). (**After Crook, 1963.**)

that the fascination of the smile to any normal adult human being, and particularly to females, is such that it in itself provides evidence for the human baby's smile having been developed and selected for, under the intense pressure of natural selection which must have operated under conditions of nomadism, where being left behind must have been one of the greatest dangers to survival. The difficulty of ignoring a crying baby may also be another example. Lorenz has also argued that the pitch and rhythm of a baby's cry are such that crying is one of the most disturbing sounds to which human beings can be exposed! In view of these facts it is perhaps surprising that infanticide by exposure has been as common and widespread as it has in the history of the human race.

Just as with sucking behaviour, so the smile has been the object of a great deal of careful research in recent years. Particularly noteworthy has been the work of Dr. Ambrose (1961). We can summarise this and other work by saying that the motor pattern of a smile can be described as instinctive, in the usual meaning of that term as I employ it in this book. Although smiles can be elicited by a range of stimuli, the baby is so biased that, from the first, some stimuli are more effective than others. From the nature of the case, the effective stimuli for the smile are far more likely to come from the baby's mother, or mother figure, and from other people in his family than from any other source. As a result of this we can say that, by processes of learning, the effective stimuli become restricted to those of human origin, notably the voice and the face. In addition we can say a baby's smile acts as a social releaser, the predictable outcome of which is that the mother responds in a loving way which prolongs social interaction between them and increases the likelihood of her exhibiting maternal behaviour in the future. So the first function of a baby's smile is to increase interaction between mother and baby and maintain them in proximity to each other.

A baby's smile develops through four main phases. First comes a phase of spontaneous and reflex smiling during which a response is elicited occasionally by any of a great variety of stimuli but is fleeting and incomplete. This phase starts at birth and usually lasts about five weeks. During this period the response is so incomplete that it leaves the spectator wholly unmoved, which is to say that it has no functional consequence. During the fourth and fifth weeks, though still very brief, it is developing slightly and becoming more complete and begins to have social effects. During the first fortnight of life almost the only condition in which a smile can be elicited from a baby is when it is in a state of undisturbed but irregular sleep (Wolff, 1963). During the second of these two weeks a brief smiling movement can sometimes be elicited by gentle stroking of the baby's cheek or belly when the baby is well fed, with eyes open just staring vacantly into space. At this time a soft light shone into the eyes and a soft sound may also have the same effect. The response is uncertain and slow. However, during this second week sounds of several different sorts may have an effect, though the human voice seems rather more reliable a stimulus than others such as a bell or a rattle. By about the fifth week, two great changes have occurred: a smile now occurs in an alert, bright-eyed baby; the movements of his mouth are broader than formerly; and his eyes "crinkle." It is now quite clear moreover that his smile is most readily evoked by a distinctively human stimulus. But it is still slow to come and brief in duration. During the fifth week the human voice, which up till now has been the most effective stimulus, loses most of its power, and thenceforward, the most usual and effective smile evoker is the sight of the human face.

Before a baby starts to smile at what he sees, he often goes through a phase, lasting several days or a week, during which he stares particularly intently at faces. He may track and follow the face with his eyes yet seem not to focus on it. While it is hard to say exactly what change has occurred, the effect on the mother, or the baby's companion, is clear—they will probably remark, "Now he can see me," or "Now he is fun to play with." By the end of the fifth week almost all babies smile at visual stimuli for increasing lengths of time.

There have been many experiments on the stimuli evoking smiles. Babies do not apparently smile at their feeding bottle, though they may smile happily at little balls of wool or celluloid. Familiarity is certainly a factor in evoking smiles but apparently only a minor one; not, as Piaget's work suggests, the chief factor.

Although the moving human face soon becomes the optimum visual stimulus, during the whole of the first half year a very rough approximation to a face will elicit smiling. The essentials that are needed are merely a pair of eye-like dots—suggesting that it is the sight of the eyes which plays a major part in eliciting smiles. It is also true that a profile picture of a face is of no interest to the baby. Even so, the baby may be extraordinarily unselective. As Ahrens (1954) found, the two-month-old infant will smile at a pair of black dots on a face-sized card and a six-dotted model is more effective than a two-dotted one! It was also found that even during the third month a baby will smile at a mask that comprises only eyes and brows with no mouth or chin. With increasing age the mask is sufficient to elicit a smile only as it provides greater and greater detail until, by eight months, nothing short of an actual human face will do. Not until he is about seven months of age can a baby begin to recognise different human faces and smile only in response to those that he has found to be satisfactory objects for the purpose and so begin to engage in proper social communication. However this must not be interpreted to mean that before this period he lacks *all* discrimination, for Polak and others (1964) found that by the end of the third month he can already discriminate a real face from a life-sized coloured photo, and that though the photo continues to be a sufficient stimulus for him to smile at, it is far from an optimum one.

Blind babies smile, and this fact provides additional valuable evidence for the innate nature of the behaviour. Babies who are born blind will smile to voice and touch particularly, and voice alone is fairly effective, but they do not smile normally until they are six months old. Previous to that time their smiles remain fleeting and are like the smiles of half-asleep normal babies during the first weeks of life.

As Ambrose (1961) has shown, whereas at thirteen weeks of age a baby may have smiled freely, even at a stranger's immobile face, a fortnight later he may not smile at it at all. At his mother, on the other hand, he smiles as freely as before and probably more so. It seems that alarm at a stranger undoubtedly plays a part during the third and fourth quarters of the first year, inhibiting smiling; and probably it is the main factor during the second quarter. In due course the mother's loving behaviour on seeing her baby smile, or even simply her familiar presence, are probably the chief influences. As the smiling behaviour develops, the baby does much else besides. He looks at the approaching figure, orients his head and body, waves his arms and kicks his legs, and also babbles. He is now rapidly developing into a social being.

The topic of babbling is dealt with below, but it is useful at this stage to mention the crying response. Since nobody likes to hear a crying baby, social stimuli have almost the reverse effect on this behaviour than they do on smiling. It is important to note that there is more than one sort of crying, each sort having its own pitch, pattern, and causal stimuli, its own terminating stimuli, and its own effects on a baby's companions. But, over and above this, recent studies with the sound spectrograph show that the cries of newborn babies are as distinctive as their fingerprints, and most mothers believe that every baby cries in his own individual way. Indeed it seems to be a fact that recognition of the baby's individual cry is achieved by many mothers within about forty-eight hours.

There are two main types of cry: crying from hunger, which starts gradually and becomes rhythmical, and crying from pain, which starts suddenly and is arhythmical. (See Formby, 1967, and Wolff, 1969.) Bowlby makes the point that the striking thing about crying is that it is effectively terminated by stimuli that, in a natural environment, are almost certain to be of human origin. These include sounds, especially the human voice,

224

and the tactile and other stimuli that arise from non-nutritive sucking and being rocked. It is interesting to note, as a number of studies suggest, that about 50 per cent of mothers consider it satisfactory to give a pacifier to their baby, and modern experts seem to agree that this has no obvious ill effects. In less developed countries the mother commonly puts a crying baby to her breast without much concern as to whether milk is available or not. It has been shown by Wolff that the presence of a comforter between the lips has an effect even when it is not sucked; and it is worth mentioning the slightly amusing fact that mothers (and fathers) are also right in believing that rocking a baby is a good way of quieting him! Finally, not until he is eleven months of age will the average baby start crying at the sight of something which he has previously experienced as having unpleasant consequences, e.g., the sight of a doctor preparing to repeat an injection that was given a few weeks earlier.

With man it is likely that erection, ejaculation in the male, and perhaps the pelvic thrusts in both sexes are properly termed "instinctive." For it seems that such movements are the expression of behavioural systems that, as regards motor pattern, are relatively little influenced, during development, by variations of environment, and at a certain phase of the life cycle are ready to be activated by whatever causal factors they are constructed to respond to. It now seems clear that fragments of sexual behaviour of a non-functional kind occur in immature members of many, perhaps all, species of primate and are also quite frequently exhibited towards parents. Bowlby (1969) says, "The component sexual instincts that are active in human infancy and childhood, and to which Freud called attention, are thus not confined to man; probably in all mammals infantile sexuality is the rule." Penile erection is quite regular, sometimes rhythmic, in babies, and Lewis (1965) has made detailed observations of the incidence of pelvic thrusts in the human infant starting at eight to ten months of age. He describes them as occurring only in conditions of maximum security. In a moment of apparent delight a child, either boy or girl, may clasp the mother, perhaps while lying relaxed on her breast, and "throwing his arms about her neck, nuzzling her chin, begin rapid rotating pelvic thrusts of a frequency of about two per second. This does not last long and is not usually accompanied by erection, and does not result in anything suggesting orgasm. Moreover it is not restricted to boys. It decreases with the gradual decrease in intimate holding contact up to or over three years of age." As Bowlby remarks, "any observer of two- or three-year-old children playing together has noticed occasions when, with much excitement, a little boy and a little girl assume positions typical of adult coitus. Neither, it is evident, has more than the vaguest idea of the post-pubertal set goal of the behaviour sequence, one bit of which they are enacting." Maternal behaviour also shows the same sort of pattern, both in little girls and sometimes also in little boys. Either sex may act in a typically maternal way towards a doll or even towards a real baby. The processes whereby these early-appearing fragments of instinctive behaviour come to be integrated into complete sequences with their normal functional consequences are discussed by Bowlby.

Vacuum Activities and Consummatory Acts

We earlier considered vacuum activities as characteristic of certain types of instinctive behaviour when under a powerful drive, forcing their way out in a stimulus vacuum, so to speak. What has been said above concerning human sexual behaviour makes it hardly necessary to add that vacuum activities are as characteristic of the instinctive parts of human behaviour as they are of those of animals. Similarly with *consummatory acts:* here again the examples of smiling and sucking serve to make it clear that similar consummatory acts are by no means lacking in the human situation.

In man, as with so many animals, the consummatory situations, or, as Bowlby calls them, *the set goals of behaviour,* are of the utmost importance. We have already seen that much of this elementary instinctive behaviour shown by human beings has been evolved by selective forces to ensure, what is from the baby's point of view, the overwhelming need and "concern" of early life, namely to maintain contact with mother, or mother substitute, the satisfier of all early needs. In short, attachment to one or two individuals, and later attachment to a group, is part of the basic nature of humanity. And loss of this attachment, particularly in the early stages of life, is one of the greatest dangers to the normal development of personality.

Much further study of attachment behaviour will be required before all its complexities will be fully understood. But a preliminary list of different forms which occur under varying conditions would include: (a) behaviour, including greeting, that initiates interaction with mother—e.g., approaching, touching, embracing, scrambling over her, burying face in her lap, calling, talking, hands-up gesture, and smiling with glee; (b) behaviour aimed to avoid separations, e.g., following and clinging and crying; (c) exploratory behaviour and (d) withdrawal (fear behaviour), also especially oriented with reference to the mother-figure. Bowlby points out that a great variety of conditions must be taken into account when studying such behaviour. Thus: (A) mother's whereabouts and movements—(1) mother present, (2) mother departing, (3) mother absent, (4) mother returning; (B) other persons—familiar persons, present or absent; strangers, present or absent; (C) non-human situation—(1) familiar, (2) a little strange, (3) very strange; (D) condition of child—(1) healthy, sick, or in pain, (2) fresh or fatigued, (3) hungry or fed. As we shall see later, the basic sociology of higher animals is in many ways extraordinarily similar to that of human beings, and it is almost impossible that we should fully understand the latter without studying the former. In fact ethology may be not too inadequately described as the sociology of animals. But before we can come to this, we must look at one other very important and most interesting feature of the development of social behaviour, namely what is known as imprinting.

Imprinting and the Sensitive Period

Imprinting provides an instructive example of the way in which the range of stimuli capable of eliciting a response can be limited and refined by experience. Spalding (1873) observed that a newly hatched duckling or gosling will follow practically any moving object it sees in the same way that it would follow its own parent. In fact, Spalding's observations did not constitute the first reference to the subject, for Pliny speaks of "a goose which followed Lacydes as faithfully as a dog"; and Reginald of Durham (1167) records eider ducks (*Somateria mollissima*) as following human beings (references Thorpe, 1963, p. 405). Unfortunately, Spalding's observations were forgotten for eighty years until rediscovered by J. B. S. Haldane.[11] In the meantime, the German ornithologist Heinroth (1910) observed the same phenomenon and had christened it *"Prägung,"* which was translated into English as "imprinting." Though there is perhaps no reason for thinking that imprinting is fundamentally different from other forms of learning, it certainly has properties which make it of particular interest. And at least some of these properties arise from the particular conditions of the imprinting situation.

Imprinting was originally defined by four characteristics: (1) as a learning period confined to a very definite and brief period of the individual's early life, which (2) once established is often very stable, and in some rare cases perhaps irreversible; (3) as a process which, though completed early, comes later in the life cycle to affect various specific reactions as yet undeveloped—such as those concerned with sexual and adult social behaviour; (4) as learning, which is generalised in the sense that it leads first to an ability to respond to the broad characteristics of a situation, though later it may enable finer discriminations to be achieved. It is clear that all these four characteristics are important and apply at least in some cases. But, from our point of view, the sensitive period and the progression from general to special

228

perception are perhaps the most interesting, since the former concerns the very important educational question of sensitive periods in learning, and the latter ties up with an equally basic topic, namely observational and exploratory learning.

As Hinde points out, the problem of sensitive periods, the occurrence of which is established in a wide variety of animals, is far more fundamental than any questions of the particular conditions of early learning and is in fact part of the problem of the development of behaviour itself. Only when the changing behaviour and abilities of the animal have been analysed in terms of its interaction with the environment at each stage can the factors which actually limit sensitive periods be understood. Present evidence indicates that differences with age in performance on *simple* learning tasks are small if motivation and reinforcement are controlled, though retention does improve with age. Performance of more complex tasks clearly changes with age. The basis for such age changes in learning include particularly the development of the nervous system and of the muscular system and the effects of rearing on the development of perceptions and of many types of skilled movements. Sensitive periods are usually not sharply defined. But the term is a good one to employ when learning is found to occur most readily at a particular stage of the life cycle. Moreover, since, as has been said, sensitive periods in learning are more likely to be evident with complex tasks rather than very simple ones, it follows that the idea is particularly important in relation to man and the higher animals, where the tasks to be learned in the ordinary development of social behaviour are very complex indeed. It is obviously for these reasons that psychiatrists such as Bowlby find the concept particularly valuable in relation to study of the development of attachment behaviour—a topic which is basic to his whole position. It seems, therefore, that the next step for us is to pass from the imprinting of birds to consider the development of affectional bonds in monkeys, where it is clear from the enormous amount of recent work that attachment behaviour is crucial.

The Development of Affectional Bonds in Primates

In later chapters we shall return to the topic in relation to the social life of monkeys and apes as they exist in the wild. But for present purposes it is more helpful to restrict ourselves to the development of affectional bonds in Rhesus monkeys as kept in captivity. For this purpose I shall be referring to the highly artificial experiments of Dr. Harlow in the United States and the much freer and therefore more natural experiments of Hinde and his co-workers in Cambridge. Harlow concludes from many years of work that affectional bonds in Rhesus monkeys are created and sustained by the operations of five basic affectional systems. They are (1) the maternal system; (2) the infant-mother system; (3) the age-mate, or peer, system; (4) the heterosexual affectional system; and (5) the paternal, or adult male, system.

1. THE MATERNAL AFFECTIONAL SYSTEM. This of course provides the infant's basic needs, as has already been seen. Thus physical and social comfort are provided by intimate bodily contact; hunger and thirst assuaged by nursing; while protection from dangerous, frightening, and unfamiliar objects is continuous. It seems likely that maternal bodily contact and breast contact and nursing are the basic features which give this affectional system its great strength.

2. THE INFANT-MOTHER AFFECTIONAL SYSTEM. This system of course includes much that may be grouped under the first heading, but as a result of bodily contact-comfort, of the soothing and comforting effect of warmth, the rocking motion and body positioning, the infant can learn to identify its own mother from all other adults and can begin to understand the meaning of items of the mother's gestural communication. An extremely important long-term socialising mechanism, which comes under this heading, is what one may call the basic security and trust which

it engenders. Both in man and monkey basic trust is of crucial importance for the development of environmental exploration, peer exploration, and *particularly* play.

3. THE AGE-MATE, OR PEER, AFFECTIONAL SYSTEM. Monkey infants or human infants placed in a secure environment first explore and manipulate inanimate playthings and then turn their attention to social objects—playmates, which are primarily peers, or age-mates. Play automatically and inevitably evolves in man and monkeys if these proper provisions are met, i.e., assorted playthings, agile and able playmates, and adequate protection. Play of course passes through increasingly complicated stages as the animals mature, and these are obviously vastly more complex and more varied in human infants than in monkey infants. This must be so if only because of the human capacity for speech. As Harlow says, "Play, be it simple or complex, be it between monkeys or between people, is always the secret of successful social development." In this system one should also mention the process whereby peer promiscuity is transformed into happy heterosexuality in both man and monkey. At the age-mate level, normal sex-differentiating behavioural patterns will mature. First they are absent altogether, then as they develop they are modified in form and in frequency even before the heterosexual system appears in its fully fledged form. It is very noticeable that homosexual friendships which are formed between peers at the age-mate stage may continue long after the heterosexual affectional system has evolved, even though this basic behaviour is not supported by effective sexual congress between the friendship partners. Homosexual behaviour is practically universal in the early stages of life of mammals and of birds. And among a great many mammals, and a few birds such as geese, peer and playmate "love" patterns are pervasive and persistent, continuing into the heterosexual stage without necessarily interfering with it.

4. THE HETEROSEXUAL AFFECTIONAL SYSTEM. The social-sexual bond uniting male and female members of a primate group may

be either profound and prolonged or perfunctory. There seems to be no consistent connexion between the degree of evolutionary development or the phylogeny of a group and the length or intensity of the heterosexual bond. For instance, whereas a great many birds mate for life, a great many mammals are polygamous or promiscuous. Again there is enormous variation in the degree of dependence on internal rhythms of male and female sex hormonal systems. The dependence of birds and of rodents on these systems, which in some cases may render previous experience and learning almost irrelevant to the development of heterosexual bonds, is very clear. But in primates, as the work of Harlow on his monkeys has shown, sexuality is destroyed by previous deprivation of affection and sexual behaviour between animals of the same age group. As he says, "Primates which have never loved early never love late. In primates 'plutonic' love, without antecedent 'platonic' love, is a maudlin myth."

5. THE PATERNAL AFFECTIONAL SYSTEM. Paternal affection expresses itself in protection against predators, protection of infants from aggression within the social group, the social ordering of females and infants who are members of the in-group structure, and even a paternal interest in, and play with, infants. The study of this system is comparatively new and there is a great deal yet to be learned about it. Yet it is remarkable, as studies both in menageries and in the wild accumulate, how important and widespread the effects of this system appear to be.

Effects of Social Isolation on Juvenile Development

Harlow's first work became familiar in ethological circles because of his experiments on the effect of social isolation in monkeys. His studies show in fact how "love can be destroyed" (1970). Social isolation is most devastating in its effect if it is instituted at birth before any affectional bonds have been formed. This is interpreted as a function of the number of affectional systems whose formation has been denied; and perhaps it is for this reason too that the devastation caused is also a function of its duration. Harlow claims that there are two types of social isolation which are qualitatively different. In the first of these, partial social isolation, the individual monkeys are placed in ranks of adjacent open cages so that they can see and hear but not physically interact with their associates. Total social isolation results from raising individual monkeys in enclosed cages where all visual and manual contact with other animals is denied. To avoid sensory deprivation as distinct from social deprivation, such monkeys are kept in well-illuminated cages without sound shielding and often provided with toys and playthings.

If monkey infants are subject to *partial social isolation,* they show excessive clinging and sucking. Locomotion and exploration fail to develop at normal rates, and repetitive stereotypes of behaviour such as rocking, cage-swinging, pacing, and circling emerge instead. As the monkey grows older, aggressive responses, both socially directed and self-directed, develop. With increasing age, the frequency of both the abnormal and normal patterns of locomotion and exploration decline till, at the end of a decade, the adult partial isolate monkeys do essentially nothing but sit at the front of their cages and stare vacantly outward. However, if stressed by external stimuli, they may break into frantic frenzies of bizarre stereotyped activity or extreme self-aggression. If monkeys have been reared in partial social isolation for the first year of life only, they show serious deficits in their subsequent social, sexual, and maternal behaviour. They rarely initiate interactions but become withdrawn and engage in disturbed and irrelevant behaviour. If, after the first year, repeated social interactions are allowed, they ultimately display the rudiments of play with other isolates. But their sexual behaviour is at best incompetent and often absent. Sexual drive may be evident, e.g., posturing and the rudiments of sexual technique; but even in the presence of a willing and experienced partner, the behaviour of such males is little more than a caricature of successful sex. Moreover few female partial isolates have become pregnant by natural means, and very rarely indeed by partial isolate males.

If they do become pregnant, they turn out to be hopelessly in-effective mothers, often indifferent or brutal, frequently to the point of destroying their offspring.

Total social isolation throughout the first three months of life leaves the monkey in a state of emotional shock. But it is sur-prising that, after three months of such isolation, subjects will make amazingly rapid and successful social adjustment to peers. Harlow says that no semi-permanent or permanent personal, social, or intellectual deficits have ever been demonstrated. It should be noted that during these ninety days isolate monkeys have been denied both normal mother love and also normal in-fant-mother love. However, being released to join age-mates at three months of age means a return to socialisation prior to the chronological period during which most age-mate interactions are initiated. If *after* three months of normal social living, monkeys are subjected to six months of total social isolation, there is relatively little social impairment, although monkeys socially iso-lated in the last half of the first year are hyperaggressive com-pared with control monkeys. *This fits in with data which indicate that aggression begins to develop during the last quarter of the first year of life.* Total social isolation for the first half year of life, or longer, leaves monkeys completely unable to interact socially with age-mates, destroys adequate heterosexuality in all males, and in most females, and eradicates normal maternal affection in monkey mothers, which of course have to be impregnated by artificial means. These effects seem to be permanent, since total social isolates, when three or four years of age, show no positive interchange with either age-mates or with monkeys half their age. Yet in spite of the enormous social sexual loss there is no "learning deficit" as measured by the standard-learning-test procedures of the laboratory. This finding even applies to mon-keys isolated for nine to twelve months. This destroys sociability with age-mates and all forms of sexuality as well as social com-munication. These phenomena are known to persist unchanged for six to seven years and are presumably permanent. Even so, no "intellectual loss" has been discovered.

Separation of infant from the mother produces, in both human and monkey infant, a period of protest and subsequently a relatively long period of despair.

If infant monkeys are subject to what Harlow calls repetitive peer separation, that is, if they are raised in groups of four and then separation is repeated say twenty times in the first nine months of life, their behaviour when mature remains frozen at an infantile level.

Another unpleasant technique developed by Harlow is to place infant monkeys in a vertical chamber, with inwardly inclined walls, for either a single thirty-day period or for a series of brief repetitive periods. When this is done, the poor animals drift into a state of deep depression in spite of the fact that there has been little or no real sensory isolation.

Thus Harlow has developed four basic techniques for producing psychopathic states in monkeys. These are (1) partial and (2) total isolation, (3) repetitive peer separation, and (4) restriction within a vertical chamber. Cruel and horrible as these experiments certainly are, they have had results of great value, since they lend themselves to the study of related biochemical and hormonal factors and to the determination of the efficiency of therapeutic techniques, either chemical or behavioural. And there is a brighter side to the picture. As Harlow says, "We now know that love at every stage and transition may be scientifically seduced and separated; but happier far, the jumbled pieces of the primate jigsaw puzzle may hopefully be reassembled."

The Harlows were in fact somewhat shocked at the unexpected and devastating success of their deliberate attempts to produce primate psychopathology. These have in fact been far more effective than they once believed possible. When this became clear, the Harlow group became increasingly interested in techniques of re-education and psychotherapy. First came the accidental discovery of social psychotherapy with "some monkeys acting as therapists and others as patients." This first observation was entirely accidental. It was observed that the infants of motherless mothers never abandoned entirely maternal ventral and mammillary search—unless of course they were actually killed by their mothers. Those infants who survived were surprisingly successful in forming maternal attachments, and after three to four months the brutal mothers ignored the infants or possibly appreciated infant-body comfort and sucking. Then came the astonishing result that almost all of these motherless monkeys who subsequently had a second or third infant were normal, or nearly normal, mothers. Their first infants had apparently psychiatrically rehabilitated them.

The first steps in experimental psychotherapy were taken with a group of monkeys previously totally socially isolated for six months (an isolation period that had actually been found to be totally socially destructive if the isolates were then paired with age-mates). In this new experiment the psychopathic monkeys were intermixed with socially normal monkeys, half their age, under home-cage conditions and also under unfamiliar conditions. The assumption was made that these youngsters would be no threat to the isolates and could eventually re-educate the abnormal animals by initiating social contacts and play. The experiment, as the Harlows report, was successful beyond all hopes or expectations. Gradually the isolated monkeys became progressively less fearful and more socially sophisticated until they usually could not be distinguished from their monkey psychiatrists. This is as far as this work has gone at the time of writing; but it clearly is of the greatest promise and will perhaps make many of the critics of the Harlows' horrible experiments take a rather different view and look at them with enlarged perspective.

Mother and Child

The very humane and more natural experiments of Hinde (1970) show the success with which natural groupings, extended families, of Rhesus monkeys can be employed as surrogates for the human social situation. In this way controlled experiments on early and brief separation from the parents, and many other

236

situations giving rise only to mild trauma, can be studied with a precision that is of course impossible with human beings.

The infant Rhesus monkey spends much of its early life attached to its mother, holding on to her chest to chest. At this stage the infant has various reflex patterns of behaviour which assist it in establishing and maintaining itself in the proper position. These behaviour patterns would however be quite ineffective if it were not for the appropriate passive and active behaviour by which the mother reciprocates. This includes cradling, nursing, grooming, restraining, and retrieving. The monkey baby appears to learn to recognise its own mother in the first week or two of life. By about three weeks the baby becomes able to do a little self-feeding and by six weeks is able to run a little way on vertical wire netting. The infant may first leave its mother briefly when about a week old. The time spent off the mother increases rapidly from the second to about the twentieth week and again just before the end of the first year. Although it continues to spend a fifth of the daylight hours awake and attached to the nipple for most of its first year, only a small proportion of this time is spent in sucking, the nipple merely serving as an additional point of suspension and as a pacifier. It is clear during all this time that the contact comfort supplied by the mother is an important issue.

As it develops, the infant's relationship with its mother gradually changes. These changes result from the growing independence of the infant, primarily as a result of changes in its own behaviour, of changes in the mother's behaviour, or both. So these stages of "growing up" can be understood as the effects of one or more of four possible simple types of change—namely an increase or decrease in the tendency of mother or infant to respond positively (i.e., other than by avoidance or aggression) to the other. A useful hypothesis in explaining the behaviour of the two animals is that they depend on only four possible measures of basic change which are shown in the table on page 242. These are: the percentage of time the infant spends off its mother; the number of times its attempts to gain the nipple are rejected by the mother (R) divided by the number of times it gains (A+M) or unsuccessfully attempts to gain (R) the nipple; the proportion of half minutes off the mother which it spends wholly more than two feet from her (two feet being about the distance the mother can reach) and the measure (%Ap−%L) of the infant's role in maintaining proximity to the mother. This last is calculated from the difference between the percentage of occasions in which the distance between infant and mother decreases from more than two feet to less than two feet (Ap), which are due to movements by the infant, and the percentage of occasions on which it increases (L) similarly. (Ap and L stand for Approaches and Leavings.) It will be found that an increase in time off the mother can be ascribed primarily to the infant if associated with a decrease in the relative frequency of rejections, and to the mother if associated with an increase. Similarly an increase in time at a distance from the mother is due to the infant if associated with a decrease in the infant's initiative in maintaining proximity and vice versa. Thus the increasing independence of the infant with age is due immediately to a change in the mother's behaviour rather than to one in that of the infant. The upshot of this is that the mother is not merely a guardian and passive provider of the infant's needs, she also plays an active part in promoting its independence.

As the infant comes to spend more time off its mother, it investigates and explores its environment more and plays more with its peers. This play consists primarily of what is called "approach-withdrawal" and "rough and tumble." Sex differences become apparent quite early on. Males not only initiate more "rough-and-tumble" play, but also show more social threat—branch-shaking and mounting behaviour—from an early age.

If an infant's mother is removed for a few days, the infant becomes depressed, showing a reduction in play behaviour and in general activity. When the mother is returned, most infants are at first intensely clinging; a complex interaction then ensues in which the mother at first accedes to the infant's demands and then rejects them until finally a more harmonious relationship is established.

Under natural conditions, of course, mother and infant live in the complex social structure of a troop. Other animals in the troop may display considerable interest in the infant, looking at, touching, grooming, or holding it, playing with it, behaving aggressively or sexually towards it. In laboratory social groups, investigatory and maternal behaviour is directed especially towards infants under twelve weeks old and subsequently decreases; females two years older than the infant are more prone to show such behaviour than females of any other age category. Mothers usually resent such attentions and protect their young either by restricting their movements, removing them, or threatening the other monkeys. Comparison between mother-infant pairs living in a social environment with mother-infant pairs living in social isolation shows that in the latter the infants spend more time off their mothers and go to a distance from them more often than in the former. Analysis of these results show that the difference is primarily due to the greater permissiveness of the mothers in the isolate mother-infant pairs. Indeed in the isolate animals the infants are primarily responsible for maintaining proximity.

The main results of very extensive and elaborate experiments by Hinde and his co-workers bring us to the conclusion that at, or soon after, birth the mother has a repertoire of maternal behaviour patterns which interlock with, and depend upon, the primarily reflex patterns of the infant. Through developing contact and experience with its general environment, the infant's perceptual, manipulative, and locomotor powers develop. As it grows, it makes greater demands on its mother and interferes more with her own maintenance and comfort activities. The care and solicitude which she shows to the newborn diminish, though she continues to care for it. The nature of the mother-infant relationship thus gradually changes, with the mother playing an important role in permitting and promoting the infant's independence. The infant is of course attracted away from the mother by its peers; these and the maternal responsiveness to the infant shown by more mature social companions have a marked influence on the mother-infant bond. In the ordinary course of events the bond gradually weakens, but sudden change, such as that of a period of separation, may change the course of development in a manner which is not fully reversible.

It seems appropriate to include at this point a brief account of some of the work on rodents carried out by Dr. V. H. Denenburg (1963). The work has many ramifications. One result of particular interest shows that if female rats are "gentled," that is to say gently stimulated by frequent caressing and handling, their treatment of their own young when born will be similarly changed from the standard control group. This results in the young themselves being of a different temperament from the control young of control mothers; and when these young themselves come to bear babies, their patterns of mothering too are different from what they would have been and reflect, in a second generation, the effects of the manual gentling which their parents had received. This has now been shown in a third generation and has been appropriately called "the grandmother effect!"

Comparison Between Monkey and Human Infant Attachment Behaviour

To conclude this chapter, it is important to make clear the close resemblance between man and monkey which is evident when we examine carefully the development of parent-offspring relations in our own species.

The work of Bowlby (1969) has shown that the development of attachment behaviour in human infants, though much slower, is of a piece with that seen in subhuman mammals. Much evidence supports this conclusion and none contradicts it. Indeed the present knowledge of the development of attachment behaviour in humans can be summarised briefly under the same eight heads that have been used to describe present knowledge of imprinting in birds:

i. In human infants, social responses of every kind are first elicited by a wide array of stimuli and are later elicited by a much narrower array, confined after some months to stimuli arising from one or a few particular individuals.

ii. There is evidence of a marked bias to respond socially to certain kinds of stimuli more than to others.

iii. The more experience of social interaction the infant has with a person the stronger his attachment to that person becomes.

iv. The fact that learning to discriminate different faces commonly follows periods of attentive staring and listening suggests that exposure learning (perceptual learning) may be playing a part.

v. In most infants, attachment behaviour to a preferred figure develops during the first year of life. It seems probable that there is a sensitive period in that year during which attachment behaviour develops most readily.

vi. It is unlikely that any sensitive phase begins before about six weeks and it may be some weeks later.

vii. At about six months, and markedly so after eight or nine months, babies are more likely to respond to strange figures with fear responses, and more likely also to respond to them with strong fear responses, than they are when they are younger. Because of the growing frequency and strength of such fear responses, the development of attachment to a new figure becomes increasingly difficult towards the end of the first year and subsequently.

viii. Once a child has become strongly attached to a particular figure, he tends to prefer that figure to all others and such preference tends to persist despite separation.

Bowlby concludes that, so far as it is at present known, the way in which attachment behaviour develops in the human infant and becomes focussed on a discriminated figure is sufficiently like the way it develops in other mammals, and in birds, for it to be included, legitimately, under the heading of imprint-ing—so long as that term is used in its current generic sense. In-deed Bowlby remarks that to do otherwise would be to create a wholly unwarranted gap between the human case and that of other species.

TABLE A. The predicted directions of the consequences on certain measures of mother-infant interaction of the four basic changes indicated on the left. The direction of the arrow indicates whether the individual under which it lies shows an increased or decreased tendency to approach the other. For explanation, see text.

		Time Off	*R/(A + M + R)*	*>2 ft only*	*%Ap − %L*
infant ←	mother	+	−	+	−
infant →	mother	−	+	−	+
infant	mother →	+	+	+	+
infant	mother ←	−	−	−	−

Chapter 7

AGGRESSIVE BEHAVIOUR

In the last chapter, we discussed affectional bonds in monkeys, as shown in the highly artificial conditions of the laboratory and also in what one might call the semi-artificial conditions of the family groups of Rhesus monkeys studied by Hinde (1970). Now, as a prelude to consideration of aggression, we will consider the social life of primates as shown by truly wild animals.

THE SOCIAL LIFE OF FREE-LIVING PRIMATE GROUPS

The Japanese and Americans have been active in this field in recent years and have established colonies of Rhesus monekys on small islands where the monkeys can develop under perfectly natural conditions and where they can be studied without interference. It soon became obvious from a great many examples that, in the immature stage, the social environment had an important effect on the determination of the future social rank of females born in the natural troop. Firstly, there is an important difference between the course of life of the young females and the young males in these colonies. As in all social animals some sort of social rank must be established, for without this there could be very little cohesion in a monkey society. Both the infant males and the infant females are of course at the centre of the family life until they become independent of their mothers at about two and a half to three years of age. Previous to that time they experience very little aggressive behaviour from adult members of the troop; and although they are disciplined by occasional cuffs and by mock bites, they are, as the work of Hinde has shown, much treasured and sought after, not merely by their own mothers but by other females in the group, particularly childless females. They are also at this stage allowed to take astonishing liberties with the dominant male without incurring any retribution.

Incidentally the function of this male leader of the troop is threefold: first, to protect the troop from invaders, second, to maintain welfare and order within the troop (settling quarrels both big and small, disciplining troublemakers, etc.), and third, to decide each concerted action of the troop—whether it should move away from a feeding place and if so where, etc. In fact, as Imanishi (1970, 1972) says, he is commander, director, and judge of the whole troop. Quite recently a number of workers have begun to provide evidence that taking his share of minding the baby is also one of the male's duties. So the leader is a kind of social institution based on the recognition by himself and other members of his troop of his peculiar position.

Primitive Proto-cultures

When the juveniles become free of the family organisation, the course of the life of males and females is very different. The young males are gradually ejected from the organisation of the group and spend their time on the outskirts only loosely attached. Females, on the other hand, are not necessarily pushed out in this way but may remain in the central part of the colony throughout life. Thus the mother-daughter relations continue as long as the dependent rank acquired by the daughters in their infancy is fixed and preserved. Wild groups observed under these conditions show gradual changes in behaviour, which may take three or

244

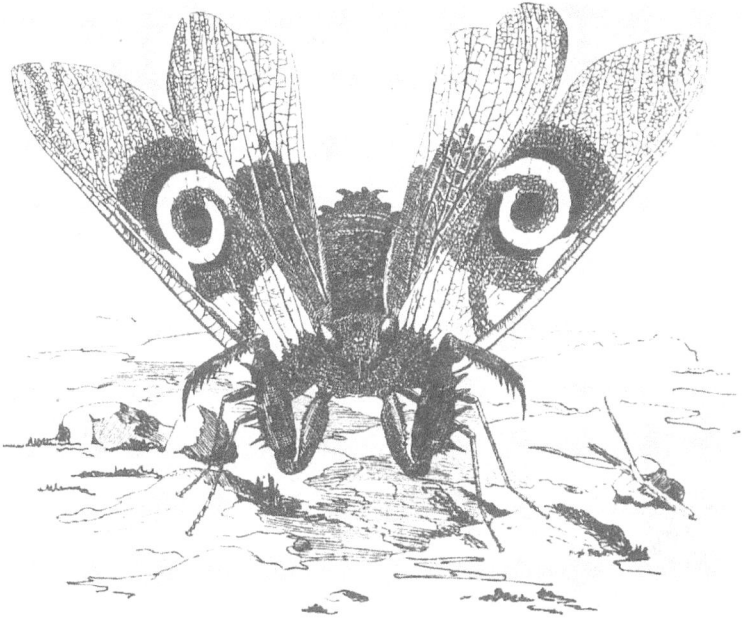

PLATE 7: Warning display of the Mantis (*Pseudocreobotra wahlbergi*). (After Cott, 1940.)

PLATE 8: Warning display of the Frilled Lizard (*Chlamydosaurus kingii*). (After Cott, 1940.)

(a)

(c)

(b)

(d)

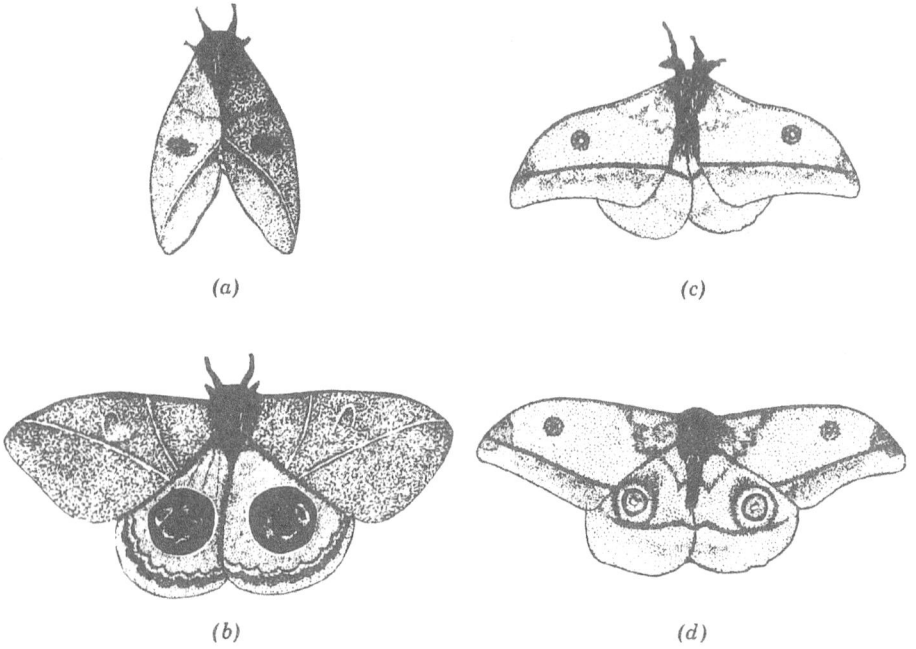

PLATE 9: Intimidation displays of moths. (a) The resting posture of an *Automeris medusae* male, (b) a female of the same species following disturbance. (c) Shows a *Nudauriela dione* male preparing for flight. In (d) the same moth in display after disturbance. (After Blest, 1957b.)

PLATE 10: Julesz random patterns.

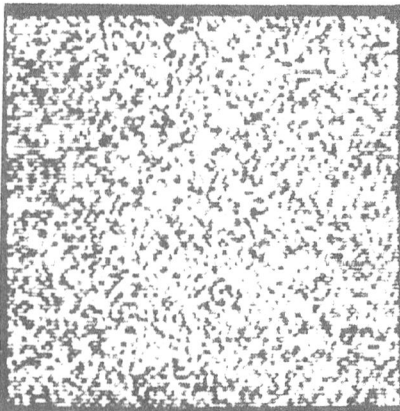

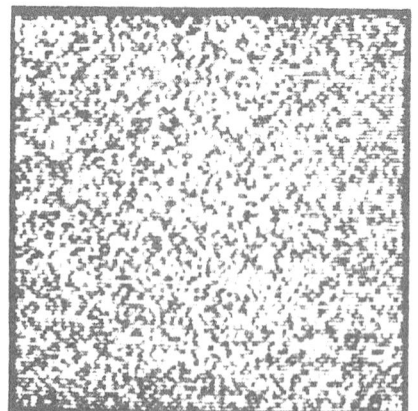

more years to spread through the colony and which are quite characteristic of a particular colony, not being shared by others. These appear to constitute learned "proto-cultures." An example of this is the tendency to wash potatoes before they are eaten; or it may be that a completely new food habit becomes established, such as that of eating wheat.

If a new habit is adopted by the dominant male, then it rapidly spreads through the group. But more often new habits are acquired by the juveniles and these are often disapproved of by the elders, who try to prevent such outrageous flouting of the established social codes! Since the juvenile females remain in the centre of the group for the whole of their lives, they will, if they acquire new and useful (or at least not undesirable) habits, be in the best position to influence others in the adoption of these. So at least in some monkey groups the young females may have a greater influence in changing social organisation than the young males. In large monkey groups, once the young male gets pushed to the periphery, and the longer he stays there, the more difficult it will be for him to make his way back into what we may call the central organisation, i.e, the group of monkeys most closely associated with the leader. Consequently, however inventive or clever he may be, it is less likely that his new patterns of behaviour will spread throughout the group. And if a male infant is a baby of a peripheral female, he will have few chances of being in contact with the leader. On the other hand a male born to a central female has far more such chances, and most of the babies cared for by the leaders are said to be those of the central females. Such babies are brought up in an environment likely to qualify for leadership since the behaviour of the leader is always before their eyes. Thus, if such early conditioning is formed in the social environment in childhood, it may produce what is termed "identification" by psychoanalysts. A male juvenile may thus become identified by his associates with the leader of the troop, and the longer and more successfully that he can stay in the centre of the establishment the more likely is he to qualify for leadership himself. This surely provides an extraordinary parallel with the training for leadership in human societies! In other words, we may say that the first few years of a young monkey's life are of paramount importance in acquiring individuality or "personality." (I use this word here in a connotation different from that which it will have when discussing human personality later in this book.) And on this "personality" his future position in the hierarchy will very largely depend. Once new habits are acquired by adults they can be propagated very widely from mother to child. And sometimes it happens that behavioural innovations established first among the group of young ones are then learnt by the younger mothers and propagated by them to the next generation. (Kawamura, in Chauvin, 1972.)

Rarity of Intergroup Aggression in Chimpanzees

This account of the behaviour of monkey troops may strike the reader as remarkable in that there is no evidence of intergroup aggression, that is to say, there is nothing in the way of clan warfare. Let us now look at the behaviour in the wild of the higher apes. After all, monkeys are far removed from man, but the chimpanzee is *biochemically* extraordinarily close, though even he is behaviourally still *very* far removed from man. To be more precise, man's relationship with chimpanzee is closer *biochemically* than that of dog with fox or cat with lion. A study of the amino-acid sequences in the haemoglobin molecule gives as between man and horse fifty-two differences, as between chimpanzee and gorilla two differences, and as between chimpanzee and man none! So it is not just wild and careless theorising that leads ethologists nowadays to spend so much time with the chimpanzee, the gorilla, and the orangutan.

Our knowledge and understanding of the true nature of chimpanzee societies has been immeasurably advanced by the pioneer work of Dr. Jane van Lawick-Goodall. For ten years or more Dr. Goodall has lived for long periods in the African forest, studying a colony of chimpanzees in what is now the Gombé

Stream National Park, on the eastern shores of Lake Tanganyika. Wild chimpanzees are of course extremely shy, but she patiently and doggedly won their confidence until she was able to sit among them and observe details of their lives never recorded before. She and her associates studied every aspect of their hierarchies and complex social behaviour and the tremendous variety of calls and gestures which served them as language. In due course she got to know almost all of the chimpanzees in her area of forest as individuals and was able to recognise them infallibly by minute peculiarities of appearance, e.g., gait, colouration, size, and degree of development, idiosyncrasies of movement, scars, injuries, and so forth.

From our immediate point of view, perhaps the most astonishing of her discoveries was the extreme lack of aggression shown by these animals. There is of course threatening behaviour, as when a male with a jerk of the head and a little cough begins to hunch his shoulders, bristle his hair, and stamp his feet. He may then get to the point of brandishing a branch or throwing stones. This is only mild threat and may perhaps correspond to verbal aggression in human beings. As Jane Goodall says, they are masters of the art of brinkmanship, seldom going to the point of actual physical violence. But even when they do so, they seldom emerge with more than a few scratches or some lost handfuls of hair. "Immediately after a clash that may send two animals rolling furiously down a slope, the antagonists are at peace again. The victim can extend its hand, the aggressor will pat its head, and then they start to groom each other" (van Lawick-Goodall, 1970, p. 7). Dr. Goodall says that she has never seen chimpanzees fight to the death, though there is on record an instance of a chimp baby being seized and eaten.

There is of course social hierarchy in these chimpanzee groups just as there is in the monkey groups we have been discussing. But the remarkable thing about Dr. Goodall's observations is that, entirely contrary to what she expected, the groups are not static or of fixed composition. Strange animals may appear, join the group, and be accepted quite normally, and then may disappear again; and so it appears that the constitution of the group changes unpredictably with time as newcomers drift in and old members drift away. It is probably true that the nucleus of the group remains the same; but there seems little limit to the amount of peripheral change. It may be of course that most of these individuals were previously known to the group. The Gombé Stream Forest covers an area of thirty square miles, and it was not possible therefore for Jane to know all the chimpanzees personally in that great area. Nevertheless *the rarity of personal aggression and the apparent complete absence of group warfare is highly significant.*

Moreover it is not as if the chimpanzees were purely vegetarian animals. For another of Dr. Goodall's discoveries was that wild chimpanzees are sometimes carnivorous and show evidence of precise co-operation in the isolation and catching of Colobus monkeys and young bush buck and bush pig. For instance, some members of the troop may be threatening the monkey from in front, while another creeps up, leaps upon it from behind, and breaks its neck. They then all join in devouring the body. Moreover they rarely fight over food, and only for much-liked items in short supply. Under natural conditions they will take fruit from a tree quietly, the higher ranking animals leaving enough for the others.

Of course there is some aggressiveness in chimpanzees; and though the female is less aggressive than the male, she is perhaps more dangerous after all. Male chimpanzees will fight and immediately forgive. The female may give way if attacked by a male, then go up to another male half an hour later and "convince him to settle the score!" (See van Lawick-Goodall, 1970, p. 8.) In parenthesis it may be said that closely similar behaviour has been observed by Hinde and his co-workers in Rhesus monkeys, where a childless female, apparently "jealous" of another member of the harem nursing a baby, would go through behaviour which suggested the pretence of being attacked and then run away squealing. The result of this was that the male in charge went in and beat up the hated rival.

It is very instructive to see what happened with Jane's chimpanzees when, in order to study their behaviour more regularly and consistently, she enticed them to come to the camp by feeding them regularly with bananas. She unwittingly acted like the snake in Eden, introducing them to "forbidden fruit." The bananas were kept in locked boxes; the animals knew that they could not get them all at once, so, at feeding time, fights resulted. She states that a dominant animal might corner the market with fifty bananas in his arms and with no intention of letting anyone else eat so much as a peel! Some of the wily youngsters found the screws that opened the locked boxes. They would sit blithely covering them with their feet until the adults went away, then they got into the banana business themselves! After a year of these handouts, the practice was stopped because it led to too much aggression.

It is striking how an accidental discovery may enable a low-ranking chimpanzee to improve his status. One of Jane Goodall's friends, called Mike, was meek and submissive until the day he picked up an empty kerosene can and found that it made a satisfactory and terrifying noise. He then found that, if he did not win friends, he could at least influence other chimpanzees and send them scurrying to the safety of the treetops when he went into his "charging display," equipped with one or more of these clattering cans. "Mike has been lording it over his fellow chimps ever since."

The Gorilla

Modern work on the gorilla, in this case by a young American, Miss Dian Fossey, is yielding comparable results. In the popular mind the gorilla epitomises terrifying ferocity and uninhibited aggressiveness (the King Kong syndrome). This is due largely to the monstrous ignorance of many of the big-game hunters of last century and of the early part of this, who, with a few notable exceptions, seem to have had a meagre and distorted knowledge of natural history. Paul du Chaillu was largely responsible for the gorilla myth, which led to the fantastic bogey of "King Kong." In fact gorillas in the wild are even more pacific than the chimpanzee. True, they have a most frightening breast-beating display; but only in the most exceptional instances, as when an animal might be cornered with its female and young, without any means of getaway, do the gorillas show any real aggressiveness. There is of course a hierarchy within the groups, maintained largely by threats which hardly ever materialise in violence; otherwise, just like the chimpanzees, the gorilla groups form and re-form with peace and amiability. And being entirely vegetarian there is not even the danger that violent methods of prey-catching may spread and infect the group behaviour. But of course in captivity both chimpanzees and gorillas become irritable, bad-tempered creatures. And it is now well known that both states of extreme isolation or overpopulation under artificial conditions, as when monkeys or apes are penned in crowded zoos, may induce a vicious circular interaction of threats generating aggression that generates more threats (Ropartz, 1970). And gang wars have been known to occur in zoos amongst animals that display no such tendencies in the wild. It is tempting to think, as Dr. Ropartz suggests, that perhaps another vicious circle exists in big cities where violent crime is on the rise. Can one argue that the violent criminal produced by crowding and then isolated in a prison cell, the opposite extreme, is possibly rendered even more aggressive than he otherwise would be? But we will return to this later.

The Causes and Meaning of Aggression

So far we have been using the term aggression quite loosely, but now we must be more precise, for an enormous amount of dangerously loose, sloppy thinking and prejudice is arising from just this source. It is highly regrettable that some of this has arisen from the recent writing of a very great zoologist, namely Dr. Konrad Lorenz. In his book, *On Aggression*, published in Vienna in 1963 and in an English version three years later,

Lorenz commits the mistake of extrapolating too readily and uncritically from the behaviour of lower vertebrates such as fish and many birds to the behaviour of the higher animals and even man himself. Lorenz regards aggression as spontaneous and inevitably finding expression in violence, independently of external stimulation. Now it is obviously quite true that aggressive behaviour does depend on aspects of the internal state, but it is also greatly influenced by external factors. There is also clear evidence that animals may actively seek for fights, in the sense that they may show behaviour which is especially likely to bring them into contact with rivals. But while the tendency to behave aggressively may increase for a short time after the encounter is over, there is no clear evidence that this increase continues until aggressive behaviour inevitably occurs—even in the virtual absence of appropriate stimulation (quoted from Hinde, 1970). This issue is obviously of the greatest importance for the control of aggressive behaviour. But if aggression *inevitably* finds an outlet, when territory or other necessities are invaded or threatened, then the only course is to try to arrange for the outlet to be a harmless one. This is the basis for the belief in catharsis; by the provision of harmless substitutes such as ball games, prize fights, and all sorts of contests, athletic and otherwise, aggressive and other socially unacceptable emotions are channelled away. But if aggression is not like that, we may be taking an unduly pessimistic view and resigning ourselves to the inevitability of the extreme form of aggression, namely war, when no such inevitability exists.

Many studies show that the nature and extent of an animal's aggressive behaviour can be much influenced by environmental factors during development, and this further study of the ontogeny of aggression seems likely to be most fruitful. The first step in all this is to separate the concept of aggression, which originally involved the idea of "stepping out" towards a new area (so suggesting the concept of a possessiveness of home or territory), from behaviour, which is directed towards physical violence in itself. So there are in fact two things here, self-assertive and go-getting behaviour, which may arise from a great many causes, particularly as we have seen from the shortage of food or undue crowding; and behaviour directed towards physical violence. We need two terms, *aggressiveness* in the normal biological sense and *violence* as behaviour definitely directed towards harming others. *Above all we must avoid the cardinal error of assuming that in the higher animals and in man group aggressiveness is the necessary and inevitable result of hereditary constitution.*

Territory Holding in Birds and Mammals

Another fertile cause of error and misapprehension is the use of the term "territory." Certain popularisers have done, and are doing, untold harm in concluding that our own territoriality is in every way comparable to that of animals. Worse still, it is argued that besides having an undoubted urge to kill, since we are descended, so it is said, from predators, we have another basic urge, the urge to have and to hold a plot of land.

Most of those who talk today about the importance of territory, and bandy about the unfortunate phrase "the territorial imperative," probably know a few basic facts about territory in bird life. But in most cases their knowledge does not extend beyond this. This is particularly unfortunate because the territory holding of birds is not equivalent to the territory holding of mammals and one should not jump lightly from one to the other.

The breeding territory of birds, in the typical case, consists of an area surrounding the nest site from which all other members of the species, except the mate, are excluded by aggressive displays, e.g., by formalised postures and movements and by song. These devices ensure that it seldom happens that the owner actually comes to physical combat with an intruder. One might say that in this context bird song is substitute fighting. Sometimes an intruder will succeed in evicting a well-established owner, but this is rare; far more often the owner maintains his freehold, though he may have to yield some marginal part of his territory to his rival. Thus territories are compressible; they are like elastic discs which can be forcibly compressed to a certain point, but will expand again if compression is withdrawn. In territorial displays we find that the intensity of the owner's display seems to be less at the territorial boundaries and to increase in strength as he is pressed towards the centre by the advance of his rival. Conversely the strength of the invader's display decreases the further he penetrates into the other's territory. In this manner a balance tends to be struck so as to accommodate economically a viable, but not excessive, number of a given species in a particular environment. But even in songbirds we find that once territorial boundaries have been settled, it often happens that the territory owners become much more tolerant to neighbours coming close to the boundary and perhaps occasionally even trespassing—a fact which seems to be dependent upon the well-known ability of birds to learn to recognise their neighbours by voice, by appearance, by their behaviour, or by all combined. Nevertheless, such tolerant territory owners drive off all trespassing strangers.

With mammals the situation tends to be very different. Mammalian territory consists not so much of a unitary area as of a number of places—first- and second-order homes, spots for sunbathing and resting, lookout posts and feeding areas—connected by a network of pathways. The owner of the territory moves along the paths to his various points of interest and activity according to a more or less fixed timetable, and the spaces enclosed by the pathway network are seldom, or never, used (Hediger, 1950; see also Leyhausen, 1970). As Leyhausen points out, in defending their territories most solitary mammals are at a great disadvantage as compared with birds. They cannot project themselves on to the highest perch and from there survey the whole of their territory; and most mammals do not "mark" their presence acoustically. So they may often fail to notice trespassers. Moreover the border areas may overlap considerably in the sense that pathways and places of interest are shared even if the first-order homes are well spaced out. As Leyhausen says, sharing in this context does not necessarily mean that the animals concerned are on good terms with each other. When they meet on disputable ground, they may fight. But with territorial behaviour being dependent upon proximity to a territory centre (first-order home), the victorious cat or wolf will not extend its pursuit of the defeated one too far into unknown territory or too far away from its own home.

Thus in many mammals, superiority gained through territorial fighting is, from the start, more or less confined to the precise locality of the fight; and after a series of such fights in different localities, the ranking between the neighbouring individuals still applies only in the border area and may even be reversed from one spot to the next, according to the distance from their respective first-order homes. Not only this. The timetable of an animal's movements about its territory is often constant enough to enable a rival, formerly beaten in a territorial fight over a certain spot or path, to adjust its schedule with regard to that spot so as to avoid the risk of an encounter with the victorious owner.

So from this we see that, quite unlike the absolute dominance of a songbird in its territory, the ranking between two individual mammals based on the outcome of territorial fighting is largely subject to locality and time. Leyhausen calls this *"relative social hierarchy,"* in contrast to the *absolute social hierarchy* of the peck order in a flock of birds, or of the dominant territory owner. Animals like cats and indeed some birds can display one kind of hierarchy in one situation and another in the second. Absolute social hierarchy is established by a cat in relation to the inhabitants of its own first-order home and to its siblings, and probably also to some rival males of the region. Here their supremacy is not challenged; and so, however badly things may go with them in fights elsewhere, they can always return home to heal their wounds and regain confidence and so are never utterly subdued—as is the lowest ranking in a permanent social group. Leyhausen states that, if in a region there are several tomcats, almost evenly matched, they have it out with each other and afterwards are very careful not to provoke any more serious fighting, which might only endanger their position. The same sort of situation appears to hold with wolves. At first this relationship resembles an armed truce, but if the animals gradually become accustomed to each other, it leads eventually to friendship, in

254

the limited sense that the animals may actually like being together for a while, and may even keep company in their pursuit of love and novice males. This sort of loose and temporary association of adult males has been called a "brotherhood" (Leyhausen, 1970).

But if mammals of this type are unduly crowded, they tend to be forced more and more towards the absolute social hierarchy position. If this is to work, there must be room for manoeuvre, for without it lasting damage to the group will result. "In short, with increasing density absolute hierarchy becomes more and more prominent and the manifestations of relative hierarchy dwindle away." (See Leyhausen, 1970.) Some mammals can live either as territorial solitaries or in more or less non-territorial groups, according to the kind of environment they are in and the season of the year. This applies to some herding animals, to lions, and probably also to the grizzly bear.

In man co-operative aggressiveness, such as war, is primarily a male function whereas no well-documented case of a culture where women were the warriors, or the hunters of large animals, is known. In fact, in man, warlike activity seems to be for men only; such female aggressiveness as there is, is not corporate. There is some evidence that this may be true of some of the feline mammals but the only case known to me of what appears to be organised gang warfare in wild animals, in a normal and unrestricted environment, is provided by the hyena (J. and H. van Lawick-Goodall, 1970), and here it seems quite evident that the corporate aggressiveness, whatever its function, is not confined to the males; indeed it seems possible that females may take a leading part. The aggressive clans of hyenas may number up to a hundred individuals and have very large group territories estimated to be up to about six square miles.

Aggression and Competition

Now that we have made clear the distinction between aggressiveness and violence, it becomes appropriate to consider more precisely the internal factors causing and controlling these tendencies. In other words, admitting that there is not any "drive for violence" as such, what are the internal and external factors which engender and control the aggressive tendency, which, though not itself violent, always provides the risk of escalation into violent forms?

I have already alluded to the fact that competition for a limited supply of food or of space, and competition for mates, may all, in mammals, lead to violence. This is especially so if the competitor is not already personally known to the defender, that is to say not individually recognised. There is a vast amount of laboratory experiment which shows that this is so, particularly with rodents (rats and mice). There is another factor which will cause aggression in captive mammals, and that is pain. Acute pain not referable to any other animal seldom occurs in the wild. A pain or defeat by a higher-ranking individual may however cause the defeated one to "take it out" on another individual of a similar or lower rank to itself. This is known as "redirected activity." It has been well shown in both rats and monkeys exposed to electric shock. The effect is for the shocked animal to behave as if its pain was caused by an associate of the same or another species and to attack it forthwith. Experimentally it has been found that monkeys held in a restraining chair and shocked in the tail will bite savagely at anything in reach, e.g., a piece of strong rubber tubing. Thus this treatment makes them aggressive in that situation and in situations directly associated with it, but not necessarily aggressive in relation to their normal cage-mates (Ulrich, 1966). The internal drives to aggressiveness are primarily due to two factors which may both be hereditary and which may both be affected by experience. They are hormones and brain mechanisms; and again it is very well known that these two themselves interact in the most elaborate manner.

Emotional Behaviour

The characteristics of behaviour controlled by an internal drive are three: (1) the effects persist, to some extent, through time; (2) various patterns of behaviour are grouped together in time in a functional manner so that the behaviour as a whole "makes sense" and does not appear random; (3) the behaviour is directive in that it continues until a certain stimulus-goal situation is achieved or a variety of behaviour patterns are alternated and used to a constant end. There is any amount of evidence that stimulation of certain parts of the brain electrically, even though absolutely painless, will cause aggressive behaviour. Similarly it is highly likely that certain regions of the brain are particularly concerned in setting aggressive behaviour in action; and if circumstances of the earlier life, or genetical or physiological defects, increase the activity of these areas, aggression may well become excessive.

In man, aggression in abnormal individuals, perhaps to some extent in all of us, is associated with strong feelings of emotion, and the idea that man has in him what has been called by MacLean (1969) "the paranoid streak" has been worked out in some detail (in Koestler and Smythies, 1969). Neurophysiological and neuropharmacological investigation of this situation is being pressed forward with great speed nowadays; and it is interesting to see how emotions and actions may become linked together in the brain, as the result of experience, in a way that could lead to excessive aggressiveness. The famous neurologist W. Penfield showed by his experiments on the stimulation of certain areas of the human cortex, during operations on the brain with unanaesthetized human subjects, that some memories are laid down in the brain together with the right emotion and that each memory is linked with its own emotional state. When the memory of a particular event in the life of an epileptic was recalled by electrical means, it came with the emotions that the person had felt at the time.

There is also the remarkable work of Delgado (1967), who has shown both with apes and with men that the brain can learn to modify its own aggressive activity. He has shown for instance that brain stimulation can not only cause aggression, e.g., make dominant individuals attack, it can also make submissive individuals more submissive. One of Delgado's experiments is most illuminating: a timid monkey had been placed in the same cage with a dominant animal equipped with a brain-stimulating device called a "stimoceiver." Also in the cage was a lever that sent a signal into the boss's brain, changing him from a "lion to a lamb." The timid monkey soon learnt how to work the lever and the results were startling. Before the use of the "stimoceiver," the dominant monkey was continually intimidating the subordinate. But after the subordinate had learnt how to work the lever, he soon had the boss cowering in the corner while he, the weakling, showed by his behaviour that he now felt himself master of the situation.

We have seen then that it is possible to evoke aggressive behaviour in animals by a considerable variety of methods. Firstly there are various social manipulations, e.g., periods of isolation, overcrowding, and frustration. Next there is pain; and thirdly we have brain lesions and brain stimulation in such areas as, for instance, the septal region. (See Krsiak and Steinberg, 1969.) None of these manipulations, with the just possible exception of the brain stimulus or lesion technique, hold out much hope of providing a method whereby human aggressiveness could be controlled. Arthur Koestler has been attracted by the idea that a drug might be found to bring into submission this paranoid streak in man and has even proposed that such a drug should be searched for.

Dr. Paul MacLean, of the National Institute of Mental Health, Bethesda, Maryland, has pointed out (1969) that emotions such as love, anger, etc., are included amongst what is known as the "general affects." These are feelings that may pertain to situations, individuals, or groups; and all may be considered in the light of self-preservation or the preservation of the species. Excluding verbal behaviour in man, there are six types of behaviour that are inferred to be guided by such general affects. These are recognised as searching, aggressive, protective, dejected, gratulant, and caressive. These may be obviously characterised by such words as desire, anger, fear, sorrow, joy, and affection.

The motive element in the paranoid streak answers the description of a "general affect." It amounts to an unpleasant feeling of fear attached to something that cannot be clearly identified. Such a feeling has the capacity to persist or recur long after the inciting circumstance and may apply to a situation, a thing, or an individual or a group. Its survival value doubtless resides in the fact that it puts the organism on guard against the unexpected.

MacLean has gone into a good deal of neurological detail which, he believes, leads to the conclusion that these general affects are part of what students of the evolution of the mammalian nervous system sometimes call the "old mammalian brain." In the modern mammals, and most strikingly in man, evolution has developed by the production of what is known as the neocortex or the new mammalian brain. This is, speaking very crudely, the tool by which man is able consciously to control the unruly activities of this evolutionary hangover of his, the old mammalian brain. In fact the old mammalian brain is represented in man and the other higher mammals by what is called the limbic system.[12] This, as is now well known, has immensely important functions in man and the higher animals—mediating, organising, and controlling, by means of its links with the hypothalamus, the drive and motivational effects arising from the subcortical parts of the brain, the sensory stimuli coming in from the various sense organs and linking them with the neocortex, the "new brain." Insofar as this is a correct, and not too simplified, estimate of the situation, it gives force to the conclusion that much of man's biological equipment, and the violent behaviour that it generates, is obsolete. It may indeed be, as some think, that man's particular problem in controlling violence is a problem inherent in the evolutionary stage through which he is passing, or which he has reached—the stage which may be regarded as the age of conflict between emotion and reason. This view suggests that the achievement of the right combination of these two influences, the rational and the emotional, is perhaps the first great task of man—a task which he is facing with particular urgency, now that he has come, or is coming, to the point where, in order to survive, he will have to manage his own social evolution. It is for these reasons that Koestler's idea that we might one day control these warring internal elements in our minds, by means of drugs, is superficially at least so attractive. What then can we expect of drugs?

Psychopharmacology in Man and Animals

Dr. Seymour S. Kety, of Harvard Medical School (1969), has discussed the possibilities of pharmacological control of the relevant brain mechanisms, which could enable the systems concerned to become more differentiated and discriminating, capable of tolerating greater delays of outcome, susceptible to more subtle grades of affect than crude pleasure and pain, and, in a species capable of symbolic conceptualisation, more sensitive to imagined, predicted, or planned outcomes, in addition to those actually perceived. He sees drugs as capable of inhibiting or facilitating the processes involved but hardly capable of generating them *de novo* and without the genetic or experiential processes which make them adaptive. In this connexion he sees as particularly promising, in addition of course to the somewhat crude effects already referred to of the influence of testosterone in the male animal, the possibility of the biogenic amines, e.g., reserpine, playing an important part in this process. Arthur Koestler in a sense summed this up in a remarkable passage:

> It is fundamentally wrong, and naive, to expect that drugs can present the mind with gratis gifts—put into it something which is not already there. Neither mystic insights, nor philosophic wisdom, nor creative power can be provided by pill or injection. The psychopharmacist cannot add to the faculties of the brain—but he can, at best, eliminate obstructions and blockages which impede their proper use. He cannot aggrandise us—but he can within limits normalise us; he cannot put additional circuits into the brain, but he can, again within limits, improve the co-ordination between existing ones, attenuate conflicts, prevent the blowing of fuses, and insure a steady power supply. That is all the help we can ask for—

but if we were able to obtain it, the benefits to mankind would be incalculable.

Waddington pointed out (1969) that, in the domestication of animals, men have succeeded in selecting genetic strains which are not aggressive but which have not lost their capacity for learning—this danger of reducing learning capacity having been raised as one of the main arguments against improvement of man's brain by pharmacological means. So Waddington argues that what the genes can do, perhaps psychopharmaceuticals might do. But of course, as Koestler points out, we do not want to do away with aggression; what we want is to control it and to prevent it spilling over into violence. If we did away with aggression, it seems highly probable that we should all become cabbages. Yet Koestler still hopes for something which might control and prevent fanaticism, that is blind devotion. But fanaticism and devotion are different. If we did away with devotion, there would be no great scientists or moralists, no great artists, no great writers or poets. But although it can be said that fanaticism is misguided devotion, it is perhaps too much for even the most optimistic to hope that the psychopharmacologist might be able to create a proper balance between emotion and reason. Or is it?

Whatever the answer, psychopharmacology is proceeding apace. Krsiak and Steinberg (1969) have studied the aggressiveness, indeed the violence, of mice under the influence of drugs and have shown that a polypeptide mixture isolated from bee venom seems to effect aggression and violence without noticeably altering any other type of behaviour. And if people are still sceptical about the jump from mice to men, it is salutary to remember (Kumar, Steinberg, and Stolerman, 1969) that rats can be readily induced to become dependent on morphine and appear to show just the same kind of withdrawal symptoms as does man when deprived of it. It seems that morphine, apart from other effects, may well produce in animals, as in man, "pleasurable" effects. If this is so, it suggests that morphine-dependent rats are indeed governed by needs which are in some ways similar to those believed to operate in human addicts and that "our animal model of dependence has many features in common with the human syndrome." Still more remarkable are Professor Steinberg's findings in connexion with the "placebo" effect, a phenomenon one might consider as characteristically human (Steinberg, 1970). A placebo effect in man has been defined as "those elements in drug effects which cannot be ascribed to pharmaco-dynamic action." They are the results of complex interaction between the patient, the drug, and the social and physical setting in which the drug is administered. Each of these can modify the effects of the others. Steinberg suggests that the results described by herself and co-workers might indeed be regarded as an animal analog of a drug-induced placebo effect and "are yet another example of how animal and human psychopharmacology can mutually reinforce each other." For further elaboration of these topics of internal factors and emotional behaviour, the work of Tobach, 1969, should be consulted.

But to my mind there is a point that is even more remarkable than these astonishing similarities between mice and men. I think we dare not hope for any "general improvement" in the human condition from surgical, electrical, or pharmacological manipulation of the human system. All we can hope for, and that indeed optimistically, is that we shall get a better control and a better balance in what we already have. This raises the extremely interesting point that, even admitting that our present civilised environment is far removed from the social circumstances which obtained during the four million years since the hominids first appeared, and the forty thousand years since *Homo sapiens* first appeared, nevertheless, during this vast evolutionary period, natural selection has undoubtedly produced a being with a brain and mind which, as far as we can see at present, is potentially, if not actually, the ideal, the standard, the norm, and perhaps we can say the paradigm of what a human mind should be! With all our failings, with all the dangers that beset us, with all our uncertainties as to how we can survive and as to whether we shall get through, we still seem to see quite plainly that we have within us potentialities which should enable us to achieve another and a better stage in social evolution. This is, to me, one of the most inspiring thoughts that comes out of the studies of this kind; and I do not think it is self-deception to believe that we have here an insight of tremendous importance—perhaps of real spiritual significance. If I may quote a passage which I wrote fifteen years ago,

> It is sound scientific common sense to see that, if only because of the existence of science itself, man displays emergent qualities far transcending those of the highest animal. The existence of his high powers of abstract reasoning and his faith, of his religious awareness and spiritual life, his appreciation of moral and aesthetic values, his self-conscious discipline and the will to achieve beauty, goodness and truth; as well as all the other manifestations of his genius that have already emerged, not only confirms this but suggests that there are also in him vast further potentialities yet to be realised.

From Aggression to War

To conclude with a few words about the step from aggression to war. I have so far been using the term aggression in the strict sense whereby I exclude violence. Now it is true that a great many of the examples I have cited do incorporate a limited amount of personal violence between individuals; but in general the organisation of the society is such that fights are extremely rare and fights to the death almost unknown. This is because there are always mechanisms of submission and appeasement, evolved (presumably) by natural selection, which ensure that violence in the society is kept within bounds. Now of course the defeated individual may lose caste and position to the extent that he can only hang on peripherally to the group. And in animals which are nomadic this is a very dangerous position indeed and may result in his death. So aggression frequently prevents certain individuals from breeding, but it very seldom leads directly to death.

We have seen how if animals are brought into captivity and

subjected to unnatural conditions such as lack of space and short-age of food, then violence, and violence which often leads to death, is frequently observed. But in nature these same animals are equipped with behavioural devices which on the whole work remarkably well in ensuring that adequate space is main-tained and adequate food is available. And we have also seen that even in the nearest relatives of man, the chimpanzee and the gorilla, group violence seems to be completely absent. Now group violence is often regarded as the intervening step between aggression and war. How then has it come about that man shows group violence and war to such an extent that the very existence of his species is threatened? Now I am certainly not able to sug-gest how this extraordinary characteristic of man has been pro-duced; and there are indeed many groups of men throughout the world—biologists, sociologists, anthropologists, psychologists, psy-chiatrists, psychopharmacologists, moral philosophers, theolo-gians, lawyers, and educationalists—who are putting their best minds to these topics of supreme importance for our society.

There are however a few points it seems to me to be worth making here, so I will tiptoe in where perhaps many angels would fear to tread. First one can say that overcrowding and lack of space do not appear to have been historically related to the occurrence of group violence. Nor does lack of food. Some primitive peoples, e.g., the Zulus, and the original inhabitants of Uganda and other parts of East Central Africa (as also of South and Central America), showed great group violence and even war when they appear to have been short neither of food nor space. The same probably applies to the incursions of westward-raiding hordes from Asia. To point to the other side of the picture, many primitive tribes and cultures, even though hunters (e.g., the Eskimo), have been and are extremely pacific. Some of them have the elaborate cultural device of "potlatch," found in several tribes of the northwest coast of America, where great feasts are given by one chief or clan to another. It is a matter of honour to accept any invitation to a potlatch and to give a grander feast in return. Refusal involves loss of prestige and rank. Sometimes the rivalry will become so intense as to amount to a dangerous drain on the resources of individuals and groups. Yet, nevertheless, it is a constructive not a destructive device which tends to bind groups together. It also serves for the repayment of debts and maintains differences of chieftainship and rank (Encyclopaedia Britannica, 1929). But even these pacific tribes (whether Bushmen or Amerindian) have shown violent reaction when their region has been invaded by unrelated tribes advancing from another region.

The next thing to be said is that, though individual violence certainly must have its part in promoting violence in small groups, it is very doubtful indeed how far individual tendency to violence is a major factor in the production of actual organised large-scale war. It is to my mind doubtful how far even individual violence in modern man is induced by crowding *per se;* for, as far as I know, some of the most crowded places on earth, e.g., Hong Kong, do not have a particularly bad record for individual violence. It is, however, true that the alienation that results from life in big conurbations, especially where the ties of family and small groups have broken and where the individual is anonymous in an anonymous crowd, undoubtedly does breed violence. But the organised violence of modern war is, so it seems to me, something different from all this. The people who find themselves at war are usually not themselves violent, nor do they come from violent groups, e.g., Korea, Viet Nam, and the Near East. But they agree to submit to the deprivation, terrors, and horrors of war, sadly and unwillingly, because they feel that, if they do not, worse things will come to them. Hence the persuaders, the Führers, the leaders, and the demagogues can hypnotise both the simple and often the sophisticated into thinking that there is some kind of glory in war. It may indeed be that such leaders are themselves personally aggressive. But how is it they can persuade non-violent, non-aggressive, peaceful people that war is glorious? It is certainly to some considerable extent a male characteristic for, even allowing for stories of Amazons, the female war-inciting demagogue appears to be non-existent. But

265

to what fantastic lengths the male can go. As Ulrich says, consider Shakespeare's speech for Henry V: "We few, we happy few, we band of brothers." They weren't few, they weren't happy, and they weren't brothers, but they fell for it all just the same!

The trouble with group violence and war in human societies is that there are no effective built-in constraints. Violence almost inevitably leads sooner or later to more violence. At a personal and small-group level, violence can be annulled and transformed by unyielding self-sacrificing love. (See Ellul, 1970, especially pp. 168–75.) But at the level of war, the scale and speed are too great for any brake to be effective unless the individual influence of saner members of society can somehow be more widely spread; and this seldom happens in time to avoid disaster. As an American biophysicist, J. R. Platt, has put it, "The world has now become too dangerous for anything less than Utopia" (Koestler, 1967). Again, as Father Mark Gibbard (personal communication) has said, speaking of sin, "there is a tragic discord at the heart of man." It is because of this discord that aggression is the terrible problem that it is. The New Testament writers saw this, and we now can easily see that a new vision of humanity is needed. Can we point to anything adequate to our condition other than the vision of the indwelling spirit which enabled Paul to say, "For as in Adam all die, even so in Christ shall all be made alive"?

Though I said that overcrowding might make cultured people feel aggressive, I doubt whether this is a major factor at present in our society. But of course if the population explosion goes on, it could well reach a point where violence increases to lethal proportions throughout society. T. S. Eliot (see Williams, 1971) foresaw, in 1930, the future of civilisation as "Internecine fighting —people killing one another in the streets." The threat of this compression, corresponding to the destruction of all the amenities which make life worth living, will indeed produce increasing fear and rightly so. As the Conservation Society says, *"Whatever your cause, it's a lost cause unless we limit population."*

The Pornography of Violence

Finally it seems to me that the factors in our society which cause the most ready acceptance of violence, and lead to personal and group violence and perhaps even to the violence of war, are those which glorify violence and at the same time, so to speak, "sanitise" it without showing its real horror and evil. Innumerable television shows do this. Newspapers and magazines do it. As Ulrich says of the United States: "You can kill five men in a movie and any five-year-old can get in to see it; but let a man and a woman show tenderness to one another and even hint that they are about to engage in the beauty of intercourse, and they won't let you in unless you're eighteen and willing to ignore the implicit and explicit banns placed on such movies in America by the churches." Many people get worked up about the pornography of sex. It may be dangerous and debasing; it may not. Many people, who indeed deserve respect, take quite opposite sides on this issue, and I feel very uncertain what the right answer is. But I do feel sure that there is a pornography of violence which constitutes a far greater danger. Now there is indeed a violent element in sex; and in many mammals (including some of our own nearest primate relatives which are promiscuous and polygamous) sex may be little more than rape. But in monogamous mammals, such as man, and in many birds (e.g., gulls), for sex to achieve its full function and fulfill its true value, the violence associated with it must be overcome and subordinated to contrary emotions.

In so far, then, as violence contaminates sexual pornography, it becomes that much more dangerous. And the more it approximates to pure violence the more dangerous it is. I have heard it stated that the most obscene and pornographic book ever published is Hitler's *Mein Kampf*, and I am prepared to agree that that is correct. For it seems to have depraved and corrupted nearly a whole nation. But while I am sure that the more we can do to control and prevent the atmosphere of violent propaganda the better; this is perhaps only one part and perhaps by far the least important part of the very profound and puzzling fact that *Homo sapiens* seems to have been infected almost from the beginning not with an instinctive drive to violence, but with a nature that makes it fatally easy for his social-control methods to slip over into violent forms. I feel more and more convinced that nothing will stop this unless mankind as a whole becomes conscious of some superordinate goal for which it must strive with all its strength. Only this perhaps could unite man and bring him to the point where he ceases to bother any more about war. A gleam of hope comes to me in this—could it be that the terrifying insistence of the increasing pollution problem will be the means of bringing him to his senses?

And if I feel depressed about it, I like to imagine myself taking a trip in H. G. Wells' "Time Machine" (or whatever its modern, space-fiction equivalent is), to view some of the many evolutionary crises which must have beset the story in the last 500 million years—crises such as the origin of the vertebrates, the colonisation of the land, the rise of the birds and mammals, the origin of the protohominids, or the establishment of man himself. At all these crises it would, I believe, have seemed to a privileged spectator that all was lost; that it was touch and go whether the stocks which were leading the way to higher and more spiritual developments could possibly survive. Yet survive and develop they did. And I feel now a great respect for, and gratitude to, Teilhard de Chardin in that he, almost alone (with his *Phenomenon of Man*, 1959, and *Man's Place in Nature*, 1956), has made clear to the ordinary reader the sound basis that exists for optimism as to the evolutionary process and the future of man. Teilhard had a bad press amongst biologists, and this was partly his own fault, for he claimed that the *Phenomenon* was to be read purely as science. In fact he was that very rare combination, an able scientist and a Christian mystical thinker of great power and depth. And these two mix with difficulty and are apt to confuse the poor biologist who comes unprepared for such a powerful potion. In fact Teilhard, in his whole vision of the future of man, is actually and avowedly restating the theology of St. Paul as this came to its fullest expression. He understands that Paul, in the last three epistles, had a vision which neither he himself, nor perhaps anyone prior to our own day, has been in a position to comprehend as fully as can now be done.

Chapter 8

THE UNIQUENESS OF MAN

In the opening chapter of this book in which we briefly considered the views of philosophers of science, such as Popper and Polanyi, we were led towards the view that something is happening in the mind, together with the brain, of man, that is in the *person* of man; something which, I think, in the foreseeable future cannot be (and I believe actually can never be) fully described in the terms of the mechanistic monism which is the scientific methodology of today. In other words we were approaching the position, which now we must attempt to amplify somewhat further, that both the old vitalism and the old mechanism are inadequate as a basis for the understanding of man. It has in the past been an arguable proposition that mechanistic monism might suffice for animals but not for man. Could it be that there is a real gulf fixed between the two? I think enough has been said in previous chapters for us to realise that, from the point of view of the features we have been discussing so far, there is no such gulf. But it is the object of the present chapter, and indeed of a considerable part of those which follow, to look at this question, so to speak, from the human side and to try to interpret the view from there.

THE DIFFERENCES BETWEEN ANIMALS AND MAN

What have been the arguments put forward in the past for the uniqueness of man? Forty or more years ago psychologists and moralists used to list a number of ways in which animals are clearly different from man. It was said (1) animals cannot learn; (2) animals cannot plan ahead; (3) animals cannot conceptualise; (4) animals cannot use, much less make, tools. (5) It was said they have no language; (6) they cannot count; (7) they lack artistic sense; and (8) they lack all ethical sense. We have already made clear that the first three of these statements do not hold. Animals can learn, often to an extraordinary degree; they can certainly plan ahead and they can certainly conceptualise, as was shown when discussing animal perceptions in relation to direction finding, territory, and so forth. So the first three distinctions are clearly invalid. We come now to consider briefly number 4, possession of tools, and at greater length number 5, the question of language. Finally, here and in later chapters, I shall have something to say about numbers 6, 7, and 8.

Ten years ago Burke, in his *The Rhetoric of Religion*, wrote a chapter entitled "On Words and the Word" in which he made the following propositions. Man is (1) the symbol-using animal, (2) the inventor of the negative, (3) is separated from his natural condition by instruments of his own making, (4) goaded by the spirit of hierarchy. Now all this of course is much less dogmatic and more reasonable than the position indicated by the eight points listed above. Burke does not deny that animals can use symbols; he does stress the positive, indeed overwhelming importance of symbol-making in the life of man. He is rather unfortunate in his final section because it is abundantly clear that a vast number of animals can be said to be "goaded by the spirit of hierarchy." In saying that man is the inventor of the negative, he is in a sense right in so far as language is concerned, but it will already be obvious that animals have ample means of showing rejection and refusal; although it is hard to argue that they have an actual word or signal standing in the abstract for "no." As we shall see, he is in effect right about "instruments of his own making," but this does not provide an absolutely firm distinction between animals and man.

BRAIN SIZE AND HUMAN EVOLUTION

Before we can usefully discuss these points of dispute much further, we must consider what are the essentials of human evolution as at present understood. First let us consider what is known about the evolutionary age of man, his relatives, and his artifacts. The present views on these questions are roughly as follows: The *first mammals* appeared on earth about fifty million years ago, the *first hominids* about *four million* years ago. The *earliest simple stone tools* are thought to date from about two million years ago. These are tools so simple that a moderately dexterous man can today learn to produce them in the course of an afternoon's practice. *Complex stone tools,* which we find need weeks or months of practice to produce rather than an afternoon, appeared about six hundred thousand years ago. Some kind of religious ritual was probably in existence seventy-five thousand years ago. *Homo sapiens* seems to date from about forty thousand years ago (about the date of the earliest cave paintings), and it is the general view amongst anthropologists and ethnologists that this must have been about the time of the appearance of true speech, that is to say verbal language—although of course languages of gestural signs and symbols must have been very much older. Finally agriculture seems to have commenced about eight thousand years ago. Previous to that, man and his hominid ancestors were probably omnivorous nomads, some of them already highly proficient hunters.*

* At the time of going to press it is beginning to appear (from the work of Richard Leakey in Kenya, Carl Johansen in Ethiopia, and Philip Tobias in South Africa) that some of the above figures will have to be greatly extended, perhaps even doubled.

Hunting and indeed being hunted provide clear and compelling reasons why natural selection should have favoured some kind of social development. These reasons apply far down the vertebrate scale and can be observed in both fish and birds. The fish school or shoal and the closely co-ordinate bird flock derive advantage from the protection such an aggregation offers when the group is attacked by a smaller number of more powerful and more active enemies. The first manoeuvre of a peregrine falcon when attacking a flock of waders, or of a marine predator attacking fish, is for the attacker to adopt tactics which will tend to split up the group or isolate one or two weaker members of it. So the first response both of the fish school and of the bird flock is to mass closer together, not to scatter. The reason for the success of this manoeuvre can be illustrated from the problems of defence against air attack in war. Any radar or other type of detector adjusted so as to aim a missile at an oncoming plane is "confused" if a large number of small objects appear close together. It can only aim into the middle of the mass and not at a single one, and hence is likely to miss. So in nature, a predator cannot concentrate on one until he has got it separated to some extent from the rest, and the ones that get separated are likely to be the less experienced or the weakest. Hence predation of this kind, and the response to it of the preyed-upon species, tends to be eugenic in that there is a strong selection for the good health and high powers of adjustment of those that survive. And if the preyed-upon animal has a means of retaliation and individuals are capable of co-ordinating their responses, then again there is safety in numbers.

This leads to a second advantage of social organisation in animals. It concerns the finding and utilisation of food. If the food sought is not evenly scattered throughout the environment but tends to be aggregated in considerable quantities in a few places, then a species seeking that food is more likely to do better if seeking is co-operative, since it will increase the chance of food being found; and when found it will increase the opportunity for its full utilisation. Once the find has been made, all can share.

If the food animal is one that is able to fight back, and has to be subdued or outwitted, once again there is advantage in the social group. Then, if evolution is taking the species towards a family organisation where the young are weak and less able to take care of themselves, and where they have to learn much before they are fully competent as foragers or fighters, then again the family or clan will be desirable in that it will provide a means of protecting the weaker young during the all-important period of their growth and education.

It is now generally assumed (although of course there has been much difference of opinion) that the Hominidae arose as offshoots from the primitive Pongidae, or ape stock, some time after the separate evolution of the Cercopithecidae or "monkeys" several million years ago). So the study of the monkeys and the apes, the way in which they develop social organisation and the nature of the social bond in these animals, is at the root of our enquiry into the social life of man.

The simplest answer to the origin of the social bond is that when feline predators, such as leopards, are about, monkeys are safer in numbers. The hypothesis has been put forward that a threefold enlargement of the brain in human stock took place during the Pleistocene. This is regarded as a reasonable deduction from the present evidence, especially after the discovery of *Zinjanthropus* by Dr. and Mrs. Leakey at Olduvai. This increase in brain size is primarily due to the growth of the cortex and might be put down to one or more of the following developments: (1) the ability to make and use tools, (2) the necessity to get to know and recognise quickly a considerable number of individuals in the same social group, and (3) the development of speech.

The gap between "man" and "ape" has been greatly narrowed in respect of brain size by the discovery of *Australopithecus* in South Africa (brain size 435 to 600 cc) and *Pithecanthropus erectus* (now recognised as a true Homo, *Homo erectus*, in Java) with a brain size of 775 to 1,225 cc. For comparison, the brain size of *Homo sapiens* is between 1,000 and 2,000 cc, thus significantly overlapping *Homo erectus*. Thus we see that the *Australopithecines* are scarcely above the level of the apes in brain size whereas *Homo erectus* has a brain between two and three times the volume of the former.

The *Australopithecines* (Vallois, 1962) are thought to be more like the apes than man, and it is assumed that there is nothing to warrant the assumption that they had speech in the way that we understand the word. But they were certainly social and bipedal and were apparently toolmakers. Perhaps this was the only character they possessed amongst the three characteristics, *namely language, fabricated stone tools*, and *war*, which are sometimes regarded as definitive of man. There is in fact evidence (Washburn and De Vore, 1962) that *Australopithecus* had a social life little developed from that of apes or monkeys, that they were probably primarily vegetarian, and that the small-brained young could have matured rapidly. But the fact that they were toolmakers, and the fact that tool using and in a sense toolmaking (not the making of stone tools, but the preparation of stick tools) have now been observed a number of times in wild chimpanzees, at first sight throws doubt on the conclusion that the development of brain size was primarily due to this characteristic. It may however be that the big change in brain size roughly coincided with the first appearance of the *elaborate* stone tools, and this could indeed be significant. But it is hard to say whether the chronological evidence is strong enough to warrant this conclusion. Chance (1953) considers that the development of brain size was primarily due to this characteristic. Admittedly there is a large, indeed enormous, gap between the toolmaking and tool using of chimpanzees (or indeed the tool using of the California sea otter and of certain birds) and the toolmaking of primitive man. Nevertheless, to attribute the immense increase in brain size for a period of about a million years (fifty thousand generations) primarily to this characteristic seems, to say the least, highly doubtful. There are also other theories which seem to me equally lacking in good evidence.

Tool Use and Tool Construction

But let us glance for a moment at the tool-using abilities of the animals. To start with I should mention that there are in fact a number of examples of tool using of a fairly primitive kind known in the insects, the crustacea, and the molluscs. However I am not going to discuss these now because for technical reasons it is very difficult to evaluate whether these really correspond to the use of tools by human beings, though they certainly strongly suggest it. Instead I will merely mention examples of tool using in birds and mammals. I assume for the purposes of this discussion that we restrict the term tool using to the manipulation of inanimate objects for a particular end. However, when we say this, we at once come up against a difficulty—the vast majority of birds manipulate grass, stems, leaves, moss, spiders' webs, etc., to make their nests. Must we then say that these are "tool users"? I think myself this is stretching the definition of tool using rather too far, since the material is part of the objective of the behaviour; and although it is manipulated in making the required structure, it is not used as a tool to *make* the structure. If we adopt this viewpoint, we rule out all those cases where a rock or stone is used as a resistance against which to break open protective shells of prey—even though the prey is dropped from a considerable height, as is the case with the Lammergeier, or Bearded, vulture (*Gypaetus barbatus*), which drops bones from a great height with the result that the marrow can be picked out from the broken remnants.

A genuine case of tool using was referred to in Chapter 5 where we discussed the way in which the satin bowerbird (*Ptilonorhynchus violaceous*) uses fibrous material as a brush with which to paint the sticks of its bower with a coloured substance made from berries or with charcoal. Still more remarkable is the tool using of one of "Darwin's finches" on the Galápagos Islands, the "woodpecker finch" (*Camarhynchus pallidus*), which feeds by picking up a cactus spine or a twig and poking it into bark crevices to extract the insects on which it feeds. Sooner or later, as a result of the "random" poking with the spine or stick, an insect or a spider runs out, whereupon the bird drops the spine and seizes the insect. Then another spine is picked up and the procedure resumed.

The large and very hard eggs of the ostriches in Africa and the emu in Australia provide tempting meals for hungry predators; but how can the eggs be broached and the contents extracted? Normally of course no predators can attack an ostrich or an emu egg when the parent is present because the bird is capable of completely protecting its eggs from attack by all comers. The Australian black-breasted buzzard (*Haemirostris melanosterna*) is said to drive the emu from its eggs and then fly aloft with a stone in its claws; this missile it drops on the eggs and then immediately swoops down to devour the contents (Chisholm, ref. in Thorpe, 1963). Much more fully reported and completely documented with photographs is the behaviour of one of the five species of vulture in East Africa, namely the Egyptian vulture (*Neophron percnopterus*) (van Lawick-Goodall, 1966). This vulture cannot drive the ostrich away from its eggs, but sometimes an egg gets rolled away or the nest is deserted, and here is a potentially sumptuous meal. The egg is too big for the vulture to pick up in the beak and much too hard to break by stabbing. Instead the vulture chooses as large a stone as it can hold in its bill and then, standing very erect, throws the stone at the egg with, when it is experienced, a fairly good aim. This stone throwing is continued until the eggshell breaks.

To come now to the mammals: the California sea otter (*Enhydra lutris nereis*) feeds on large "shellfish" such as the "abalone." The animal dives to the sea bottom, say about two fathoms, and returns to the surface carrying a small boulder or a large stone with one arm and one of the abalones with the other. The animal floats on its back in the water, rests the stone on its chest, and hammers the mollusc on the stone until the shell is broken and the meat can be devoured. As soon as the meat is fully available the stone is dropped and then, when ready, the otter returns to the bottom for another mollusc and comes up again with the same or another stone. The whole process has been carefully analysed, and it is quite clear that there is intentional selection of a stone for the purposes of a tool and that all the behaviour shows striking evidence of at least elementary planning and foresight. (See Hall and Schaller, 1964.)

But although, in the above examples, objects are chosen as tools, they are not worked or modified. Can we find, in wild animals, any genuine case of special preparation of a tool? The answer now is, Yes, we can. Chimpanzees in the wild use both sticks and leaves as tools. Sticks are used for various purposes, but in particular they are employed during the time of year when the chimpanzees feed on termites or white ants. When preparing for a termite-gathering expedition, they set out, apparently first visiting a particular tree with which they are familiar, and break off a suitable branch. They then strip the leaves off and carry the tool so formed to the termites' nest. The sticks are then thrust into the nest entrance so that the termites cling to it. When withdrawn they come out covered with termites. The chimpanzees then put the sticks in their mouths and draw them through, wiping the clinging termites off with their lips and eating them. Here we have the very simple form of tool preparation required for this rather special activity of feeding upon termites.

Let us now return to the main problem of the increase in brain size during the evolutionary history of man. If tool using and toolmaking are not the keys to the problem, how far could it be understood by the assumption that with the development of social life the ability to get to know and recognise quickly a considerable number of individuals became essential? Chance himself suggests that a somewhat similar solution is rendered plausible by the study of present-day macaques and baboons. In these species there is intensive competitive behaviour. This is correlated with the breeding premium which implies a very rapid rate of selection of the characteristics that lead to dominance. Chance points out that the most important of these characteristics is the ability to control emotive expression at high levels of social excitement. This facility, if, as is probable, it were dependent upon an enlargement of the amygdala, would also be a predisposing mechanism for the development of tameness; and so it is suggested that "tameness" is the basis (together with individual recognition) upon which co-operative social life can emerge in hunting communities. And so perhaps it is after all more plausible to suggest that the clue lies not in progressive increases in tool-making ability but rather in the development of true social organisation. This is, as we have seen, organisation in which not only a certain individual is dominant and others submissive but in which each member of the group must know personally each of the others. Such societies involve, as we find in wolves and many social birds, not merely dominance but submission and leadership, which are much more subtle relationships. On the other hand the very existence of these faculties in birds and in the Canidae gives one pause. Because here there is nothing to suggest the necessary connexion between a high degree of social organisation and a massive development of the cortex or analogous brain structures.

It has been argued by the protagonists of the toolmaking theory that bipedal gait released the hand for a more specialised, and far more finely adjusted, series of activities, and that tool-making is the most likely explanation of the process. Chance and Meade (1953) suggest that the control of emotive expressions, with its concomitant enlarged amygdala, would itself be a pre-disposing mechanism for the development of tameness, and that this is the basis upon which co-operative social life can emerge in hunting communities. They think it may have been only a phase in man's development, but that it probably antedated the period of maximum cortical expansion. It might have served as a necessary preliminary period of selection, assisting the background rearrangement of hereditary factors that could dispose man's ancestors for the rapid change that occurred during the Pleistocene. If it were known whether Australopithecus had a large amygdala, it might be possible to decide whether this type of selection did precede Pleistocene enlargement of the cortex.

As we shall see, when we come to consider the development of language a little further, the development of a hunting, as distinct from a vegetarian, community might be a tremendously strong factor in the development of human society. In the development of hunting, mutual help would certainly become of high selective value. Here again I think those who have written on this subject are insufficiently alive to the extent to which this already occurs in prehuman stocks. It has only recently been found (van Lawick-Goodall, 1968) that wild chimpanzees are sometimes carnivorous and show evidence of precise co-operation in the isolation and catching of Colobus monkeys. And, after all, nowhere in the living apes is there evidence of mutual co-operation of the degree shown in the hunting behaviour of lions and wolves, or the reproductive and defensive behaviour of the elephants and the dolphins. So as a result of our survey of mammalian behaviour generally, one cannot but feel less and less convinced about the adequacy of any of these three alleged causes of the increase in brain size.

I myself think that we may have to look at the matter in a somewhat different light, as indeed did Washburn and his co-workers in an earlier and, I cannot help feeling, more balanced assessment of the situation. (See also Dobzhansky, 1962.) To my mind it seems likely that much of what we think of as "human" evolved long after the use of tools. It is probably more correct to think of much of our structure as the result of culture than it is to think of men anatomically like ourselves slowly developing culture.

Ritual Anthropophagy

We have already discussed elementary cultures in birds and in the establishment of new habits in monkeys. As was pointed out, there seems little doubt that different monkey colonies, even of the same species, have different learned proto-cultures. With this kind of example in mind let us consider again the evidence for cultures in early man. Schultz (1962) has an ingenious suggestion as to the way in which the attitudes of subhuman primates might have given rise to some of the most characteristic examples of early human cultural traditions. He points out that every zoo and primate laboratory has witnessed instances of the pitiful devotion of simian mothers to their sick infants. Every zoo director has experienced the long and painful struggle which the keeper has to take a dead, or even decomposed, baby away from its mother, who will clutch the corpse to her breast day after day. Sick or wounded juvenile or adult monkeys that are incapable of keeping up with the group search for a hiding place—perhaps in a cluster of dead foliage or, if they have fallen to the ground, in the deepest niche amongst roots or rocks. If they reach a cave, they will soon be found in the farthest, darkest corner. There they will remain, still and quiet, until they recover or die.

It seems plausible that, like monkeys and apes, the early hominids withdrew to the best available hiding places as soon as they became too weak from one cause or another to live with their groups. It was not until the later hominids became encouraged by the light and protection of fire that they began to use caves, instead of trees, as a nocturnal retreat for those healthy individuals who could be sheltered thus. Schultz argues that the primary role of caves for primates, connected with illness and death, may very well have induced the later behaviour of cave men, especially their attitudes towards skeletons found in their innermost recesses.

Acts of ritual anthropophagy (Bergounioux, 1962) seem to have been associated in a number of cases with a cult in which the occipital hole of the skull was enlarged with blows from a club. The brain was then devoured, presumably by those who wished to assume the virtues and merits of the dead man. Similar anthropophagous tribes in Central Africa apparently practised mutilation rituals for a long time. Thus the presence of broken jaws and skulls indicates a funerary cult. Bergounioux asks, What can be the significance of this? What did these men think about before a dead body? What would be the meaning of the rigidity, the cold, and impressive stillness? The dead man is there, but he does not speak, he appears not to see or hear, he is all the more formidable; he seems to be jealously guarding a terrible secret which none can take from him without assuming part of his substance. So it is natural to think that the organ of command, so expressive in life and now fixed in rigidity, should be an object of special veneration; and so they carried a few bones of the deceased about the person like a talisman. And so it seems that the kind of behaviour that occurred in *Homo erectus* was retained, or again developed, without substantial modification, through hundreds of thousands of years.

It is all of course highly conjectural, but it is hard not to believe that during these millennia secret psychical activity was ceaselessly exercised. That cultures of such persistence must have very powerfully affected the pressures acting upon the individual cannot be doubted. Perhaps we shall never know enough about the cultures of prehistoric man and his forebears to be able to get the picture very much clearer than it is at present; but it is plain that the ritual mutilation of the base of the skull was performed by early and late Neanderthal man for a period estimated at about a quarter of a million years. The stability of this and other evidences of culture can only be explained in terms of the power of tradition and of cultural continuity through evolving human races which, meanwhile, changed body type and most certainly changed genetic constitution. I think that the ethologists, taking a wide view of animal behaviour, would tend (perhaps surprisingly to the anthropologist) to emphasise, in cultural development, *the psychic factors as more important than any other one feature in determining the evolutionary course of the hominids.* And we must remember that the earliest formal burials, of adults and children in graves, together with food and stone tools (for the afterlife?), date from at least 70,000 years ago (Neanderthal man).

There is one point which deserves emphasis at the conclusion of this discussion. It has often been pointed out that modern man, as an individual, is weaker than at least many of his ancestors, and that, biologically, one of the most striking features of mankind is helplessness at birth and for the long period of childhood. Why did selection lead to the formation of a species with individuals of a more infantile and therefore less robust structure? Bergounioux quotes a Russian anthropologist, Roginsky, who answered this question by saying that it is just this weakness of the individual which favoured the establishment of a more organised and more substantial collective group in which each of its members is first of all seeking protection at the core of this collective group and in the second place is capable of submitting to its exigencies.

FROM LANGUAGE TO SPEECH

Learning Chimpanzees "Speech"

We discussed the essentials of communication in Chapter 3 and described the system of "design features" elaborated by Hockett and Altmann. We must now consider recent studies on the training of chimpanzees to "talk," in relation to what was said there. There have been, in the past, several attempts to train chimpanzees to use human language. It is not putting it too strongly to say that they have been monumental failures. The best-known was that of Hayes and Hayes (1952, 1955) with the young chimpanzee "Viki." I was fortunate to be able to spend some days with Dr. and Mrs. Hayes and Viki, in 1952, and have vivid memories of their experiments and the immense care and the sophisticated psychological technique which they employed in their attempts to teach Viki to talk. The result was that in six years Viki learned only four sounds that approximated to English words and even then the approximation was somewhat tenuous. As Gardner and Gardner (1969) point out, human speech sounds are unsuitable as a medium for communication for the chimpanzee, whose vocal apparatus and vocal behaviour are different from ours. These animals do make many different sounds, but generally vocalisation occurs in situations of high excitement and tends to be specific to the exciting situation. Undisturbed chimpanzees are usually rather silent when in captivity. It is consequently improbable that a chimpanzee could be trained to make refined use of its vocalisations.

With this problem in mind, the Drs. Gardner adopted an infant female chimpanzee at an age between eight and fourteen months and proceeded to attempt to teach this animal a gesture language known as the American Sign Language (ASL). This is the language widely used in the United States for communication between deaf human beings, and it is systematically taught to deaf children. It is entirely different from the deaf-and-dumb language of Great Britain, which essentially is a method of spelling—an alphabetical means of communication. Such systems of finger spelling are of course widely used by the deaf and dumb in conjunction with, and to supplement, sign languages.

ASL is in fact composed of manually produced visual symbols, called signs, which "are strictly analogous to words as used in spoken languages" (Gardner and Gardner, 1971). The Gardners point out that as words can be analysed into phonemes, so signs can be analysed into what have been call "cheremes" by Stokoe. A system of fifty-five cheremes has been devised for ASL. Nineteen of them identify the configuration of the hand or hands making the sign, twelve the place where the sign is made, and twenty-four the action of the hand or hands. Thus the configuration of pointing the hand yields one sign when near the forehead, another near the cheek, another near the chin, yet another near the shoulder and so forth. At any given place the pointing-hand signal yields one sign if moved towards the signer, another if moved away, another if moved vertically, and yet another if moved horizontally, and so on. But if the "tapered hand signal" is used, instead of the pointing hand, a whole new family of signs is generated.

This summary shows that ASL satisfies the criteria for Hockett's design feature 13 (p. 74) in that there are arbitrary, but stable, meaningless signal elements and that these are arranged in a series of patterns which constitute minimum meaningful combinations of those elements. The formal analysis of the ASL language by linguists is still in a relatively elementary state. But it is already clear that ASL has a syntactical structure of its own that is different from English. It will surprise non-linguists to learn that the complete linguistic analysis of spoken English is even yet incomplete, so, as the Gardners point out, it will be a long time before a precise comparison of ASL with English, in regard to syntax, can be established. But while such precise comparison is not yet possible, it is nevertheless clear that ASL is a language in essentially the same sense that English is a language, and that if a chimpanzee can be taught ASL to such a degree that it can carry on some or most of the normal communicative activities of its life by that means, then that chimpanzee has learned a language. The process of teaching ASL to a chimpanzee has the further very great advantage that the animal's achievements can be compared directly with the achievements of normal young children in their acquisition of English and with deaf children of the same ages in their acquisition of ASL.

The basic situation employed was as follows. A young chimp (named "Washoe") was kept in a room that contained most of the usual items of a modern human dwelling; that is to say the environment was as interesting as possible and the training programme was made an integral part of this environment throughout the waking hours of the ape. There was, however, no attempt to make the chimpanzee into a normal member of a human family. The work was planned so that during the whole of her waking hours Washoe was in the presence of one or more human companions with whom she took part in the routine activities of the day—feeding, bathing, dressing, etc.—and with whom she played games, examined new objects, was shown picture books and magazines, and so on. However the only form of verbal communication that was used in Washoe's presence was ASL; all her human companions had to master ASL sufficiently well for them not to need to use any other form of verbal communication, with the exception of finger spelling for unusual or technical words. But apart from the prohibition on the use of spoken language, there was no rule of silence. Vocalisation was permitted if it was not verbal or if the sounds were sounds that Washoe could imitate, such as laughter and cries of pleasure and displeasure. Washoe's attention was obtained by clapping the hands and many other noises, and there was also music. Burglar alarms and boat horns were used to frighten Washoe away from forbidden places. After the first thirty-nine months of this work the results are briefly as follows:

One of the most widespread hypotheses invoked to explain the development of language in the human infant may be called, for convenience, the "babbling hypothesis." This assumes that the "random" babbling and jabbering of the human baby comprise a great variety of sounds and so will include most if not all of the sounds which are employed in the language of whatever culture it happens to be reared in. Mothers often talk or croon to their children when attending to them, and so the sound of the mother's voice will become associated with comfort-giving measures. From this it is to be expected that when the child, alone and uncomfortable, hears his own voice, this will likewise have a consoling, comforting effect. So it is supposed (e.g., by Mowrer, 1950) that the infant will be rewarded for his own first babbling and jabbering without any necessary reference to the effects produced upon others. Before long, however, the infant will learn that if he succeeds in making the kind of sound his mother makes, he will get more interest, affection, and attention in return; so the stage is set for the learning of language. There are, in fact, a good many difficulties in the way of this theory; perhaps the major one of these is the difficulty, if not impossibility, of characterizing the kind of reinforcing event which could adequately account for the acquisition of language in such a learning situation. In fact, as will be made clear in other sections of this book, Chomsky (1957) has shown, with seemingly incontrovertible argument, that such a theory cannot possibly account for the basic events in the child's acquisition of language.

Nevertheless, at the commencement of the work with Washoe

it was assumed that the infant chimpanzee would in fact show a great deal of "manual babbling" in the form of random or accidental gestures, which would come so close to the cheremes of ASL that they could be readily enhanced and shaped by the methods planned for the experiment. However, during the earliest months of the project the amount of manual babbling was very small. The ape would manipulate objects, poke at them with her fingers, and so forth, but seldom engaged in the kind of manual play that had been expected, such as wiggling her fingers before her eyes or poking the fingers of one hand at the other hand. As time went on cheremic and incipiently cheremic gestures seemed to increase in frequency, and during this period the ape acquired several signs which she could use appropriately. Moreover she seemed to be paying more and more attention to the signs made by her human companions and showed that she could comprehend the meaning of many of these signs. Manual babbling was encouraged by the experimenters as much as possible, and one sign which did appear to be learned largely in this way was the ASL "word" for funny. Washoe was fond of touching her nose or her friends' noses with her index finger, and in the "funny" sign the extended index and second fingers are brushed against the sides of the nose. Washoe herself introduced a variation which consisted of snorting as the nose was touched, and gradually she came to make the "funny" sign in "funny" situations without any prompting. Although manual babbling did appear to play its part at this stage, it declined as time went on, and its function in the total process of acquiring ASL seems to have been comparatively slight and rather doubtful.

Particularly in the later stages of the learning, imitation was playing a greater and greater part in the process (a fact that in any case could have been anticipated by the striking powers of manual imitation shown by Viki). One of the signs which was clearly corrected by imitation was that for "flower." In the acceleration of ASL acquisition, observational learning, as distinct from imitation, was almost certainly the prime factor. But Gardner and Gardner remark (1971), "However, if Washoe could reach a point at which she asks us for the names of things, then imitative guidance might become the most practical method of introducing new signs."

Some of the signs developed by Washoe seem to be best described as straight inventions. They are quite different from the signs which had, until then, been modelled for her, and their occurrence throws a particularly strong light upon the animal's mental processes. One example will suffice. The experimenters sometimes could not find an ASL equivalent for an English word which they wished to use. In such cases they would adapt a sign of ASL for the purpose: the sign for "bib" was one of these cases. They happened to use the ASL sign for "napkin" or "wiper" to refer to bibs as well. This sign is made by touching the mouth region with an open hand and a wiping movement. During the eighteenth experimental month, Washoe had begun to use this sign appropriately for bibs, but it was still unreliable. "One evening at dinner time, a human companion was holding up a bib and asking Washoe to name it. She tried 'Come-gimme' and 'please,' but did not seem to be able to remember the 'bib' sign that we had taught her. Then, she did something very interesting; with the index fingers of both hands she drew an outline of a bib on her chest—starting from behind her neck where the bib should be tied, moving the index fingers down along the outer edge of her chest, and bringing them together again just above her navel." The authors remark, "A high level of cognitive ability must be possessed by a creature that can represent the concept of a bib by drawing an outline on its chest with its fingers."

A number of instances have recently come to light which demonstrate that many animals, at least including the birds and the mammals, must possess greater powers of conceptualisation than hitherto seemed credible. Among the pioneers in this field were Herrnstein and Loveland (1964), whose work showed quite dramatically that the domestic pigeon is capable of forming a broad and complex concept when placed in a situation that demands one. The pigeons used by these workers were in fact taught to respond to the presence or absence of human beings in photographs. They were trained to peck one disc if there was any sign of a human being in the photograph, and another if there was no sign. It was found that the most fragmentary, and presumably unfamiliar, aspects of the human being, or parts of the human being, were sufficient to cause the birds to give a positive response. (For similar recent work on monkeys, see Lehr, 1967.) Accordingly, it was not surprising that the ape Washoe often showed this kind of ability. Many of the items for which Washoe learned the names and the appropriate ASL signals could of course be classified into meaningful groups. Thus there were six items, "brush," "clean soap," "comb," "oil," "lotion," and "toothbrush," that could be classified as grooming articles; five, namely "bird," "bug," "cat," "cow," and "dog," which could be classified as animals; and four, "banana," "drink," "meat," and "sweet," that could be classified as foods, and so on. When Washoe made errors it was possible to show that these were governed by the category of item that was actually presented. Thus in one set of experiments in which Washoe made errors in twelve trials, seven of the twelve were the signs for other items in the appropriate category—in this case the category of grooming articles. Similar results were found for other categories of items. In fact these errors revealed just the kind of conceptualisation referred to above.

This was further displayed in Washoe's ability to learn the use of pronouns. When she was being taught, the experimenters often had to use a few specific instances of the appropriate referent: a few items of clothing for "pants," a few examples of her companions' possessions for "yours." When Washoe transferred the sign to another referent, or when she used it in a new combination, she produced examples of the usage that went beyond the ones that had been taught to her. It was from these that it is possible to infer and evaluate her meaning. It would never have been possible to show Washoe all the persons she should designate as "you," nor all the actions that "you" was capable of performing. Yet it appeared that Washoe used the pronouns appropriately, that is, for any companion and in combination with a wide variety of signs for action and for attributes. She began to use the two pronouns "you" and "me" in January 1968. In spring 1968, she had signed "you me out" in a doorway situation and later produced many variants such as "you Roger Washoe out," "you me go out," "you me go out hurry."

At the time of the latest report Washoe does not have signs for words that can be used to join members of combinations—e.g., "and," "for," "with," "to." But it is significant perhaps that words of this type are noticeably absent from the early sentences of young children (Brown and Bellugi, 1964; see also Brown, 1970).

According to the information available at the time of going to press, Washoe, in the approximately three years since the experiment commenced, has reliably mastered the use of eighty-seven signs included in, or of a type similar to, those which make up ASL. Let us remind ourselves that in a comparable period, the chimpanzee Viki, belonging to Dr. and Mrs. Hayes, acquired a vocabulary of four vocalisations, one of which was still rather doubtful. Nothing further needs saying to stress the impact and significance of this new approach to the understanding of the communicative abilities of the higher animals.

The Question of Syntax

We must now come to what is in many respects the key question in this whole topic, namely the question of syntax. From what was said above, it will be already clear that the popular notion, derivable from any dictionary, that syntax is a set of rules governing sentence construction will not carry us very far at the present day. In fact Chomsky's *Syntactic Structures* (1957) was, so to speak, a signpost marking the direction of the new road. The problems raised by the advances and developments resulting from the work of Professor Chomsky have been discussed elsewhere (Hinde, 1972) and need not be entered into here. But it is still necessary to enquire, as far as we can, whether and in what senses of the word the achievements of Washoe can be described as syntactic. Certainly Washoe combines words meaningfully. In the thirty-eight months following April 1967, the experimenters recorded 294 different two-sign combinations used by this animal. In arriving at this total, different sequences of the same signs, e.g., "open please" and "please open," and again "gimme food" and "gimme food gimme," were tabulated as the same two-sign combinations. It was soon noticed that the vocabulary seemed to be divided into a small group of words called "pivots," which are found in the bulk of the two-word utterances, and a larger group which are seldom found in two-word utterances unless they are paired with one of the pivots. All the 87 word signs were scored according to the number of different two-sign combinations in which they appeared. It was found that at least one of the twelve highest-ranking signs occurred in 240 of the 294 different two-sign combinations. These twelve word signs, in descending order of their scores, were "come," "gimme," "please," "you," "go," "me," "hurry," "more," "up," "open," "out," "in," and "food." As Gardner and Gardner point out, if the tabulation had been based on the total number of two-sign combinations that Washoe produced, it would only indicate that she had some favourite signs and perhaps some favourite combinations. But in this tabulation, each two-sign combination was counted only once, no matter how many times it was used by Washoe, and moreover, reversals of order and repetitions of the same sign were not counted. This indicates that the sample is a sample of types, and the finding that at least one out of a small number of signs appeared in most of the combinations indicates that certain types of combinations were more permissible (according to Washoe's own "rules") than others. This fact suggests, to a non-specialist, the beginnings of an approach to "syntax."

Since Washoe's achievements, significant though they are, are so far removed from the achievements of a fully articulate human being, Gardner and Gardner very wisely proceeded by comparing Washoe's two-sign combinations with children's two-word combinations in a way that follows the scheme proposed by Brown (1970). First they listed the 87 signs and grouped them into six categories. This analysis is shown in Table V. It will be seen that the six categories, which are "Appeal," "Location," "Action," "Object," "Agent," and "Attribute," overlap to a considerable extent. But for Washoe it was found necessary to establish an additional category, namely the first one, "Appeal," which does not appear in Brown's scheme for children's two-word combinations. As Brown suggests, further analysis may make it possible to fit these four signs, "gimme," "hurry," "more," and "please," into the other five categories.

A further point of interest appears. Apart from the pronouns "me" and "you," most readily combined signs are all to be found amongst the "Appeals," "Locations," and "Actions." This suggests that these more readily combined signs serve certain constructive functions. It is quite evident, from a study of the records of characteristic dialogues between Washoe and one or other of her human associates, that if, in response to an initial word from Washoe—for instance the sign "please" or the sign "come"—the human partner asks the question, "What you want?" Washoe elaborates by adding a second word in the form of an answer; and this answer expresses considerably more than the initial one-sign utterance. Thus in response to these questions, the commonly formed two-sign combinations that Washoe uses are as follows: "please out," "come open," "more tickle." Leading questions indicate what the human partners in this project, Washoe's linguistic community, would accept as completed ASL utterances, and it is clear that she gives them.

Just because infant human beings and infant chimpanzees cannot act as "informants" in the way that native speakers serve as informants when an unknown human language is being studied, lists of the attempts so far made to analyse children's early language for structure have used the utterances themselves as raw data. And this must obviously be the method employed in the study of the communications between Washoe and her associates. Table VI compares Washoe's achievements with the structure of the earliest two-word combinations of children. The essence of the scheme for children is the notion that the con-

Table V. Washoe's signs grouped into six overlapping categories. (From Gardner and Gardner, 1971.)

Appeal	Action	Location	Object	Agent	Attribute
gimme hurry more please	in, out, up come, go, help bed, brush, catch look, oil, tooth-brush ride clean, comb, cover, dirty, drink, food, listen hug kiss, open, peek-aboo, spin, tickle	there down	baby, banana, berry cheese, climb, clothes hurt, key, leaf spoon, string, sweet bib, bird, book, bug, car, cat, chair cow, dog, flower, fruit, grass, hammer, hat light, meat, pants, pencil, shoes, smell, smoke tree, window	me you Washoe Dr G. Mrs G. Greg Naomi Roger Susan Wende	black green red white enough funny good quiet sorry mine

293

junction of two words can express a relationship that is independent of the particular words in the pair. The comparison set forth in the table is discussed in detail by B. T. and R. A. Gardner (1971), and readers who wish for a more detailed discussion of the problems and difficulties it raises must seek it there.

It seems safe, however, to say that Brown's scheme shows that the types of construction which can be distinguished in the earliest combinations of young children do express relationships that are somewhat independent of the specific words that appear in the combinations. That is to say, to some extent children's utterances are characterised by structure at this level of development. From the data available to Gardner and Gardner, at the time of writing, it is estimated that between 70 and 85 per cent of the two-word combinations in the children's samples can be accounted for by the Brown scheme. In the sample of Washoe's 294 two-sign combinations, 228, or 78 per cent, can be accounted for by the scheme that the Gardners have derived from Brown's schemes. "At this level of analysis, then, Washoe's earliest two-sign combinations were comparable to the earliest two-word combinations of children." (See Gardner and Gardner, 1971.) There remains the question whether this structure represents the first emergence of syntax or whether it is a stage of semantic structure that precedes the first stage of truly syntactical construction. The present view of the Gardners is that this question remains open.

We may now turn to another recent series of experiments with a chimpanzee using a quite different technique. It will be obvious that the ability to develop an association between two objects or events in contiguity is part of the basic learning repertoire of every animal that can at least establish a conditioned response. Every dog can learn to associate a sound or a gesture with an object which it desires or fears. Premack (1970a, b), in a remarkable series of experiments with "Sarah," another young female chimpanzee, has developed an ingenious technique for teaching language by means of plastic "words." Each "word" is a metal-backed piece of plastic, of a given and unique com-

Table VI. Parallel descriptive schemes for the earliest combinations of children and Washoe. (From Gardner and Gardner, 1971.)

Brown's (1970) scheme for children		The scheme for Washoe	
Types	Examples	Types	Examples
Attributive Ad + N	big train, red book	*Object—Attributable*	drink red, comb black
Possessive: N + N	Adam checker, mommy lunch	*Agent—Attribute*	Washoe sorry, Naomi good
		Agent—Object	clothes Mrs G., you hat
N + V	walk street, go store	*Object—Attribute*	baby mine, clothes yours
		Action—Location	go in, look out
Locative N + N	sweater chair, book table	*Action—Object*	go flower, pants tickle
		Object—Location	baby down, in hat
Agent—Action: N + V	Adam put, Eve read	*Agent—Action*	Roger tickle, you drink
Action—Object: · V + N	put book, hit ball	*Action—Object*	tickle Washoe, open blanket
Agent—Object: N + N	mommy sock, mommy lunch	*Appeal—Action* *Appeal—Object*	please tickle, hug hurry gimme flower, more fruit

bination of shape, size, texture, and colour, which adheres lightly to a magnetised slate. Association between the plastic "word" and the object (e.g., an apple) which it is to represent is readily taught to the animal by simple reward. From this simple beginning, Premack, by an elegant series of steps, has been able to teach Sarah to "speak," by tokens, to a degree not inferior to Washoe and in some respects superior. The work has not yet been reported in sufficient detail to enable a full comparative assessment to be made, nor is it possible here to describe Premack's method in detail. But not only does Sarah's vocabulary now exceed that of Washoe, her use of it is in many respects more sophisticated and complex. Thus Sarah has a vocabulary of 112 plastic "words" which comprise eight names of persons (or chimps), twenty-one verbs, six colours, twenty-one foods, twenty-six miscellaneous objects, and thirty "concepts, adjectives, and adverbs."

Exact comparison with Washoe is of course misleading in that the "words" are made for Sarah; she does not have to learn to make them herself. Nor does she have the free choice of actions open to Washoe; she can manipulate what is given to her but not invent or choose others. Nevertheless, the work with Sarah gives even stronger suggestions of syntax than does that with Washoe. Premack says, "We feel justified in concluding that Sarah can understand some symmetrical and hierarchical sentence structures and is therefore competent to some degree in the sentence function of language."

Another achievement of Sarah that is worthy of mention is her ability to answer questions about her classification of objects. It is possible for instance to ask her "A is what to A?" or "A is what to B?" Two object words are put on the board with the question symbol between them; Sarah's task is to replace the question mark with the right word "same" or "different." A second question may be translated "A is the same as what?" or "A is not the same as what?"

Finally Sarah can be asked a variety of yes-no questions thus: "Is A the same as A?" "Is A not the same as A?" and so on. Sarah, it is claimed, learned to answer all three types of questions for an essentially unlimited variety of items, words, and concepts. There are indeed objections which can be made as to how far these are true questions; this cannot be discussed here, but there is interesting evidence that the chimp thinks of the word not as its literal form (say, a piece of blue plastic) but as the thing it represents (e.g., a red apple).

Finally we come to the thorny question of language and its relation to speech. The general colloquial use of the term "language" is so vague as to be of little value. But there has been for many years a widespread tendency, both among students of animal behaviour and a good many physiological psychologists (e.g., Teuber, 1967), to use the term language for many of the more elaborate examples of communication amongst animals, especially for the transfer of social information and particularly when the transfer is vocal or auditory. While there is much to be said for this, the usage in the past has perhaps been too naïve (Thorpe, 1968). Hebb and Thompson (1954) proposed that the minimal criterion of language is twofold. First, language combines two or more representative gestures or noises purposefully for a single effect, and secondly, it uses the same gestures in different combination for different effects, changing readily with circumstances. It will be quite obvious from this book that not only the communication of Washoe with her associates but also the communication of many birds and some other animals comes within this definition of language. There remains, however, the problem of intent or purpose, a topic which is discussed elsewhere in the present book (e.g., Chapter 1). To express my own view, and I do not wish to in any way saddle the Drs. Gardner with it, I would say that no one who has worked for a long period with a higher animal such as a chimpanzee, particularly in the circumstances of the Gardners' work, is justified in doubting the purposiveness of such communication. I believe such purposiveness is also clear to the experienced and open-minded observer with many of the Canidae; with some, probably many, other mammals; and with certain birds (Thorpe, 1966, 1969). Some of the philosophical depth and significance of this question of purposiveness, both for students of animal behaviour and for philosophers such as Price and Whitehead, will be found in Pantin (1968).

It would no doubt be easy to devise definitions of language such that no examples of animal communication could readily find inclusion therein. There have always been, and no doubt there will continue to be, those who resist with great vigour any conclusions which seem to break down what they regard as one of the most important lines of demarcation between animals and men. We must surely be justified in accepting such preconceived definitions only with the utmost caution. One of the tasks of the scientific student of animal behaviour is to attempt to establish whether or not there are such hard-and-fast dividing lines, and if so, what and where they are. Of one thing we can be certain: it is that work such as that of the Gardners and of Premack is only the beginning of the application of an important and powerful new technique from which we stand to learn much in years to come. I believe that no one should have anything to fear from its cautious and objective application. Personally I believe it is safe to conclude that, if chimpanzees had the necessary equipment in the larynx and pharynx, they could learn to talk at least as well as can children of three years of age, and perhaps older.

Number and Abstraction

The next question is, "Could they count?" The answer is, I believe, "Yes, up to the number seven." This problem will be next considered.

We must recognise a fact that is too often forgotten, namely that visual signals are as important and as complex in man as in any animal. And many domestic animals, even though they may have little power of understanding niceties of vocal communication, can nevertheless often recognise the intentions of their masters with uncanny precision—as was shown by the famous calculating horses that so puzzled comparative psychologists in the early years of this century. What then is the difference, if any, between such visual signals and the language of human beings? It is not at first sight merely a question of symbolism because the visual signals of animals may become so reduced as to be little more than "symbolic." I have seen a bull European bison intimidate a junior and subordinate male in its herd by the very slightest sideways flick of its head, indicative of the tossing and goring movements. Nor is it, as used to be argued, that animal language is emotive only, whilst human language is supposed to be emotive *and* propositional.

We may ask, then, does the human ability to symbolise—in the sense of representing completely abstract or general ideas by words which in themselves have nothing of the essential characteristics of the concepts which they denote—provide us with a difference? For example, the word "three" has nothing triple about it, nor is the word "four" quadruple; but man can learn to understand absolutely general meanings of this kind. Can animals do the same? As far as we yet know for certain, no animal language, however much information may be conveyed, involves the learnt realisation of completely general abstractions. Otto Koehler and his pupils, in their famous studies of the recognition of number, showed that animals, especially birds, can "think unnamed numbers"—that is (and this is also true of squirrels) they have a prelinguistic number sense; to some extent they think without words. But perhaps some examples of their number training do involve something more than a special association between given numbers and particular signals; and there is now some evidence for the ability to arrive at a general solution indicating the comprehension of a numerical series.

Lögler (1943) carried the investigation of the problem of number sense in animals a step further by his extremely thorough and painstaking work on counting in the Grey parrot. Extending the earlier investigation of Koehler and his pupils, he found that a parrot, "Jako," was able to recognise the successive presentation of a number of optic stimuli as a signal for the task of performing the same number of actions. The bird, having been shown, say, four or six or seven light flashes, was then able to take four or six or seven (as the case might be) of irregularly distributed baits out of a row of food trays. Not even numerous random changes in the temporal sequence of signal stimuli impaired the percentage of correct solutions. Having learnt this task, a signal of successive light flashes was replaced by successive notes of a flute. The bird was, however, able to substitute immediately, without further training, and the change from light flashes to flute notes had no effect on the number of correct solutions. Nor was the accomplishment hindered by the completely arhythmic presentation of stimuli, or by a change of pitch. This parrot was not able to accomplish a task which represented a combination of the two faculties of learning numbers presented successively and simultaneously— e.g., he could not respond to numbers presented visually and simultaneously after hearing the same number of acoustic stimuli presented successively—yet when he had learnt to "act upon" two or one, after hearing two sounds simultaneously or a single sound, he was spontaneously able to open a lid with two spots on it or a lid with one spot, according to the same acoustic signals. That is to say, he was able to transpose from the simultaneous-successive combination to the simultaneous-simultaneous in twenty experiments without relearning. It seems then that this remarkable work does bring our estimate of the counting achievements of birds a step nearer that of man, though it is still not true counting in the fully human sense.

Also of great interest is the extensive work of Rensch (1962, 1967), during which he showed that a Civet cat (*Viverricula malaccensis*) could learn to choose between pairs of patterns, one composed of even, the other of odd, numbers of spots or signs of various sorts, but otherwise having nothing in common, thus suggesting averbal concepts of odd and even.

MAN'S SPEECH AS UNIQUE

Perhaps the most reasonable assumption at present is that, however great the gulf which divides animal communication systems from human language, there is no single characteristic which can be used as an infallible criterion for distinguishing between animals and men in this respect. Human speech is unique only in the way in which it combines and extends attributes which, in themselves, are not peculiar to man, but are found also in more than one group of animals. We have evidence that animals can use conceptual symbols, but to a limited degree; and that here, as in so many other instances, the difference between the mind of animals and men seems to be one of degree—often the degree of abstraction that can be achieved—rather than one of kind. But man can manipulate abstract symbols to an extent far in excess of any animal, and that is the difference between bird "counting" and our mathematics. I think we can sum up this matter by saying that although no animal appears to have a language which is propositional, fully syntactic, and at the same time clearly expressive of intention, all these features can be found separately (to at least some degree) in the animal kingdom. Consequently, bearing in mind the work on chimps discussed above, we can say that the distinction between man and animals, on the ground that only the former possess "true language," seems far less defensible than heretofore. Yet, as argued elsewhere in this book, there comes a point where "more" creates a "difference."

ART AND A SENSE OF VALUES

Artistic appreciation and artistic creativeness are surely two of the facets of man's nature which most readily come to mind when thinking of his uniqueness. So it seems appropriate to round off this chapter by giving a little thought to the topic in relation to the world of nature and in particular to the higher animals. I have no intention, of course, of trying to summarise man's thought on the vast problem and significance of the beauty of animate nature as perceived by our senses. Countless works by philosophers, theologians, aestheticians, artists, scientists, and moralists have been written upon it. So I wish simply to state my general approach to this field, the one which seems to me most fundamental and to give most satisfaction. This is that "significant form" is the essential quality common to all works of art; whether it be visual art, musical art, or the art of the sculptor which, though it is normally visually observed, can often, and especially in the case of small sculptures, be better apprehended by touch and feeling. This summary view, it is true, arouses difficulties in relation to colours and still greater difficulties in connexion with the olfactory sense, since these two fields of experience are not usually thought of as involving a concept of "form." However, I do not think this need be an insurmountable obstacle since in music we have to bring in the idea of time. So in thinking of our sensations of colour we can think of the relationships of the solar spectrum and the colour perception and sense of colour contrast mediated by our eyes. And even an aesthetic of olfaction and gustation, if it ever comes into being, will have to be treated as an aesthetic of subtle combinations, simultaneous and successive, of, primarily, olfactory sensations.

Significant Visual Form

Where we speak of significant form in nature, we come at once to the mathematical relationships which are at the basis of the form of organised matter and which a very great zoologist, D'Arcy Thompson (1942), unravelled with masterly insight and perception in his great work, *On Growth and Form*. There he dealt with the basis for beauty in innumerable exquisite structures produced by the plant and animal worlds and showed how some of them can be reduced to fairly simple mathematical forms such as the logarithmic spiral, which is found in the shells of many molluscs and occurs widely throughout organic nature.

But for us the question first arises, How far do the beauties of animal colour and form—particularly those displayed by the adornments of so many insects and birds—imply something like aesthetic appreciation in the sensory systems of the species themselves? Does the fact that the wings of lepidoptera and the plumes of birds have been evolved as devices to influence and attract the other sex of the same species imply that we must credit them with something like our own taste and standards of beauty? On this point I will let Sir Alister Hardy (1965) reply. Where he is discussing the selection which has produced both the extraordinary cases of natural camouflage and the marvellous examples of mimicry found so widespread amongst the insects and some other invertebrate groups, he says:

> I would point out a difference between the kind of selective action producing camouflage and that producing mimicry. Camouflage is the result of predators *failing* to perceive the typically coloured forms; the mimics on the other hand are not imitating natural objects in the usual sense, like leaves or twigs, but are "copying" what are much more like the designs of the abstract artist, brilliant colour patterns of arresting beauty, which have been evolved by the action of the predators themselves, i.e., selecting such "designs" as aids to *their* "memory": striking devices (like warning signals) to enable them to perceive the presence of danger (noxious taste or sting, etc.) before it is too late. I have put the word memory, you will note, in quotes; whatever our views are about memory, however, we must recognise that the evolution of the mimics implies a constant *matching* of remarkably detailed patterns by the *perceiving* predators: the "careful" comparison of one design with another which they have previously seen and, from their experience, *learnt* to avoid. It can only be this matching, with an extraordinarily exact "visual memory" image, which could produce the "photographic" mimetic copies we are dealing with.

> I think it likely that there are no finer galleries of abstract art than the cabinet drawers of the tropical butterfly collector. Each "work" is a symbol, if I must not say of emotion, then of vivid life; they are either arresting signs to warn hungry hunting predators, vertebrates like ourselves, of danger, or they are glowing courtship colours flaunted by male insects to attract and coax coy mates to submission. It is often, I believe, the fascination of this abstract colour and design, as much as an interest in biology or a love of nature, that allures the ardent lepidopterist, although all these may be combined; he has his favourite genera and dotes upon his

different species of *Vanessa* and *Parnassius* as the modernist does upon his examples of Matisse or Ben Nicholson (p. 151).

But we must leave the general topic, the beauty inherent in animate nature, at that point and come to a special aspect of it which concerns us much more closely. In Chapter 3 I alluded to the activities of certain bowerbirds who appeared to display some artistic sense in decoration of their bowers. It is also relevant to mention the "paintings" which chimpanzees have produced in captivity, which again suggest the glimmerings of artistic sense, and also the powers of abstraction and generalisation shown by primates in comparing and choosing elaborate visual patterns, often preferring those patterns which seem to us artistically more attractive or in some obscure sense "better." But I went on from there to refer to the problem of the musicality of bird songs and remarked on the number of instances in which the song of an individual bird (e.g., the blackbird) will continue to develop and improve towards the end of the breeding season—a time when we can be virtually sure it has no further biological function. So in these instances we are faced with the problem not merely of appreciating and preferring objects or patterns which strike the human observer as beautiful; much more than that, we are concerned with the apparent elements of artistic creation which go into the activities of these creatures! Because of my particular interests and because of the remarkable nature of the bird song examples, I restricted myself to the discussion of these. Of course the musical talent of birds, if indeed it exists, is certainly minuscule compared with the musical achievements of human beings. Nevertheless in my view it is large enough to warrant serious consideration as "absolute music." (See Thorpe, 1972.)

Significant Musical Form

Now let us look at the significance of musical form and consider the basis of musical aesthetics. The first thing to say is that music is pre-eminently non-representative even in its classical example and its highest attainment (Langer, 1951). As Langer says, "It exhibits pure form, not as an embellishment but as its very essence." In pure music we have practically nothing but tonal structures before us—no scene, no object, no fact. Music then is pure form and is essentially non-representative. Music has, however, a sort of vocabulary in that, in any particular culture, certain sounds seem natural to joy and others to grief or despondency, some to tenderness and love, and so on. But even the most blatant "programme music," such as Richard Strauss's *Till Eulenspiegel,* is not really descriptive. Nor does Beethoven's *Pastoral Symphony inevitably* bring to the mind of the musical listener the pastoral scenes which the composer himself had in mind when writing the work. In other words music is not a language in the sense that it can, or could ever, be learnt to the point of supplanting a description in words. As Langer says (p. 242), "a programme is simply a crutch. It is a resort to the crude but familiar method of holding feelings in the imagination by envisaging their attendant circumstances. It does not mean that the listener is unmusical, but merely that he is not musical enough to think in entirely musical terms." While of course we cannot fully understand a composer's intentions if we listen to the music of an opera without knowing the story or seeing the work on the stage, yet the music itself, even if completely divorced from the stage setting, can be just as worth while without it. Music then is in some way symbolic of feeling; but it cannot formulate and represent a logical picture. Moreover, to follow Susanne Langer, music is transcendent or perhaps rather one should say transformational, in the sense that all artistic creation is but a transmutation and every artist a transformer.

Music in fact reveals the rationale of feelings and in so far as it does this it is a force in our mental life, our awareness and understanding, and not merely our affective experience. Therein lies at least part of the relationship to mathematics. Since algebraical letters are pure symbols, we see numerical relationships not in them but through them. As Langer says, they have the highest "transparency" that language can attain. There is, I think, no doubt about this. When we are moved by music we perceive and appreciate something which could not have been revealed to us by language alone, although of course poetry can reveal the unspeakable in the same kind of way. So music articulates forms which language cannot set forth, and music, and indeed probably all art, is essentially untranslatable. I think we can say that a great symphony, a great painting, or indeed a great poem can give us for ourselves something of what the artist himself experienced in the creation. *Music is telling us something which cannot be named but which it can symbolise.* Facts and the contents of ordinary discursive thinking can be verbalised and subjected to the laws of language. Artistic symbols, on the other hand, are untranslatable. They are always implicit.

Now to produce a work of art, the artist must of course have felt at least subconsciously the emotional content, the emotional values of the work. But there is another aspect which Langer calls aesthetic emotion. And this springs from the intellectual triumph provided by overcoming the resistance and recalcitrance of the medium with which he is working, whether it be paint and canvas or the inherent limitations of musical instruments and the human voice. But Langer argues that the emotive content of the work is much deeper than any intellectual experience, more essential, prerational and vital; as she says, something of the life rhythms we share with all growing, moving, and fearing creatures.

The Problem of Musical Sense in Birds

Now Langer does bring herself to consider the problem of bird music, and instantly dismisses it for the, to me, curious reason that the singing of birds is unconscious and therefore it is not art! I think I have said enough in this book to make the reader at least doubt the wisdom of considering the behaviour of any of the highest animals as completely "unconscious," and I am sure that to do so leads us into an impasse in our task of understanding behaviour. And if, as I believe we are justified in thinking, the activities of the higher vertebrates at least are in some degree and in some sense conscious, we are faced at once with the question of whether these few creative creatures are really artists in the profound sense which I have just been discussing as implicit in the work and achievements of human artists. I think we must provisionally answer "Yes"! The compositions elaborated by the most musical of birds and the artistic constructions of captive chimps are, as I have already suggested, of great simplicity, perhaps verging on the trivial, when compared with our own achievements as we like to regard them. But all I can say is this, the more we study and intensively analyse the creative achievements and the apparently artistic perception of the higher animals, the more convincing becomes the assumption that here we have art at least in its embryonic form. And such increased familiarity, from long study, certainly for me, increases my conviction that our judgment that bird songs, in some instances and in some degree, represent music is not mistaken. But even granting this, we are left with a tremendous chasm—intellectual, artistic, technical, linguistic, moral, ethical, scientific, and spiritual—between ape and man. And we have no clear idea as to how this gap was bridged. Man is unique in all these aspects, and we may never know how this happened.

Chapter 9

PROBLEMS OF CONSCIOUSNESS

THE MEANING OF CONSCIOUSNESS

The term "consciousness" has many overtones of meaning but involves three basic components. First an inward awareness or sensibility—what might be called "having internal perception." Second, an awareness of self, of one's own existence. Third, the idea of consciousness includes that of unity; that is to say it implies, in some rather vague sense, the fusion of the totality of the impressions, thoughts, and feelings which make up a person's conscious being into a single whole. As Lashley put it, the process of awareness implies a belief in an internal perceiving agent— an "I" or self which does the perceiving. This leads inevitably to the conclusion that this agent selects and unifies elements into a unique field of consciousness. The belief in a perceiving self, or, to use Eccles' term, "experiencing self," has two other important consequences: (a) the self transcends time and space, since memory brings into immediate relation events remote from one another in these dimensions; (b) in man it makes possible the creation of aesthetic and ethical values held to be absolute.

Consciousness is indeed a well-trodden field. Whole libraries have been written on what is generally known as the "mind-body problem"; and by far the larger part of these libraries has been produced by philosophers, psychologists, and moral scientists, and only a very small part by physiologists and biologists. But there have been such big developments in the neurology and neurophysiology of brain in recent years that I feel it essential, in view of the contemporary climate of opinion, that we should try to approach this perennial problem from this aspect.

After Descartes, four main possibilities were open to philosophers (Beloff, 1962; Smythies, 1965). These are as follows: (1) Accepting the Cartesian dichotomy as essentially valid, in which case one is of course committed to dualism; and this may be of two types or intensities: (a) one that allows a two-way causal interaction between mental and physical events, and this we may call strong form of dualism, or (b) weak form, which allows mental events to be effects but never causes. (2) Acknowledging mental entities as real (this was Berkeley's position) and regarding material entities as at best a convenient abstraction. (3) Acknowledging material entities as real but instead dismissing mental entities as an abstraction. Finally (4) asserting that certain events are at one and the same time both mental and material; the mental, so to speak, being the interior view of what has a physical exterior. This is usually known as the Identity Hypothesis and has appeared in a number of forms under the title of Double-aspect Theory.

As to alternative (2) above, it would be very difficult to find people today who would support Berkeley's view in anything like its original strict form, and indeed most scientists and perhaps most philosophers would regard it as verging on the absurd. Similarly I think we can say that alternative (3), material entities are real but mental entities an abstraction, is clearly false since, applied in its rigid form, it negates the whole of experience. This leaves us with (1) and (4), (1) being the Interactionist Theory and (4) the Double-aspect Theory. I am afraid it is true, however, that quite a number of physiologists, even some learned and distinguished ones (and still more scientists who have not thought deeply about the matter at all), are found to accept alternative (3), attracted I think by the practical economy, tidiness, and convenience of it.

POPPER'S THREE-WORLD THEORY

Sir Karl Popper has recently extended and elaborated his views (1972) as to the existence of worlds 2 and 3 (outlined in Chapter 2 above), describing himself as a pluralist rather than a Cartesian dualist. Popper agrees I think with most students of animal communication that consciousness of selfhood, that is a fully self-reflective consciousness, is absent in animals. All animal language, indeed almost all animal behaviour, has a communicative or signalling function; but human language has besides some further functions which make it a language in a narrower and more important sense of the word. In addition to the characteristics of language listed by Hockett, Bühler referred long ago to the basic descriptive functions of human language, and Popper adds to this the argumentative functions. Popper does not think that any of these functions are reducible to any of the others. Least of all does he regard the two higher functions of description and argument as reducible to the two lower ones as an expression of communications. His thesis is, of course, that with the higher functions of the human language the new world, the world 3, emerges. He calls the world of physical matter, fields of forces and so on "world 1"; the world of conscious and perhaps also subconscious experience "world 2"; and "world 3" is the world of spoken, written or printed language—"storytelling, myth-making, theories, theoretical problems, and arguments including perhaps the world of artistic products and of social institutions."

Psycho-physical Parallelism

He explains that he introduces these terms in order to emphasise the limited autonomy of these regions. Most materialists, physicalists, or reductionists assert that, of these three worlds, only world 1 really exists, and that it is therefore autonomous. They replace world 2 by behaviour and world 3 more particularly by verbal behaviour. This, Popper says, is just one of those all too easy ways of solving the mind-body problem; the way of denying the existence of the human mind and of the human consciousness of self—that is, of those things which may be regarded as some of the most remarkable and astonishing in the universe. He adds, "the other equally easy way out is Berkeley and Mach's immaterialism; the thesis that only sensations exist and that matter is just a construct out of sensations." Coming to the question of a thoroughgoing parallelism between mental states and states of the brain (psycho-physical parallelism), he rejects this because, like epiphenominalism, it robs consciousness of any biological function. Popper states that his own position is that a brain-mind parallelism is almost bound to exist up to a point. Certain reflexes such as blinking when seeing a suddenly approaching object are to all appearances more or less parallelistic in character: the muscular reaction (in which no doubt the central nervous system is involved) repeats itself with regularity when the visual impression is repeated. Nevertheless he believes that the thesis of complete parallelism is a mistake, probably even in some cases where mere reflexes are involved. He thus adopts a form of psycho-physical interactionism which for his three-world theory involves the thesis that the physical world 1 is not causally closed but open to the world 2 of mental states and events. He regards this as a somewhat unattractive thesis for the physicist but one that is supported by the fact that world 3 acts upon world 1 via world 2. He is willing to accept the view that whenever anything goes on in world 2 something connected with it goes on in world 1 (in the brain); but in order to speak of a complete authoritarian parallelism we would have to be able to assert that the same mental state or event is always accompanied by an exactly corresponding physiological state and vice versa. And this, he thinks, cannot be maintained.

Popper shows that in his opinion the talk about strictly parallel physiological processes loses all content. He also remarks that since we have reason to believe that if one region of the brain is destroyed another region can often take over without or with very little interference with world 2, we have another argument against parallelism. He adds, "All this sounds, of course, very anti-reductionist; and as a philosopher who looks at this world of ours, with us in it, I indeed despair of any ultimate reduction. But as a methodologist this does not lead me to an anti-reductionist research programme. It only means that, with the growth of our attempted reductions, our knowledge and our un-solved problems will expand." He argues that philosophical re-ductionists must in the end be reduced to denying the existence of worlds 2 and 3, and with this human technology (especially the existence of computers which make so much use of world-3 theorems) becomes incomprehensible. Trying to follow out the results of such a reductionist position, he comes to the con-clusion that they are absurd and that philosophical behaviourism (or the philosophy of the identity of mind and body) is in-evitably reduced to the absurdity of attributing all modern tech-nology to a pre-established harmony built ultimately into hy-drogen nuclei. He adds, "This seems to me to stray too far from common sense." Hardly, I think we shall agree, an overstatement!

Neuronal Mechanisms in Perception

Almost all the major difficulties involved in this problem centre around the theory of perception, about which I had something to say earlier. It was very refreshing when Sir Charles Sherrington, in his famous Gifford Lectures in Edinburgh (1940), described the brain as the organ of liaison—that is, liaison between mind and body. He has a wonderful passage describing the problems of perception involved when we look at a star.

> For instance a star which we perceive. The energy scheme deals with it, describes the passing of radiation events into the eye, the little light image of it formed at the bottom of the eye, the ensuing photo-chemical action in the retina, the trains of action potentials travelling along the nerve to the brain, the further electrical dis-turbance in the brain. . . . As to our *seeing* the star, it says noth-ing. But to our perception it is bright, has direction, has distance. That the image at the bottom of the eyeball turns into a star over-

head, a star moreover that does not move, though we and our eyes as we move carry the image with us, and finally that it is the thing, a star, endorsed by our cognition—about all this, the energy scheme has nothing to report. The energy scheme deals with the star as one of the objects observable by us; as to the perceiving of it by the mind, the scheme puts its finger to its lips and is silent. It may be said to bring us to the threshold of the act of perceiving and there to bid us "good-bye." Its scheme seems to carry up to and through the very place and time which correlate with the mental experience, but to do so without one hint further.

Let us then approach the topic by considering the neuronal mechanisms involved in perception. The first thing to say is that the recent progress of neurology and neurophysiology has shown the brain to be of a complexity beyond imagining and far outside the field of thought of even Sherrington in 1940. The result of this is that all early writings on the mind-brain problem with, as Eccles says, "their self-assured efforts to give accounts of brain structure and function," seem naïve in the extreme.

The essential structure of the brain, from our present point of view, is the cerebral cortex, which is the folded surface sheet of densely packed nerve cells that are estimated to number about ten thousand million. These cells communicate with each other by particular regions of close contact called synapses. Each cell receives many thousands of these contacts by branches (axons) coming from other nerve cells, and in turn each nerve cell influences many hundreds or thousands of other nerve cells when it is triggered to discharge an impulse along its own efferent pathway, the axon, with its numerous branches (Eccles, 1966, 1970, p. 153). *At first glance* the cerebral cortex appears a neuronal network somewhat like a vast telephone exchange of 10 thousand million elements—each nerve cell having converging on to it contacts with hundreds of other nerve cells and each nerve cell in its turn spreading its influence by divergence over hundreds of other nerve cells. It is now well established that there are two kinds of junctions or synapses. One is excitatory; and if there is sufficiently intense bombardment by excitatory synapses the recipient nerve cell will be stimulated to discharge impulses along its own axon. The other kind of synapse is inhibitory. These counteract the excitatory connexions and tend to silence the nerve cell which receives them. Thus each nerve cell is continually subjected to bombardment by these two types of stimulus, and so its responses derive very largely from the total effect, the total impact, of its neighbours upon it.

It is now well known that the essential time of action of the nerve cell, in an operative linkage, is about one-thousandth of a second for cells with short axons. This represents the total time that elapses between the reception of the excitation that triggers the discharge and the action of this impulse on other nerve cells. If one thinks for a moment, it will be seen that once activity arises in a population of nerve cells it is potentially capable of almost explosive spread throughout the neuronal network—through millions of cells in a few milliseconds. And as Eccles says, "Inhibitory synaptic activity mercifully can restrain this explosive spread which would otherwise result in a convulsion." He adds that it is still impossible to conceive the manner of operation of the neuronal network in a more global manner and involving tens of millions of neurones, which of course is continually proceeding in the cerebral cortex during all kinds of conscious experiences such as memories, thoughts, dispositional intentions, and so forth. This account concerns the cerebral cortex alone; but it is enough to show what a staggering problem in neurophysiology the attempt to understand the action of the brain involves.

When we look at the way in which the brain is informed of what goes on in the external world (which may of course be external or internal to the body), things are not quite so difficult. Thus electro-magnetic radiations with wavelengths between about 400 and 700 microns are transduced in the retina to give discharges of nerve impulses along the optic nerve fibres. These are brief all-or-nothing electrical events which travel along a million or so nerve fibres in the optic pathway without any interference in the way of cross talk from their neighbours. Information from a sense organ, such as the retina, is transmitted to the visual cortex in coded form, both by the frequency of impulse-repetition in the fibre and by the topographic relationship of retinal origin and of cortical termination. This afferent pathway, which is in effect the optic nerve, does not connect retinal point to cortical point, but signals more symmetrical geometrical arrangements such as edges, lines, angular orientations, and so forth.

Now what can we imagine to be proceeding in the machinery of the cerebral cortex when some image is projected on the retina as in Sherrington's example? Firstly there are bursts of discharges in cells that respond to lines or edges in the visual field and in various specific orientations—this itself is quite a complex business when we realise that there are three hundred million neurones in the visual cortex alone. So there are cells which are particularly sensitive and responsive to the lengths and widths, lines and slits, angles and so on. And it looks as though, in due course, cells will be found responding to more and more complex patterns; and it may be that eventually cells will be discovered that selectively respond to abstract forms, such as, for example, triangularity. And if this happens, this will to some extent explain our ability in the recognition of abstract forms (Eccles, 1970, p. 160).

Let me here quote Sherrington again. "We might imagine this principle pursued to culmination in final supreme convergence on one ultimate pontifical nerve cell, a cell the climax of the whole system of integration." This indeed would be a not-un-reasonable supposition in view of the fact that the phenomenon of hierarchy is very obvious when we study the behaviour of the nervous system. Sherrington continues, "Such would be a spatial climax to a system of centralisation; it would secure integration by receiving all and dispensing all, as unitary arbiter of a totalitarian state. But convergence towards the brain offers in fact nothing of that kind. The brain region, which we may call 'mental,' is not a concentration into one cell but an enormous expansion into millions of cells. They are, it is true, richly interconnected. But where it is a question of 'mind,' the nervous system does not integrate itself by centralisation upon one pontifical cell. Rather it elaborates a millionfold democracy whose each unit is a cell."

As Eccles says, the dynamic properties of patterned activity in tens of millions of neurones with the connectives that we have been describing defeats not only the imagination but, so far, any attempt at mathematical treatment. (However, there are daring and exciting theories now in the field; see, for instance, D. Marr, 1970.)

It must be emphasised now, once again, that there is no immediate experience of a perception when the visual cortex is activated. This, as the quotation from Sherrington indicates, is just one stage on the way to the much more elaborate patterned activity that must be associated with consciousness. It is interesting to note that these initial stages of activation, namely the electrical responses of the cortex, are unaltered even in relatively deep anaesthesia; and, with just perceptible flashes of light, at least 0.2 seconds of cortical activity may be needed before a perception is registered. Professor Libet and his colleagues in the Department of Physiology, at the University of California, San Francisco (Eccles, 1966), have found in their work on that part of the cerebral cortex which is sensitive to stimulation of the surface of the body that there was a delay of at least half a second before the onset of the experienced sensation whatever the conditions of threshold stimulation. So, clearly, there is time for an enormous elaboration of neural activity in the most complex spatio-temporal patterns during what Eccles calls the "incubation period" of conscious experience at threshold level. This implies what is well known from the detailed work of Moruzzi (1966, see *Brains and Conscious Experience*, ed., J. C. Eccles) that only an extremely small fraction of the total sensory impact to our brains is actually experienced. For example, during sleep there is a continuing overall activity of cortical nerve cells, and in some regions there may even be increased activity at that time.

Another aspect of the problem of consciousness is approached by modern physiological studies on the old problem of sensation and perception. Gibson (1966) quotes with approval Thomas Reid's (1785) statement that "the external senses have a double province; to make us feel and to make us perceive; to furnish us with a variety of sensations and to give us a conception of external objects." Yet Gibson himself, like the present author, has argued that sensations are not the basis of perception but rather that, as William James proposed, perception is primary whereas sensations are secondarily isolated parts thereof, at least in mature human beings, which is also the traditional view of the "best *alt*" psychologists. But it may be that, in the more primitive animals, the beginning of consciousness was in some way connected with the first appearance of the ability to combine different sensory modalities to provide an elementary map of the environment so that, for the first time in evolutionary history, animals could "find their way about." (See Thorpe, 1963, Pantin, 1968.) In that it suggests that the development of proprioception marks an especially important stage, this view receives much support from recent work in the U.S.S.R. summarised by Razran (1971), who comes to the conclusion that "the entire reach of consciousness inheres in the proprioceptive sequelae, or kinestheses, of sensory-orienting reactions: liminal consciousness, or sensation, in those of unintegrated or even individual reactions; and organised consciousness, or perception, in the integrated transforms of the reactions." He goes on to propound the view that the liminal consciousness of a sensation is anchored to a particular modality or quality, whereas perception is largely inter- or rather super-modal in quality. He also quotes with approval Gibson's statement that "Proprioception or self-sensitivity is . . . an overall function, common to all systems, not a special sense and that the activity of orienting, exploring, and selecting extracts the external and internal information from the stimulus flux while registering the change as subjective feeling."

This highly simplified and very brief account of the development of a conscious experience will serve to refute dramatically the view implied by the identity hypothesis that as soon as neural activity lights up in the cerebral cortex there is a conscious ex-

317

perience. In fact there is an intense ongoing activity in the cortex of the awake subject in the total absence of any specific sensory inputs; and as everyone knows there is even activity during sleep, an activity which is enhanced during periods of dreaming. So it is clear that time is required both for synaptic transmission and for the enormous development and elaboration of neural patterns which are apparently needed to establish conscious experience.

Then it must be recognised that intention comes into the picture. Only a very small fraction of the complex ongoing patterned response of the cerebral neurones is experienced. The remainder fades away unobserved; and of course it is essential that it should do so, for one can imagine the confusion that would result if we actually experienced the totality of the cerebral patterns in our cortex. Now a very obvious feature of our conscious experience is that with training and learning, from infancy upwards, we have the power of relegating many very elaborate actions and responses to the subconcious or unconscious levels where they are, so to speak, so automated that they can take charge of an enormous preponderance of our life activities, to our great relief and contentment. Everyone knows how car driving becomes automatic, just as does piano playing, with the result that we can drive safely while at the same time conversing and observing the scenery, with just enough unconscious or subconscious attention to the highway to arrive safely. Then, when an accident threatens, suddenly consciousness takes over; and many who have been in this unenviable situation report that time seems suddenly to have stretched until seconds apparently become minutes so that at least we feel we have ample time to decide on the best strategy.

Sherrington dramatically imagines the behaviour of the cortex as like a loom weaving "a dissolving pattern, always a meaningful pattern, though never an abiding one; a shifting harmony of sub-patterns." This is his "enchanted loom." So we have all the unimaginable complexities of operation in a neuronal machinery of the brain generating a level of complexity transcending any

318

human evaluation. Over against this there is the problem, defined by Sherrington, of the conscious experiences that are quite different in kind from any goings on in the neuronal machinery; nevertheless the events in the neuronal machinery are, *as far as the physiologist is concerned,* assumed to be a necessary condition for the experience. Here I agree with Eccles that, though they are a necessary condition, they are not a sufficient condition; for even the most complex dynamic patterns played out in the neuronal machinery of the cerebral cortex are in the matter-energy world, whereas transcending this level, and in emergent relationship from it, is the world of conscious experience.

CONSCIOUSNESS IN MAN AND ANIMALS

These remarks, as well as some in other chapters, make clear the importance, indeed the absolute necessity, of attention and awareness in building up our own mental unity and individuality throughout our lives from babyhood onwards. We are in fact creating our minds step by step all our lives. Some of this creation, perhaps much of it, is certainly at the subconscious level, particularly in our earlier days. But although the subconscious or unconscious mind can do marvellous things and can cope with much learning of the elementary conditioning sort, it is unthinkable that anything like a mature, responsible, fully socialised human being could develop without the continual and overriding control established by our conscious will. Thus, although looked at from the strictly neurophysiological point of view, interactions may seem to be one way—from neurological states to conscious experience—they must in fact be two ways, for if it were not so, no human being could ever develop. So whatever theory we may hold, no thinking person in his senses can deny the existence and the importance of consciousness. If I may quote a few remarks that I made in a discussion on this topic in 1966:

> Consciousness is a primary datum of existence and as such cannot be fully defined. The evidence suggests that at the lower levels of

319

the evolutionary scale consciousness, if it exists, must be of a very generalised kind, so to say unstructured. And that with the development of purposive behaviour and a powerful faculty of attention, consciousness associated with expectation will become more and more vivid and precise.

As these remarks reveal, I am thinking all the time of the possibility of the existence of consciousness in animals other than ourselves. And, as you will have gathered from earlier chapters, I do indeed find it essential to assume something very similar to consciousness and conscious choice in many of the highest animals.

So to me one of the important considerations is (even admitting that organisational changes and developments, including those of great complexity, can occur in both the human and animal brain below the level of consciousness) that conscious choice and awareness have an absolutely essential function in individual development, and therefore, I think we can confidently assert, in, at any rate, the later stages of evolutionary process. So one of the key questions to be asked (a topic worth brooding on) is how far and at what levels can we regard the development of consciousness as a valuable factor conferring selective advantage in the evolution of animals and men? William James in 1890 said, "Consciousness is what we might expect in an organ, added for the sake of steering a nervous system grown too complex to regulate itself." This now sounds to us very naïve; so much of the complex steering systems of the higher animals having been explained on reasonably self-regulating and automatic bases. And where there are adequate cybernetic principles at work, consciousness may seem redundant. Indeed if self-regulation was the chief or sole criterion as evidence for consciousness, then all animals and plants must be conscious—a conclusion which strikes the modern biologist as absurd. The evolutionary problem is as follows: Given a brain of a given degree of elaboration, is it likely to be a more effective mechanism—more effective in an evolutionary sense—if it has consciousness, so to speak, attached, than if it has not?

Karl Popper (1972) points out that the idea of problem-solving is quite foreign to the subject matter of non-biological sciences but seems to have emerged together with life. Even though there is something like natural selection at work prior to the origin of life, we cannot say that for atomic nuclei survival is a "problem" in any sense of the term. Nor can we say that crystals have problems of growth or propagation or survival. But life, as Popper says, is faced with the problem of survival from the very beginning; indeed we can describe life, if we like, as problem-solving, and living organisms as the only problem-solving complexes in the universe. This of course does not mean that we have to suppose that in all life there is a consciousness of the problems that have to be solved; that is obvious nonsense. Yet Popper agrees that there can be little doubt that animals possess consciousness, and they can be, at times, even conscious of a problem. But, he says, *"The emergence of consciousness in the animal kingdom is perhaps as great a mystery as the origin of life itself."* He agrees however that there can be little doubt that consciousness in animals has some function and can be looked at as if it were a bodily organ. We have therefore to assume, "difficult as this may be, that it is a product of evolution, of natural selection." Of course for the behaviourists who tend to deny the existence of consciousness altogether (a position quite fashionable at present), there is no problem. But as Popper says, "a theory of the non-existence of consciousness cannot be taken any more seriously than a theory of the non-existence of matter." These theories, he says, solve the problem of the relationship between body and mind by a radical simplification. It is the denial either of body or of mind; but I agree with Popper that such a solution is, to say the least, too cheap. In fact there seems to be no prospect whatsoever of reducing the human consciousness of self and the creativeness of the human mind to any other explanatory level. Here Jacques Monod (1971) would appear to agree with Popper in that he calls the problem of the human central nervous system "the second frontier," comparing its difficulty with the "first frontier," the problem of the origin of life itself. Popper indeed believes that the reduction of biology to physics or of physics to chemistry, reduction to physiology of the conscious or subconscious experiences which we may ascribe to animals, and still more, the reduction of human consciousness itself and the creativeness of the human mind to animal experience are all projects the complete success of which seem most unlikely if not impossible.

DEPENDENCE OF MAN'S HIGHER FACULTIES ON INTACT BRAIN STRUCTURES

The extraordinary elaboration and specialisation of brain structure, which modern researches have revealed, brings to mind at once the moral problem engendered by the dependence of our highest faculties on the integrity of our brain structure. This of course is no new problem. Ever since the realisation that the brain is in some way the seat of the mind or soul, the occurrence of such hereditary disasters as microcephalic idiocy has been a grave stumbling block for moralists interpreting the world as the expression of the activity of a beneficent creator. That great and devout naturalist, John Ray, felt it acutely in the seventeenth century; and it is with us very much today in a period of ever-increasing road accidents, and other disasters, resulting in irreparable brain damage. We indeed know much more about this than we did, but the knowledge is not very comforting! A child or adult can, as we all know, be reduced to an "unconscious" vegetable existence; and even when the damage does not go as far as this there may nevertheless be many bizarre and crippling consequences.

Although the activities of the human cortex are not *initially* highly localised, they may become localised in the cortex as the result of experience, and in other parts of the brain as a result of the hereditary make-up. Consequently quite local damage may produce extraordinary results. This is nowhere more striking than in the effects of brain injury on body image. There are many cases of patients who, as the result of a lesion in the posterior part of the right half of the brain, fail even to recognise as part of the body, the limbs on, say, the left side. One such patient dried only the right side of his body when he had a bath. The surprising thing about this is not that the patient should be unable to feel one half of the body normally, but that he should have apparently forgotten that he ever possessed it! He not only disregards it, he doesn't seem to know that he is disregarding it. So the conclusion is inescapable that somehow the lesion has destroyed not only the patient's present awareness of his body image but also his ability to retain memories previously linked with it. Sometimes, however, it appears (Williams, 1970) that the patient has not forgotten that he had parts of his body—on the contrary, the actual body image may remain undisturbed, that is, the concept such patients have of their bodies, the image due to past experience, is still present. But it is the awareness of the real body and its present position which seems to be at fault. This information fails to reach consciousness and so is not becoming integrated with other mental acts. The patient is, as it were, carrying around a phantom of himself and, in the absence of severe or prolonged external stimulation, lives with this phantom instead of reality. The existence of phantom limbs, sometimes very painful and distressing, is well known as following on amputation. There the patient, who is mentally normal, cannot convince his subconscious self he has lost the limb at all. In due course, in most cases, the erroneous perception of the phantom limb fades and ceases to cause trouble, but it may suddenly recur as the result of administration of certain drugs, such as mescalin, and can indeed be brought back by cerebral lesion. An old phantom limb may reappear as the result of epileptic attacks, even though many years have passed since the injury was suffered.

Another very distressing result of certain types of disease or injury is inability to speak and use words normally. In many of these cases, however, it appears that the words are not actually lost, but, as a result of the lesion or disease, have become relatively inaccessible. It is now known that the memories of words are stored in groups rather than as individuals and that a single item, for instance the word "hands," is stored several times over for each of its various contexts. But there is some relationship between these independent stores since arousal of a word in one context can arouse it in others too. It is also known that the written and spoken forms of a word are stored separately, and yet with connexions between them. I could give much space to the discussion of extraordinary details of the effects of factors of various kinds upon a person's consciousness. Suffice it to say that there is hardly any behavioural, mental, or moral activity of which human beings are capable which cannot be eliminated or distorted to a greater or lesser extent by cerebral accidents.

THE RELEVANCE OF BRAIN SURGERY

It is here appropriate to refer to the extraordinary results reported by the famous brain surgeon Penfield as a result of electrical stimulation of the exposed cortex, carried out, of course, with the patients' consent when the brain was exposed for operations for the relief of certain types of epilepsy or brain tumours. When points on the superior surface of the temporal lobe were stimulated, it was found that forty different patients (over a total series of somewhat over a thousand investigated) experienced an extraordinarily vivid and complete recall of some long-forgotten events (together with the appropriate emotional concomitants) of their past life. Recall is so clear that even small changes in the present sensory input coming from eye and ear are recognised. The patient finds it difficult or impossible to believe that he has not been temporarily transported into a period of his past life.

In one case, that of D.F., the patient heard a song played by an orchestra each time the stimulating electrode was applied at a specific point. This point was stimulated over and over again and each time she heard an orchestra playing the same song which began at a particular verse and went on to the chorus. When asked to do so, she hummed the air accompanying the music she was made to hear. The tempo of her humming was what would be expected from such an orchestra. She could not remember when she had heard it before, but the experience was extremely vivid. So much so that she afterwards became convinced that a record had been played to her, surreptitiously, by the surgeon. Another patient, B.R.A., was made under similar circumstances to hear a certain piece of music. She did remember the occasion. It was Christmas Eve in Amsterdam where she had lived. She seemed to be in church. It was during the war and there were Canadian soldiers there. (She married a Canadian soldier later and so came to live in Montreal.) The choir sang and she felt again how beautiful it was, even as she lay on the table in the Montreal operating room. Yet another case, a young South African, J.T., was stimulated. He realised where he was and cried out in astonishment, "Yes, Doctor! Yes, Doctor! Now I hear people laughing, my friends, in South Africa." After the electrode was withdrawn, he discussed the experience with Penfield. He had seemed to be with two young women, his cousins, on their family's farm. He saw them; they were laughing and he was laughing with them. Yet still he knew he was really in Montreal and could still speak to the surgeon. Sometimes the recall is both visual and auditory. Sometimes there is a strong emotional involvement; but often the time recalled was neither significant nor important.

These cases are so remarkable and so unexpected that Penfield, at the time, felt driven to the conclusion that he was accidentally tapping a sort of continuous film-strip-plus-tape-recorder version of the patient's emotional life. The memories were certainly *not* lodged in the particular area of the cortex he was stimulating; he has very good reasons for thinking them to be elsewhere, and deeper in the brain. He came to think that perhaps all our conscious experiences are perpetually and indelibly recorded somewhere in the brain, and it is the recall of these which is difficult or impossible under normal conditions of life.

UNIQUENESS OF PERSONAL EXPERIENCE

It has often been supposed (e.g., Monod, 1971) that the uniqueness of the individual's personal experience is derived ultimately from the uniqueness of his genetic constitution, but this is an unthinkable conclusion, as is shown by the following summary of a passage from Eccles (1970, see pp. 80–83).

We may take it as certain that my conscious self depends uniquely on my brain and not on other brains. This unique interdependence between a brain and a conscious self raises a problem that has always been of great interest. It has been expressed by the great American biologist H. S. Jennings (1930) in a speculative chapter entitled "Biology and Selves." However, the climate of opinion has been so unfavourable to such speculations that Jennings' ideas have been almost universally neglected. Yet they are very relevant to the problems raised, namely, the uniqueness of the conscious experiences that each of us enjoys and their relationship to the neuronal activities of our brains.

Two questions may be asked, What is the nature of this consciously experiencing self? and How does it come to be related in this unique manner with a particular brain? Eccles states that for him these are the most fundamental and important questions that can be asked; and he adds that he has held this belief since he was eighteen years old, when a sudden illumination of these problems occurred which has driven him on by their interest and urgency to spend his life studying the nervous system.

Jennings formulated with a masterly and lucid style two problems that to him were quite unanswerable. Both were related to the superficially attractive hypothesis that the uniqueness of the self derives from the uniqueness of the particular gene combination belonging to that self, or, as he expresses it, "the assumption that it is diversity of gene combination that gives origin to distinctiveness of selves."

In the first place, of course, that assumption is refuted by the distinctiveness that is experienced by identical twins with their identical gene combinations. Alike as these twins are to external observers, each in its own conscious experiences and selfhood is as distinct from its fellow twin as it is from any other self. Evidently, identity of gene combinations must be compatible with distinctiveness of experiencing selves.

The second problem has a universal reference to all conscious selves—to each one of us. It was formulated by Jennings in relation to the genetic theory that any individual (except identical twins) is a genetically unique and never-to-be-repeated knot of strands of genes (Dobzhansky, 1962, 1967) that has come by inheritance through countless individuals from the remote past. Jennings asks:

> What is the relation of my self, identified as it is with one particular knot in the great network that constitutes humanity, to the other knots now existing? Why should I be identified with one only? To an observer standing apart from the net, it will not appear surprising that the different knots, since they are formed of diverse combinations of strands, should have different peculiarities, different characteristics. But that the observer himself—his total possibility of experience, that without which the universe for him would be non-existent—that he himself should be tied in relations of identity to a single one of the millions of knots in the net of strands that have come down from the unbeginning past—this to the observer appears astonishing and perplexing. Through the operation of what determining causes is myself, my entire possibility of experiencing the universe, bound to this particular one of the combination of strands, to the exclusion of some millions of others? Would I never have been, would I have lost my chance to participate in experience, would the universe never have existed for me, if this particular combination had not been made?

If the existence of "me" is thus tied to the formation of a particular combination of genes, one may enter upon calculations as to the chances that I should ever have existed. What are the chances that the combination which produced me should ever have been made? If we depend on the occurrence of the exact combination of genes that as a matter of fact produced us, the odds are practically infinite against my existence or that of any of my readers.

And what about the selves that would have come into existence if other combinations of genes had been made? If each diverse combination yields a different *self*, then there existed in the two parents the potentialities, the actual beginnings, of thousands of billions of selves, of personalities, as distinct as you and I. "Each of these existed in a form as real as your existence and my existence before our component germ cells have united. Of these thousands of billions, but four or five come to fruition. What has become of the others?"

And of course to go further backwards in our genetical tree makes the problem even more preposterously fantastic. Hence on both these grounds we must reject this materialistic doctrine that the uniqueness of my conscious experiencing self is derived from the uniqueness of my genetic make-up. What then determines the uniqueness of myself?

A frequent and superficially plausible answer to this question is the statement that the determining factor is the uniqueness of the accumulated experiences of a self throughout its lifetime. And this factor is also invoked to account for the distinctiveness of uniovular twins despite their genetic identity. It is readily agreed that my behaviour, my character, my memories, and in fact the whole content of my inner conscious life are dependent on the accumulated experiences of my life; but no matter how extreme the change that can be produced by the experiences of circumstance, I would still be the same self, able to trace back my continuity in memory to my earliest remembrances at the age of one year or so, the same self in a quite other guise. Thus the accumulated experiences of a lifetime cannot be invoked as the determining or generating factor of the unique self, though naturally they will enormously modify all the qualities and features of that self.

Jennings must have appreciated the fallacy of attempting to derive the uniqueness of self from the experiential history of an individual, for in searching for an explanation he develops the following remarkable speculations:

> To work this out in detail, one would apparently have to hold that the human self is an entity existing independently of genes and gene combinations, and that it merely enters at times into relations with one of the "knots" formed by the living web. If one particular combination or "knot" should not occur, it would enter into another. Then each of us might have existed with quite different characteristics from those we have—as our characteristics would indeed be different if we had lived under different environments. . . . It could be held that there is a limited store of selves ready to play their part, that the mere occurrence of two particular cells which may or may not unite has no determining value for the existence of these selves, but merely furnishes a substratum to which for reasons unknown they may become temporarily attached. . . . And what interesting corollaries might be drawn from such a doctrine, as to the further independent existence of the selves after the dispersal of the gene combinations to which they had been attached! Certainly no one can claim that biological science establishes or indeed favours such a doctrine. But since biology itself furnishes no positive doctrine of the relation of selves to gene combinations, the question is a fair one. Does biological science make the holding of that doctrine impossible?

BRAINS AND COMPUTERS

We must come now to the question of the supreme control of the brain, the organising system whereby we have freedom of choice. Donald MacKay, Professor of Communication at the University of Keele, has developed his theories about this as a result of the consideration of arguments, so frequently and blithely, not to say ignorantly, put forward by popular writers and others that the mind is nothing but a giant and excessively complex computer. The first thing to say is that the mind is more than a calculational or representational mechanism in that it involves self-consciousness. Karl Popper has shown that even a computing machine of unlimited capacity would be unable completely to predict the future of a physical system *of which it was itself a part*. He showed that such machines are incapable of answering all questions because it is impossible for them to possess completely up-to-date initial information about themselves. If self-consciousness is in any sense a fact, then minds have a fundamental quality which distinguishes them from computers; calculators cannot "think." To the question, Can computers think? the answer is not "Yes" or "No" but "Don't be silly." In the case of human beings we do not say that brains think, but that people do. Computers, as mechanisms in metal, are logically on the same footing as brains (mechanisms in protoplasm), and to say that they think is simply to drop a philosophical brick. Computers manipulate not ideas, but tokens for our ideas (as, presumably, do brains). Employing the arguments used by Popper, Professor MacKay concludes that no information system can embody within it an up-to-date and detailed representation of itself, *including that representation*. He points out first that it is a working assumption of neurophysiologists studying the brains of animals and men that all conscious human activity and experience—choosing, seeing, believing, etc.—has a correlate in corresponding neural activity. It follows that if all cerebral changes were physically determined by prior physical functions, including other cerebral changes, then the future content of conscious experience would in principle be predictable from these factors.

FREE WILL

It would seem to follow from this that our conviction of having "free will" is an illusion. Really we are bound to do what we do because the "choice" has actually been forced upon us by our brains. Professor MacKay believes this to be a mistaken conclusion by virtue of the exact argument which Karl Popper has used. The key point is that if what a man believes affects correspondingly that state of his organising system, that is, part of his brain, no complete up-to-date account of that organising system could be believed by him without being, by that very fact, out of date. By the same token, given even the most complete current data, no complete prediction of the future state of the organising system is deducible upon which both the agent (that is, the person who does the thinking—the I) and the observer could correctly agree. A prediction made secretly by a totally detached observer could well be valid for the observer and his fellow observers, but upon the agent himself it has no logical binding force; and so we come to the extraordinary conclusion that, on the contrary, the agent would be mistaken if he believed it, even though the observers were apparently correct to believe it! Supposing I now decide to raise my little finger—there, that was an example of "free will!" I could have chosen not to do that.[13] Now imagine there is some master scientist, some mythical determinist at work, unbeknown to me, using a marvellous new invention, a kind of glorious microscope plus cinema which could photograph everything that is happening in all the ten thousand million cells in my brain at every moment. He then comes along and shows me his film and says, "Look here, you don't really have free will. I can prove you don't by this film I have just taken. What you did just now was not a free choice, but was determined by the state of your organising system." Well, any picture that he arrived at by that machine would of necessity leave out the internal representation that I have by means of what I believe to be free will.

Suppose that all the relevant facts on the workings of my brain could be made available, without disturbing it, to a computer system capable of predicting its future behaviour from these facts and the environmental forces acting upon my nervous system. Suppose in other words that my brain were as mechanical as clockwork and as accessible to deterministic analysis. What then? MacKay argues that even then—even with this wildly idealised pre-Heisenberg conception of a physically determined brain—the denial of human freedom in general would not only be unfounded but demonstrably mistaken. This is a very curious and extremely important kind of logical relativity principle. In order that the observers may validly believe what they do about the agent's brain, it is necessary that the agent should believe something else, for if he believes what they do, it would not be valid for him or for them. In fact no prediction of a typical choice could be believed by the agent without affecting its own validity. To call an action "free" in this sense is therefore to deny the existence of any determinate specification that is binding on (valid and definitive for) everyone, *including the agent,* before he makes up his mind.

It is this kind of freedom, so it is supposed, that underlies human responsibility. In a given initial state, on the same mechanistic assumptions, there may exist not just one but a whole range of potential state descriptions, any one of which would become correct *if accepted by the subject.* From a mechanistic point of view, "this will happen whenever, given this acceptance, the equation of state has several self-consistent solutions." From the standpoint of the subject, it means that a corresponding range of options are all really open to him, so there is no one outcome which he would be correct to regard as the only possible one. It would be equally consistent with mechanistic theory to accept any one of them as describing his immediate action, and whichever he accepts will in fact determine the action. So, coming back to our imagined determinist and his ciné film, we reach the following conclusions: (1) his evidence proves that he was correct, and indeed bound by mechanistic considerations, to expect me to choose as I did, but (2) it does not retrospectively prove that I was mistaken beforehand in believing my action to be undetermined, because (3) though the prediction is demonstrably binding on him, I would have been mistaken in believing it before I made up my mind. Moreover (4) when I came to make up my mind, the different possibilities I contemplated were still demonstrably open to me on his mechanistic assumption; that (5) if I was disposed to deny that I were free to choose between them, his mechanistic evidence could in principle demonstrate the reality and extent of my freedom.

Let me give one other example demonstrating another point —that in fact no conceivable method of observation could be certain of not upsetting the system observed unpredictably. Suppose you were taking a Gallup poll of the expected results of a forthcoming election and, instead of taking a very small sample —10 per cent or whatever it is—you took a sample of the vast majority of the constituency—80 or 90 per cent. Suppose you had asked them, each person privately, which way he was going to vote. You kept the results quite secret, added them all up and came out with the private prediction that Candidate "A" was going to be elected. By the very fact of asking them you might have caused them to think again and to change their minds. Thus it is never possible for a prediction of that kind to be absolutely certain. By the very fact of making the investigation, you have upset the mechanism which you are supposing is operating in a person's organising system. If MacKay is right, the understanding of mind will not come by finding some unexplained details of physical analysis, but by some quite new understanding of the significance of brain and bodily activity together. It seems that what we call "mind" has a working contact with "matter" more intimate than one form of energy upon another. They seem to be truly complementary in some very mysterious way, and this mysterious unity is what we know as "personal agency." I consider that it is absolutely essential to stress this idea of a personal agent if we are to begin to get to grips with the problem of the mind and its place in nature, and this of course is the very essence of our topic, the uniqueness of man.

More recently (1970) Professor MacKay has shown that even if a person's behaviour is predictable by us, this does not mean that his behaviour was inevitable for him. It cannot be so, for it cannot produce a specification of the outcome that the agent will be unconditionally correct to accept before he made up his mind. In this sense, no matter how many detached observers could predict the outcome, the agent and you and I are *free* in choosing. We cannot logically escape (or be denied) re-

sponsibility for our choices on the grounds of their predictability by non-participant observers.

DIMINISHED RESPONSIBILITY

As MacKay says, all this has an obvious bearing on the use
of evidence from brain science to determine whether a criminal
should be denied responsibility for his actions. If the argument
is correct, it is clearly not enough to prove that an action had a
physical cause, or could have been predicted by non-participants.
What matters is whether its causes were such that, before it
took place, they determined the *outcome inevitable for the man
himself*. There could of course be many cases in which the chain
mesh of cause and effect in the brain was as tight as we please,
but no such inevitable outcome could have been specified in
advance. If, however, as in certain kinds of brain damage—epileptic seizures, *force majeure,* or the like—the cognitive system
is by-passed or overridden, the situation is quite different. There
may well exist now a specification of a future action with an
unconditional take-it-or-leave-it claim on the man's assent; in
other words the outcome is *not* now open for him to determine,
but inevitable. MacKay suggests a possible mechanistic criterion
of diminished responsibility. Clearly there could be a whole range
of intermediate cases in which what we believe about the outcome of our choice would have progressively less effect on its
predictability for us. Think, for example, of the slow stages by
which a drug may take over control of a man's faculties. In
such cases we can usefully think of responsibility as diminished
in proportion as the outcome becomes unconditionally specifiable
for the man concerned. Ideally, it is about this that we want
the psychiatrists or the brain scientists to tell us. Evidence that
the outcome was predictable by *others* is not enough in itself
to justify depriving anyone of the right to be treated as a responsible agent.

Perhaps because it questions deep-rooted habits of thought.

334

the present argument is easily misunderstood as proving only that we are free subjectively, but determinate objectively. It is particularly important to see the mistake in this, since the essence of the argument is that in treating people as free we are recognising an objective fact about them: namely the non-existence of an unconditional specification of their future actions, *for them and for us.* The point is that when we are in dialogue with another individual, our brains form a mutually coupled system. Thus not only is your immediately future brain state necessarily indeterminate in detail for you; it is also indeterminate for *me* when I am in dialogue with you. So in social interaction the individuals concerned are objectively correct in recognising that each is indeterminate (in detail) for *all* members of the dialogue. Not even the most fully equipped of non-participant observers could produce a completely detailed specification of the future of the community that could survive the scrutiny, let alone claim the unconditional assent, of any member of it.

Professor MacKay goes on to say that it may seem almost suspiciously strange that this logical oddity should turn up in connexion with the brain, when we have not run into it elsewhere; but it is easy to see that in fact it belongs to a family of related oddities which beset us in science whenever a factor classically treated as negligible has turned out not to be so. Broadly speaking, the process of gaining scientific knowledge has three stages, in which information is respectively (1) generated, (2) transmitted, and finally (3) absorbed. At each we have to pay for our information by accepting limitations which were classically thought to be trivial. (1) Generation of information requires *interaction.* This interaction cannot be reduced below the limit set by Planck's constant. Then (2), transmission of information requires *time.* This time cannot be reduced below the limits set by the velocity of light. In each of these cases, when the scientific spotlight has been turned upon the process itself, we have had to realise that the corresponding costs could no longer be neglected. The result, says MacKay, has been the familiar paradoxes of quantum theory and relativity theory.

335

The basis of the present argument is that on the assumption made by mechanistic brain theory itself (3) absorption of information requires a *change in brain state*. Thus when the scientific spotlight is turned upon the process of cerebration itself, we need hardly be surprised that this cost in turn proves no longer to be negligible. It is by reckoning with it constantly, he suggests, that we can see the bankruptcy of all attempts to use brain science to deny human responsibility.

THE LIMITS OF MIND

We must now give brief consideration to paranormal experiences since one cannot discuss the limits of mind from the scientific point of view (leaving out for the time being the religious or theological point of view) without being as fair to modern parapsychology as one can. As Beloff (1962) has pointed out, reactions to the findings of parapsychology can be divided into four well-known types. He gives each of these types a label: (1) the agnostic, (2) the sceptical, (3) the conservative, and (4) the radical. The first attitude, that of the agnostic, is simply that any decision on the evidence so far available would be premature; and therefore it is wiser to suspend judgment altogether and to say nothing whatever about the problem. The agnostic does not claim that there is some specific flaw in the evidence, nor does he argue that anyone is acting in bad faith. He only alleges that the results are so queer and their implications so subversive for science, in short that they recall so much magic and superstition, that in the hope that they will go away they had better *not* be taken seriously. This is perhaps an entirely honourable attitude for the working scientist—*provided of course he is a really scientific materialist* and thereby deliberately wearing blinkers. We can say, as I would say, that no scientist has the evidence to be *philosophically* a scientific materialist; but if our agnostic does not trouble to go into that aspect of the matter one can hardly expect him to consider parapsychology. That philosophers should ignore parapsychology is perhaps more reprehensible; and it is indeed astonishing, as Beloff remarks, that so many contemporary philosophers are content to theorise about the mind in complete disregard of both physiological and parapsychological findings. To come now to the position of the *sceptic*, the sceptic does not suspend judgment; he just takes up a dogmatic a priori attitude that paranormal events are impossible and consequently anyone who alleges that they exist must either be deceived, deceiving himself, or deceiving others. The *third* attitude, *that of the conservative*, is to make the best of a bad job. He acknowledges that the results are very odd, very disconcerting, perhaps even deplorable. But it is cowardly and unwise to ignore them, and so commendably he sets out to try, so far with little success, to make the paranormal appear a little more normal than before. *Fourthly*, the radical attitude involves the acceptance of the results at their face value.

PARANORMAL COGNITION

This last view is the view that I hold because I believe it can be said that, on straightforward grounds of scientific evidence, the existence of some forms of ESP was settled a long time back. (For a valuable recent summary, see Koestler 1972.) Since then the real question has been (and still is) "How does it work?"[14] That the phenomena are difficult to repeat, and the attainment of precise observations elusive, is no argument against the overwhelming evidence for its existence—any more than the rarity of supernova in the experience of astronomers of an earlier period, and impossibility of forecasting their appearance, was reason for disbelieving in their existence. Perhaps ESP observation will become fully repeatable when the circumstances of occurrence have been more perceptively analysed. Dr. Grey Walter's work on the "readiness wave" (see note 13) may, as Koestler suggests, provide a clue. One of the difficulties with ESP is our inability to control the unconscious processes underlying it. It seems likely that "a paradoxical compound of detachment and excitement" is needful. Koestler (1972), in a valuable discussion, points out that,

> Spontaneous paranormal experiences are always bound up with some self-transcending type of emotion, as in telepathic dreams or in mediumistic trance; and in the laboratory, too, emotional rapport between experimenter and subject is of decisive importance. The subject's interest in the mystery of ESP in itself evokes a self-transcending emotion; when that interest flags at the end of a long ESP sitting, there is a characteristic falling-off in the number of "hits" on the score sheet. This "decline effect" is regarded as an additional proof for the reality of ESP. There is also an overall decline in the performance of most subjects after a prolonged series of sittings. They get bored. Most normal skills improve with practice. In ESP the opposite is the case.

A further argument relating to the apparent *rarity* of paranormal phenomena (see also note 14) was put forward by the late Professor C. D. Broad in an article in *Philosophy* (1949, vol. 24):

> If paranormal cognition and paranormal causation are facts, then it is quite likely that they are not confined to those very occasions on which they either manifest themselves sporadically in a spectacular way, or to those very special conditions in which their presence can be experimentally established. They may well be continually operating in the background of our normal lives. Our understanding of, and our misunderstandings with, our fellow men; our general emotional mood on certain occasions; the ideas which suddenly arise in our minds without any obvious introspectable cause; our unaccountable immediate emotional reactions towards certain persons; . . . and so on; all these may be in part determined by paranormal cognition and paranormal causal influences.

Professor Price (1967) added an interesting suggestion regarding the apparent *capriciousness* of ESP:

> It looks as if telepathically received impressions have some difficulty in crossing the threshold and manifesting themselves in consciousness. There seems to be some barrier or repressive mechanism which tends to shut them out from consciousness, a barrier

which is rather difficult to pass, and they make use of all sorts of devices for overcoming it. Sometimes they make use of the muscular mechanisms of the body and emerge in the form of automatic speech or writing. Sometimes they emerge in the form of dreams, sometimes as visual or auditory hallucinations. And often they can only emerge in a distorted and symbolic form (as other unconscious mental contents do). It is a plausible guess that many of our everyday thoughts and emotions are telepathic or partly telepathic in origin, but are not recognised to be so because they are so much distorted and mixed with other mental contents in crossing the threshold of consciousness.

Adrian Dobbs (1967), commenting on this passage, raised an important point:

This is a very interesting and suggestive passage. It evokes the picture of either the mind or the brain as containing an assemblage of selective filters, designed to cut out unwanted signals on neighbouring frequencies, some of which get through in a distorted form, just as in ordinary radio reception.

THE THEORIES OF PRICE AND BROAD

As to the relationship between mental and physical, Broad (1923) and Price (1965) have each made significant theoretical contributions. Price suggested that the difference between mental events and physical events lies not in the fact that the latter are spatial, whereas the former are not, but in the fact that they are both spatial but have different spatial locations. That is to say, he suggests that there is one physical space in the world containing stars, planets, human bodies, and brains, and in addition a number of other spaces, one for each human individual, that contains his thoughts, images, and sense data. And if I am right we should now have to add one for each of many animal individuals. Price points out that we have been so conditioned for centuries by the Cartesian theory that we find it difficult to grasp the possibility of there being more than one space in the world. However there is no a priori reason why there should not be more than one space; and it is fairly easy to grasp his idea that physical objects are in one space and images, etc., in other spaces. The question is, How are these to be related to one another? So far, Price's theory is very similar to that of Broad's. But Price suggests that there are temporal and causal relations between the events in two systems, but no spatial relations. This of course introduces a new twist into our ideas of causal relations—since scientists up to now recognised only one spatial system, causal relations have always been described between objects in this system. Price argues that this is not logically necessary and indeed that it is logically possible to have events linked by causal, but not by spatial, relations.

Broad's theory suggests that physical space time and the various space times may all form cross sections of an n-dimensional space where n can equal any number larger than four, since there are many different ways of assembling a number of three spaces in one common space. Any point in physical space time can be specified completely by four co-ordinates, and any point in someone's perceptual field can be specified by four co-ordinates. Broad's theory suggests, therefore, that the axes from which these co-ordinates are obtained are not the same in the two cases except the time axis. The advantage is that the causal relations postulated between brain events and mind events do not incur the concept of action across a "non-space," but merely that the geometry of space is more complex than we had thought.

Figures 51 and 52 show diagrammatically the difference between Broad's theory and Price's theory. In Broad's theory the entire three-dimensional physical world is represented by one plane "A" and the space of one person's mind by a second plane "B" that intersects the first figure. Thus, showing himself an early precursor of Karl Popper, he argues that man's physical body and brain will be in "A," his conscious world will be in "B." This enables us to imagine the visual field as something like the screen of a television set, and similarly for the other sensory fields. The ego's view of the physical world will thus be mediated by a mechanism working just like television. Smythies (1969) suggests some interesting implications of this. (1) Events in mental space would seem to satisfy many, if not all, criteria for being "material" as specified for events in the physical world. The events would be, clearly, spatially distributed and organised. Thus the theory is to that extent thoroughly materialistic. It is just that there is more matter in the n-dimensional universe than there would be in the 4-dimensional one. (2) Consciousness as here defined would not be located *in* the brain at all, as in the Double-aspect Theory, but *outside* it altogether in a space of its own. So Smythies would argue that the reason the perceptual field looks nothing like any part of the cortex would be that it is not any part of the cortex but a separate piece of the human mechanism in its own right. The brain thus becomes not the total mechanism of mind but merely a part of it.

In essence, Broad's theory, of course, requires a radical change in physics and cosmology. But, unlike previous changes, this

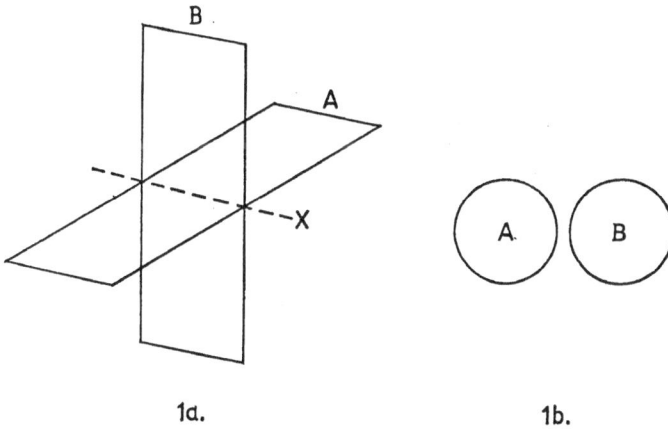

1a.   1b.

Figure 51

1(a). Broad's Theory.

   A represents the 3-dimensional physical world, and B represents the mental world. X represents the volume of their intersection.

1(b). Price's Theory.

   A represents the entire physical world, and B one person's entire mental world. The "space" on the paper between them should be regarded as non-existent.

(From Koestler and Smythies, 1969.)

is not an internal rearrangement of the present system but the addition of a whole new system. Indeed if one surveys the present state of physics, one should not be surprised at this request, and Broad's theory is evidently a possible cosmological theory—for there is no a priori reason why space must be three-dimensional; that is, we are not compelled by logic to locate every event in the universe by using only four space-time axes. Smythies suggests that these new theories produced by Broad and Price, which are closely linked with two theories of perception, are worthy of serious consideration by those grown weary of the eternal debate between dualism and monism. These theories are neither dualistic nor monistic in the old sense; nor do they ask us to believe in any ghosts in the machine. They merely

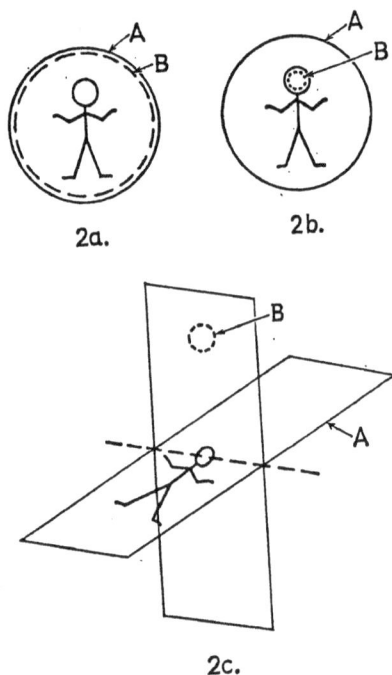

2a.   2b.

2c.

Figure 52   2(a). Naïve Realism.
            2(b). Psychoneural Identity.
            2(c). Broad's theory -----Physical world *a* -----Perceptual world
                  (of consciousness) B.
            (From Koestler and Smythies, 1969.)

suggest that many of the old metaphysical arguments can be avoided if we pay more attention to the geometry of the space time in which we live. There has been much interesting critical comment on these theories (Koestler and Smythies, 1969, pp. 246–57). They are, of course, extremely provisional and tentative. Some commentators say they are perfectly happy dualists; others are more cagey. Some feel happy at the prospect of a new cosmology which would really cope with the world as we experience it by including, or rather making room for, what we can surely say is the most remarkable fact in the universe to our present ways of thinking; namely that of the existence of mind.

There is however one final point to be made. I stated above my belief that the existence of *some* forms of ESP was settled long ago. But now, over and above this, we are faced by the increasing refinement of technique which seems to be providing impressive evidence for clairvoyance as distinct from precognitive telepathy. If this trend is indeed established, and it certainly becomes increasingly difficult to ignore, it will once again open wide the whole question of the relation between mentality, mental perception, and physiological mechanism. It may indeed be, as Eccles has argued in relation to the problem of free will, that physics, physiology, and parapsychology are yet in too primitive a state to allow even a proper formulation of the problems, let alone their solution. The brain is so stupendously complex and its organisation so refined and elaborate that, as Eccles says, there may be an unimaginable richness of properties in the active cerebral cortex, giving it the power of being a detector in liaison with dispositional intentions in the world of conscious experience. So perhaps indeed present theorising may turn out to be of only a very limited significance. If so, it will at least be no new experience for science!

WAYS OF KNOWING

Finally, to say a few provisional words on the topic of different and complementary ways of knowing. I am convinced that if scientists are ever to cope with the gigantic problems which seem to be bearing down upon them, as a result of recent developments both in biology and physics, a new approach with new conceptual tools, perhaps a new orientation of mind, will have to come. I think scientific advance is essentially unpredictable. No one can tell what forms the new tools will take. But I am prepared to risk a very strongly backed bet that enlightenment will only come with a further development of creative imagination—some new development in imagination similar to the creative intuition and perception of the artist. I think something akin to this creative intuition and perception of the artist and the poets is going to become as necessary to the future of science as are, and as will remain, the skills of deductive inference and experimental prowess. All this is looking very far into the future. But I am convinced that scientific advances of the future will not come from pessimistic adherence to misunderstood views as to the nature of past science; neither will they come from an attempt to make the experimental methods of science into a philosophy of science. They are much more likely to come from what Polanyi is all the time advocating and pointing out: an acceptance of the view that man's intellect acquires knowledge by a real act of *personal* faith; a readiness to believe in the reality of inspiration and its possibilities in guiding the dedicated spirit to new synthesis and new peaks of vision.

That great physiologist Claude Bernard once said: "*Dans les champs de l'observation le hasard ne favorise que less esprits préparés.*" Well, what kind of preparation is going to be needed for the scientific advances in the future? I think all will probably accept that the essence of external reality is unattainable. If we look at art, we find that all painting rests on a series of conventions which gradually become accepted by painter and beholder alike. The history of perspective painting shows how conventions gradually accumulate and how artists apply what they have learned. Hinshelwood (1961) says: "At no stage is there any strict meaning in saying that artists paint what they see." The part played by the imagination of the viewer is an essential one and the picture represents equivalents to nature rather than "likeness." That is to say, the evolution of painting has been a continuous voyage of discovery. If the painter seeks the vision of nature, it is by analysis and by re-creation. The vision, however splendid, always remains partial. Hinshelwood (1961) makes the profound observation: "That is why the contemplation of the greatest works of art can be tinged with sadness and a subtle feeling of frustration."

The desire to grasp and represent in art corresponds in science to the desire to enquire "Why" and "How" when confronted by nature. And art and science in that respect have a similar root. They seek to forge the union of man with nature. And it is for theology to treat the relation of man to God. Here we are again led on to poetry: "When those whose minds are not attuned to mathematics seek the translation of its symbols into metaphor (and this is now very common in physics), they are coming close to poetry." I suspect that a great deal of modern theoretical physics is much nearer to poetry than to science. The poetic simile is not the right one for sciences; the idiom is wrong. Poetic vision relates the elements of the external world to the human mind, but not in a way which helps to relate them in any general or consistent way to one another. With nature, it is the coherent vision as a whole—and that is what science is after, is seeking to give, and by its own methods is gradually giving. Here Hinshelwood again comes to the profound human instinct to seek something personal behind the processes of nature: "People are led both by intellectual and by emotional paths to the contemplation of religious questions. In so far as men seek to fuse their own personal worlds with the impersonal element in the external world, they are pursuing the vision of nature; in their desire for communion with the universal and personal they pursue what, I suppose through the ages, they have meant by the vision of God." Paths, then, of art and poetry, of science and religion, are the means by which man grasps the universe, surrenders himself to it, identifies himself with it, loses himself in it.

The final sections of Dante's *Il Paradiso* come as near as is humanly possible to achieve the ultimate goal of great poetry. Dante there describes the ultimate fusion of beauty and truth and goodness in the supreme vision and his own beatific union with it.

But I would like to give the last word not to Dante but to Coleridge, who says: "The primary imagination I hold to be the living power and prime agent of all human perception, and as a repetition in the finite mind of the eternal act of creation."

Chapter 10

EMERGENCE AND THE
HUMAN SPIRIT

EMERGENCE AND TRANSCENDENCE

This last chapter is intended as an attempt to pull together and correlate a number of the themes which have been put forward in varying degrees of detail during those which have gone before and to carry the story forward to the highest reaches of man's nature. One could, perhaps with some advantage, have replaced the word "emergence" with the word "transcendence." Emergence has been in use for so long in this context that it has had time to accumulate a good many undesirable overtones, though having been, from time to time, associated with somewhat ill-conceived and inadequately supported theories of evolution. But I am convinced that there are features in the natural world, features which we encounter in the process of evolution, which are truly emergent in something like the original sense.

The strict form of emergent theory was outlined by Broad (1923) as follows: It is the theory that the characteristic behaviour of the whole *could* not, even in theory, be deduced from the most complete knowledge of the behaviour of its components, taken separately or in other combinations, and of their proportions and arrangements in this whole. Broad goes on to point out that if we want to explain the behaviour of any whole in terms of its structure and components, we *always* need two independent kinds of information. (a) We need to know how the parts would behave separately, and (b) we need to know the law or laws according to which the behaviour of the separate parts is compounded when they are acting together in any proportion and arrangement. As Broad points out, it is extremely important to notice that these two bits of information are quite independent of each other in every case.

But transcendence does not necessarily imply intrinsic irreducibility of the human or biological phenomena; it does mean that new patterns of phenomena have emerged which it is not only permissible, but indeed necessary, to study as new patterns (Dobzhansky, 1967, 1969). And indeed, as we shall see, a mere change of scale may result in entirely new emergent qualities which could not previously have been foretold.

THE REFUTATION OF REDUCTIONISM

The concept of reductionism and that of determinism are related in some contexts and are interchangeable. But one must be careful because the term "determinism" in philosophy has shades of meaning and many implications which I am not prepared, nor indeed able, to discuss. When I use the term "determinism," it is primarily Scientific Determinism that I mean, and it is this form of determinism which has received such violent (and I think lethal) critical shocks in recent decades. In the first chapter, I mentioned a number of biologists and physicists of great eminence, such as Paul Weiss, Michael Polanyi, Walter Elsasser, and Sir John Eccles, and I also discussed in other connexions the equally strongly worded criticisms of Sir Charles Sherrington. All these are presumably dualists, though some of them at least might qualify this and restrict their dualism to certain circumstances only, such as the difference between mind and brain.

Amongst philosophers and logicians, particularly amongst those who have given special attention to scientific problems, many names could be mentioned, including that great thinker L. T. Hobhouse, whom I like to mention first because I owe so much to his writings. When Hobhouse speaks of what he calls "the correlation of governing principles"—a concept which involves the recognition of abstract moral law and eternal values which are good in themselves—he has surely passed far beyond the possibility of any form of scientific reductionism. Again I have discussed at some length the views of Sir Karl Popper and the logician William Kneale, as in some sense at least unashamedly dualist. The former indeed sees no future at all for philosphical reductionism. To these I might have added the name of Professor Stephan Körner, and finally that bright comet in the present-day firmament which according to certain observers comes trailing dazzling clouds of uncertain composition, namely Dr. Noam Chomsky. And I should recall also that admirably argued book by a philosophical logician, Dr. M. R. Ayers, entitled, *The Refutation of Determinism* (1968).

It will strike the reader at once that I have not mentioned in this connexion Whitehead and his followers. Whitehead came to a position of what could be called "panpsychism." Philosophically this is of course eminently respectable and indeed most attractive. As a biologist I have long been immensely impressed by, and beholden to, Whitehead's philosophy of organism (*Process and Reality*), in that it seems to me that, as I understand him, he is the first great philosopher who really took trouble to comprehend the biological developments of his time. My trouble with panpsychism, as advanced by Whitehead and, for instance, his disciple Hartshorne, is that I see no conceivable scientific possibility of investigating its significance. It is easy enough to assume some sort of psychic element in the ultimate physical particles; indeed Eddington himself toyed with that idea. It may be, as Carl von Weiszäcker (1968) has boldly suggested, that since the concept of a particle itself is just the description of a connexion which exists between phenomena,

349

there may, if we are prepared to jump into strict metaphysical language, be no reason why what we call "matter" should not in fact be "spirit." This I think amounts to saying that not only physical theories but biological theories portray not nature itself but our knowledge of nature. Again the trouble here is that I see no conceivable scientific possibility of confirmation. Nor does the combination of physical units, in so far as modern physics reveal them, suggest to us how, or by what laws, psychic units could similarly combine and so produce what we recognise as the mental. Moreover the results which I discussed in Chapter 9 do *not* indicate parallelism between the laws of the combination of physical units and the development of mind. We can indeed say that if reductionism were right, in the sense that the mental and spiritual, artistic, and ethical values which we experience really are in any sense "in" the electrons and other primary components of which the world is made, then they don't *appear* to be there. It follows that a great and unjustified leap of faith is required to believe it—a leap without, so it seems to me, any scientific evidence. Thus in fact reductionism requires at least as great a faith, if not much greater faith, than does any form of syncretism or organicism. In the first we are required to believe what we can in no way detect; in the second we are required to believe in a source of value added to, or injected into, a natural process, as complexity develops, which we are unable to understand. Is it too wild to suggest that reductionism leads to deism and/or mechanism, while organicism leads to theism and/or mysticism?

One might choose many different examples to illustrate the basic problem of reductionism and its refutation. However, I think that, rather than come at once to biology, one secures a better perspective by starting with physics. First, we must say that, as a working hypothesis, reductionism is the major basic tool found to be in use among the great majority of active experimental scientists. And with good reason: for when and where it is successful, it achieves the most impressive of all scientific advances. In fact as a working tool it is indispensable, and all of us use it all the time. But many scientists go on from there to accept it without question, not merely as a tool but as a philosophy—that is, they assume that all the activities of our minds and bodies, all the changes and complexities shown in the study of animate or inanimate matter, are controlled by the same set of fundamental laws.

There are in physics certain extreme conditions where this does not seem to be true, but for the moment they can be ignored. To the ordinary working scientist there is an obvious course of action; perhaps one should call it a temptation. Having first assumed that there is a basic set of fundamental laws, the temptation is to proceed from there to what seems an obvious corollary, that is, that everything obeys the same fundamental laws. Then the only scientists who are studying anything really fundamental are those who are working on these laws. A physicist colleague of mine, to whom I am much indebted (Anderson, 1972), has pointed out, in a discussion of the topic, "More is Different," that if this were so, then the only scientists who would certainly be regarded as carrying out "fundamental" work would be some astrophysicists, some elementary particle physicists, some logicians and other mathematicians, and a few more. This reductionist point of view which seeks knowledge by analysis almost inevitably leads its proponents to assume, quite unwarrantably, that all that is then required is to work out the consequences of these laws by the prosecution of what is called "extensive science" whereupon all truth will be revealed!

But there is a tremendous fallacy here. For the success of the reductionist hypothesis in certain areas does not by any means imply the practicability of a "constructionist" one: to reduce everything to simple fundamental laws does *not* imply the ability to start from those laws and reconstruct the universe. In fact "the more the elementary particle physicists tell us about the nature of the fundamental laws, the less relevance they seem to have to the very real problems of the rest of science, much less of society." (See Anderson, 1972.) The constructionist hypothesis breaks down in the twin difficulties of scale and complexity.

351

The behaviour of large and complex aggregates of elementary particles, so it turns out, is not to be understood as a simple extrapolation of the properties of a few particles. Rather, at each level of complexity entirely new properties appear, and the understanding of these new pieces of behaviour requires research which is as fundamental as, perhaps even more fundamental than, anything undertaken by the elementary particle physicists.

Anderson starts from the laws which govern the motion of individual atoms and electrons and attempts to understand how large collections of them—particularly macroscopic solid bodies —behave. He finds it a truism, in physics at least, that as we look at phenomena of a very different scale we often find that the basic laws which govern the motion change. For example, on the cosmic scale, Newtonian mechanics has been replaced by the more accurate Einstein theory; on the atomic scale, Newtonian mechanics has been replaced by quantum mechanics, and on the subnuclear scale, the laws are still changing. In fact, he says, it is a mistake to be too analytical in one's approach and to assume that all new and fundamental laws come from logical analysis. They do not. Take the arguments for the building of a thousand-billion-electron-volt accelerator. We often hear it argued that, in short, intensive research goes for the fundamental laws, extensive research for the explanation of phenomena in terms of known fundamental laws. Thus on this view ordinary physicists are applied particle physicists, chemists are applied physicists, biologists are applied chemists, psychologists are applied biologist, social scientists are applied psychologists, etc. Anderson (1972) states,

> I believe this is emphatically not true: I believe that at each level of organisation, or of scale, types of behaviour open up which are entirely new, and basically unpredictable from a concentration on the more and more detailed analysis of the entities which make up the objects of these higher level studies. True, to understand worms we need to understand cells and macromolecules, but not mesons and nucleons. And even the comprehension of cells and

macromolecules can never tell us all the important things that need to be known about worms.

At each level in fact there are fundamental problems requiring intensive research which cannot be solved by further microscopic analysis but need, as Anderson says, *"some combination of inspiration, analysis, and synthesis."*

Another point is that clearly fundamental questions always seem to cluster around just those areas where the scale changes. Thus in biology exciting things seem to occur at the interfaces with chemistry and with psychology—both scale changes in the sense intended. To take another example, aerodynamics: turbulence represents a real problem in principle because it spreads in scale from atomic to microscopic; meteorology is enormously interesting and difficult because the scales of importance stretch from very local to world-wide; and yet in both cases the fundamental laws of motion of the air have been known for decades or centuries.

Popper (1974), in a recently published consideration of the problem of scientific reductionism, commences by asking three questions: 1. Can we reduce, or hope to reduce, biology to physics or to physics and chemistry? 2. Can we reduce to biology, or hope to reduce to biology, those subjective conscious experiences which we may ascribe to animals, and if question 1 is answered in the affirmative, can we reduce them further to physics and chemistry? 3. Can we reduce, or hope to reduce, the consciousness of self and the creativeness of the human mind to animal experience, and thus, if questions 1 and 2 are answered in the affirmative, to physics and chemistry?

Before proceeding to answer these questions, Popper makes the following points: First he suggests that scientists have to be reductionists in the sense that nothing is as great a success in science as successful reduction. Indeed it is perhaps, as has been said above, the most successful form conceivable of all scientific explanations since it results in the identification of the unknown with the known. Secondly Popper suggests scientists have to be

353

reductionists in their methods—either naïve or else more or less critical reductionists, sometimes desperate critical reductionists, since, as he points out, hardly any major reduction in science has ever been completely successful. There is almost always an unresolved residue left by even the most successful attempt at reduction. Thirdly Popper contends that there do not seem to be any reasons in favour of philosophical reductionism. But nevertheless the working scientist should continue to attempt reductions for the reason that we can learn an immense amount even from unsuccessful attempts at reduction and that problems left open in this way belong to the most valuable intellectual possessions of science. In other words, emphasis on our scientific failure can do us a lot of good.

Popper proceeds to discuss some of the classical examples of reductionism. Einstein wrote in 1920, "according to our present conceptions the elementary particles (that is, electrons and protons) are *nothing else* than condensations of the electromagnetic field, . . . our view of the universe presents two realities . . . namely, gravitational ether and electromagnetic field or—as they might also be called—space and matter." By using the term *nothing else* here, Einstein implied that this was an example of complete reduction. As Popper says, "reduction in the grand style." Einstein was not the only one; and by 1932 almost all leading physicists, Eddington, Dirac, Einstein, Bohr, De Broglie, Schrödinger, Heisenberg, Born, and Pauli, accepted uncompromisingly the reductionist view. Popper gives a quotation from R. A. Millikan in which that physicist says that nothing more beautifully simplifying has ever happened in the history of science than the whole series of discoveries culminating about 1914 which finally brought about practically universal acceptance of the theory that the material world contains but two fundamental entities, namely, positive and negative electrons. But, as Popper points out, this reductionist passage was written in the very nick of time (1932); for it was in the same year that Chadwick announced his discovery of the neutron and that Anderson (1933) first discovered the positron. Nevertheless many of the greatest physicists, such as Eddington (1936), continued to believe that with the advent of quantum mechanics the electromagnetic theory of matter had entered into its final state and that all matter consisted of electrons and protons. Popper (1972) points out that, though we still believe in the repulsive forces as being electromagnetic and still hold Bohr's theory of the periodic system of elements in a modified form; everything else in this beautiful reduction of the universe to an electromagnetic universe with two particles of stable building blocks has by now disintegrated. An immense number of important new facts has been learnt, but the simplicity of the reduction has disappeared. This refutation of the reductionist position started with the discovery of neutrons and positrons and has continued ever since with the discovery of new elementary particles. But particle theory is not even the main difficulty. "The real disruption is due to the discovery of new kinds of forces, especially of nuclear forces irreducible to electromagnetic and gravitational forces." So now we have at least four very different and still irreducible kinds of forces in physics—gravitation, weak decay interactions, electromagnetic forces, and nuclear forces.

In discussing Pauling's work on the nature of the chemical bond, Popper further remarks that even letting us suppose that we have a fully satisfactory theory of nuclear forces, of the periodic system of the elements and their isotopes and especially of the stability and instability of the heavier nuclei, have we thereby a fully satisfactory reduction of chemistry to physics? The answer is "No." For an entirely new idea had to be brought in, an idea which is somewhat foreign to physical theory: the idea of evolution, of the history of our universe, of cosmogeny. This is so because the present theory of the periodic system explains the heavier nuclei as being composed of lighter ones, and ultimately as being composed of hydrogen nuclei (protons) and neutrons (which might in turn be regarded as a kind of composition of protons and electrons). This theory assumes that the heavier elements have properties which can only actually result from a very rare process in the universe which makes several hydrogen nuclei fuse into heavier ones. These heavier elements are at present regarded as products of supernovae explosions. The present estimate is that since hydrogen forms 25 per cent of all matter by mass and helium 75 per cent of all matter by mass, all the heavier nuclei appear to be extremely rare—not more than 1 or 2 per cent by mass. Thus the earth and presumably the other planets are made of extremely rare materials.

The present most widely accepted theory of the origin of the universe—that of the hot big bang—claims that most of the helium is the product of the big bang itself and occurred within the very first minute of the existence of the expanding universe and that the background radiation, which is now being studied so intensively, provides some evidence of the date of this initial explosion. Moreover it is only under the circumstances of the intense gravitational contraction which leads to supernovae outbursts that the heavier elements can have been formed. Two things of great interest emerged from these considerations. First, in the conditions of the once supposed uniform, universally distributed primeval nebula, existence of gravitational forces could never have been envisaged, and consequently the existence of heavy elements could never have been predicted. These can thus be regarded as genuine emergents in the strict sense. In so far as chemistry has been reduced it has not been reduced to physics but to cosmology (or as Popper says, even to cosmogeny) rather than to physical theory. And present views seem to imply that the possibility of ever reducing chemistry to physics is remote indeed.

Popper points out that nuclear forces are thus potentialities and become operative only under conditions which are extremely rare, namely tremendous temperatures and pressures. He goes on to suggest that this comes very close to a theory of essential properties which have the characteristics of predestination or pre-established harmony. At any rate "a solar system like ours depends, according to present theories, on their pre-existence." The same close approach to the idea of pre-established harmony applies to the production of heavy metals by gravitational forces, and if this is the best that can be done, then any philosophy of pre-established harmony is an admission of the failure of the method of reducing one thing to another. "Thus the reduction of chemistry to physics is far from complete even if we admit unrealistically favourable assumptions. Rather, this reduction assumes a theory of cosmic evolution or cosmogeny and in addition two kinds of pre-established harmony in order to allow sleeping potentialities, or relative propensities of low probability built into the hydrogen atom to become activated. Thus we are operating with emergent properties." In fact the so-called reduction of chemistry is to a physics that assumes evolution, cosmology, and cosmogeny and the existence of emergent properties.

The argument against reductionism from the biological point of view is perhaps well set out by stating that one can never hope to observe the whole repertoire of an organism if it is kept and observed solely in an artificially simplified environment. Thus a honeybee could never be fully understood, that is to say its possible responses and reactions could never be elucidated and itemised, if it were studied in isolation in an experimental cage or chamber. This is because the range, elaboration, and specialisation of conditions and stimuli which it encounters in its natural life could *never* be duplicated experimentally without having first observed them in nature, and certainly not fully even then. Similarly a nerve cell from the brain of a higher vertebrate could never be put through all its paces isolated in a tissue culture or other experimentally simplified situation. The fact is that a highly complex organ, or system, has capacities and potentialities that are the properties of the system and not merely of the components of the system.

Obviously as we go up the physicochemical scale into biology we come up against the crucial problem at issue, namely that of form or complexity and especially its transmission from one individual to another. Anderson (1972) approaches this from the point of view of homogeneous systems which have full symmetry and so little information and less homogeneous systems, or

357

less symmetrical systems, which are nevertheless regular and therefore contain information.

This brings us back to an example given in the first chapter of this book; namely that very curious question as to why is a thunderstorm not an organism. The core of that difference amounted to the fact that a thunderstorm, as contrasted with an organism (although in terms of the number of molecules involved vastly larger than many organisms), does not contain and transmit vast amounts of coded information. In all examples of objects which we unhesitatingly accept as alive the amount of information is enormous. Anderson estimates it at a quantity of the order of "bits" per molecule!

So as we go up the scale we find ourselves talking not about decreasing symmetry but about increasing complication; and, ascending the hierarchy of the sciences, we find many fundamental questions leaping out at us at each stage as we try to fit together the less complicated pieces into a more complicated system and as we try to understand the basically new types of behaviour which can result. Thus students of animal behaviour find themselves concerned about sensitivity, contractility, habituation, learning, perception, memory, orientation, perceptual synthesis, and mind—all topics which can be illuminated but not fully resolved by reductionist techniques. Coming up to the human level, since human beings can build and programme electronic computers it is *incontestable* that a human being is intrinsically a more complicated machine than a computer— "for instance, he has the possibility of *choosing* to do this thing himself, which the computer does not."

At the end of his discussion Anderson (1972), as a theoretical physicist, returns again to the fundamental laws of physics as an example of one other symmetry which is always broken in large systems. The fundamental laws of physics are completely independent of the sign of time. An electron cannot tell whether it is heading from tomorrow into yesterday or vice versa—cannot tell in any way. On the other hand we can tell time subjectively and in fact any large enough piece of matter can tell the time objectively. The rain falls down, not up; the sun shines, does not absorb light, and so on. This is the arrow of time referred to in an earlier chapter in connexion with evolution (p. 242). Finally Anderson comes back to the old argument about free will versus determinism. And he injects into this argument a new twist which some will dispute and which will no doubt require much debate. *In principle* it might still be argued that if a Cartesian superbrain really knew the wave function of the universe *now* it could calculate its subsequent history for ever. But the point is that the complication of this universe is so great that the superbrain or supercomputer would (and this is an exact statement) have to be infinitely bigger than the universe it was computing and would never even be capable for gathering the appropriate information (cf. the MacKay and Popper arguments once again, pp. 329–36). So our computer, infinitely bigger than the universe, would keep falling behind just because it would be unable to transmit information faster than light.

Anderson ends his discussion with the remark that when he was asked to write something about his personal scientific philosophy he discovered for the first time that he had one! Moreover he found that one of the central tenets was entirely different from what he would have expected, namely that the whole can be greater than, and very different from, the sum of its parts. Physicists and others who do not bother to ask themselves what their own philosophy really is fail to realise the fascinating things that can be discovered by looking at both the whole and the part, but most of all at their relationship to one another. This conclusion once more brings us back to the question of hierarchy and the architecture of complexity.

HIERARCHY

There is I think no doubt whatever that the idea of hierarchy is absolutely fundamental to the understanding both of evolution and of the composition of organisms. As Simon (1962) has pointed out, the word hierarchic is generally used to refer to a complex system in which each of the subsystems is subordinated by an authority-relation to the system it belongs to. This is to say each of the subsystems has a boss who is the immediate subordinate of the boss of the system. This is an idea which has been very illuminatingly worked out by Arthur Koestler in more than one of his recent books. I would refer particularly to the Alpbach Symposium (edited by Koestler and Smythies, 1969). Science can in fact pass beyond reductionism just because its reality is hierarchically arranged, and so the process of continuing analysis, which is what reductionism is about, can be balanced, illuminated, and to some degree superseded by this very hierarchical principle, according to which we focus our attention on the relationship between the whole and its parts—or, as Koestler would put it, between the whole and its sub-wholes or "holons" which, according to the hierarchic principle, are "Janus-faced" in that when seen from above they appear and act in some respects as parts; seen from below they appear and act in some respects as wholes. Anderson recalls a well-known passage: Scott Fitzgerald: "Ernest, the rich are different from us." Hemingway: "Yes. They have more money!" To turn from the ridiculous to the sublime, look again at the quote from Whitehead given at the beginning of Part Two of this book (p. 211).

REDUCTIONISM AND NIHILISM

By this time, I hope my readers will agree that determinism and reductionism, in so far as they appear as bugbears in the scientific world picture, are well and truly vanquished. So much so that you may wonder whether I have not spent too much time discussing the issue, even though it carries such immense philosophical import. The fact is that it has great social and spiritual import also. In his Gifford Lectures in Aberdeen, 1964–65, Sir Alister Hardy remarked that he could only regard the present-day monistic views of so many scientists and humanists as exceedingly dangerous for the future of civilisation in that it makes man's spiritual side simply the superficial by-product of a material process. He regards this as an entirely unwarranted dogma as unreasonable as any dogma of the medieval church. But let us see its effect in a field I have not yet talked much about, namely the field of psychiatry.

There seems little doubt that the belief in reductionism—subconscious though it may be, and perhaps all the more serious for that—has an effect on the mental health and indeed the sanity of modern man which is difficult to exaggerate. Dr Viktor Frankl, Professor of Psychiatry in the University of Vienna and widely known for his therapeutic work, finds that one of the major threats to health and sanity is what he calls the existential vacuum. He describes (1969) how more and more patients, in all parts of the world, crowd into the clinics and consulting rooms disrupted by a feeling of inner emptiness, a sense of the total and absolute meaninglessness of their lives. And he believes this is the direct and disastrous result of the denial of value which is regarded as characteristic of modern scientifically oriented society. It is the result, so he argues, of a widespread assumption that since science in its technique is largely reductionist, reductionism is the only philosophy in which one can believe.

Dr. Frankl gives some very telling examples: he says that L. J. Hatterer, a Manhattan psychoanalyst, pointed out in a paper that "many an artist has left a psychiatrist's office enraged by interpretations which suggest that he writes because he is 'an injustice collector,' or a sadomasochist; acts because he is an exhibitionist; dances because he wants to seduce the audience sexually, or paints to overcome a strict bowel training by free smearing." Frankl says that the unmasking of motives is indeed perfectly justified, but it *must stop* where the man who does the unmasking is finally confronted with what is genuine and authentic within a man's psyche. If he does not stop there, what this man is really unmasking is his own cynical attitude to his own nihilistic tendency to devaluate and depreciate that which is human in man. Frankl argues that there is an inherent tendency in man to reach out for meanings to fulfil and for values to actualise. Alas, man is offered (to quote two outstanding American scholars in the field of value psychology) the following definitions: "Values and meanings are nothing but defence mechanisms and reaction formations." Frankl adds that for himself he is not willing to live for the sake of his reaction formations and even less to die for the sake of his own defence mechanisms. (It is perhaps worth mentioning that Dr. Frankl spent some time in a concentration camp where he lost his wife and family.) He goes on to say that reductionism today is a mask for nihilism. Contemporary nihilism, he says, no longer brandishes the word "Nothingness"; today nihilism is camouflaged as "Nothing butness." Human phenomena are thus turned into mere epiphenomena. He argues that contrary to a widely held opinion, even existentialism is not nihilism; the true nihilism of today is reductionism. The true message of existentialism is *not* nothingness, *but* the no-thingness of man—that is to say *a human being is no thing*, a person is not one thing amongst other things.

Frankl gives another example of his own experience as a junior high school student when his science teacher used to walk up and down the class explaining to the pupils that life in its final analysis is nothing but combustion, an oxidation process. In this case reductionism actually took the form of oxidationism! The boy Frankl at once jumped to his feet and said, "Dr. Fritz, if this is true, what meaning then does life have?" At that time he was twelve. Now imagine what it means that thousands and thousands of young students are exposed to indoctrination along such lines, are taught a reductionist concept of man and a reductionist view of life.

Frankl points out that it is clear that about 20 per cent of neuroses today are noogenic (originating in thought) by nature and origin. He defines the existential vacuum as the frustration of what we may consider to be the most basic motivational force in man, and what we may call (by a deliberate oversimplification) *"The will to meaning"*—in contrast to the Adlerians' will to power and the Freudians' will to pleasure. There is also some evidence in the same direction produced by the results of brain surgery. Dr. Hyman, a California brain surgeon, states that he is again and again confronted with patients whom he has completely relieved from intractable pain by stereotactic brain surgery, and who then say to him: "Doctor, I am free from pain— but now more than ever I ask myself what the meaning of my life is, because I know that life is transitory, particularly in my situation." *The argument seems to be that people do not care so much for pleasure and avoidance of pain, but they do care profoundly for meaning.*

So this demand for meaning, particularly in the face of death, leads us on to our next topic, namely man as a religious animal.

MAN AS A RELIGIOUS ANIMAL

What then is man? What divides him from the animals? The anthropologist Bidney (1953) has suggested that man alone has the ability to objectify himself, to stand apart from himself as it were, and to consider the kind of being he is and what it is that he wants to do and to become. He continues, "Other animals may be conscious of their affects and the objects perceived; man alone is capable of reflection, of self-consciousness, of thinking of himself as an object." I think we have here to be very careful about the use of our terms. I certainly do not think that we can deny to all animals the attribute of being, to use Eccles' term, "experiencing selves." As I have already said earlier, no one who works for a long period with higher animals such as apes, monkeys, or even dogs and cats can, I believe, assert without fear of contradiction that these species, and possibly many others, are entirely devoid of consciousness. This conclusion I think extends beyond consciousness of their affects and the objects perceived. To some extent therefore I consider animals to be capable of reflection and to that extent of self-consciousness. If this is so, they must to some extent think of themselves as objects. However I personally feel equally sure that no animals can reflect about themselves, about the abstract quality of their natures, their long-term aims, in short their past and future history; or certainly not in anything even remotely like the way and to the extent that can man. That is I do not conceive that animals can be said to "philosophise."

Now, our attribution of self-awareness and mind-like qualities to other human beings is primarily achieved by understanding their behaviour—including of course their language. Nevertheless we do not hesitate to attribute to men of some primitive culture, of whose language we understand not a word, the same essential self-experience that we have ourselves. And although we can only be said to "talk with animals," perhaps in the one case of the chimpanzee "Washoe" who has learned American sign language, we certainly do not feel that chimpanzees are the only self-experiencing beings other than ourselves. What I do feel convinced about, as I have already mentioned, is the lack in animals of the appreciation of what Hobhouse called the correlation of governing principles. In other words I am prepared to deny to animals, on present evidence, the ability to hold quite general concepts of right and justice.

In a recent statement by A. I. Hallowell (see Dobzhansky, 1967) a profound truth gleams through the jargon of cultural anthropology. He says, "What occurred in the psychological dimension of hominid evolution was the development of a human personality structure in which the capacity for self-awareness, based on ego functions, *became of central importance.*" (My italics). Now I think we must admit (and this creates a formidable problem for Christian moralists and many others) that this, like all other steps in evolution, as far as we know, occurred by extremely gradual increments so that, if we had the whole evolutionary story of mankind displayed before us in every detail, we should have the greatest difficulty in deciding exactly at what point "MAN" had appeared. Nevertheless the absolute moral imperative is experienced by truly cultured man to the extent that, as Wittgenstein says, we are aware of duties from which, irrespective of conditions, not even death itself can absolve us. So I would say that perhaps the first and most important characteristic in which man is unique, and is I would like to think still evolving, lies in this conviction of the extreme and all-pervading value of such central beliefs.

Dostoyevsky somewhere said, "If God did not exist, all would be permitted." And I think Baillie (1962) is correct when he sees in this kind of statement—whether it comes from scientists, philosophers, or artists—the ultimate ground for the sense, which all share, of the reality of the corporeal world, strict "proofs" for which are so unsatisfactory. This sense in fact is dependent upon the apprehension of the world as shared, in some way derivative from the sense of reality of other selves; and of course above all the sense of a sustaining spirit. Woods (1962) has given what seems to me an admirable expression of this. He argues that there is an irreducible distinction between seeing that something is so and seeing that it ought to be so. The two judgments, he says, cannot possibly be the same. There is a fundamental Christian conviction that somehow there is a realm in which what ought to be is what is; and I believe he is right when he argues that it is impossible to conceive absolute moral judgments being made where there is no moral agent; and a moral agent implies personality.

The Concept of the Soul

The discussion of these matters brings one to the concept of the soul as in some sense a transcendent of the continuing self-awareness of man, the superego if one cares to use that term—potentiality for which is instilled by the grace of God in every normal human being. By the willing acceptance of that grace, each of us according to our circumstances can develop into a continuing spirit which transcends human life in all its other aspects, a process by which a continuing self in this world is developed and translated into a spirit inhabiting, in some sense which we can only very vaguely understand, eternity. I speak about such things with the greatest hesitation because I am at least aware of the vast range and ramifications of this theological topic. In the standard works of Christian theology I have yet to find anything more rigorous and profound than Tennant's lengthy chapter in Volume 1 of his *Philosophical Theology*. He ends that chapter with a quotation from Sir Thomas Browne, "There is a something in us that can be without us and will be after us; though indeed it hath no history [as to] what it was before us and cannot tell how it entered into us." Then, nearly three hundred years later, one of the greatest of neurophysiologists, Sir Charles Sherrington, said, "For me now the only reality is the human soul." (Quoted by Eccles, 1970, p. 174.)

After Tennant, there appears to be little that is relevant for today's scientifically oriented enquirer until the recent lecture by Hick (1972), and it is to be hoped that his study marks a tendency for return to this surely central topic of theological enquiry. Be this as it may, I find Professor Hick's study so admirable that a fairly full summary seems justified here in that he writes with knowledge and understanding of the present-day climate of opinion and is able to see the relevance of the modern biomedical revolution with its attendant new ethical and social problems. One of the documents of the First Vatican Council of 1869–70 declared, in reaffirmation of an ancient doctrine, "God creates a new soul and infuses it into each man." About this traditional doctrine Hick makes the point that if it is to have any substance at all, so as to be worth either affirming or denying, it must entail that there are characteristics of the self that are derived neither from genetic inheritance nor from interaction with the environment. The modern view implies that the body to which the soul is said to be attached already contains genetic information selecting the personal characteristics that can and cannot be developed; and this information is part of the range of environmental factors amid which the soul is placed when it is inserted into the body. In other words we must bracket inheritance and environment together as jointly constituting the soul's world. The problem facing the traditional soul-theorist, then, is to indicate an adequate content and function for the soul after genetics has pared so much away.

Hick of course presupposes a real (though limited) human freedom; for, as we have seen, however strong the arguments for universal determinism may appear to be, the claim to *know* that one is totally determined must always be self-refuting—since the concept of knowledge embedded in our language presupposes that the cognising mind is not totally determined. In discussing the nature of "personality"—i.e., the basic personal nature in virtue of which the individual exercises his freedom in one way rather than in another—Hick identifies the soul "with certain fundamental dispositional characteristics—presumably our basic moral and religious attitudes." He then comes to the conclusion that the material and social world of which we are a part sets the problems in the tackling of which the soul's earthly career consists, whilst our genetic inheritance, together with our acquired training and experience, furnish the tools with which we tackle those problems. "On this view the soul remains as the core of the individual's being, his essential nature, consisting in a structure of personal and ethical characteristics which inhere, presumably, in some kind of persisting substratum or frame."

After considering Indian views as to the nature of the soul, Hick turns to the Western idea of the soul as a metaphysical reality which God individually creates and attaches to the body; and he asks what hangs upon the traditional insistence on the special divine creation of each soul; it is the concept of the human being as a unique individual who is valued and sustained by his Creator and who in virtue of his relationship to the Eternal may enjoy an eternal life. Religiously the high point in the development of the idea occurred in Jesus' teaching about God as our heavenly Father, who knows each of His human children so that the very hairs of our head are numbered. He cares for each like a shepherd seeking a lost sheep, or a needy widow searching for a lost coin, and He lavishes His love upon each like a father welcoming back a long-lost son. "Philosophically, the high points are Plato's *Phaedo*, affirming the immortality of the rational soul; Descartes's *cogito ergo sum*, taking the existence of individual self-consciousness as the necessary starting point for thought; and Kant's founding of ethics upon the free, autonomous person seen as an end in himself." He points out that in politics the idea of the inherent value of the individual human being has worked itself out in the demise of feudalism, the eventual abandonment of slavery, the gradual growth of democracy, and in the advance of women towards full social equality with men. The common theme here is the idea of the unique value of the human person as a child of God, made in the divine image, and destined to an eternal life in fellowship with God. Hick continues:

> As well as setting aside, as I think we must, the temptation to locate God's activity in the still unmapped intricacies of the genetic process, we have also seen reasons to abandon the notion of the soul as a divinely created and infused entity. This does not however necessarily mean that the term "soul" can no longer have any proper use, but only that it should not be used as the name of a spiritual substance or entity. But we also commonly use the word as an indicator of value.

Hick indeed believes it will be found that the word "soul" normally has a valuational connotation and that it could well be that this feature of our ordinary use of the term, as connoting what is of the greatest value, points to its primary meaning within human communication; and that the metaphysical theories of the soul are secondary, as speculative or mythological ways of affirming the *unique* value of the individual human person.

> If we accept this suggestion we shall not be opposed to the continued use of soul language, or even to speaking of human beings as souls, or as having souls, for such language will express that sense of the sacredness of human personality and of the inalienable rights of the human individual which we have already seen to be the moral and political content of the Western idea of the soul.

Nor, he says, need the Church cease to strive to save souls; but the souls to be saved are simply people and not some mysterious religious entity attached to them. To speak of man as a soul is, then, to speak mythologically, but in a way which is bound up with important practical attitudes and practices. "The myth of the soul expresses a faith in the intrinsic value of the human individual as an end in himself."

Hick then proceeds to ask whether this valuation of humanity can continue to be religiously based once the *metaphysical* conception of the soul has been abandoned? He attempts to answer this question by, very wisely, speaking from within the context of Christianity, as the faith which has historically particularly cherished and taught the idea of the sacredness of human personality and the value of men and women as rational and moral ends in themselves. He says:

> Speaking, then, as a Christian theologian, it appears to me that *the time has come to complete the shift of emphasis in theological anthropology from the question of origins to the question of ends. It is not what man has come from but what he is going to that is important.*

He assumes that the picture being built up by the natural sciences of the origin of man, both individually and as a species, is basically correct and is progressively becoming more adequate and accurate as research continues. He accepts that each human individual comes about through the partially random selection of a specific genetic code out of the virtually infinite range of possibilities contained even in the portion of genetic material lodged in his parents. This is, he says, in broadest outline, the picture of man's beginning, as it emerges from the physicists', chemists', and biologists' researches. And Christianity does not offer a different or rival account of our human origins. It says, in its Hebraic myth of man's genesis, that he has been created out of the dust of the earth; though the details of the creative process, from "dust" to the immensely complex religious and valuing human animal, are for the relevant sciences to trace.

If soul language expresses a valuation of mankind, so that the soul is the human person seen and valued in this special way, then, so Hick argues, we must be prepared to renounce the idea that whereas the body has been produced by natural processes the soul has been produced by a special act of divine creation.

> We have to say that the soul is a divine creation in the same sense as the body—namely through the instrumentality of the entire evolution of the universe and within this of the development of life on our planet. Distinctively human mentality and spirituality emerges, in accordance with the divine purpose, in complex bodily organisms. But once it has emerged it is the vehicle, according to Christian faith, of a continuing creative activity only the beginnings of which have so far taken place.

But this is not to say, in any sense, that the soul is nothing more than a complex material being, any more than the mind is a complex material brain. We have already seen how erroneous that argument is. Both the mind and the soul are, in my view, completely new and unforeseeable emergents.

While the biblical myth of Adam and Eve and their fall from grace of course cannot, except by outrageous chicanery (sophistry), be made to accommodate these new insights, yet there is, as Hick points out, an alternative strand of Christian theology, exemplified by some Greek Fathers of the second century A.D., which, he says, can readily absorb the new "empirical" knowledge. Thus Irenaeus distinguished between what he called the image of God and the likeness of God and suggested a two-stage conception of the divine creation of man. "The *imago dei* is man's nature as a rational, personal, and moral animal. Thus man in society—man the ethical being, man the creator of culture—exists in the image of God." It has taken many hundreds of millions of years of biological evolution to produce him, and yet even so he is only the raw material for the second stage of the creative process, which is the bringing of man, thus fashioned as person in the divine image, into the finite likeness of God. This latter state represents the fulfilment of the potentialities of our human nature, the completed humanisation of man in a society expressing mutual love. Whereas the first stage of creation is an exercise of divine power, the second stage is of a different kind. "Human life as we know it is the sphere in which this

second stage of creation is taking place; though it seems clear
that if the process is to be completed it must continue in each
individual life beyond our earthly three-score years and ten,
whether by the survival of the mind after the death of the body
or through the reconstitution of the total psychophysical being."

Hick continues:

> The final meaning of man's life lies in the future state to which,
> in God's purpose, he is moving. And from this point of view man's
> lowly beginnings are not in contradiction with his high destiny. The
> origin of life out of the "dust of the earth"—the emergence of the
> human species from lower forms of life to form the apex of the
> evolutionary process; the programming of the individual genetic
> code through an unpredictable rearranging of the chromosomes;
> and again the unpredictable selection of one out of hundreds of
> millions of sperm to fertilise an ovum are the ways in which man
> has been brought upon the stage. They do not in themselves tell us
> what he is here for or what his future is to be. The religions, how-
> ever, do profess to tell us this. The Christian faith, in the Irenaean
> version of its theology, suggests that this complex process whereby
> man has been created as a personal being in God's image makes
> possible his cognitive freedom in relation to his Maker. Finding
> himself as part of an autonomous natural order, whose functioning
> can at all points be described without reference to a creator, man
> is not compelled to be conscious of God. He has an innate tendency
> to interpret his experience religiously, but if he gives rein to this
> tendency his resulting awareness of the divine is the kind of
> partially free awareness that we call faith. Thus man's existence as
> part of the natural order ensures his status as a relatively free being
> over against the infinite Creator.

Hick argues that God wills to exist an autonomous physical
universe, structured towards the production of rational and personal life—an organisation of matter which may, for all we know,
be developing only on this earth or alternatively perhaps on millions of planets of millions of stars in millions of galaxies.

> The virtually infinite complexity of the cosmic process makes it
> to us, as finite minds existing within it, a law-governed realm which
> however includes randomness and unpredictability in its details;

and as such it constitutes an environment within which we may grow as free beings towards that fullness of personal life, in conscious relationship to God, which (according to Christianity) represents the divine purpose for us.

The Knowledge of Death

Any belief in an eternal soul is of course inconceivable without an understanding of the nature and problem of death. So I would say that full death awareness is another feature in which man is unique. But here again there seems to be no justification for saying that full awareness of this fact sprang *suddenly* into being at some point in the evolutionary history of man. We can certainly not say at what point it became a dominant feature of man's mental world. But we do know that at some point in the story man began to not only bury his dead but to enact elaborate symbolic rituals in connexion with the process. As Pfeiffer (1969) says, archaeological excavations rarely provide direct information about the feelings of our remote ancestors; usually the most we can do is to make more or less shrewd guesses. But sometimes the past leaves patterns whose significance cannot be mistaken. Neanderthal man had elaborate burial rituals at least 70,000 years ago. *Homo erectus pekingensis* practised ritual anthropophagy which probably implies some sort of funerary cult involving perhaps ideas about a future life and almost certainly an awareness, and possibly some understanding of, the fact of death. This suggests a dating in the later Pleistocene of perhaps 700,000 years ago. Leakey and others now, it seems, have a true *Homo* in the Lower Pleistocene, 3,000,000 years ago. Finally it seems quite likely that there were true hominids in the Pliocene, say 4,000,000 years ago. (N.B. These figures may now need extension.)

Such evidence cannot be made to bear any great weight of theoretical conclusion. But it at least suggests (and is not inconsistent with the idea) that there was a reasonably steady development of "religious" belief over enormously long periods of time.

About one hundred years ago anthropologists gave up hope of

ever finding really primitive men. With this they of course also relinquished the hope of finding primitive culture, language, and primitive religion. All languages and all religions known have certainly had long periods of development. But many anthropologists such as Marett and Eliade find evidence for faith, hope, and charity in some of the most primitive religions accessible, even though these features may be overlaid by much that is secondary, superstitious, and probably corrupt.

But whatever the facts in regard to the above matters, it is surely impossible to suppose that religious belief of some kind has not been essential to *Homo* for a period at least of the order of 1,000,000 years. Can anyone reasonably argue that religious beliefs are no longer a needful part of a stable and balanced human society entering the new era in which evolution is coming within our control? During the early 1900s such evidence was uncovered at Le Moustier, about thirty miles west of La Chapelle-aux-Saints. It shows that Neanderthal man had developed a new way of thinking, a new attitude towards life and death. A boy of about fifteen or sixteen years had been buried in a cave. He had been lowered into a trench, placed on his right side with knees slightly drawn and head resting on his forearm in a sleeping position. A pile of flints lay under his head to form a sort of stone pillow, and near his hand was a beautifully worked stone axe; around the remains were wild-cattle bones, many of them charred, the remnants of roasted meat, which may have been provided to serve as sustenance in the world of the dead. Not far away in another cave—discovered by a road-building crew —was a set of nine little mounds arranged neatly in three rows. One of the mounds contained the remains of a small infant, perhaps stillborn, and three flint tools. The other eight were empty. One possibility is that this may have been a family cemetery since the graves of three children and two adults were found near the infant's grave. Neanderthal man appeared approximately 75,000 years ago and persisted for about 35,000 years. I find something intensely moving in the thought of these little groups of men, very widely scattered and isolated as they must have been, in the incredibly severe conditions of the next to last glaciation, somehow becoming aware of their mortality and of their destiny.

We all know the Advent hymn with its line "Late in time behold Him come." The hymn writer was of course thinking of the four thousand years supposed to have elapsed between the Creation and the birth of Jesus. But we today realise Jesus was not four thousand years late but more than seventy thousand years late. And moreover it looks as if, even at that time, there had been something like a loving family life as indeed we have seen there can be in its counterpart in monkeys and apes. There may well indeed have been other "Christs" or earlier "Sons of God," some earlier representatives of the Holy Spirit which brought joy and succour to these lonely people.

Perhaps it is idle to speculate like this, but I do feel convinced that a Christian theology which failed to take into account the immense age of mankind and the evidence for the spiritual development, as it evidently existed 75,000 years ago, can hardly command the full respect of present-day thinkers. It may of course be argued that this is no new problem, and the medieval Church and medieval system of thought, as expressed by Dante in the *Divine Comedy*, were deeply concerned with the problem of the good Pagan and his fate. One recalls Dante's cry of joy when his lifelong doubts and anxieties are set at rest by finding the souls of Ripeus, the virtuous Trojan, and the great and saintly Roman Emperor Trajan in Paradise. (See *Paradiso*, Canto XX, especially line 82.) Yet some may feel that however adequate the medieval position over this may be interpreted to be, there is a somewhat indefinable difference (perhaps spurious) between a period of four thousand years following upon the fall of man as described in *Genesis* on the one hand; and on the other the indefinite number of thousands of years which now appear to us to have elapsed since the first appearance of death awareness upon the earth, and something like a spiritual response to it. As will have been apparent from the general tenor of this book, I personally feel inclined still further by this problem to look upon the living world as expressing, in an especial and perhaps unique way, a dimension of creation through which especially the creative spirit of God, an insight into his nature, can be made available to us. I think in fact this comes very near to what I mean by Natural Religion. I do indeed agree with Dobzhansky when he says that if the zoological classification were based not on anatomical and chemical grounds but on psychological grounds, then Man, far from being a mere anthropoid Primate, would comprise a separate Phylum or even a unique Kingdom.

The Concept of Creation

All this leads us to the concept of creation. The old form of the argument from design as expressed by William Paley and later P. H. Gosse is clearly inapplicable to our thought today. The latter author, in his famous book *Omphalos*, admitted freely all the evidences of geology in favour of the antiquity of the world, but got out of the difficulty in a manner all his own. He argued that when the Creation took place everything was constructed *as if* it had a past history. Thus Adam and Eve had navels just as if they had been born in the ordinary way, and similarly everything else was created as if it had grown. On this view the rocks were filled with fossils just as they would have been if they had been due to volcanic action or to sedimentary deposits, and as Bertrand Russell (1935) said, we might all have come into existence five minutes ago, provided with ready-made memories, holes in our socks, and hair that needs cutting! Of course, however strongly entrenched the argument from design, nobody could believe that the universe was really designed like that; hence the discomfiture of poor Gosse.

In a recent book, *Chance and Necessity*, which has received wide publicity, Jacques Monod argues that the molecular organisation at the basis of life (the DNA-RNA system) implies that the whole story of life and of the universe as fit for life is based on chance and chance alone. It has long been argued by geneticists that the gene mutations which provide the raw materials for evolution by natural selection are random in respect of the immediate and foreseeable requirements of the stock. As Sir Ronald Fisher argued in 1950, the process of natural selection acting on "random" mutations is a true process of creation, proceeding throughout the history of the living world and as active today as ever it was. The discovery of the genetic code, chemically arbitrary as it appears to be, has emphasised the truth of this view and Monod is obviously correct in his statement that the sequences of residues which encode the structures of proteins (which are the essential "building blocks" in the construction of organisms) are indeed random in the strictly mathematical sense within the limits of the chemical mechanism involved.

But is this, can this be, the whole story? There are serious objections, coming both from geneticists and others: Monod scorns or ignores them all. Instead he extrapolates from the genetic code to the whole universe and concludes that "chance" is a basic law of nature. But he admits that science can neither say nor do anything about a unique occurrence and that the origin of life *may have been* a unique occurrence. But since we *know* little about the age, dimensions, or complexity of the universe, we cannot estimate the probability of any such occurrence. Thus the statement "all is chance" amounts to saying that we can know nothing whatever about the matter. Nor has he anything to say concerning the monstrous problem (see above, pp. 26–27) posed by the coding of the genetic code's self-reproductive powers—to which no one has as yet the glimmerings of an answer.

As Dobzhansky says (Dobzhansky and Ayala, 1974), in looking at evolution at close quarters one inevitably loses sight of the forest (the progressiveness of evolution) for the trees (the turmoil of particular evolution). Now evolutionary progress includes increase in receipt, conveyance, and processing of information and *consciousness*. And all these steps in their turn play their part in selecting and constructing non-random, directive trends upon the various types of mutation and recombination which the genetic mechanism provides. And the last point, namely the establishment of self-reflective consciousness, with all the characteristics it possesses and which are outlined in this chapter, finally removes any reason for considering evolution *as a whole* to be a chance process. For with the coming of a fully conscious social life based on ideals and spiritual aspirations, man has increasingly taken over his own psycho-social evolution with potential consequences which at present can be only dimly seen.

Fitness of the Environment

There is a modern form of the old argument from design which is once again coming to the fore. Obviously one could envisage a form of the argument from design in which the design consists solely in the establishment of the initial conditions of the universe and all else is programmed to follow from the single first act of creation. Of course this leads us straight into deism and to the concepts of scientific reductionism which I have been at such pains to controvert. Now as I have already indicated, it is becoming increasingly clear that the physical environment is peculiarly fit for life. As Pantin pointed out (1951), the organism is built up of standard parts with unique properties. The older conceptions of evolutionary morphology stressed the graded adaptation of which the organism is capable, just as putty can be moulded to any desired shape. But we should rather consider the organism as like a model made from a child's engineering constructional set; a set consisting of standard parts with unique properties, of strips, plates, and wheels which can be utilized for various functional objectives, such as cranes and locomotives. In Pantin's words, "models made from such a set can in certain respects show graded adaptability, when the form of the model depends on a statistically large number of parts. But they also show certain severe limitations dependent upon the restricted properties of the standard parts of the set." For Pantin the crux of the argument is whether we can or cannot discern design in the properties of the units which make such an organism possible. These properties of units are not solely the result of selection in the Darwinian sense, and Pantin finds it hard to escape from the conclusion that if we see design in them, we must say with du Bois-Reymond: "Whoever gives only his little finger to teleology will inevitably arrive at Paley's discarded natural theology." He continues, "Natural selection bowed Paley and his argument from design out of the front door in 1859 and here he would come climbing in through the back window saying that he owns the title deeds of the whole estate."

Dobzhansky (1962), one of the greatest living authorities on genetics and evolution, sees design both in the initial conditions and in the course of evolution. He then says, "Christianity is a religion that is implicitly evolutionistic in that it believes history to be meaningful: its current flows from the Creation, through progressive revelation of God to man, from man to Christ and from Christ to the Kingdom of God. St. Augustine expressed this evolutionistic philosophy most clearly." It is for this reason that I have argued elsewhere that amongst the world religions only Christianity shows signs of being able to meet the demands of a scientific world view cognisant of evolutionary biology; and only Christianity (as a religion which is both historical and eschatological) can serve a mankind fully conscious of its past and of the evolutionary possibilities of its future. For only the Judaeo-Christian tradition attributes value to the creation as an essential part of God's revelation.

IDEA OF THE SUPERNATURAL

I consider man as essentially a religious animal. And in this context we can agree with Hobhouse that religion is "progressive apprehension of the spiritual." It seems, as we have seen, to have begun *at least* 70,000 years ago with ritual burials and perhaps enormously earlier with ritual anthropophagy. If so, it may well have been concomitant with the early stages of the increase in brain size.

So I am groping after the view that the development of religious awareness is the most characteristic of all the distinguishing features of MAN. This means that for at least 100,000 years man has found religion necessary for survival and development. If so, do people seriously believe that now we can dispense with it? Is it not more likely that it is due to perform an ever-increasing purpose in the story of man?

Views of this kind constantly and inevitably bring us into contact with the idea of the supernatural as over against the natural. If we come to see man and nature as part of one creative act continuing in time—a view similar to that approached by Teilhard de Chardin—we must assume that there is in man at least the divine spirit which is over and above the physical forces of evolution—prior to them, in fact—but which is in ever-increasing measure capable of assuming control of the physical process, thus conferring upon them progressively greater value. In this sense the spirit of man may be seen as supernatural. Yet does not the whole include both within its unity?

One of the severe difficulties which face the humanist when he tries to understand religious thought is essentially this, the concept of the supernatural: and it is posed particularly by the term "mysticism." Use this word in conversation with the average scientist and he is apt to look at you as if he thinks that perhaps you are really not quite nice to know or else, with pitying condescension, because he thinks you quite barmy. All this is due to the quite incorrect opinion held by many ordinary people and many scientists among them that the word "mysticism" denotes something spurious if not indeed deliberately designed to confuse (Misty Schism). But of course the correct meaning of the word "mysticism" is very close to that of the word "religion" itself. Religion means the belief that interpenetrating the natural environment perceived by our senses, there extends beyond it a larger environment without which the visible environment cannot be fully comprehended and to which men must relate themselves. This is what Tillich calls "ultimate concern," which is manifest in all creative functions of the human spirit. And it is interesting that Dobzhanksy's perhaps most powerful book is entitled *The Biology of Ultimate Concern.*

Mysticism then is concerned with the awareness of values, in part at least, above and beyond the scope of current symbolism to express; in particular the intense awareness of the whole within the unity of all things. In fact it involves essentially the idea of the numinous or the holy; and for guidance in this field I always turn to Rudolf Otto's renowned book *The Idea of the Holy.*[15] In fact the holy is a form of awareness that is neither that of ordinary perceiving nor of ordinary conceiving. It interests me to find that one of the most justly renowned of the St. Andrews Gifford Lectures, namely the 1926 to 1928 series by A. E. Taylor, *Faith of a Moralist,* contains a remarkable chapter on the supernatural. It is significant that Taylor evidently at first found much to criticise and correct in Otto's work; but he comes in the end to the conclusion that no amount of criticism will really seriously shake Otto's central position, in that "it is this immediate recognition of the numinous, the wholly other and transcendent, in persons, things, events, which is at the root of worship, and so of religion."

Arthur Koestler (1972) speaks of "that oceanic feeling" captured in varying degrees by the artist and the mystic and relates it in an illuminating discussion to ideas of synchronicity and seriality. These he regards as the modern derivatives of the archetypical belief in the fundamental unity of all things, transcending mechanical causality. This links on to his ideas about "holons" (discussed earlier in this book, p. 360) which he finds neatly expressed by Pico della Mirandola (1557) in the words: "Firstly there is the unity in things themselves whereby each thing is at one with itself. Secondly there is the unity whereby one creature is united with the others, and all parts of the world constitute one world."

But there are many mysticisms and perhaps all have some value for the world. So I welcome the suggestion of Professor Hick that theology should be concerning itself more and more with religions other than Christianity. Nevertheless I believe that

380

Christianity as a moving, living, developing faith has a message of central and unique value for mankind in this era of perhaps his greatest crisis. And my conviction of this is in line with that of Teilhard de Chardin (1960) when he says that "in relation to all the main historical forms assumed by the human religious spirit, Christian mysticism extracts *all* that is sweetest and strongest circulating in all human mysticisms, though without absorbing their evil or suspect elements."

NATURAL RELIGION

I would like in conclusion to refer to some previously expressed thoughts of mine and to quote a modern theologian who was particularly helpful to me. It is my view that a deeper probing into the relation between biology and those fundamental ideas which lie at the basis of moral and ethical judgments must be largely based upon the idea of natural religion and a consideration of its relation to "revealed" religion. In considering this subject, it is necessary to realise that in the last hundred years there has been a change in the generally accepted meaning of the term "natural religion." Cardinal Newman, writing in 1870, regarded the conclusion as obvious that Christianity is merely the completion and supplement of natural religion and of previous revelations; and he shows that this was what Jesus and the Apostles taught. But natural religion for Newman implied knowledge coming through our own minds, through the voice of mankind, and thirdly through the course of human life and human affairs. He was not, I think, in any way concerned with the view that science as an objective study of natural phenomena, let alone the theory of evolution by natural selection, could provide any unique or necessary knowledge of the ways of the Creator. Still less did he imagine that the objective study of mental processes and of human and animal behaviour, which constitutes the disciplines of ethology and psychology today, could lead to knowledge at least as important and profound as that obtained through introspection.

Towards the end of the nineteenth century and in the decades of the present century, there was a strong and encouraging tendency in the direction of acceptance, by theologians and philosophers, of the implications of evolution theory for religion. This was exemplified particularly by the writings of Whitehead, Lloyd Morgan, Pringle Paterson, Alexander, and Stout amongst philosophers, and Gore, Barnes, Tennant, Oman, and Raven amongst theologians. But it was one of the disasters of the First World War, and the forty years that followed, that this far-seeing and enlightened tendency amongst theologians was largely smothered. Canon Raven indeed spoke of the great blight which descended upon theology when it accepted "the religion of despair" of Carl Barth and Reinhold Niebuhr; and I think he hardly exaggerates the disastrous effect of this when he speaks of Christ's religion becoming "almost wholly confined to Scripture treated as the single means of revelation and to liturgy as the single activity of the Church." I therefore feel particularly indebted to Bezzant (1963) who says,

> . . . intellectual objections to Christianity nowadays, and the fact that there are no convincing answers to them, in my judgment both grow out of one root. This is that there is no general or widely accepted natural theology. I know that many theologians rejoice that it is so, and seem to think that it leaves them free to recommend Christianity as divine revelation. *They know not what they do.* For if the immeasurably vast and mysterious creation reveals nothing of its originator, or of his and its attributes and nature, there is no *ground* for supposing that any events recorded in an ancient and partly mythopoeic literature, and deductions from it, can do so.

The only possible basis for a reasonably grounded natural theology is what we call scientific. The difficulty is that there is no such actuality as "science"; there are many and increasing sciences. Their deliverances are not as yet mutually consistent. This is the root difficulty in constructing a natural theology. For myself I cling to the hope that it will, in time, become possible.

382

Meanwhile I think there is nothing that can be called "knowledge" or "reasonable belief" which implies that there is or can be anything in the human mind that can possibly justify the passing of such a colossal condemnation of this inconceivably vast and mysterious universe as is implied in the judgment that it has no meaning or enduring value. Bezzant continues,

> Further I think it is entirely reasonable for any man who studies the spirit of the facing of life as Christ faced it, and studies his recorded teaching, to decide that by him he will stand through life, death or eternity rather than join the possible triumph of any evil over him. Whether or not any Church will regard such a man as a Christian is nowadays wholly secondary and manifestly relatively unimportant: any Church which refuses so to recognise him may be harming itself; it cannot harm him and he should accept the refusal with regret but with equanimity.

THE SUPREME DUTY OF MAN

Finally I would like to paraphrase some remarks of Polanyi (1959).

So far as we know, we are the supreme bearers of thought in the universe; some would say the only bearers. Five million centuries of evolution, groping upwards along numberless paths, have led to this result only in us, in us human beings. And ours has as yet been but a brief venture. After five million centuries of evolution, we have been engaged only for fifty centuries in a literate process of thought. It has all been the affair of the last hundred generations or so.

This task then appears to be the particular calling of literate man in this universe. . . .

"If this perspective is true, a supreme trust is placed in us by the whole creation, and it is sacrilege then even to contemplate actions which may lead to the extinction of humanity or even its relegation to earlier or more primitive stages of culture."

Polanyi concludes with the words: "I believe that no one who

383

thankfully acknowledges man's calling in the universe, be he religious or agnostic, can avoid this ultimate peremptory conclusion." And if we do acknowledge this conclusion we can hardly fail to be doubly conscious of the immense responsibility that rests upon all literate men of good will, and particularly perhaps those with scientific expertise, to take every opportunity, in and out of season, of bringing home to mankind better understanding of the stupendous evolutionary process of which they are both the spearhead and custodians. Thus the task of mankind is perhaps greater and his activities for good or ill more momentous now than ever before in the history of the world. It is tragic that such multitudes are today oppressed and rendered impotent and ineffective by a failure to find meaning in their lives when in fact the potential fullness of human life has never been greater or more obvious for those who have eyes to see. It is indeed both a joy and a terror to be living in times such as these—joy at the fullness of life and the opportunities for greater enlightenment; terror at the danger and disasters threatened by evil forces—for never has the human race had greater opportunity than now to rise above itself and to bring the human spirit to new levels of transcendence. To do this we must be inspired by a glimpse of the timeless vision of Dante (*Paradiso* XXXIII, ll. 70–90) who saw in the ineffable climax of his pilgrimage, in perhaps the greatest poem in the history of man, that all creation and all time are bound up, like the pages in some vast volume, in God— "the love that moves the Sun and the other stars."

NOTES

1. Donne is here referring to the fact that the new astronomers of the time, Tycho, Rotman, Kepler, etc., by their new doctrine of the heavens are "exploding in the meantime those elements of fire, those fictitious, first watery movers, those heavens I mean above the firmament, which Delrio, Ludovidius Imola, Patricius and many of the fathers affirm" (Burton, *Anatomy of Melancholy*, Part 2, section 2, mem. 3). They have abolished, that is to say, the fire which surrounded the air, as that air surrounded the water and the earth (all below the moon); they have also abolished the Crystalline sphere and the Primum Mobile which were supposed to surround the sphere of the fixed stars, or the firmament. See *Donne's Poetical Works*, edited by H. J. C. Grierson, Vol. 2, Introduction and Commentary, p. 190. Oxford: Clarendon Press, 1912.

2. As Professor Thoday (1970) has recently pointed out, it is, to say the least, somewhat remarkable that we are still asking these questions today. William Bateson (1913) wrote as follows:

> We must not lose sight of the fact that though the factors operate by the production of enzymes, of bodies on which these enzymes can act, and of intermediary substances necessary to complete the enzyme-action, yet these bodies themselves can scarcely be themselves the genetic factor but consequences of their existence. What then are the factors themselves? Whence do they come? How do they become integral parts of the organisms?

And again:

> We have little idea even of the haziest sort as to the nature of living organisms, or of the proximate causes which determine their forms, still less can we attempt any answer to those remoter questions of origin and destiny which form the subject of the philosopher's contemplation. . . . It may well be that, before any solution is obtained, our knowledge of the nature of unorganised matter must first be

increased. For a long time yet we may have to halt, but we none-theless do well to prepare ourselves to utilise any means of advance that may be offered, by carefully reconnoitring the ground we have to traverse.

A possible line of explanation of the way in which the genes in mammalian chromosomes may have their action controlled in specific ways linked with the production and organisation of specific tissues is given by J. Paul, et al. (1970). These workers have shown that with mammalian cells (but not so far as I know with cells of any other organisms), when cell division is induced in mouse liver and kidney, a very early event is a change in "masking" in chromatin. This "masking" precedes changes in RNA populations, and both precede DNA synthesis. This means that DNA is masked in an organ-specific way *in vivo*, and the masking is preserved in isolation: implying that the RNA from one of these organs is different from the RNA from other organs, although it cannot be distinguished from natural RNA from the same organ as the chromatin. The authors have shown that chromatin can be accurately reconstructed from DNA, histones, and non-histone pro-teins. Experiments using this system indicate that histones non-specifi-cally mask DNA whilst non-histone proteins are essential for the reversal of masking in a specific way.

3. Still more relevant from the point of view of our present dis-cussion is the recent work of T. M. Sonneborn (1970) on "Gene action in development." Sonneborn has worked especially with the protozoan *Paramoecium aurelia*. He has studied a number of the structures in *Paramoecium* which are revealed under the microscope, particularly the structures known as the basal bodies, at the point of origin of the cilia, and the mouth region and gullet, which occur at one end of the organism. He shows that the information for the positioning and orien-tation of the developing parts of the unit territory from which the cilia arise is located *within* the unit itself and, when experimentally altered, reproduces in the altered orientation which cannot be corrected by gene action. This hereditary aspect of development is determined by an unbroken chain of self-reproducing arrangements of cortical parts. *The search for DNA in the cortex gave negative results*. The con-clusion was that, for all regions of the cortex examined, development is hereditarily determined by existing and self-reproducing cortical arrangements: the genes (or DNA) doubtless control synthesis of the molecular building blocks, but not their site of assembly or position, orientation, and number of assemblies. Passing on to the flatworm

Stenostomum he found that here too hereditary developmental control by self-perpetuating structural arrangements must have occurred. He concludes that "whether similar processes occurred in the inheritance of the developmental decisive organization of the amphibian egg is still open to question," but that the processes he has described certainly constitute only one of the many options available for hereditary control of development.

4. Professor J. L. Brachet (1971) has conveniently summarised recent developments in part of this field in a review lecture entitled "Nucleocytoplasmic interactions in morphogenesis." He considers first the morphogenesis and synthesis of macromolecules in the total absence of the nucleus. This is very well displayed in the alga *Acetabularia* where the morphogenetic substances produced by the nucleus are distributed along a decreasing apicobasal gradient as is shown by the accompanying figure, Figure 1, page 230. In eggs he finds that sea urchin and amphibian eggs can undergo repeated cleavage in the absence of the nucleus. It appears, therefore, from these experiments that the cytoplasm from sea urchin and amphibian eggs contains information sufficient for a few abnormal cleavages. But this process cannot get very far, and the presence of a normal nucleus is absolutely required for further development. Moreover there is very little evidence so far that DNA synthesis is possible in the absence of the nucleus. Considering nucleocytoplasmic interactions during cogenesis and maturation, he finds from studies on amphibia that, during the early stages of development, changes between the nucleus and cytoplasm can occur in both directions. Some of the RNA synthesised in the nucleus migrates to the cytoplasm, but many of the proteins built up in the cytoplasm move into the nuclei where they may have important regulatory functions. It appears that nucleocytoplasmic interactions in the fertilised egg may eventually shed some light on the biochemical and morphogenetic properties of the cell surface material. During later development it seems differentiation is preceded by the synthesis in the nuclei of short-lived messenger RNAs. In regard to late differentiation, cell fusion *in vitro* in the laboratory holds out great promise for further elucidation of this extremely tricky problem. It looks as if there might be selective gene amplification during cell differentiation. And certainly in some forms, the cytoplasm can exert a positive contol, as in the inactive hen erythrocyte nucleus. So it can at least be said that many controls, both positive and negative, are probably necessary in order to ensure cell differentiation. This is perhaps a modest conclusion; but it does underline the extraordinary complexity of the organisation of the developing

387

plant or animal—a complexity far in excess of that first envisaged when the DNA/RNA story was unravelled.

5. For those who are not familiar with the basic DNA/RNA story, the following summary may be helpful. An essential feature of the reduplication of organisms is the reduplication of chromosomes. This reduplication can now, in turn, with high probability be assigned to the reduplication of the particular kinds of DNA molecule characteristic of the organism. Deoxyribonucleic acid (DNA) has been established as the carrier of heritable "information." Metabolic processes can eventually be traced to enzymes, which must themselves be synthesised but cannot duplicate themselves. The proteins of an organism are specific and this specificity is heritable; heredity is carried in the chromosomes, in which DNA is always present; DNA is present in mitochondria, but these are at least in part autonomously replicating, and here again the role of DNA is doubtless as a blueprint, the same as it is in chromosomes.

The serially particulate character of inheritance is that correlated with the serially particulate character of the arrangement of a molecule of a particular sort. By implication from the results of genetical studies, these molecules must have two powers: (1) on some occasions they must reproduce other molecules of precisely the same sort and in the same ordered arrangement, and (2) on other occasions they must set in motion the ordered production of substances which will determine the successive direction of the metabolic processes of the cell so as to synthesise another living individual of the same kind as the parent.

The sequence of operations which results in the formation of the individual is thus supposed, and with great probability, to be held as a "code" in the ordered DNA molecules. It has been one of the triumphs of molecular biology that Watson and Crick on the basis of X-ray and crystallographic data were able to prepare a molecular model which has already repeatedly been shown to be consistent with the known chemical, cytological, and genetical requirements of the reduplicating system.

As a molecule, the nucleic acid DNA is of enormous length. It consists of a chain of parts, nucleotides. There are in fact only four sorts of these nucleotides, and in each sort of DNA molecule these are arranged in a different serial order, just as four sorts of beads can be arranged along a string in an enormous variety of serial orders. Such a serially ordered uniqueness can be compared to a linear code bearing information.

In Watson and Crick's model, the DNA strands occur in pairs, arranged side by side along their length. Indeed the double thread or helix (for the two strands are twisted round each other corkscrew-wise) can be considered as a minute elongated aperiodic crystal. That the two DNA strands can be held together in this way is possible because the four kinds of nucleotide beads of which they are composed are not identical but happen to exist as two sets of complementary parts. The succession along one thread resembles the projections and hollows of the edge of a key, and the succession along the companion thread resembles the wards of a lock. When reduplication occurs, each of the DNA threads separates from its partner, and each is able to assemble a fresh replica of its companion by the collection, in the right place and order, of new beads of nucleotide units from the nucleotides in the surroundings.

The reduplication of nucleic-acid chains is of course only the first, though essential, part of the machinery of reduplication of a whole organism. In the living cell, the DNA templates not only have the power to reduplicate themselves but to manufacture other components of the cell such as a strand of RNA (containing ribose instead of deoxyribose) which, while not usually able to reproduce itself, can carry the information as to the particular sequence of amino-acids. This, by a series of steps, can serve as a template which by the action of other substances such as enzymes (catalyst proteins) can ensure the synthesis of the corresponding protein. These operations again require a supply of energy which is derived from an energy-rich molecule, adenosine triphosphate, which is itself a nucleotide combined with further phosphoric acid.

The production of these various substances takes place in an ordered manner in time and position, to make the cells, the tissues, and the organism. All this sequence is coded in the original pattern of the DNA. We can make an analogy with the ordered sequence of events in a game of chess, from the opening gambit with a configuration of individual pieces to the complex pattern of functional implications in the end game.

This then was the basic picture round about 1960. Now, more than ten years later, its prime author (F. Crick, 1971, A general model for the chromosomes of higher organisms, *Nature, 234:* 25–27) has produced a supplementary scheme or model which, it is hoped, will cope with the many inevitable problems and difficulties which the furious rate of research has turned up in a decade. It is especially an attempt to account for some of the difficulties already alluded to earlier in the present chapter. (See p. 34 above.) It will be some time before it is clear how far it is successful in this aim. The theory is highly complex and it may prove far from easy to design experiments by which it may be satisfactorily tested.

6. An account of the structure and behaviour of *Microstomum* will be found in *The Invertebrates,* Vol. 2, by L. H. Hyman, New York, 1951. A bibliography of the many papers by Kepner and his associates will be found on p. 426.

7. In this passage Bronowski speaks of the physical world evolving in the same way as the biological world evolves. I have given reasons elsewhere why I consider this usage incorrect since physical structures do not, in the biological sense, reproduce themselves, are not "born," and do not "die." Hence there can be no natural selection of such structures in the biological meaning of the term.

8. Behaviourism—the primarily American school of psychology, virtually founded by J. B. Watson. According to this, the behaviour of organisms, including animals and men, comprises the whole content of psychology. It renounces all mental concepts and all ideas of innate urges or "instincts" and seeks to explain all by a theory of the mechanical compounding of stimuli, based upon the results of Thorndike and of Pavlov. B. F. Skinner is generally regarded as the present-day leader of the Behaviorist School.

9. Chuang-tzu and Hui-tzu were strolling on the bridge over the Hao. Chuang-tzu said: "The white fish stroll out freely; this is fishes' delight." Hui-tzu said: "You are not a fish. How can you know fishes' delight?" Chuang-tzu said: "You are not I; how can you know I do not know fishes' delight?" Hui-tzu said: "If, because I am not you, I do not know you, then since you are not a fish, your ignorance of fishes' delight is total." Chuang-tzu said: "Please go back to the beginning of your discussion. When you said, 'How do you know fishes' delight?', you asked me knowing already how I knew it. I knew it from my pleasure in strolling over the Hao while the fishes strolled under the Hao." (From the book known as *Chuang-tzu,* compiled about 290 B.C. Translation kindly supplied by Dr. L. E. R. Picken.)

10. For a valuable summary of the present state of knowledge concerning communication in fishes, see Tavolga (1960) and Moulton (1969).

11. Dr. M. D. Shalter has recently recalled that Sir Thomas More, in his *Utopia* (first published in Latin in 1516), gives the following account of a practice in Utopia:

> "They breed vast numbers of chickens by almost extraordinary method. Instead of leaving the hens to sit on the eggs, they hatch out dozens at a time, applying a steady heat to them—with the result that when the chicks come out of the shells, they regard the poultry-man as their mother, and follow him everywhere!"

One wonders whether More's allusion to imprinting was derived from then-existing knowledge, applied perhaps in some foreign land, or was the product of his own observations and imagination.

12. Dr. J. D. French, a distinguished brain surgeon (Professor at the University of California, Los Angeles), has summarised the function of the reticular activating system, which is comprised in the limbic system, as follows: "It awakens the brain to consciousness and keeps it alert; it directs the traffic of messages in the nervous system; it monitors the myriads of stimuli that beat upon our senses, accepting what we need to perceive and rejecting what is irrelevant; it tempers and refines our muscular activity and bodily movements. We can go even further and say that it contributes in an important way to the highest mental processes—the focussing of attention, introspection, and doubtless all forms of reasoning." (See also H. W. Magoun, *The Waking Brain*, Springfield, Illinois: C. C. Thomas, 1958.)

13. W. Grey Walter (1969) in *Observations on Man, his Frame, his Duty and his Expectations* (the 23rd Eddington Memorial Lecture. Cambridge University Press) has described how his study of "brain waves," by means of electroencephalograph, has revealed objective evidence that spontaneous impulses to explore and the evocation of imaginary experiences are preceded and accompanied by clear and substantial electrical events. He says, "It is an eerie experience to discern through an electric machine the genesis of a person's intentions, to predict his decisions before he knows his own mind. Even more impressive is the experience, when one is oneself harnessed to such a machine, to find that by an effort of will one can influence external events with movement or overt action, through the impalpable electric surges in one's own brain." As a physiologist he finds it embarrassing to have to introduce such a phrase as "will power." This is what we feel subjectively when we say "I wish" and "I will." He says, "It may be the fate of physiologists that they can merely provide increasingly de-

tailed corroboration of faculties which the wise have always known we possess."

14. Those who have not looked critically at the scientific evidence for "telepathy" may well feel sceptical. So perhaps it is worth briefly recounting the extraordinary results of some of the great number of experiments which have been conducted with the utmost care and precision. In the famous Pratt-Pearce experiment, during the early years of the Duke University department, the number of calls made by the percipient, Hubert Pearce, was 1,850. The most probable number of "hits," or correct guesses, on the hypothesis of "pure chance," is 370. The actual number of correct guesses exceeded this by 188. The odds against obtaining such a deviation by chance alone are quoted as being well over 8 million million million to 1 (actually 8×10^{26} to 1). Again a series of experiments carried out by Dr. Soal in London, in 1941, with Basil Shackleton as percipient had an even more astonishing result. An earlier pilot experiment had shown that Shackleton seemed to be guessing not at the card at which the agent was looking, but the card ahead of that. In the confirmatory series of experiments nearly 4,000 guesses were made. During this time, Shackleton continued to guess successfully at the card ahead, getting about 300 hits above the mean chance expectation of 800. The odds against the chance hypothesis are indeed astronomical, namely 10^{36} to 1. It has been estimated that in order for the deviation observed in the Soal-Shackleton experiment to turn up by chance, we would require more experiments than the whole history of the world would allow time for!

In 1969 Dr. Helmut Schmidt reported results hardly less striking. In one precognition experiment, the subjects were faced with four coloured lamps which were lit in a random sequence governed by a radioactive source. The subjects were required to guess which of the four lamps would light up next, and to press the button corresponding to this lamp. In a series of nearly 74,000 guesses, three subjects succeeded in making about 900 more correct guesses than would be expected by chance. In the task of predicting which of the lamps would *not* light up, two subjects were able to score strikingly *below* chance expectation. This below chance or negative deviation in 9,000 trials was over 200. The probability of obtaining these scores by chance is less than 1 in 10,000 million.

One of the best-attested features of the classical type of card-guessing experiment, which has been evident from the very commencement of such studies by J. B. Rhine in the 1930s, has been the fact that percipients may, at the beginning of an ESP test, score beyond chance, only to score at the chance level as the test continues. Scoring rate may indeed decline over a long period of testing, or there may be a decline in scoring within an experimental occasion which is followed by a pick-up in the scoring rate at the start of the next occasion. These have been called "long-term declines," a phenomenon which tends to be permanent for the particular percipient; while the second has been called an "episodic decline." (See Robert Harvie in Alister Hardy, R. Harvie, and Arthur Koestler, *The Challenge of Chance*. London: Hutchinson, 1973, pp. 137–38.)

R. Harvie (op. cit., pp. 144–50) has carried out a number of experiments with series of numbers obtained from random tables prepared by the most exact possible methods, under critical supervision, for avoiding any degree of systematic ordering; and critical tests have shown that his sources do *not* possess such ordering. Yet when he came to carry out matching tests, it was concluded that the complete absence of pattern in the tables did not in fact preclude scoring significantly beyond chance expectation. The non-randomness of the target digits having been most minutely determined, and the possibility that the experimenters were guilty of inaccuracy in the matching scores having been excluded, only one alternative seemed to remain; namely that of paranormal causation. But this, he concluded, can only involve a circular argument since it would be based on the assumption that *any* deviation from chance observed in a purely statistical experiment, where all other causes are absent, must be due to paranormal causation. As he says, "If it were shown that highly significant deviations from chance expectation could be obtained in the absence of any possible normal or paranormal cause, then our commonsensical notions of chance are in for a rude shock." This very interestingly takes us back to the results of George Spencer Brown (who was working with Professor Alister Hardy in Oxford), which were published in his book *Probability and Scientific Inference* (London: Longmans, 1957). Spencer Brown attributed the appearance of extraordinary results of this kind, where non-random effects appeared with no conceivable parapsychological influences tenable, to a vagueness in the very concept of randomness itself. In other words he was beginning to doubt the universal applicability of classical frequency-probability theory. Dr. Brown's work was subject to a good deal of criticism; some of it apparently cogent. But Spencer Brown did suggest that perhaps some apparently successful ESP experiments are indeed pointing to an unknown property of that insubstantial territory which we call "randomness."

At this point some recent studies from the Massachusetts Institute of Technology become highly relevant. Dr. Stewart Kauffman ("Metabolic Stability and Epigenesis in Randomly Constructed Genetic Nets," *Journ. Theor. Biol.* 1969, Vol. 22, pp. 437–67) studied the behaviour of randomly constructed systems, or "nets," of binary elements. These nets, which were simulated computer, were comprised of elements, analogous to switches, each of which could be either "on" or "off."

The interconnexions between the elements of a net were at random. Each element scanned the input ("on" or "off") from two other elements, and had an output ("on" or "off") to one other element. The response, or output, from each element was prescribed by a randomising device.

Nets containing between fifteen and two thousand elements were found to behave in a surprisingly orderly manner. For any such net there is a finite but very large number of possible states. A net containing N elements has 2^N possible states. Starting from an arbitrarily chosen initial state, in which the elements are placed on or off at random, one would expect a randomly constructed system to pass through a sequence of all possible states, returning eventually to the initial state, and then to traverse the whole cycle again, and so on indefinitely. Far from this being the case, the nets tended to cycle through a very small number of states. Furthermore, the number of different configurations displayed by the system when started from different initial states was unexpectedly small. Again, as the systems cycled through successive states (after they had been arbitrarily perturbed by reversing one element) they exhibited a surprising stability. In 90 per cent of cases the system returned to the cycle of states from which it had been disturbed—like a missile homing in on its target returns to its original path when subjected to minor, random interference. These networks of disorderly construction gave every appearance of orderly patterning and stability in behaviour.

Kauffman suggests that the metabolic activity and development of contemporary organisms may be governed by large randomly connected nets of genes which interact in a similar fashion to randomly constructed networks of binary elements. The behaviour of such nets displays the stability characteristic of, and necessary for, life. This hypothesis is supported by the accuracy of predictions with regard to, for example, the rate of cellular differentiation and cell replication observed in organisms of varying complexity, which Kauffman based on the observation of his binary nets. In concluding this argument Kauffman writes:

> A living thing is a richly connected net of chemical reactions. One can little doubt that the earliest proto-organisms aggregated their reaction nets at random in the primaeval seas; or that mutation continues to modify living metabolic nets in random ways. *Evolution, therefore, probably had as its initial substrata the behaviour of randomly aggregated reaction nets.* [Italics mine—ed.]

It is a fundamental question whether two billion years of survival

pressure have succeeded in selecting from a myriad of unorderly reaction nets those few improbable, that is non-random and ordered,
metabolic nets which alone behave with the stability requisite for life;
or whether living things are akin to randomly constructed automata
whose characteristic behaviour reflects their unorderly construction
no matter how evolution selected the surviving forms. . . . Large,
randomly assembled nets of binary elements behave with simplicity,
stability, and order. It seems unlikely that Nature has made no use of
such probable and reliable systems, both to initiate evolution and protect its progeny.

The upshot is that the study of random nets seems to point to a forma-
tive tendency present in apparent disorderliness. The accepted theory of
evolution is that Nature shapes out of chaos, through the processes of natural selection, the intricate and highly organised forms of living organisms.
In contrast to inanimate matter, *the living world is one of increasing*
orderliness. While the physical universe, like a runaway horse, tends
towards increasing entropy, or disorder, the living world flows against this
current by constantly creating order, or negative entropy. *Is not the orderliness emerging from the free-for-all antics of Kauffman's automata* remi-
niscent of the processes which take place within the living organism?

It all recalls the synchronicity principle which has been so well described and discussed in Arthur Koestler's *The Roots of Coincidence*
(London: Hutchinson, 1972).

Finally there are some recent, quite bizarre experiments, which, if substantiated, seem to throw still more light on the possible biological value
of "capricious randomness." (Abstracts of these will be found in *J. Para-
psychol.* Vols. xxiv and xxv for 1970 and 1971.)

Walter J. Levy and Eve André, working at the Institute for Parapsychology, placed newly hatched chicks under a heat lamp coupled to a randomising device governed by a radioactive source. At set intervals the
lamp was switched on or off, according to the dictates of the randomiser.
The number of "offs" and "ons" was recorded automatically. With the
lamp on the chicks were "relaxed and showed every sign of enjoyment";
with the lamp off they were "huddled and peeping miserably." The chicks
were left with this automated "hen" for a number of nights; on each occasion the number of "ons" was significantly greater than the number of
"offs." However, when the apparatus was left to run by itself with no
chicks under the lamp, the number of "off" and "ons" were equal—in
accordance with chance expectation.

An even more remarkable experiment was carried out by Levy. Using the same apparatus, not chicks, but fertile chicken eggs were placed under the heat lamp. The lamp came on or stayed off every twenty-four seconds, according to the selection of the randomiser. When no eggs (or only hard-boiled eggs!) were present, the number of "offs" equalled the number of "ons." When fertile eggs were placed in the incubator, the lamp came on more often than not. In the first experimental series of 4,500 trials the light came on 2,358 times, as opposed to the 2,250 times expected by chance. In the second series of 6,506 trials the lamp came on 3,416 times whereas the chance expectation is 3,253. The adaptive value of these chance deviations, if confirmed by further work, is clear in a way that is not obvious in the general run of guessing experiments.

15. R. Otto, *The Idea of the Holy,* translated by J. W. Harvey, London, 1923. For a further discussion of Otto's work see J. Oman, *The Natural and the Supernatural,* London, 1931, especially pp. 60–64 and Appendix A, p. 474.

REFERENCES

CHAPTER 1

Agar, W. E. (1943). *The Theory of the Living Organism.* Victoria: Melbourne Univ. Press.

Bastin, T. (1971), ed. *Quantum Theory and Beyond.* London: Cambridge Univ. Press.

Bohm, D., et al. (1970, 1971). *Quanta and Reality.* In Bastin (1971) and Waddington (1970). London: Hutchinson.

Bronowski, J. (1969). *Nature and Knowledge.* Eugene and London: Univ. of Oregon Lecture Publications.

Crick, F. H. C., and Orgel, L. E. (1973).

Elsasser, W. M. (1966). *Atom and Organism.* Princeton: Princeton Univ. Press.

Hinde, R. A., ed. (1972). *Non-Verbal Communication.* London: Cambridge Univ. Press.

Koestler, A., and Smythies, J. R., eds. (1969). *Beyond Reductionism.* London: Hutchinson.

Linney, D. S., and Weiszäcker, C. F. von (1971). In Bastin, ed. See especially pp. 229, 331.

MacKay, D. M. (1972). In Hinde, ed.

Monod, J. (1971). *Chance and Necessity.* London: Collins.

Pantin, C. F. A. (1968). In *Relations Between the Sciences,* A. M. Pantin and W. H. Thorpe, eds. London: Cambridge Univ. Press.

Pattee, H. (1970). In C. H. Waddington (1970).

Pattee, H. (1971). In Bastin, ed.

Polanyi, M. (1967). *The Tacit Dimension.* London: Routledge & Kegan Paul. Garden City, New York: Anchor Books.

Popper, Karl (1972). *Objective Knowledge: An Evolutionary Approach.* Oxford: Clarendon Press.

Schrödinger, E. (1944). *What Is Life?* London: Cambridge Univ. Press.

Thom, R. (1970). In Waddington, ed.

397

REFERENCES

Thorpe, W. H. (1963). *Learning: Instinct in Animals*. London: Methuen.

Toulmin, S. E. (1966). In P. H. Oehser, ed., *Knowledge Amongst Men*. New York: Simon & Schuster.

Waddington, C. H., ed. (1970). *Towards a Theoretical Biology. 3 Drafts*. Edinburgh: Edinburgh Univ. Press.

Weiss, P. (1969). The living system: determinism stratified. In Koestler and Smythies, eds.

Whittaker, E. (1949). *From Euclid to Eddington*. Cambridge and London: Cambridge Univ. Press.

Woodger, J. H. (1960). Biology and physics. *Brit. J. Phil. Sci.*, 11, No. 42, p. 89.

CHAPTER 2

Bateson, W. (1913). *Problems in Genetics*. New Haven: Yale Univ. Press.

Batham, E. J., and Pantin, C. F. A. (1950). Inherent activity in the Sea-anemone *Metridium senile. J. Exp. Biol.*, 27, 290–301.

Binet, A. (1891). *La Vie Psychique des Micro-organismes*. Paris.

Bouvier, E. L. (1918). *La Vie Psychique des Insectes*. Paris.

Brachet, J. L. (1971). Nucleo-cytoplasmic interactions in morphogenesis. *Proc. Roy. Soc. London B.*, 178, 227–43.

Bronowski, J. (1969). *Nature and Knowledge*. Eugene, Oregon, and London: Univ. of Oregon Lecture Publications.

Commoner, B. (1968). Failure of the Watson-Crick Theory as a Chemical Explanation of Inheritance. *Nature*, 220, 334–40.

Corning, W. C., and Riccio, D. (1970). *Molecular Approaches to Learning and Memory*. New York: Academic Press.

Eccles, J. C. (1970). *Facing Reality*. Berlin and New York: Springer-Verlag.

Fleischman, T. (1970). The Chemical Basis of Inheritance. *Nature*, 225, 30–32, and Hershey, A. D. (1970). Genes and Heredity Characteristics. *Nature*, 226, 697–700.

Gardner, R. A., and Gardner, B. T. (1971). Two-way communication with an infant chimpanzee. In A. Scheier and F. Stollinit, eds., *Behavior of Non-human Primates*. New York: Academic Press.

Hershey, A. D. (1970). Genes and hereditary characteristics. *Nature*, 226, 697–700.

Grene, M. (1966). *The Knower and the Known*. London: Faber & Faber.

Hobhouse, L. T. (1915, 2nd ed.). *Mind in Evolution*. London: Macmillan.

Hobhouse, L. T. (1913). *Development and Purpose*. London: Macmillan.

Jennings, H. S. (1899). The Psychology of a Protozoan. *Amer. J. Psychology*, 10, 1–13.

Jennings, H. S. (1906). *The Behaviour of the Lower Organisms*. New York: Columbia Univ. Press.

Lashley, K. S. (1938). The Experimental Analysis of Instinctive Behaviour. *Psychol. Rev.*, 45, 445–71.

Münsterberg, H. (1900). Grundzüge der Psychologie. See Vol. 1.

Pantin, C. F. A. (1968). *The Relations Between the Sciences*. London: Cambridge Univ. Press.

Paul, J., et al. (1970). Organ-specific gene masking in mammalian chromosomes. *Proc. Roy. Soc. London B.* 176, 277–85.

Popper, K. R. (1968a). Epistemology without a knowing subject. In *Logic, Methodology and Philosophy of Sciences*, 3rd ed. Van Rootselaar and Staal, eds. Amsterdam: North-Holland Publishing Company.

Popper, K. R. (1968b). On the theory of the objective mind. Wein: *Akten des XIV Internationalen Kongresses für Philosophie*, Vol. 1.

Popper, K. R. (1972). *Objective Knowledge: An Evolutionary Approach*. Oxford: Clarendon Press.

Pratt, J. R. (1962). A "Book Model" of genetic information transfer in cells and tissues. In M. Kasha and B. Pullman, eds., *Horizons in Biochemistry*. London: Academic Press.

Salisbury, F. B. (1969). Natural Selection and the Complexity of the Gene. *Nature*, 224, 342–43.

Sonneborn, T. M. (1970). Gene action in development. *Proc. Roy. Soc. London B.*, 176, 347–66.

Spetner, L. M. (1970). Natural Selection versus Genetic Uniqueness. *Nature*, 226, 948–49.

Thomson, J. Arthur (1920). *The System of Animate Nature*, 2 vols. London: Williams and Norgate.

Thoday, J. M. (1970). In Discussion. *Proc. Roy. Soc. London B.*, 176, 249–50.

Thorpe, W. H. (1963). *Learning and Instinct in Animals*. London: Methuen. Cambridge, Mass.: Harvard Univ. Press.

Thorpe, W. H. (1965). *Science, Man and Morals*. London: Methuen.

Waddington, C. H. (1969). The theory of evolution today. In A. Koestler, and J. R. Smythies, eds., *Beyond Reductionism*. London: Hutchinson.

Wolpert, L. (1970). In *Towards a Theoretical Biology*. C. H. Waddington, ed. Edinburgh: Edinburgh Univ. Press.

CHAPTER 3

Section I

Adler, H. E., ed. (1971). Orientation: sensory basis. *Ann. N. Y. Acad. Sci.,* **188**, 1–408.

Alexander, R. D. (1960). Sound communication in Orthoptera and Cicadidae. In Lanyon and Tavolga (1960), 38–93.

——— (1967). Arthropods. In Sebeok (1968), 167–215.

Altevogt, R. (1957). Untersuchungen für Biologie, Ökologie und Physiologie indischer Winkerkrabben. *Z. Morph. Ökol. Tiere,* 46, 1–110.

——— (1959). Ökologische und Ethologische Studien an Europas Winkerkrabbe. *Uca tangeri. Z. Morph. Ökol. Tiere,* **48**, 132.

Boeckh, J., Kaissling, K.-E., and Schneider, D. (1965). Insect olfactory receptors. *Cold Spring Harbor Symp. Quant. Biol.,* 30, 263–80.

Bonner, J. T. (1959). *The Cellular Slime Moulds.* Princeton: Princeton Univ. Press.

Bossert, W. H. (1968). Temporal patterning in olfactory communication. *J. theor. Biol.,* 18, 157–70.

Böttger, K. (1962). Zur Biologie und Ethologie der einheimischen Wassermilben. *Arremurus (Megaloiracarus) globator* (Müll.), 1776, *Piona nodata nodata* (Müll.), 1776, *Eylais infundibulifera meridionalis* (Thou), 1899 (*Hydrachnellae,* Acari). *Zool. Jb. (Syst.),* 89, 501–84.

Bristowe, W. S. (1939–41), *The Comity of Spiders.* London: The Ray Society.

Bull, H. O. (1928–39). Studies on conditioned responses in fishes. *J.M.B.A. and Dove Marine Laboratory Reports,* Parts I–IX.

Butler, C. G. (1967). Insect pheromones. *Biol. Rev.,* 42, 42–87.

Capranica, R. R. (1968). The vocal repertoire of the bullfrog. *Behaviour,* 31, 302–25.

Carlisle, D. B., and Knowles, F. (1959). *Endocrine Control in Crustaceans.* London: Cambridge Univ. Press.

Cloudesley-Thompson, J. L. (1958). *Spiders, Scorpions, Centipedes and Mites.* London: Pergamon Press.

Cott, H. B. (1961). Scientific results of an inquiry into the ecology and economic status of the Nile crocodile in Uganda and Northern Rhodesia. *Proc. Zool. Soc. London,* 29, 211–356.

Crane, J. (1943). Display breeding and relationships of fiddler crabs *Brachyura* genus *Uca* in the N.E. United States, *Zoologica,* 28, 217–23.

—— (1949). Comparative biology of salticid spiders of Rancho Grande, Venezuela, IV. An analysis of display. *Zoologica*, 34, 159–214.

—— (1957). Basic patterns of display in fiddler crabs *Ocypodidae* genus *Uca*. *Zoologica*, 42, 69–82.

—— (1958). Aspects of social behaviour in the fiddler crabs, with special reference to *Uca maracoani* (Latreille). *Zoologica*, 43, 113–30.

Crisp, D. J. (1961). Territorial behaviour in a barnacle settlement. *J. exp. Biol.*, 38, 429–46.

—— and Mellers, P. S. (1962). The chemical basis of gregariousness in Cirripedes. *Proc. Roy. Soc. London*, B, 156, 500–20.

Davenport, D. (1966). The experimental analysis of behaviour in symbioses. In *Symbiosis*, 381–429. S. M. Henry, ed. New York and London: Academic Press.

—— and Norris, K. S. (1958). Observations on the symbiosis of the sea anemone *Stoichactis* and the pomacentrid fish *Amphiprion percula*. *Biol. Bull.*, 115, 397–410.

Delco, E. A., Jr. (1960). Sound discrimination by males of two cyprinid fishes. *Tex. J. Sci.*, 12, 48–54.

Dietrich, G. (1963). *General Oceanography*. New York: Wiley.

Eibl-Eibesfeldt, I. (1967). *Grundriss der vergleichenden Verhaltensforschung*. Munich: Piper.

Evans, L. T. (1961). Structure as related to behavior in the organization of populations in reptiles. In *Vertebrate Speciation*. W. F. Blair, ed. Austin, Texas: Univ. Texas Press.

Frings, H., and Frings, M. (1968). Other invertebrates. In Sebeok (1968), 244–70.

Frisch, K. von (1941), Über einen Schreckstoff der Fischhaut und seine biologische Bedeutung. *Z. vergl. Physiol.*, 29, 46–145.

—— (1946). Der Tanz der Bienen. *Östrr. Zool. Zeit.*, 1, 1–48. A further summary in the same year was given in *Experienta*, Basel, 2, 197–404.

—— (1954). *The Dancing Bees*. London: Methuen.

—— (1967a). *The Dance Language and Orientation of Bees*. Cambridge, Mass.: Harvard Univ. Press.

—— (1967b). Honey bees: Do they use the information as to direction and distance provided by their dances? *Science, N.Y.*, 158, (3804), 1072–75.

—— (1968). Do bees really not understand their own language? *Allg. dt. Imkerztg.*, 2(2), 35–41.

—— (1969). The foraging bee: How she finds and exploits sources of food. *Bee World*, 50, (4), 141–52.

REFERENCES

Frishkopf, L. S., and Goldstein, M. H., Jr. (1963). Responses to acoustic stimuli from single units in the eighth nerve of the bullfrog. *J. acoust. Soc. Am.*, 35, 1219–28.

Froloff, J. P. (1925). Bedingte Reflexe bei Fischen, I. *Pflüg. Arch.*, 208, 261–71.

—— (1928). Bedingte Reflexe bei Fischen, II. *Pflüg. Arch.*, 220, 339–49.

Galloway, T. W. (1908). A case of phosphorescence as a mating adaptation. *School Sci. and Math.*, 8, 411–15.

—— and Welsh, P. S. (1911). Studies on a phosphorescent Bermudan annelid *Odontosyllis enopla* Verrill. *Trans. Am. microsc. Soc.*, 30, 13–39.

Galtsoff, P. S. (1938). Physiology of reproduction of *Ostrea virginica*, II. Stimulation of spawning in the female oyster. *Biol. Bull.*, 75, 286–307.

Gould, J. E., Henerey, M., and MacLeod, M. C. (1970). Communication of direction by the Honey bee. *Science, N.Y.*, 169, 544–54.

Harris, C. G., and Bergeijk, W. A. van (1962). Evidence that the lateral line organ responds to near-field displacements of sound sources in water. *J. acoust. Soc. Am.*, 34, 1831–41.

Hasler, A. D., and Wisby, W. J. (1951). Discrimination of stream odour by fishes and its relation to parent stream behavior. *Am. Nat.*, 85, 223–28.

Hinde, R. A. (1970). *Animal Behaviour: A Synthesis of Ethology and Comparative Psychology*, 2nd ed. New York: McGraw-Hill.

—— ed. (1972). *Non-verbal Communication*. London: Cambridge Univ. Press.

Hockett, C. F. (1960a). Logical considerations in the study of animal communication. In Lanyon and Tavolga (1960), 392–430.

—— (1960b). The origin of speech. *Sci. Amer.*, 203, 89–96.

—— and Altmann, S. A. (1968). A note on design features. In Sebeok (1968), 61–72.

Johnson, D. L. (1967). Communication among Honey bees with field experience. *Anim. Behav.*, 15, 487–92.

Lanyon, W. E., and Tavolga, W. N., eds. (1960). *Animal Sounds and Communication*. Washington, D.C.: Am. Inst. Biol. Sci.

Leslie, C. J. (1951). Mating behavior of leeches. *J. Bombay Nat. Hist. Soc.*, 50, 422–23.

Lindauer, M. (1961). *Communication Amongst Social Bees*. Cambridge, Mass.: Harvard Univ. Press.

—— (1967). Recent advances in bee communication and orientation. *A. Rev. Entomol.*, 12, 439–70.

Lissmann, H. W. (1951). Continuous electrical signals from the tail of a fish, *Gymnarchus niloticus* Cur. *Nature, Lond.,* 167, 201–2.

—— (1958). The function and evolution of the electric organs of fish. *J. exp. Biol.,* 35, 156–91.

—— (1963). Electric location by fishes. *Sci. Amer.,* 208 (3), 50–59.

Lloyd, J. E. (1966). Studies on the flash communication system in *Photinus* fireflies. *Univ. Michigan Mus. Zool. Mis. Publ.,* 130, 1–95.

Lutz, B. (1947). Trends towards aquatic and direct development in frogs. *Copeia,* 4, 242–52.

Marler, P., and Hamilton, W. J. (1966). *Mechanisms of Animal Behavior.* New York: Wiley.

Michelsen, A. (1968). Frequency discrimination in the locust ear by means of four groups of receptor cells. *Nature, Lond.,* 220, 585–86.

Michener, C. D. (1969). Comparative social behavior of bees. *A. Rev. Entomol.,* 14, 299–342.

Moulton, J. M. (1969). The classification of acoustic communication behavior amongst teleost fishes. In *Approaches to Animal Communication.* T. A. Sebeok and A. Ramsay, eds. Mouton: The Hague.

Parry, D. A. (1965). The signals generated by an insect in a spider's web. *J. exp. Biol.,* 43, 185–92.

Ross, D. M. (1960). The association between the hermit crab *Eupagurus bernhardus* (L) and the sea anemone *Calliactic parasitica* (Couch). *Proc. Zool. Soc. Lond.,* 134, 43–57.

Schneider, D. (1963). Electrophysiological investigation of insect olfaction. In *Olfaction and Taste,* 85–103. Y. Zotterman, ed. New York: Macmillan.

Sebeok, T. A., ed. (1968). *Animal Communication.* Bloomington, Ind. and London: Indiana Univ. Press.

Shaffer, B. M. (1953). Aggregation in cellular slime moulds: *in vitro* isolation of acrasin. *Nature, Lond.,* 171, 975.

—— (1956a). Properties of acrasin. *Science, N.Y.,* 123, 1172–73.

—— (1956b). Acrasin, the chemotactic agent in cellular slime moulds. *J. exp. Biol.,* 33, 645–57.

—— (1957a). Aspects of aggregation in cellular slime moulds. I, Orientation and chemotaxis. *Am. Nat.,* 91, 19–35.

—— (1957b). Properties of slime mould amoebae of significance for aggregation. *Q. J. microsc. Sci.,* 98, 377–92.

—— (1957c). Variability of behaviour of aggregating cellular slime moulds. *Q. J. microsc. Sci.,* 98, 393–405.

Smith, M. (1954). *The British Amphibians and Reptiles,* 2nd ed. London: Collins.

REFERENCES

Stout, J. (1963). The significance of sound production during the reproductive behaviour of *Notropus analostraneus* family Cyprinidae. *Anim. Behav.*, 11, 83–92.

Tavolga, W. N. (1956). Visual, chemical and sound stimuli as cues in the sex-discriminatory behaviour of the Gobiid fish *Bathygobius soporator*. *Zoologica*, 41, 49–64.

—— (1958). The significance of underwater sounds produced by males of the Gobiid fish *Bathygobius soporator*. *Physiol. Zool.*, 31, 259–71.

—— (1960). Sound production and underwater communication in fishes. In Lanyon and Tavolga (1960), 93–136.

Thorpe, W. H. (1949). Orientation and methods of communication in the Honey bee and its sensitivity to the polarisation of light. *Nature, Lond.*, 164, 11.

—— (1972). The lower vertebrates and invertebrates. In *Non-Verbal Communication*, Ch. 5, R. A. Hinde, ed. London: Cambridge Univ. Press.

—— and Davenport, D., eds. (1965). Learning and associated phenomena in the invertebrates. *Anim. Behav. Supplement No. 1.*

Tinbergen, N. (1953). *Social Behaviour in Animals.* London: Methuen.

Wenner, A. M. (1967). Honey bees: Do they use the distance information contained in their dance maneuver? *Science, N.Y.*, 155, (3764), 847–49.

—— and Johnson, D. L. (1967). Honey bees: Do they use the direction and distance information provided by their dancers? *Science, N.Y.*, 158, (3804), 1076–77.

—— Wells, P. H., and Rohlf, F. J. (1967). An analysis of recruitment in Honey bees. *Physiol. Zool.*, 40 (4), 317–24.

Wever, E. G., Hepp-Reymond, M.-C., and Vernon, J. A. (1966). Vocalization and hearing in the leopard lizard. *Proc. Nat. Acad. Sci.*, 55, 98–106.

Wilson, E. O. (1968). Chemical systems. In Sebeok (1968), 75–102.

—— and Bossert, W. H. (1963). Chemical communication among animals. *Recent Progr. Hormone Res.*, 19, 673–716.

CHAPTER 3

Section II

Ashmole, N. P., and Humbertotova, A. (1968). Prolonged parental care in Royal terns and other birds. *Auk*, 85, 90–100.

Beer, C. G. (1970). Individual recognition of voice in the social behavior of birds. *Adr. Study Behav.*, 3, 27–74.

Bertram, B. C. R. (1970). The vocal behaviour of the Indian hill mynah, *Gracula religiosa. Anim. Behav. Monog.*, 3, Pt. 2.

Brémond, J.-C. (1967). Reconnaissance de schémas réactogènes liés à l'information contenue dans le chant territorial du Rouge-gorge. *Proc. 14th Int. Ornith. Congr.*, 217–29. Oxford: Blackwell.

Busnel, R.-G. (1968). Acoustic communication. In Sebeok (1968), 127–53.

Chomsky, N. (1967). The general properties of language. In *Brain Mechanisms underlying Speech and Language*, 63–88. C. H. Millikan and F. L. Darley, eds. New York and London: Grune & Stratton.

——— (1968). *Language and Mind.* New York: Harcourt, Brace & World.

Coulson, J. C. (1966a). The influence of change of mate on the breeding biology of the kittiwake. *Anim. Behav.*, 14, 189–90.

——— (1966b). The significance of pair-bond and age on the breeding biology of the Kittiwake gull (*Rissa tridactyla*). *J. Anim. Ecol.*, 35, 269–79.

Falls, J. B. (1969). Functions of territorial song in the White-throated sparrow. In Hinde (1969), 207–32.

Gibson, J. J. (1968). *The Senses Considered as Perceptual Systems.* London: Allen Unwin.

Griffin, D. R. (1958). *Listening in the Dark.* New Haven, Connecticut: Yale Univ. Press. (For more recent references, see Adler, H. E. [1971]. Orientation: sensory basis. *Ann. N. Y. Acad. Sci.*, 188, 1–408.)

Hall-Craggs, J. (1962). The development of song in the Blackbird (*Turdus merula*). *Ibis*, 104, 277–300.

——— (1969). The aesthetic content of bird-song. In Hinde (1969), 367–81.

Hartshorne, C. (1958). The relation of bird song to music. *Ibis*, 100, 421–45.

——— (1973). *Born to Sing:* An Interpretation and World Survey of Bird Song. Bloomington and London: Indiana University Press.

Hinde, R. A. (1958). The nest-building behaviour of domesticated canaries. *Proc. Zool. Soc. Lond.*, 131, 1–48.

Hinde, R. A., ed. (1969). *Bird Vocalizations.* London: Cambridge Univ. Press.

Hooker, T., and Hooker, B. I. (Lade) (1969). Duetting. In Hinde (1969), 185–205.

REFERENCES

Hutchison, R. E., Stevenson, J., and Thorpe, W. H. (1968). The basis for individual recognition by voice in the Sandwich tern (*Sterna sandvicensis*). *Behaviour*, 32, 150–57.

Konishi, M. (1963). The role of auditory feedback in the vocal behaviour of the domestic fowl. *Zeit. f. Tierpsychol.*, 20, 349–67.

Lack, D. L. (1939). The behaviour of the Robin. *Proc. Zool. Soc. Lond.*, 109, 169–78.

Lade, B. I., and Thorpe, W. H. (1964). Dove songs as innately coded patterns of specific behaviour. *Nature, Lond.*, 202, 366–68.

Marler, P. (1955). Characteristics of some animal calls. *Nature, Lond.*, 176, 6–7.

—— (1960). Bird songs and mate selection. In Lanyon and Tavolga (1960), 348–67.

—— (1967). Comparative study of song development in Emberizine Finches *Proc. 14th Int. Ornith. Congr.*, 231–44. Oxford: Blackwell.

—— (1969). Animals and man: communication and its development. In *Communication*, J. D. Roslansky, ed., Amsterdam: North-Holland.

—— (1970). A comparative approach to vocal learning: song development in white-crowned sparrows. *J. comp. physiol. psychol., Monogr.*, 71, 1–25.

Nicolai, J. (1959). Familientradition in der Gesangentwicklung des Gimpels (*Pyrrula pyrrhula* L.). *J. f. Orn.*, 100, 39–46.

Nottebohm, F. (1968). Auditory experience and song development in the Chaffinch (*Fringilla coelebs*): Ontogeny of a complex motor pattern. *Ibis*, 110, 549–68.

—— (1970). The ontogeny of bird song. *Science, N.Y.*, 167, 950–56.

Schwartzkopff, J. (1960). Vergleichende Physiologie des Gehörs. *Fortschr. Zool.*, 12, 206–64.

Smith, W. J. (1968). Message-meaning analysis. In Sebeok (1968), 44–60.

Stevenson, J., Hutchison, R. E., Hutchison, J., Bertram, B. C. R., and Thorpe, W. H. (1970). Individual recognition by auditory cues in the Common tern (*Sterna hirundo*). *Nature, Lond.*, 226, 562–63.

Teuber, H. L. (1967). Lacunae and Research Approaches to Them. In *Brain Mechanisms underlying Speech and Language*, 204–16. C. H. Millikan and F. L. Darley, eds. New York and London: Grune & Stratton.

Thielcke, G. (1969). Geographic variation in bird vocalization. In Hinde (1969), 311–39.

Thorpe, W. H. (1958). The learning of song-patterns by birds, with especial reference to the song of the Chaffinch, *Fringilla coelebs*. *Ibis*, 100, 535–70.

—— (1961). *Bird Song: The Biology of Vocal Communication and Expression in Birds*. London: Cambridge Univ. Press.

—— (1963). Antiphonal singing in birds as evidence for avian auditory reaction time. *Nature, Lond.*, 197, 774–76.

—— (1966). Ritualization in the individual development of bird song. *Phil. Trans. Roy. Soc.*, B. 251, 351–58.

—— (1967). Vocal imitation and antiphonal song and its implications. *Proc. 14th Int. Ornith. Congr.*, 245–63.

—— (1968). Perceptual bases for group organization in social vertebrates, especially birds. *Nature, Lond.*, 220, 124–28.

—— (1972). Duetting and antiphonal song in birds: its extent and significance. *Behaviour: Monograph Supplement* No. 18, 1–197.

—— (1973). Duet-singing Birds. *Sci. Am.* 229, 70–79.

—— and North, M. E. W. (1965). Origin and significance of the power of vocal imitation with special reference to the antiphonal singing of birds. *Nature, Lond.*, 208, 219–22.

—— and North, M. E. W. (1966). Vocal imitation in the Tropical Bou-Bou shrike (*Laniarius aethiopicus Major*) as a means of establishing and maintaining social bonds. *Ibis*, 108, 432–35.

Tschanz, B. (1968). Trottellummen. *Zeit. f. Tierpsychol. Suppl.*, 4.

White, S. J. (1971). Selective responsiveness by the Gannet to played-back calls. *Anim. Behav.*, 19.

—— White, R. E. C., and Thorpe, W. H. (1970). Acoustic basis for individual recognition in the Gannet. *Nature, Lond.*, 225, 1156–58.

CHAPTER 4

Adrian, E. D. (1950). The control of nerve cell activity. *Symposia of the Society of Experimental Biology* No. 4: 85–91. London: Cambridge Univ. Press.

Brillouin, L. (1962). *Science and Information Theory*. 2nd ed. New York: Academic Press.

Bullock, T. H. (1961). The origins of nervous discharges. *Behaviour*, 17, 48–50.

—— (1966). Nervous and hormonal mechanisms of integration. *Symposium No. 20 Society for Experimental Biology*. London: Cambridge Univ. Press.

Darwin, C. (1872). *The Expression of the Emotions in Man and Animals*. London: John Murray.

Hebb, D. O. (1953). Heredity and environment in mammalian behaviour, *Brit. J. Animal Behaviour,* 1, 43–47.

Hinde, R. A., ed. (1969). *Bird Vocalizations: Their Relation to Current Problems in Biology and Psychology.* London: Cambridge Univ. Press.

Hinde, R. A. (1970). *Animal Behaviour: A Synthesis of Ethology and Comparative Psychology.* 2nd ed. New York and London: McGraw-Hill.

——, ed. (1972). *Non-Verbal Communication.* London: Cambridge Univ. Press.

Konishi, M. (1965). The role of auditory feedback in the control of vocalization in the white-crowned sparrow. *Zeit. f. Tierpsychol.,* 22, 770–83.

—— (1966). The attributes of instinct. *Behaviour,* 27, 316–28.

Lorenz, K. Z. (1969). The innate basis of learning. In K. H. Pribram, ed., *On the Biology of Learning.* New York: Harcourt, Brace & World.

Smith, S. (1960). Models and Analogues in Biology. *Symposia of the Society for Experimental Biology, No. 14,* London: Cambridge Univ. Press.

Thorpe, W. H. (1951). The Learning Abilities of Birds. *Ibis,* 93, 1–52, 252–96.

—— (1961). *Bird Song: The Biology of Vocal Communication and Expression in Birds.* London: Cambridge Univ. Press.

—— (1963). *Learning and Instinct in Animals.* London: Methuen; and Cambridge, Mass.: Harvard Univ. Press.

Wertheimer, M. (1912). Experimentelle Studien über das Sehen von Bewegung. *Z. Psychol.,* 61, 161–265.

CHAPTER 5

Adler, H. E., ed. (1971). Orientation: sensory basis. *Ann. New York Acad. Sci.,* 188, 1–408.

Armstrong, E. A. (1969). Aspects of the evolution of man's appreciation of bird song. In Hinde (1969).

Billings, S. M. (1968). Homing in leach's petrel. *Auk,* 85, 36–43.

Croze, H. (1970). Searching image in carrion crows. *Zeit. f. Tierpsychol.,* Supplement No. 5.

Dubos, R. (1970). *So Human an Animal.* London: Hart-Davis.

Fisher, H. I. (1971). Experiments on homing in the laysan albatross, *Diomedia immutabilis. Condor,* 73, 389–400.

Gilliard, E. T. (1969). *Birds of Paradise and Bower Birds*. London: Weidenfeld & Nicholson.

Griffin, D. R. (1969). The physiology and geophysics of bird navigation. *Quart. Rev. Biol.*, 44, 255–76.

Hall-Craggs, J. (1962). The development of song in the blackbird (*Turdus merula*). *Ibis*, 104, 277–300.

—— (1969). The aesthetic content of bird song. In Hinde (1969).

—— (1972). Musical aspects of the vocalizations of *Laniarius aethiopicus and L. ferrugineus*. In Thorpe (1972), Ch. VIII, 134–61.

Held, R., and Hein, A. (1963). Movement-produced stimulation in the development of visually guided behaviour. *J. Comp. Physiol. Psychol.*, 56, 872–76.

Herrnstein, R. J., and Loveland, D. H. (1964). Complex visual concept in the Pigeon. *Science*, 146, 549–51.

Hinde, R. A., ed. (1969). *Bird Vocalizations: Their Relation to Current Problems in Biology and Psychology*. London: Cambridge Univ. Press.

—— (1970). *Animal Behaviour: A Synthesis of Comparative Psychology and Ethology*. London and New York: McGraw-Hill.

Köhler, W. (1921). *Intelligenzprüfungen an Menschaffen*. Berlin.

Lehr, E. (1967). Experimentelle Untersuchungen an Affen und Halbaffen über Generalisation von Insekten—und Blütenabbildungen. *Zeit. f. Tierpsychol.*, 24, 208–44.

Matthews, G. V. T. (1955, 1968). *Bird Navigation*, (1st and 2nd eds.). London: Cambridge Univ. Press.

Thorpe, W. H. (1958, 1963). *Learning and Instinct in Animals* (1st and 2nd eds.). London: Methuen.

—— (1972). Duetting and antiphonal song in birds: Its extent and significance. *Behaviour*, Monograph Supplement No. 18, p. 197. Leiden: Brill.

Tickell, W. L. N. (1962). The Dove Prion (*Pachyptila desolata*) Gmelin. *Falkland Island Dependencies Survey Sci. Reports*, No. 33.

CHAPTER 6

Ahrens, R. (1954). Beitrag zur Entwicklung des Physiognomie-und Mimikerkennes. *Z. exp. angew. Psychol.* 2: 412–54.

Ambrose, J. A. (1961). The development of the smiling response in early infancy. In *Determinants of Infant Behavior*. Vol. 2, Foss, B. M., ed. London: Methuen. New York: Wiley.

REFERENCES

Bailey, S. (1842). *A Review of Berkeley's theory of vision designed to show the unsoundness of that celebrated speculation.* London: Ridgeway.

Berkeley, G. (1709). *An Essay towards a New Theory of Vision.* In A. C. Fraser, ed., *The Works of George Berkeley,* Vols. I and II. Oxford: Clarendon Press (1901).

Bowlby, J. (1969). *Attachment and Loss.* Vol. I. London: Hogarth Press.

Bridger, W. H. (1962). Ethological concepts and human development. *Recent Advances in Biological Psychiatry,* 4, 95–107.

Carmichael, L. (1970). The onset and early development of behavior. In P. H. Mussen, ed., *Carmichael's Manual of Child Psychology.* Vol I, 447–563.

Coleridge, S. T. (1885). Quoted by L. Carmichael (1970). *q.v.*

Denenburg, V. H., and Smith, S. A. (1963). Effects of infantile stimulation and age upon behavior. *J. Comp. Physio. Psychol.,* 56, 307–12.

Dubos, R. (1970). *So Human an Animal.* London: Hart-Davis.

Eibl-Eibesfeldt, I. (1967). Concepts of Ethology and their significance in the study of human behavior. In H. W. Stevenson, E. Hess, and H. S. Rheingold, eds., *Early-Behavior: Comparative and Developmental Approaches.* New York: Wiley, pp. 127–46.

Formby, D. (1967). Maternal recognition of infant's cry. *Dev. Med. Child Neurol.,* 9, 293–98.

Gibson, J. (1958). Visually controlled locomotion and visual orientation in animals. *Br. J. Psychol.,* 49, 192–94.

Gunther, M. (1961). Infant behavior at the breast. In B. M. Foss, ed., *Determinants of Infant Behavior,* Vol. 1. London: Methuen. New York: Wiley.

Harlow, H. F. (1970). *Love Created—Love Destroyed—Love Regained.*

———, and Harlow, M. K. (1965). The affectional systems. In A. M. Schrier, H. F. Harlow, and F. Stollnitz, eds., *Behaviour of Non-human Primates.* Vol. II. New York and London: Academic Press.

Heinroth, O. (1910). Beitrage zur Biologie, namentlich Ethologie und Physiologie der Anatiden. *Verhl. 5 Int. Orn. Kong.,* 589–702.

Hinde, R. A. (1970). *Animal Behavior: A Synthesis of Ethology and Comparative Psychology.* New York and London: McGraw-Hill.

Hirsch, J. (1962). The contributions of behavior genetics to the study of behavior. In F. H. Kallmann, ed., *Expanding Goals of Genetics in Psychiatry,* pp. 25–31. New York: Grune & Stratton.

Lewis, W. C. (1965). Coital movements in the first year of life. *Int. J. Psycho-Anal.,* 46, 372–74.

Pastore, N. (1965). Samuel Bailey's Critique of Berkeley's Theory of Vision. *J. Hist. Behavior. Sci.,* 1, 321–37.

Peterson, F., and Rainey, L. H. (1910). The beginnings of mind in the newborn. *Bull. Lying-In Hosp. City of New York,* 7, 99–122.

Polak, P. R., Emde, R., and Spitz, R. A. (1964). The smiling response to the human face. *J. Nerv. Ment. Dis.,* 139, 103–9, 407–15.

Prechtl, H. F. R. (1958). The directed head turning response and allied movements in the human baby. *Behavior,* 13, 212–42.

Shalter, M. D. (1972). Imprinting. *Nature,* 237, 297.

Spalding, D. A. (1873). Instinct with original observations on young animal. *McMill. magazine,* 27, 282–93. (Reprinted *Brit. J. Animal Behav.,* 2, 2–11.)

Thorpe, W. H. (1963). *Learning and Instinct in Animals,* 2nd ed. London: Methuen.

Tomkins, S. D. (1962–63). *Affect, Imagery, Consciousness Vol. I. The Positive Affects. Vol. II. The Negative Affects.* New York: Springer. London: Tavistock Publications, 1964.

Wolff, P. H. (1963). Observations on the early development of smiling. In B. M. Foss, ed., *Determinants of Infant Behavior.* Vol. II. London: Methuen. New York: Wiley.

——, The natural history of crying and other vocalizations in early infancy. In B. M. Foss, ed., *Determinants of Infant Behavior.* Vol. IV. London: Methuen. New York: Wiley.

CHAPTER 7

Behrman, D. (1970). Understanding man's aggressiveness. *UNESCO Courier,* August–September, 7–19.

Carpenter, C. R. (1958). Territoriality: A Review of Concepts and Problems. In A. Roe and G. G. Simpson, *Behavior and Evolution.* New Haven: Yale Univ. Press.

Delgado, J. M. R. (1967). Social rank and radio-stimulated aggressiveness in monkeys. *J. Nerv. Ment. Dis.,* 144, 383–90.

Eliot, T. S. (1930). Quoted in Williams (1971), p. 70.

Ellul, J. (1970). *Violence: Reflections from a Christian Perspective.* London: S.C.M. Press.

Encyclopaedia Britannica (1929). 14th ed. Art. *Potlach,* 18, 336.

Hediger, H. (1950). *Wild Animals in Captivity.* London: Butterworth.

REFERENCES

Hinde, R. A. (1970a). *Animal Behavior: A Synthesis of Ethology and Comparative Psychology*, 2nd ed. London and New York: McGraw-Hill.

———— (1970b). Aggression in animals. *Proc. Roy. Soc. Med.*, 63, 162–63.

Hitler, Adolf (1935). *Mein Kampf*. Berlin. (First English ed., London: 1939.)

Imanishi, K. (1957). Social behavior in Japanese monkeys. *Psychologia*. Vol. 1, 47–54.

———— (1972). In R. Chauvin, ed. (1972), *Modèles Animaux du Comportement Humain*. Paris: Éditions du Centre National de la Recherche Scientifique.

Kawamura, S. (1972). In R. Chauvin, ed. (1972), *Modèles Animaux du Comportement Humain*. Paris: Éditions du Centre National de la Recherche Scientifique.

Kety, S. (1969). New perspectives in psychopharmacology. In Koestler and Smythies (1969).

Koestler, A. (1967). *The Ghost in the Machine*. London: Hutchinson.

———— and Smythies, J. R., eds. (1969), *Beyond Reductionism: New Perspectives in the Life Sciences*. London: Hutchinson.

Krsiak, M., and Steinberg, H. (1969). *J. Psychosomatic. Res.*, 13, 243–52.

Kumar, R., Steinberg, H., and Stolerman, I. P. (1969). *Scientific Basis of Drug Dependence*. London: Churchill.

Lawick-Goodall, J. van (1967). Mother-offspring relationship in free-ranging Chimpanzees. In D. Morris, ed., Primate Ethology. London: Weidenfeld & Nicholson. Garden City: Anchor Books.

———— (1970). Quoted by Behrman (1970).

———— (1968). Behavior of free-living chimpanzees of the Gombé Stream area. *Animal Behavior, Monograph 3*.

———— and Lawick, H. van (1970). *Innocent Killers*. London: Collins.

Leyhausen, P. (1956). Verhaltensstudien an-Katzen. Beih. *Zeit. f. Tierpsychol.*, 2.

———— (1965). The communal organization of solitary mammals. *Symp. Zool. Soc. London*, 14, 249–63.

———— (1970). The sane community—a density problem? *UNESCO Courier*, August–September, 26–32.

Lorenz, K. (1963). *Das Sogenannte Böse: zur Naturgeschichte der Aggression*. Vienna: Borotha-Schoeler. English translation (1966), *On Aggression*. London: Methuen.

MacLean, P. D. (1969). The Paranoid Streak in Man. In Koestler and Smythies (1969).

Ropartz, P. (1970). Quoted Behrman (1970), p. 16.

Shakespeare, W. (1599). *King Henry V*.

Steinberg, H. (1970). *Chemical Influences on Behavior.* In B. Porter and J. Birch, eds., *CIBA Foundation Study, Group No. 35,* 199–206.

Teilhard de Chardin, P. (1959). *The Phenomenon of Man.* London: Collins.

—— (1966). *Man's Place in Nature.* London: Collins.

Tobach, E., ed. (1969). Experimental approaches to the study of emotional behavior. *Ann. New York Acad. Sci.,* 159, 621–1121.

Ulrich, R. E. (1966). Pain as a cause of aggression. *Amer. Zool.,* 6, 643–62.

Waddington, C. H. (1969). The theory of evolution today. In Koestler and Smythies (1969).

Wells, H. G. (1895). *The Time Machine.* London: Lane and Penguin Books.

Williams, D. (1971). *Trousered Apes.* London: Tom Stacey.

CHAPTER 8

Bergounioux, F. M. (1962). Notes on the mentality of primitive man. In S. L. Washburn, *Social Life of Early Man,* 106–18. London: Methuen.

Brown, R. (1970). The first sentences of child and chimpanzee. *Selected Psycholinguistical Papers.* New York: Macmillan.

—— and Bellugi, U. (1964). Three processes in the child's acquisition of syntax. *Harvard Educational Review,* 34, 133–51.

Burke, K. D. (1961). *The Rhetoric of Religion.* Boston: Beacon Press.

Chance, M. R. A., and Mead, A. P. (1953). Social behaviour and primate evolution. *Symp. No. 7. Soc. Exper. Biol.*

Chomsky, N. (1957). *Syntactic Structures.* The Hague: Mouton.

Dobzhansky, T. (1962). *Mankind Evolving.* New Haven and London: Yale Univ. Press.

Gardner, R. A., and Gardner, B. T. (1969). Teaching sign language to a chimpanzee.

—— (1971). Two-way communication with an infant chimpanzee. In A. Scheier and F. Stollinitz, eds., *Behaviour of Non-human Primates.* New York: Academic Press.

Hall, K. R. L., and Schaller, G. B. (1964). Tool-using behaviour of the California Sea Otter. *J. Mammal.,* 45, 342–65.

Hardy, Alister (1965). *The Living Stream.* London: Collins.

Hayes, K. G., and Hayes, C. (1952). Imitation in a home-raised chimpanzee. *J. Comp. Physiol. Psychol.,* 45, 450–59.

—— (1955). In G. J. D. Wayne, ed., *The Non-Human Primates and Human Evolution.* Detroit, Michigan: Detroit Univ. Press.

REFERENCES

Hebb, D. O., and Thompson, W. R. (1954). The social significance of animal studies. In G. Lindzey, ed., *Handbook of Social Psychology*. Cambridge, Mass.: Addison-Wesley.

Herrnstein, R. J., and Loveland, D. H. (1964). Complex visual concept in the pigeon. *Science*, 146, 549–51.

Hinde, R. A., ed. (1972). *Non-Verbal Communication*. London: Cambridge Univ. Press.

Langer, S. K. (1951). *Philosophy in a New Key*. Cambridge, Mass.: Harvard Univ. Press.

Lawick-Goodall, J. van (1968). Behaviour of free-living Chimpanzees of the Gombé Stream area. 8 *Anim. Behav. Monogr.*, 3.

——— and Lawick-Goodall, H. van (1966). Use of tools by the Egyptian Vulture, *Neophron percnopterus. Nature*, 212, 1468–69.

Lehr, E. (1967). Experimentelle Untersuchungen an Affen und Halbaffen über Generalisation von Insekten-und Blütenabbildungen. *Zeit. f. Tierpsychol.*, 24, 208–44.

Lögler, P. (1943). Versuche zur Frage des "Zahl"-Vermögens an einem Graupapagei und Vergleichsversuche an Menschen. *Zeit. f. Tierpsychol.*, 5, 575–712.

Mowrer, O. H. (1950). On the psychology of talking birds: a contribution to languages and personality theory. In *Learning Theory and Personality Dynamics*. New York: Ronald Press.

Pantin, C. F. A. (1968). *The Relation Between the Sciences*. A. M. Pantin and W. H. Thorpe, eds. London: Cambridge Univ. Press.

Premack, D. (1970a). A functional analysis of language. *J. Exp. Analysis. Behav.*, 14, 107–25.

——— (1970b). The education of Sarah. *Psychology Today*, 4, 55–58.

Rensch, B. (1962). *Gedächtnis, Abstraction und Generalisation bei Tieren*. Arbeitsgemeinschaft für Forschung des Landes Nordrhein-Westfalen. *Heft*, 114, 1–57. Westdeutscher Verlag: Köln und Opladen.

——— (1967). The evolution of brain achievements. In *Evolutionary Biology*, T. Dobzhansky, M. K. Hecht, and W. C. Steere, eds. New York: Appleton-Century-Crofts.

Schultz, A. H. (1962). Some factors influencing the social life of Primates in general and early man in particular. In S. L. Washburn, ed., *Social Life of Early Man*. London: Methuen.

Teuber, H. L. (1967). Lacunae and research approaches to them. In C. H. Millikan and F. L. Darley, eds., *Brain Mechanisms underlying Speech and Language*, 204–16. New York and London: Grune & Stratton.

Thompson, D'Arcy W. (1942). *On Growth and Form*, 2nd ed. London: Cambridge Univ. Press.

414

Thorpe, W. H. (1963). *Learning and Instinct in Animals.* London: Methuen.

—— (1966). Ethology and consciousness. In J. C. Eccles, ed., *Brain and Conscious Experience,* 470–505. New York: Springer-Verlag.

—— (1968). Perceptual bases for group organization in social vertebrates, especially birds. *Nature,* 220, 124–28.

—— (1969). Vitalism and organicism. In D. J. Roslansky, ed., *The Uniqueness of Man,* 71–99. Amsterdam and London: North-Holland Pub. Co.

—— (1972). Duetting and antiphonal song in birds: its extent and significance. *Behaviour,* Monogr. Supplement, No. 18, 1–197.

Vallois, H. V. (1962). Social behaviour of baboons and early man. In S. L. Washburn, ed., *The Social Life of Early Man,* 214–36. London: Methuen.

Washburn, S. L., and De Vore, I. (1962). Social behaviour of baboons and early man. In S. L. Washburn, ed., *The Social Life of Early Man.* London: Methuen.

CHAPTER 9

Beloff, J. (1962). *The Existence of Mind.* London: Macgibbon & Kee.

Broad, C. D. (1923). *The Mind and its Place in Nature.* London: Kegan Paul, Trench and Trubner.

—— (1937). *The Mind and its Place in Nature.* London: Kegan Paul, Trench and Trubner.

Dobbs, A. (1967). The feasibility of a physical theory of E.S.P. In *Science and E.S.P.* J. R. Smythies, ed., London: Routledge & Kegan Paul.

Dobzhansky, T. (1962). *Mankind Evolving.* New Haven and London: Yale Univ. Press.

—— (1967). *The Biology of Ultimate Concern.* New York: New American Library.

Eccles, J. C. (1965). *The Brain and the Unity of Conscious Experience.* (XIX Eddington Memorial Lecture.) London: Cambridge Univ. Press.

—— (1966). Conscious experience and memory. In J. C. Eccles, ed. *Brain and Conscious Experience.* Berlin, Heidelberg and New York: Springer.

—— (1969). The experiencing self. In J. D. Roslansky, ed. *The Uniqueness of Man.* Amsterdam: North-Holland Publishing Co.

—— (1970). *Facing Reality.* Berlin, Heidelberg and New York: Springer.

415

REFERENCES

Gibson, J. J. (1966). *The Senses Considered as Perceptual Systems.* London: Allen & Unwin.

Hinshelwood, C. M. (1961). *The Vision of Nature.* (XV Eddington Memorial Lecture.) London: Cambridge Univ. Press.

James, W. (1890). *The Principles of Psychology.* New York: Holt.

Jennings, H. S. (1930). *The Biological Basis of Human Nature.* New York: W. W. Norton.

Koestler, A. (1972). *The Roots of Coincidence.* London: Hutchinson.

—— and Smythies, J. R., eds. (1969). *Beyond Reductionism—New Perspectives in the Life Sciences. The Alpbach Symposium.* London: Hutchinson. New York: Macmillan.

MacKay, D. M. (1967). *Freedom of Action in a Mechanistic Universe.* (XXI Eddington Memorial Lecture.) London: Cambridge Univ. Press.

—— (1970). The Bankruptcy of Determinism. *New Scientist.* July 2.

Marr, D. (1970). A theory for cerebral neocortex. *Proc. Roy. Soc. Lond. B.,* 176, 161–234.

Monod, J. (1970). *Le Hasard et la Nécessité.* Paris: Éditions du Seuil. Translated as *Chance and Necessity.* New York: Knopf (1971) and London: Collins (1972).

Pantin, C. F. A. (1968). *The Relations Between the Sciences.* A. M. Pantin and W. H. Thorpe, eds. London: Cambridge Univ. Press.

Penfield, W. (1966). Speech, perception and the uncommitted cortex. Being Chapter IX, pp. 217–37 of J. C. Eccles, ed. *Brain and Conscious Experience.* Berlin and New York: Springer.

Popper, K. (1972). *Objective Knowledge: an Evolutionary Approach.* Oxford: Clarendon Press.

Price, H. H. (1967). Psychical research and human personality. XXX In J. R. Smythies, ed. *Science and E.S.P.* London: Routledge & Kegan Paul.

—— (1965). Survival and the Idea of another world. In J. R. Smythies, ed., *Brain and Mind.* London: Routledge & Kegan Paul.

Ray, J. (1961). *The Wisdom of God Manifested in the Works of Creation.*

Razran, G. (1971). *Mind in Evolution.* Boston: Houghton Mifflin.

Reid, T. (1785). *Essays on the Intellectual Powers of Man.*

Sherrington, C. S. (1940). *Man on his Nature.* London: Cambridge Univ. Press.

Smythies, J. R., ed. (1965). *Brain and Mind: Modern Concepts of the Nature of Mind.* London: Routledge & Kegan Paul.

——, ed. (1967). *Science and E.S.P.* London: Routledge & Kegan Paul.

416

——— (1969). Aspects of consciousness. In A. Koestler and J. R. Smythies, eds., *Beyond Reductionism*. London: Hutchinson.

Thorpe, W. H. (1963). *Learning and Instinct in Animals*. London: Methuen.

——— (1966). Ethology and consciousness. Chap. XIX, 470–519. In J. C. Eccles, ed., *Brain and Conscious Experience*. Berlin: Springer.

Williams, M. (1970). *Brain Damage and the Mind*. London: Penguin.

CHAPTER 10

Anderson, C. D. (1933). The positive electron. *Physical Review*, 43, 491–94.

Anderson, P. W. (1972). More is different: broken symmetry and the nature of the hierarchical structure of science. *Science*, 177, 393–96.

Ayers, M. R. (1968). *The Refutation of Determinism*. London: Methuen.

Baillie, J. (1962). *The Sense of the Presence of God*. London: Oxford Univ. Press.

Bezzant, J. A. (1963). Intellectual objections. In A. R. Vidler, ed., *Objections to Christian Belief*. London: Constable.

Bidney, D. (1953). *Theoretical Anthropology*. New York: Columbia Univ. Press.

Broad, C. D. (1923). *The Mind and its Place in Nature*. London: Kegan Paul, Trench and Trubner.

Dobzhansky, T. (1962). *Mankind Evolving*. New Haven and London: Yale Univ. Press.

——— (1967). *The Biology of Ultimate Concern*. New York: New American Library.

——— (1969). The pattern of human evolution. In J. D. Roslansky, ed., *The Uniqueness of Man*. Amsterdam: North-Holland.

——— and Ayala, F. J., eds. (1974). *Problems of Reduction in Biology*. London and New York: Macmillan.

Eddington, A. (1936). *Relativity Theory of Protons and Electrons*. London: Cambridge Univ. Press.

Frankl, V. E. (1969). Reductionism and Nihilism. In A. Koestler and J. R. Smythies, eds. *Beyond Reductionism*. London: Hutchinson.

Hardy, Alister (1966). *The Divine Flame*. London: Collins.

Hick, J. (1957). *Faith and Knowledge*. New York: Cornell Univ. Press.

——— (1972). *Biology and the Soul*. (XXV Eddington Memorial Lecture.) London: Cambridge Univ. Press.

Koestler, A. (1972). *The Roots of Coincidence*. London: Hutchinson.

417

REFERENCES

Monod, J. (1972). *Chance and Necessity*. London: Collins.

Newman, J. H. (1870). *A Grammar of Assent*. London: Burns, Oates & Co.

Pantin, C. F. A. (1951). Organic design. *Br. Assn. Adv. Sci.*, 8, 138–50.

———— (1968). *The Relations Between the Sciences*. A. M. Pantin and W. H. Thorpe, eds. London: Cambridge Univ. Press.

Pfeiffer, J. E. (1969). *The Emergence of Man*. New York and London: Harper & Row.

Popper, K. (1972). *Objective Knowledge: an Evolutionary Approach*. London: Oxford Univ. Press.

Polanyi, M. (1959). *The Study of Man*. Chicago and London: Univ. Chicago Press.

Russell, B. (1935). *Religion and Science*. London.

Simon, H. A. (1962). The Architecture of Complexity. *Proc. Amer. Philos. Soc.*, 106, 467–82,

Teilhard de Chardin, P. (1960). *Le Milieu Divin*. London: Collins.

Whitehead, A. N. (1929). *Process and Reality*. New York: Macmillan.

Weiszäcker, C. von (1968). *Theoria to Theory*, 3, 7–18.

Woods, G. F. (1962). The idea of the transcendent. In A. R. Vidler, ed., *Soundings*. London: Cambridge Univ. Press.

INDEX

For Product Safety Concerns and Information please contact our EU
representative GPSR@taylorandfrancis.com
Taylor & Francis Verlag GmbH, Kaufingerstraße 24, 80331 München, Germany